CALIFORNIA POLITICS AND PARTIES

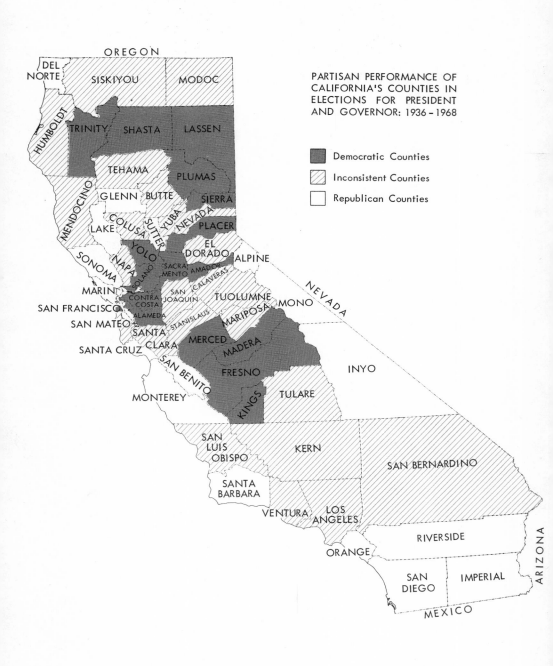

PARTISAN PERFORMANCE OF
CALIFORNIA'S COUNTIES IN
ELECTIONS FOR PRESIDENT
AND GOVERNOR: 1936-1968

Democratic Counties
Inconsistent Counties
Republican Counties

california politics and parties

JOHN R. OWENS
EDMOND COSTANTINI
LOUIS F. WESCHLER
The University of California, Davis

THE MACMILLAN COMPANY
COLLIER-MACMILLAN LIMITED, LONDON

First Printing

Library of Congress catalog card number: 77–97764

The Macmillan Company
Collier-Macmillan Canada, Ltd., Toronto, Ontario

Printed in the United States of America

FOR A. M. O., B. H. B., A. L., A. C., J. W.

preface

his book is about California politics. It deals with voting in primaries and elections, political parties and politicians, campaigns and candidates, interest groups and legislative lobbying—with all the important forces that seek to control California government and determine its policies. The purpose of this book is to acquaint people with the dynamics of California politics, to tell them something about the state's political tradition and how it developed, and to examine the ways in which various interests attempt to shape and distribute political power in the most populous state in the nation. In doing so we hope to dispel some of the chronic confusion about California politics in the minds of many people.

It is our contention that California politics are important, not only to Californians, but also to the people of the nation as a whole. Everyone is aware of the growing impact of California on national politics. The President of the United States is a native Californian, and after 1970 the state will have more electoral votes and more representatives in Congress than any other state in the union. But it is also interesting to note how other states are increasingly becoming more like California in their politics. Many of the features of California politics that set the state apart in the past—for instance, the absence of urban political machines and bosses—are spreading elsewhere.

Although a number of books on California government are presently available, this book should not be confused with them. They are concerned primarily with the constitutional-legal system of California government, with formal institutions such as the executive or the courts, and with substantive governmental policies. They deal in a limited and perfunctory way, probably in one chapter, with the subject of partisan politics. In contrast our book is concerned almost exclusively with the politics of partisan offices and elections in California.

We have learned from working on this book that it is not a simple matter for three people to write one book. Differences in personality and temperament, in time schedules and work habits, in research methods and writing styles constantly complicated our efforts to produce a book. Responsibility for writing individual chapters was distributed as follows: Edmond Costantini wrote Chapters 1, 3, and 4; John Owens wrote Chapters 5 and 8 and collaborated with Edmond Costantini on Chapter 6; Louis Weschler wrote Chapters 2 and 7. Still this book is a collective enterprise involving collaboration at every point; we have read and criticized each others' work often to the point of endangering friendships. We have sought to develop an integrated book, one consistent in content, interpretation, and style.

We wish to acknowledge the assistance of a number of people who helped us in many ways. Bernard and Margaret Teitelbaum read most of the manuscript and offered us valuable counsel and editorial assistance. John Owens and Louis Weschler wish especially to thank Harlan Demuth, a former graduate assistant and now a teacher of political science, for his indispensable research and editorial help. They also wish to thank their colleague Alvin Sokolow for the privilege of using his extensive research materials on the California legislature. Edmond Costantini wishes to acknowledge the help of Gene Smith, a graduate student at the University. The coauthors, individually and collectively, wish to thank Roberta Kenney for her expert typing and for working long hours so that we could meet our deadlines. Finally, all of us wish to acknowledge financial assistance to do this research from the Research Committee, University of California, Davis.

J. R. O.

E. C.

L. F. W.

contents

C H A P T E R   1

california: politics and people

alifornia offers a fascinating focus of study for students of American politics. Not only is it the most populous state in the nation, but tradition and people have combined with other factors to give a distinctive style to its political life. It is a style that for some is exhilarating and alluring and for others repelling and unappealing. Most of all, it is a style observers are likely to find bewildering and confusing. They are puzzled by the unpredictable voting behavior of an electorate that registers three to two Democratic, yet persistently elects Republicans to its highest offices. They are confused—sometimes amused—when movie actors without significant political experience suddenly become prominent in California politics. They are amazed at the state's high-priced, extravagant campaign spectacles managed by hired public relations specialists who merchandise candidates like cigarettes and automobiles. They see exceptionally weak and chronically fragmented political parties sharing their major functions with volunteer political groups having no official party status. They are bewildered by a political climate that nurtures political extremes ranging from free sex, Third World Liberation Fronts, and Maoist communism to theocracy, John Birchism, and the Minutemen.

antipartyism and california politics

California is so large, its population so varied and mobile, and its society so diverse that it is difficult to generalize about the state's politics. Nevertheless, a certain recurring theme or leitmotif runs through that politics, an understanding of which brings some order to what otherwise appears senseless and unpredictable. The theme is perhaps best characterized by the term *antipartyism*. Primarily a legacy of the Progressive era of a half-century ago, antipartyism has been largely responsible for California's distinctive political character. In general, it involves a distrust of politics and the politician, a fear of strong political parties, and a conviction that political independence is a virtue.

The antiparty theme weaves its way in and out of this book. At this point it will suffice to outline the central features of California's antipartyism.

PERSISTENT INTRAPARTY FACTIONALISM

Internal party discipline and unity have been elusive luxuries in California for Republicans and Democrats alike. Fratricidal conflicts, free-for-all primary contests, and bitter public clashes among their leaders have persistently plagued both parties. In large part the seeds of factionalism are sown during periods of one-party control when factions within the dominant party assume the role of dissent normally played by the opposition party. California politics in this century was, until 1958, generally Republican politics. This success was largely the result of the Republicans' ability to appeal across party lines and of the willingness of the party's leaders to eschew the open expression of narrow partisan interests in carrying out governmental responsibilities. Such a bipartisan strategy involves the danger of disenchanting party regulars imbued with the traditional party ideology. Thus Republican dominance during the first half of this century led to factionalism within the party, and the divisions established in this early period have persistently plagued the GOP ever since. Similarly, vigorous factional conflicts afflicted the Democratic party during its recent period of sustained success and have carried over even now when the party has fallen upon harder times.

INDEPENDENT AND BELEAGUERED VOTERS

The California voter tends to be a political independent who lacks strong partisan loyalties and votes for a man rather than a party. Thus, for example, each Republican success in campaigns for statewide office since 1934 has been achieved despite the existence of a substantial Democratic majority among registered voters. In fact, during this period, Republicans carried the state in six of the nine gubernatorial elections and nine of the thirteen senatorial elections. Ronald Reagan's overwhelming victory in 1966 required no less than 900,000 registered Democrats to cross party lines and vote for him over their own party's gubernatorial candidate. Richard Nixon received a minimum of 430,000 Democratic votes while carrying the state against Hubert Humphrey in the 1968 presidential election.

The California voter is also among the most burdened in the nation. Distrustful of the ability or vision of parties and political leaders, California calls directly upon its citizens to make an unusually large number of important political decisions. At each statewide election they pass on a variety of initiative and referendum ballot measures and consider candidates for a large number of elective offices. Thus, in the last gubernatorial election voters across the state were asked not only to elect a Governor, state and national legislators, and various local officials, but to vote for Lieutenant Governor, state Attorney General, Secretary of State, Controller, and Treasurer, for five justices of the State Supreme Court, for a member of the state Board of Equalization, and for a nonpartisan state Superintendent of Public Instruction. Additionally, they were asked to vote on a bond issue and sixteen propositions regarding public policy questions of varying degrees of complexity and importance.

As if the task of voting in general elections is not onerous enough for the beleaguered California citizen, he is also called upon to participate in primary elections far more significant than those in most states outside the one-party American South. Among the several factors accounting for this significance—and they will be explored in Chapter 3— is the fact that persistent intraparty factionalism in California means many vigorous primary contests. At the same time, California's system of local nonpartisanship, another aspect of the state's antiparty tradition, means that election to many nonpartisan governmental positions occurs at the primary.

WEAK PARTY ORGANIZATIONS

California's antipartyism reveals itself most directly in the official organizations of its political parties. They are, quite simply, weak and ineffectual. Indeed, for many observers familiar with politics in other large urban states, they scarcely deserve to be called "organizations" at all. The official California party is the victim of a number of factors. Some are social in nature and subject to neither control nor encouragement. Thus, population mobility within the state and heavy in-migration from without the state make the development of stable, locally based party organizations difficult. Other factors are statutory in nature and in large part deliberately designed to produce organizational debility. Four measures adopted by the Progressives a half-century ago have particularly served to place California's parties in a legal strait jacket. First, the system of nonpartisan local elections has acted as a deterrent to the development of strong party organizations at the grass roots level. Second, the establishment of a comprehensive civil service system has made it impossible to build strong party organizations through the distribution of patronage. Third, provisions for direct legislation through the initiative and referendum have diminished the role of parties in the formulation of public policy. Fourth, the crossfiling system of making nominations for partisan office allowed members of one party to run in the primary of the other party and to receive its nomination for even the highest public office while the official party was forced by law to sit idly by. Even today with crossfiling abolished, the official party organizations are prohibited from making preprimary endorsements of or otherwise assisting candidates seeking partisan nomination.

Largely because of these limitations on the official parties, unofficial mass membership organizations, unparalleled in other states, emerged within both major parties—the California Democratic Council and the California Republican Assembly being the most significant examples. Although loosely affiliated with the official party, the extralegal nature of these organizations has permitted them to endorse candidates in party primaries. Now generally in decline, California's unofficial party groups injected new vitality—both ideologically and in terms of grass roots activity—into party politics in the Golden State.

PERSONALIZED POLITICAL CAMPAIGNS

A system in which intraparty factionalism often creates enmities preventing collaboration between copartyists, in which the voter is highly independent, and in which party organizations are without muscle—such a system suggests a special style of political campaigning.

California campaigns are highly personalized extravaganzas. Candidates for major public office invariably create their own campaign organizations because they cannot rely on existing weak parties. They are likely to conduct their campaign efforts independent of other candidates on the same party ticket, thus running without the advantages or disadvantages of a "party slate." Given the nature of the electorate, a high value is placed on the candidate who can present a charismatic image and a glittering personality, and who can establish his credentials as a political independent and/or political amateur. The major campaign battlegrounds in California are the mass media—television, radio, mass mailings, roadside billboards—rather than in the precincts in old-style, face-to-face encounters with the voters.

Independently organized, personality-oriented, and mass media-conducted campaigns are highly expensive. As a result, money and the money-raiser assume high importance in California elections. And so too does the skill possessed by the professional public relations expert, the high-priced image-makers who have usurped a role traditionally assumed by professional politicians.

POWERFUL PRESSURE GROUPS

Nearly thirty years have elapsed since California's leading lobbyist proclaimed before a county grand jury, "I'm the governor of the legislature. To Hell with the Governor of the State." Although lobbying activities in California have been extensively regulated since Artie Samish made this arrogant assertion, pressure group politics continues to play an unusually important role in the state. Joseph Harris concludes that "nowhere are pressure groups more highly organized and more potent than in California."[1] Is it any wonder? With political parties weak and ineffective, a power vacuum has existed which pressure groups have moved to fill. Not only have they been aggressive at the state capital, but they have participated significantly in campaigns for public office—with money, research, information, personnel, and equipment; with all the resources naturally required by campaign organizations.

If weakened parties have opened up opportunities to pressure groups so have California's initiative and referendum procedures by which the public participates directly in the formulation of public policy. Interest

---

[1] *California Politics,* 4th ed. (San Francisco: Chandler, 1967), p. 84.

groups can and do use these procedures to take their case to the people—
at times with extraordinary financial expenditures and with the most sophisticated campaigns. And they have not always returned empty-handed.

LOCAL NONPARTISANSHIP

Elections below the state level in California are conducted on a nonpartisan basis. Candidates for local office run without benefit of party
label on the election ballot and have usually not been recruited, sponsored, or otherwise assisted by party organizations. In fact, they are
reluctant to draw attention to their party affiliation in election campaigns
for fear of alienating the independent-minded voter.

Advocates of nonpartisanship expected that under such a system the
voter would judge candidates on the basis of individual merit rather
than being misled by party labels. They argued further that election
issues would be local in nature and irrelevant national issues, upon
which party allegiances are based, would be properly ignored. In general, government officials would be dedicated to serving the public interest rather than the narrow and at times avaricious interests allegedly
represented by parties.

The lofty expectations of the advocates of nonpartisanship have not
been fully realized. Moreover, nonpartisanship has contributed heavily
to the weak position in which California's political parties have found
themselves. It is largely through participation in local elections that
grass roots party organizations are built. Deprived of an opportunity
to contest these elections, party organizations have withered on the
vine. At the same time, nonpartisanship has presented serious difficulties
for parties in the fulfillment of their function of leadership recruitment:
Local politics has been less effective than in many other states as a proving ground for individuals aspiring to higher office and as an arena
where leaders can demonstrate through a proper apprenticeship that
they deserve further recognition and reward from their party.

WEAKNESS OF PARTY-IN-GOVERNMENT

Critics of the American political system frequently point with dismay
to the lack of cohesiveness and unity within parties at the governmental
level. Public policies are not the product of well-disciplined party groups
seeking to fulfill clear pledges to the voters but are instead the result of
compromise and logrolling between governmental parties and between
the executive and legislative branches.

California is no exception to this situation. The state legislature con-

siders few bills where the members of one party are neatly arrayed
against the members of the other party; different alignments develop
on almost every controversial issue. Moreover, the organization of the
California legislature hampers partisanship in a number of significant
ways. For example, in contrast to the United States Congress, members
of both parties, not just the majority party, serve as chairmen of standing
committees. Also, the Speaker of the Assembly and the President pro
tempore of the Senate, unlike their counterparts in the United States
Congress, are frequently elected by coalitions formed by members of
both parties. Finally, passage of the state budget—the single most
authoritative statement of any administration's policy goals—requires a
two-thirds majority vote in the legislature and thus is usually the
product of cross-party compromising.

California's Governor has traditionally been limited in his ability to
act as a strong party leader and to use his office as a vehicle for ensuring
party unity. Although national executive power is concentrated in the
hands of the President, California's Governor must share his executive
authority with five other independently elected officials. These constitutional officers may have been candidates of the other political party, or,
if from the Governor's party, may be his political enemies. The Governor
also has relatively little opportunity to distribute patronage with an eye
to vitalizing his political party or asserting party leadership as there is
so little patronage in California to distribute; the state's extensive merit
system restricts any Governor's potential to build or strengthen political
organization through the distribution of government jobs.

The foregoing phenomena—party factionalism, independent voting,
weak party organizations, personalized campaigns, powerful pressure
groups, local nonpartisanship, and ineffective parties-in-government—
all contribute to California's distinctive political style. However, many
of the features associated with its antiparty tradition are encountered
with increasing frequency throughout the nation. Old-style party
precinct organizations are disappearing. The merit system is nearly
universal in state governments and as a result political machines can no
longer be glued together with the rewards of patronage. Professional
public relations firms, while prototypically Californian, are increasingly
utilized in campaigns in other states. And, whereas California may have
been among the first states to adopt nonpartisan local elections, today
more than half of America's cities elect their government officials on
a nonpartisan ballot. Indeed, many observers have looked on California
as a sort of political "Kingdom Come," as a place where the future
patterns of American politics first unfold themselves. It may well be
that as a result of changes occurring elsewhere, much that has been

distinctive about California politics is becoming commonplace nationally.

Coincidental with these national changes, California politics is assuming increasingly partisan overtones. The state's parties have been waging their protracted war with antipartyism with some degree of success. A decade ago crossfiling was abolished and one party's primary is no longer open to raids by another party's candidates. Both parties have been revitalized by the development of extralegal mass membership organizations. Local elections more and more take on partisan overtones. Party lines are drawn with increasing frequency in the state legislature. Pressure groups have been newly regulated by state legislation. In sum, California may be shedding many of the features of its antiparty tradition, just as the rest of the nation is beginning to assume some of the features of this same tradition.

However, antipartyism in California is more than a product of a historical tradition. It is also deeply rooted in the very nature of contemporary California society, most prominently in the character of the state's population.

population mix

Population is an important factor in the political equation of any society. In the case of California, of course, the *size* of that population gives the state a very special significance in national politics. In addition, the *character* of the California population contributes mightily to the durability of its political style. Several features of the state's population mix do much to sustain the antiparty tradition.

A STATE OF NEWCOMERS

Most Californians are not. Rather they are newcomers, "outsiders," men and women who "were born somewhere else and then came to their senses." The process John Steinbeck called "westering" brings more people to California from other states yearly than immigrate into the entire United States. They come seeking a better life, attracted by climate, recreational opportunities, employment and income advantages, and educational possibilities. The Nobel Laureate from the great eastern university, the illiterate from the Deep South, the displaced border state farmer working in an urban industry for the first time, the engineer sent by his firm, the old-timer looking for a pleasant place to end his days, the young man seeking quick fame or easy fortune, families hoping to escape from racial discrimination—whatever the motives, they arrive by the hundreds daily.

Almost 60 per cent of California's residents were born out of the state. Approximately the same percentage of the annual growth in population in recent years has resulted from net migration (the number of persons entering the state minus those leaving) as from net natural increase (the number of births minus deaths). Between 1950 and 1960 the population of California increased by 3,145,000 as a result of immigration alone. Of the other states only Florida achieved a net migration increase of over one million (1,625,000) during the decade. Twenty-one other states had more immigrants than emigrants, and their combined net migration increase did not equal that of California.

The newcomer, whose trip to California already demonstrated his adventuresomeness, is likely to be politically fickle. He is, as Alan Cranston explains, "making a new start—professionally, socially, and culturally. Politically, his inclinations are in flux."[2] This is not the kind of person upon whom stable political organizations can thrive. Moreover, the newcomer is likely to bring with him a party affiliation that is based on the prevailing ideological orientations of his former state's parties rather than on those of California. Thus, he is apt to add a discordant note to his California party, contributing to its factionalism and disunity. As a voter it is not unlikely that he is an independent Democrat or independent Republican, willing to vote against his party and for those candidates, regardless of party, whose ideas are more like his own. Finally, without deep and long-standing involvement in civic affairs and community organizations, the newcomer tends to depend heavily on the mass media for his political information and to be responsive to personalized election appeals.

A STATE ON THE MOVE

Californians are a people in motion. There are more airline passengers, passport holders, licensed drivers, and automobile owners than in any other state. With approximately one motor vehicle for every two residents, California has two and one-half million more automobiles than the next leading state. Movement in California involves an amazing disposition to change one's residence. Californians move two or three times more often than other Americans, with some 45 per cent of the

---

[2] Alan Cranston, "Democratic Politics," in Eugene P. Dvorin and Arthur Misner, eds., California Politics and Policies (Reading, Mass.: Addison-Wesley, 1966), p. 51.

TABLE 1–1 CALIFORNIA POPULATION MOBILITY: 1955–1960

		Per Cent
Total population five years old and over in 1960	13,974,000	
1960 population residing in same house in 1955	5,216,000	37
1960 population residing elsewhere in 1955		
Moved from abroad	364,000	3
Moved from a different state	1,938,000	14
Moved from a different county within California	1,488,000	11
Moved from within the same county	4,668,000	33
Moved, but previous residence unknown	300,000	2
		100

state's population in 1960 having moved within the state during the previous five years. This intrastate mobility involves more than two and one-half times the number of persons who arrived as newcomers to California in that same five-year period. (See Table 1–1.) Utility company records reveal that one out of two families in some northern California urban areas change their residence in a year's time. In some southern California areas the number jumps to as many as two out of three families. It has aptly been said that as a result of population movement nothing is more useless than last year's Los Angeles telephone book.

Mobility within California has much the same effect politically as in-migration. Both contribute to those features of California politics—weak party organizations, and so on—which shape its frenzied, erratic political style. Professors Turner and Vieg conclude, "the constant migration into the state and the tendency for Californians in urban areas to move from place to place have had a pervasive influence on California government and politics. This growth and mobility of the population have created an electorate with weak social and political ties, with little time to engage in partisan activities and with little knowledge of political conditions or personalities. The growth and mobility have also contributed to the tradition of nonpartisan politics and to the independence of the California voter."[3]

---

[3] Henry A. Turner and John A. Vieg, *The Government and Politics of California*, 3rd ed. (New York: McGraw-Hill Book Company, Inc., 1967), p. 34. One observer ties Ronald Reagan's 1966 gubernatorial victory to in-migration and mobility rates: "All this movement to California and within it suggests that Californians are strongly motivated to escape. . . . Thus, when an election came up during a time of rapid social change and increasing problems, the people of California fled reality." "Paradise Reagan-ed," *The Nation*, CCIII (Dec. 5, 1966), p. 596.

A STATE DIVIDED BY REGION

California is physically a big state—the third largest in the nation. The whole of New England would fit within its borders. So, too, would each of seventy-five members of the United Nations, with California's 160,000 square miles making it larger than such major nations as Great Britain, Italy, Japan, and West Germany. With 800 miles separating its Oregon and Mexican borders, California, if laid along the nation's east coast, would stretch from Boston, Massachusetts to Charleston, South Carolina.

Given this kind of geographic expanse and the resulting topographic and climatic variations, it is little wonder that regional differences characterize California's political culture. There are actually several Californias. The Great Central Valley, the San Francisco Bay area, southern California, the Sierra Nevada mountain counties, the coastal regions north and south of the Bay area, all have different economic and social characters and consequently different political interests and outlooks.

The clearest and politically most conspicuous regional cleavage in the state is between northern and southern California. The cleavage cuts across party lines and has prompted one political scientist, Eugene C. Lee, to write of "The Two Worlds of California Politics."[4] Each of these two sections has a great city serving as its sociopolitical nucleus— Los Angeles in the south and San Francisco in the north, both among the dozen most populous cities in the nation.[5]

The northern part of the state was well-settled long before people began pouring into southern California. By the 1860s the San Francisco Bay area had become a thriving urban center and had already estab-

---

[4] "The Two Arenas and Two Worlds of California Politics," in Eugene C. Lee, ed., *The California Governmental Process* (Boston: Little, Brown and Company, 1966, pp. 46–53. Lee concludes that one cannot observe politics in California without noting "the underlying truth of the differences existing in each party— personal, organizational, and ideological—between the two political worlds of North and South California." (p. 53)

[5] The two and three-quarters million residents of the city of Los Angeles compose 15 per cent of California's population. An additional 20 per cent reside elsewhere in Los Angeles county, making this county more populous than any of the more than 3,000 in the nation. The state's second largest county, San Diego, also is found in southern California, as is its fastest growing county, Orange.

San Francisco Bay area counties include another one fourth of the state's population, with the city and county of San Francisco providing 5 per cent of the total California population. Although the Bay area is the sociopolitical hub of northern California, this section also includes other distinctive geographic subsections, most notably the Great Central Valley, California's agricultural heartland where more than 10 per cent of the state's population is located.

lished the basis for its relatively rich tradition, while the south could claim little more than a few quiet villages. As late as 1900, less than one quarter of the state's population resided in the southern part of the state. Today, on the other hand, about 60 per cent of California's population lives in the South, i.e., in the eight of the fifty-eight counties lying south of the Tehachapi Mountains.[6] Changing power relationships brought about by these changing population patterns have intensified traditional antagonisms between the regions. Thus, for example, the recent reapportionment of the state Senate on the basis of population occasioned the revival of proposals in the north to permanently divide California into two states. Regionalism is furthered by differences in the kinds of people residing in the two areas. The southern Californian is more mobile than the northerner, more likely to be a newcomer to the state, and, if a newcomer, more likely to be an emigré from the American Middle West, the South, or a border state. His pattern of life tends to betoken instability and independence, and his politics has a style to match.

The north/south cleavage is nurtured by differing public policy needs. Conflicts over such issues as the distribution of the state's water, the apportionment of revenues from the state's gasoline tax for the purpose of highway construction, and the purchase and development of recreational land have resulted in regional divisions in the state legislature cutting across party lines. Geographer David Hartman summarizes the situation, "In recent years [north/south] factionalism has been inflamed by the water needs of California Man, since the greatest supply of water is found in northern counties with the greatest demand in the south. . . . Aside from the politics of water rights, north and south factionalism has demonstrated itself in many ways in the state legislature, so that a vote very often will be decided by North/South divisions rather than party affiliation."[7]

The political parties have attempted to adjust organizationally to the north/south division in the state. The chairmanship of each party state central committee rotates biennially between a northerner and a southerner. Statewide party tickets are usually balanced with candidates from both regions. Statewide election campaigns tend to be bifurcated, with the individual candidate usually mounting separate organizational efforts in the north and the south. Until George Murphy's election in 1964,

---

[6] Throughout this book, *southern California* is defined by the authors to include the counties of Imperial, Los Angeles, Orange, Riverside, San Bernardino, San Diego, Santa Barbara, and Ventura.

[7] *California and Man* (Dubuque, Iowa: William C. Brown, 1964), p. 6.

the pattern of party nominations had traditionally resulted in one United States Senator coming from northern California and one from the South.

DIVERSIFIED ECONOMY

There is hardly a major area of economic activity in which California is not among the nation's leaders. The state ranks second in the nation in manufacturing, with over 20 per cent of its work force engaged in this activity. Chemicals, concrete, cosmetics, electrical equipment, furniture, paper, plastics, rubber, textiles, and countless other items are among California's potpourri of industrial products.[8] The state's food processing industry is first in the nation and so is its wood products industry. There are more automobile workers in California than in Michigan.[9] The state's aircraft industry is second to none. Over one third of California's manufacturing is concentrated in production for defense and space uses. Indeed, no state is so closely tied to the defense needs of the nation; in recent years almost 25 cents of every defense dollar has been spent in California and more than 50 per cent of all space contracts have been awarded here. In large part defense monies continue to find their way to California because the space and military establishments find a vast manpower pool of trained and talented scientists and technicians—more than 100,000 in the San Francisco and Los Angeles areas alone.[10]

Almost one eighth of the California work force is composed of civilian government employees, the largest number being part of the great edifice of educational institutions for which the state has been noted. No state and not even the District of Columbia has more federal employees within its borders than California.

With a high per capita income, a high degree of urbanization, and a perennial population boom, a relatively greater percentage of the California work force is engaged in services and in retail and wholesale trade. The construction industry, for example, is first in the nation in both construction volume and employment.

Sixty-five separate ports and three major harbors at San Francisco,

---

[8] Given the state's remarkable growth rate in manufacturing during the last 25 years—the number of factories and plants, for example, have more than tripled—California should move to first place in the near future.

[9] Winston Crouch et al., *California Government and Politics,* 3d ed. (Englewood Cliffs, N.J.: Prentice-Hall, Inc., 1964), p. 4.

[10] Fully one half of all American scientists and technicians who are involved in space research and development and one quarter of all of her mathematicians and physicists are in this state.

Los Angeles, and San Diego make California's four billion dollar annual foreign trade tops in the nation. Further, the state is the financial center of the west and includes even more stockholders than New York. Nature's bounty has served California's economy well. It has been estimated that timber-based industries add more than two billion dollars annually to the gross state product. Each of the state's fifty-eight counties contributes to its mineral production and no other state has such a wide variety of mineral products as California. Third in over-all mineral production, it is second only to Texas in oil production. It leads the nation in total fish catch. The tourist and recreation industries have always played an important part in the California economy, with out-of-state visitors attracted by California's scenic and climatic wonderments and spending more than a billion dollars annually in the state.

California is the second most urbanized state in the nation.[11] However, while less than 5 per cent of the population is engaged in farming, it is still the number one agricultural state. With 3 per cent of the nation's farm acreage, it produces 12 per cent of its farm product and generates 15 per cent of its farm income. Agriculture contributes over $3 billion a year to the economy, easily more than agriculture contributes in any other state. Vineyards, dairies, orange groves, cotton fields—California's agricultural variety is vast. Every major American crop, with the exception of tobacco, is produced for the commercial market, and the state actually leads the nation in the production of approximately thirty major crops.[12]

The Aerojet engineer from Sacramento and the steel worker at Fontana, the lumberjack from Eureka and the Covina computer technician, the Carmel motel owner and the missile maker from Pomona,

---

[11] More than 90 per cent of the state's population lives in cities. California now has more cities (six) with a population of over 100,000 than any other state and it is the only state with two cities among the twelve largest in the nation. City planning expert William Wheaton concludes that California "has enjoyed or suffered from the most rapid rate of urban growth ever experienced in the history of western civilization. Every year 200 square miles of once rural land—140,000 acres—are bulldozed into the streets, houses, factories, and shopping centers of an urban landscape." ("Peril and Promise: The Urbanization of California in the '60's," *California: The Dynamic State* [Santa Barbara: McNally Loftin, 1966], p. 50.)

[12] In the case of some crops, California accounts for 90 per cent or more of the nation's output, e.g., in almonds, dates, figs, grapes, lemons, lettuce, olives, tomatoes, walnuts. Forty per cent of all the fruit and 30 per cent of the truck crops marketed in the United States are California raised. The city of Fresno calls itself the "raisin capital" of the world and Petaluma in Sonoma County the "egg basket of the world," Shafter in Kern County is the "potato capital," Castroville in Monterey County the "artichoke capital," Holtville in Imperial County the "carrot capital," Santa Paula in Ventura the "lemon center," Lindsay in Tulare county the "olive capital."

the grape grower from Modesto and the retired millionaire in San Marino, the stock-broker in San Francisco and the aircraft worker from Inglewood, the physicist from Cal Tech and the shipyard worker from San Diego—all of these people are strangers to each other. Their interests, backgrounds, and aspirations are likely to differ and so, too, their political attitudes. The clash and counterpoint that characterize California's economic fabric contribute to the richness of the state's pressure group activity and to the inability of political parties to build a unified organizational edifice and eliminate costly factional conflict.

ETHNIC DIVERSITY

Californians are a people divided by ethnic background, just as they are by state of origin, geographic region within the state, and economic activity. They include representatives of every ethnic group in the nation. According to the 1960 census, over 25 per cent of the California population was either foreign born or had one or both parents who were foreign born. Among the four million who were thus foreign stock, 600,000 or almost 4 per cent of the total California population were of east European ancestry and 1,400,000 were divided in origin between the United Kingdom, Germany, Italy, and Canada in approximately equal portions. Those of oriental ancestry number 300,000, more than one half of the nation's oriental-Americans living outside of Hawaii. Of those of foreign stock, the state's 700,000 Mexican-Americans are California's largest ethnic group. Indeed, approximately one of every ten Californians has a Spanish surname and the city of Los Angeles has the largest Mexican population outside of Mexico City. In addition to those nationality groups, Negroes comprised 5.6 per cent of the California population in 1960.

In the great urban states of the East, states upon which most of the generalizations concerning ethnic politics have been based, ethnic groups are the building blocks of party organizations and serve as the stable bedrock of a party's electoral support. Ethnic politics in California, however, differs significantly from ethnic politics in the East. First, California's ethnic population is somewhat smaller. For example, in the nine-state area comprising the Northeast, extending from New Jersey and Pennsylvania in the south to Maine in the north, 33.5 per cent of the population in 1960 was of foreign stock, compared to 25.4 per cent of the California population. The percentage of Negroes in the Northeast was 6.9 per cent compared to 5.6 per cent in California; and the proportion of Negroes in most of the major cities in America, e.g. Chicago,

Cleveland, Washington, Philadelphia, Detroit, and St. Louis, was more than 5 per cent over that of either Los Angeles or San Francisco.

Second, a significant portion of California's ethnic population is distributed in rural areas rather than being concentrated in urban centers. Those of foreign stock comprise a greater percentage of the state's rural farm population than of its urban population.

Third, even within the large urban centers of California various forces militate against strong ethnic identifications, bloc voting, and party organizational activity along nationality lines. The ethnic neighborhood is less frequently encountered here than in the East, especially in the cities of southern California where high rates of population mobility tend to destroy neighborhood solidarity and stability. Moreover, California's cities tend to be built horizontally rather than vertically, with single- or two-family homes, often owner-occupied, standing in marked contrast to the densely populated, high-rise apartment houses of a city such as New York.[13] Fourth, in addition to the greater physical dispersion of ethnic groups in California, the ethos of the state stresses individual effort rather than one's heritage, personality rather than group ties and is orientated more to the future than to the past. Such an ethos clearly runs counter to the perpetuation of ethnic group identities.

Richard Harvey summarizes the situation, "In contrast to many other major areas of the nation, parties here have not received consistent support from otherwise reliable population elements. Those racial and religious factions that march to the polls at the party's beck and call in Boston, New York, and Chicago are less prone to bloc balloting in a highly mobile society where their group identifications are diminished."[14]

---

[13] The old adage that Los Angeles is a collection of suburbs in search of a city is still in many ways valid and indeed applies to one extent or another to all urban centers in the state; each has the element of two-dimensionality common to suburbia rather than the three-dimensionality of the eastern metropolis.

[14] "California Politics: Historical Profile," in Eugene P. Dvorin and Arthur Misner, eds., *California Politics and Policies* (Reading, Mass.: Addison-Wesley, 1966), p. 19.

One prominent political scientist describes growing up in Los Angeles in appropriate terms, "The social structure did nothing to change the individualistic orientation of life. People had no identities except the personal identities, no obvious group affiliations to make possible any reference to them by collective nouns. I never heard the phrase 'ethnic group' until I was in graduate school. . . .

"The absence of such group identities and of neighborhoods associated with these identities may be one reason for the enormous emphasis on 'personality'. . . . To be 'popular' and 'sincere' was vital [for a candidate for office in a Los Angeles high school.] In a New York high school, by contrast, personality would have to share importance in such contests with a certain amount of bloc voting among the Irish, Italians, and Jews. . . .

"[Similarly in public elections] 'bloc voting' and group preferences were unheard of and, when heard of, unthinkable. And the idea that political parties ought to

first among equals

California is a state thoroughly committed to primacy and super-eminence. It has been able to claim for its own the biggest trees, the tallest mountains, the most beaches, the lowest point, the highest water-falls of any of the states. It is considered the "brain capital of the world," with more Nobel Laureates, more members of the National Academy of Sciences, more technicians involved in space research and develop-ment, more high school graduates, more students enrolled in institutions of higher education than in any other state. California's system of high-ways is the most extensive in the nation, includes the longest bridges, and accommodates the most automobiles per capita. In volume of foreign trade, of agricultural production, of electric power output, of business investments, of new jobs created annually, California leads the way. Indeed, when separated statistically, California's economy ranks seventh among the nations of the world—behind only the United States, the Soviet Union, West Germany, the United Kingdom, France, and China. California, it often seems, has the best, the most, the greatest, or the biggest in just about anything its citizens care to discuss.

Population size has now been added to the California catalogue of superlatives. Ascendancy in 1963 to the status of the nation's most populous state reflected a long process of population escalation, the dimensions of which have been unparalleled in human history. California quadrupled in size in the first decade following its admission to the Union in 1850 and it has since approximately doubled its population every twenty years. Its growth rate in the twentieth century has been three times that of the nation as a whole and in recent years has ap-proximated over 1,300 people each day. In the 1960s California's popula-tion increase alone will exceed the total population of all but seven of the fifty states.[15] California's growth has indeed been phenomenal and

---

do anything besides help add up preferences was most heterodox—the worst thing that could be said about it was that it was 'Eastern.' The well-known institutional features of California's political system—weak parties, the extensive use of the referendum to decide policy issues, nonpartisanship—were perfectly matched to the political mentality that was nurtured in Southern California." James Q. Wilson, "A Guide to Reagan Country," *Commentary*, XLIII (May 1967), p. 39.

[15] Some population projections stagger the imagination. The Population Reference Bureau, for example, has recently estimated that one hundred years from now California's population will approximate 1,500,000,000 (one and one-half billion!) persons or about one half the present population of the entire planet. (*continued*)

TABLE 1–2 CALIFORNIA POPULATION: A HISTORY OF GROWTH

Year Census	California	U.S.	Ten-year Per Cent Increase Calif.	U.S.	Calif. Rank	Calif. Per Cent of U.S.
1850	93,000	23,192,000	—	—	29	0.4
1860	380,000	31,443,000	310.4	35.6	26	1.2
1870	560,000	38,558,000	47.4	22.6	24	1.4
1880	864,694	50,189,209	54.3	30.1	24	1.7
1890	1,213,398	62,979,766	40.3	25.5	22	1.9
1900	1,485,053	76,212,168	22.4	20.7	21	1.9
1910	2,377,549	92,228,496	60.1	21.0	12	2.6
1920	3,426,861	106,021,537	44.1	15.0	8	3.2
1930	5,677,251	123,202,624	65.7	16.2	6	4.6
1940	6,907,387	132,164,569	21.7	7.3	5	5.2
1950	10,586,223	151,325,798	53.3	14.5	2	7.0
1960	15,717,204	179,323,175	48.5	18.5	2	8.7
1970 (est.)*	20,654,000	202,490,000	31.4	12.9	1	10.2

* The 1970 estimates are based on data in California Department of Finance, *Estimated and Projected Population of California, 1960–2000.* Sacramento, June 1968.

its twenty million residents make it more populous than the twenty smallest states combined and more populous than one hundred United Nations members. One of every ten Americans may be found within its borders. (See Table 1–2.)

This extraordinary population achievement has great consequences for California's role in national politics. The state is assured a significant place in the quadrennial process of President-making and in the Congressional power system, because at almost every turn—at presidential nominating conventions, in the Electoral College, in the House of Representatives—a state's representation is related to its population.

Although California has yet to send the largest delegation to a national party convention, its importance in presidential nominations is beyond dispute. For example, at the 1964 Republican convention the California delegation held 13 per cent of the vote needed to win the

---

Geographer D. B. Luten discusses the statistics of California's population growth in terms that are similarly disquieting. "Simple arithmetic," he writes, "shows that if California maintains its growth rate at the traditional 3.8 percent a year and the nation maintains its rate at 1.6 per cent . . . then in about 110 years, say 2070, the population of both the United States and California would be about a billion. That is, all Americans would live in California." He assures us, however, that "this seems unlikely." He concludes that "California will stop growing one day because it will have become just as repulsive as the rest of the country." (In Carey McWilliams, ed., *The California Revolution* [New York: Grossman, 1968].)

nomination and represented the largest single bloc going to the man emerging as the party's presidential nominee, Senator Barry Goldwater.

California's presidential primary is the most important in the nation. A potential presidential nominee can add more pledged votes to his convention arsenal by winning that primary than by winning any other. Victory may bring him new prominence as a serious contender as it did Estes Kefauver in 1952. It may even propel him to an eventual nomination as it did Adlai Stevenson in 1956 and Barry Goldwater in 1964, and as it might have done for Robert Kennedy had he not been tragically assassinated on the night of his 1968 California primary victory. On the other hand a defeat may dash all hopes of achieving the presidential nomination, as it did Kefauver in 1956 and Nelson Rockefeller in 1964.[16]

California now has 40 of 538 Electoral College votes, second in number to only New York.[17] The College operates on a winner-take-all basis within each state; the presidential candidate who wins in a state is given all of its electoral votes regardless of his popular vote margin. As a consequence of this system, a presidential candidate could carry every one of the eleven smallest states in the nation by the greatest of popular pluralities and still not receive as many electoral votes as he would if he carried California by but a single popular vote. Little wonder that every four years California's voters are generously treated to the most advanced forms of political seduction available to presidential aspirants and that the favor of its leading politicians is carefully curried by those aspirants.

Indeed, given the power of California in the nominating conventions and in the Electoral College, the state's leading politicians must be given every possible consideration for a place on a presidential ticket. Hiram Johnson, Herbert Hoover, Earl Warren, and Richard Nixon are Californians who, in this century, have appeared on such a ticket. (See Table 1–3.) The only election year since World War II in which a son of the state was not a presidential or vice-presidential candidate was 1964.

After 1970, when California's population primacy will be officially registered by the United States Census, California's electoral votes should

---

[16] Prior to his victory over Rockefeller in the 1964 California primary, Goldwater summed up the situation quite accurately when he concluded that "the man who wins the California primary will win the nomination."

[17] A state's electoral vote is equivalent to the number of Representatives and Senators on its delegation to the U.S. Congress. It is thus a function of the relative size of its population at the previous census.

TABLE 1–3   CALIFORNIANS AND PRESIDENTIAL POLITICS

1856–1864	In 1856 John C. Fremont, former military Governor of California and delegate to the U.S. Senate before statehood, is nominated as the Republican Party's first presidential candidate. Fremont plays a prominent part in Republican presidential politics in the two succeeding presidential elections.
1912–1924	Governor Hiram Johnson is Theodore Roosevelt's running mate in his 1912 bid for the presidency on the Progressive Party ticket. Johnson is prominent at the Republican National Conventions of 1920 and 1924, seriously considered as a vice-presidential prospect.
1920–1924	U.S. Senator William McAdoo, Woodrow Wilson's son-in-law, leads in the early convention balloting for the Democratic presidential nomination in both 1920 and 1924, only to fall victim to the two-thirds rule then in effect at Democratic conventions.
1928–1932	Having emerged as an important convention figure in 1924, California engineer Herbert Hoover is nominated by the Republicans and elected President in 1928, renominated but defeated in 1932.
1944–1948	Governor Earl Warren is considered a possible presidential candidate in 1944 but instead agrees to serve as Keynoter at the GOP National Convention. In 1948 Warren is nominated as Republican vice-presidential candidate. Rejected by Eisenhower for the same role in 1952, he is appointed to the U.S. Supreme Court shortly after Eisenhower's victory and serves as Chief Justice until 1969.
1952–1960	Richard Nixon is nominated twice to the vice-presidency, a position in which he serves during Eisenhower's two terms as President. In 1960 Nixon achieves the Republican nomination for the presidency only to be defeated by John Kennedy.
1968	Governor Ronald Reagan's last-minute attempt to capture the GOP presidential nomination fizzles. Nixon, now a New Yorker, is nominated and goes on to win the election and to become 37th President of the United States.

increase to forty-six and possibly to as many as fifty. At the same time, in view of current population trends, it seems likely that each of the other states now in the top five in terms of population will suffer a decline in electoral votes. California's gain, then, will be at the expense of the other populous states, because, in contrast to California, their population growth rate is smaller than that of the nation as a whole.

California's importance in presidential politics is enhanced by the fact that it is a "doubtful" state, one in which the candidate of either party has a good chance of winning. During the last half century, beginning with the election of 1916, Californians have preferred a Republican presidential nominee eight times and a Democrat six times. Four of these Republican victories occurred in the post-World War II period and were thus achieved in the face of wide but obviously deceptive Democratic margins in the state's party registration.

The closeness with which presidential elections are contested in California is revealed in the distribution of its popular vote in the three election years since World War II in which the outcome nationally remained in doubt to the very end. In 1948 a shift of a mere 9,000 California voters (two tenths of 1 per cent of the total vote) would have given Dewey rather than Truman the state. In 1960 a shift of 18,000 California voters (three tenths of 1 per cent of the total vote) would have given Kennedy rather than Nixon the state. In 1968 if 115,000 of the three-and-one-half million Californians who voted for Nixon had instead voted for Humphrey, Nixon would not have received the state's electoral votes or a majority in the Electoral College. The election would have gone into the U.S. House of Representatives.

There can be no question: California's importance in presidential elections is guaranteed by its size and enhanced by its status as a "doubtful" state. A political party dare not ignore California in its candidate selection process, dare not consider it lost or won as a foregone conclusion, and dare not assume election victory can be achieved without its big bloc of electoral votes.

If California is increasingly important in the making of Presidents, it is also increasingly important in the making of Congress. (See Table 1-4.) The 38-member delegation currently sent to the House of Representatives exceeds in size the combined delegations of the eighteen smallest states in the nation and is second only to that of New York. Following the 1970 census, California will probably be entitled to forty-four congressmen. This would not only make its delegation the largest at the nation's Capitol but would represent almost twice as many seats as now occupied by the congressmen from the six New England states combined, more seats than presently held by no less than six Deep South states combined, and only five less than the combined total of

TABLE 1–4 CALIFORNIA AND THE UNITED STATES HOUSE OF REPRESENTATIVES—APPORTIONMENT OF MEMBERSHIP

	California Delegation	Total House Membership	California Per Cent of Total
1850	2	237	0.8
1860	3	243	1.2
1870	4	293	1.4
1880	6	332	1.8
1890	7	357	2.0
1900	8	391	2.0
1910	11	435	2.5
1930	20	435	4.6
1940	23	435	5.3
1950	30	435	6.9
1960	38	435	8.7
1970 (anticipated)	44	435	10.1

Note: There was no reapportionment based on the 1920 census.

seats now held by California's seventeen westernmost neighbors (exclusive of Texas).

A state's potency in the congressional scheme of things is measured by more than the size of its delegation. It is measured, too, by the nature of the committee assignments received by the members of that delegation, by the extent to which they are elevated to committee chairmanships, and by the extent to which they achieve elected positions in the congressional party leadership structure.

In terms of committee assignments, California congressmen have fared quite well. In the Ninety-first Congress (1969–1971), for example, eight Californians received assignments to the three most important standing committees in the House of Representatives—James Corman and James Utt to the twenty-five member Ways and Means Committee, B. F. Sisk and H. Allen Smith to the fifteen member Rules Committee, and Jeffrey Cohelan, Glenard Lipscomb, John McFall, and Bruce Talcott to the fifty member Appropriations Committee.

In terms of elevation to committee chairmanships, Californians have been able to assume three House (but no Senate) chairmanships since 1950, each of them quite appropriate given California's social and economic fabric. Clair Engle, before he went to the U.S. Senate in 1959, had served for four years as chairman of the House Interior and Insular Affairs Committee—an achievement appropriate for a Californian as federal land in the state approaches 50 per cent of its total land area and is exceeded in acreage only by that in Alaska. George P. Miller has served as chairman of the House Science and Astronautics Committee since 1961, and Chet Holifield has been senior House member on the Joint Committee on Atomic Energy since 1961 and therefore its chairman during alternate Congresses. These latter two positions, like Engle's chairmanship, are appropriate for Californians given the state's leadership in the space sciences and in nuclear research and development, a leadership in large part resulting from and sustained by the largesse of the federal government. (Five Californians in the Ninety-first Congress are ranking Republican members of committees—House Administration, Merchant Marine and Fisheries, Rules, Veterans' Affairs, and Joint Atomic Energy. They presumably would have been selected as committee chairmen if their party had captured control of the House of Representatives in the 1968 elections.)

Despite these achievements, it should be noted that the number of committee chairmen produced by California has never been commensurate with the size of its congressional delegation. Seniority is the avenue to a chairmanship and seniority is elusive for a state as politically unsettled and volatile as this, where congressmen have uncommon difficulty in surviving successive election challenges. Before 1900 no Californian had been in the House of Representatives for more than four years and in the Senate only one Californian had ever been reelected. In the Ninetieth Congress, only three Californians were included among the ninety-one most senior members of the House of Representatives. Of the sixteen states having ten or more members in the House, only four (Michigan, New Jersey, Georgia, and North Carolina) had fewer congressmen who had served without interruption since 1950.

Election by party colleagues to positions in the congressional party organizations is an additional mark of success in achieving leadership status in the congressional system. California's political potency has been duly recognized in this respect. Senator Thomas Kuchel was selected by the Republican caucus in the Senate as Assistant Minority Leader (or party Whip) and was serving in that capacity when defeated for re-election in 1968. Senator George Murphy has served as chairman of the Republican Campaign Committee in the Senate just as Bob Wilson has served as chairman of the counterpart committee in the House. John Moss has served as Assistant Democratic Whip in the House. Harry Sheppard was chairman of the Democratic Patronage Committee at the time of his retirement from Congress in 1965. William Knowland was Republican Minority Leader when he left the Senate in 1959.

The designation of these individuals is more than a recognition of their abilities—which are no doubt considerable. It is also a recognition of California's importance as a state, one that has fast approached and has now achieved a position of first among equals in the nation.

The plain fact is that size is among California's most important politically salient characteristics. It brings a special kind of potency to the state in national politics—in presidential conventions, in the Electoral College, in the House of Representatives. The political business of California is perforce the nation's business and what happens in California politics inevitably has a significant impact on the politics of the entire nation.

Although population size and rapid population growth are important power resources for California in national politics they also raise special problems for the state. With a new resident arriving either obstetrically or vehicularly every minute of every day, the state must add the equivalent of another San Diego or Oakland yearly. It must build a new school building a day, create 4,000 new jobs a week, construct 25,000 new homes a month, and 2,000 miles of highway a year. The problems of overcrowded classrooms, of air and water pollution, of urban blight and suburban sprawl, of insufficient recreational opportunities and inadequate employment opportunities—these are problems faced by governments across the nation. But in California, population size and growth give them an added dimension and a greater sense of urgency. What is required are politicians of extraordinary ingenuity and foresight and political institutions capable of developing and utilizing that ingenuity and foresight.

CHAPTER 2

partisan politics
in perspective

he history of partisan politics in California is rich and
exciting. A corrupt and monolithic statewide political
machine once ran the government as its own prerogative.
Radical political movements have been common. Political
reform and nonpartisan politics have left their imprint
upon the state's political heritage. Independent and forth-
right men have served the people of California; political
hacks also have had their day. Colorful third parties have
challenged the Democratic and Republican parties. Such
unusual issues as irrigation and independent nationhood
for "the Republic of California" have divided parties and
partisans. Yet, within this diversity of political experience,
three major facts stand out: the dominance of the Republican party in partisan politics, the vital importance
of intraparty factions, and the lasting impact of the
Progressive Movement upon California political practice.

The Republican party has dominated California politics
for most of this century. Only two Democratic Governors,
Culbert Olson and Edmund Brown serving a total of
twelve years, have been elected since the Republican

victory of 1894. California's most famous politician, Hiram Johnson, who served the state from 1910 to 1945 as Governor and U.S. Senator, was a Progressive Republican. Although California voters have supported every Democratic presidential victor except John F. Kennedy,[1] the Democratic party did not regain full control of the state government until the 1958 triumph of Governor Brown. California's political legacy is truly one of Republican dominance.

In most states, competition among factions within a party is more important than competition between parties. California is no exception. Republican rule in California has rested upon the ability of Republican leaders to reconcile the factional differences within their party and to attract disaffected Democratic factions to their cause. Factional conflicts, especially between liberals and conservatives, have continuously plagued both parties, but until the 1958 election, Democrats were less successful than Republicans in overcoming the centrifugal tendencies of factionalism.

Conflicts between factions within parties have been fostered by the Progressive ethos and reforms created early in this century to combat the political machine of the Southern Pacific Railroad. The Progressives cherished a nonpartisan ideology that is still operative today. Furthermore, they buttressed the ideology with constitutional reforms that tore away the roots of partisan political organization in California. Home rule, nonpartisan elections at the local level, the direct primary, and crossfiling effectively did away with the local political organizations that were the backbone of the railway machine. These reforms also enabled the Progressives to wrest control of the Republican party from the machine-dominated party caucus. Reform measures and their attendant ethos not only wrecked the Southern Pacific Railroad's political machine but also promoted conditions that ultimately caused California political parties to be weak, decentralized, and factious.

These three crucial political facts—Republican dominance, intraparty factions, and Progressive reforms—are the primary features of a rich political history. Beneath these basic contours lies a substructure filled with vital and interesting events. Our purpose is to present a brief historical overview of California partisan politics, which coterminously stresses the importance of the three outstanding features and provides a taste of the state's rich political experience.

---

[1] California did not cast its electoral votes for Woodrow Wilson in the 1912 election, but it did support him in his second election.

background to reform: 1849-1900

The gold seekers of the 1840s found California to be a strange and challenging environment. Their old ways had to be changed to meet the demands of the vast and isolated frontier. Adaptation to the demands of the new environment produced a distinctive pattern of culture that differed from the past experiences of the migrants. Violence, lawlessness, and a tendency toward mob action fostered a toughness and single-mindedness usually associated with frontier life. The forty-niners found opportunity in politics as well as in the gold fields. As tough men entered the mining towns in search of precious metal, equally tough men entered political life in search of power. Some of the fortune hunters saw California as a wide-open opportunity to achieve economic success through politics. Few of the early politicians were disappointed miners. Most of them immigrated to California to help shape a fluid political environment to their liking.

A DECADE OF DEMOCRATIC RULE[2]

Most of the migrants who came to California seeking political fortune were either Whigs or Democrats, the two leading national parties of the period. The frontier culture of the mining camps and the boom towns favored the party of Andrew Jackson, and those aspiring politicians who claimed allegiance to the Democratic party were more successful than those who followed the ways of Daniel Webster and Henry Clay. Although the nation had turned toward the Whigs with the victory of General Zachary Taylor in the presidential election of 1848, California overwhelmingly supported Democratic candidates in the first state election in 1849. By the time California was admitted to the Union in September of 1850, Democrats constituted a majority in both houses of the state legislature, a majority of the California delegation to the House of Representatives, and held the governorship and one U.S. Senate seat. Strangely enough, the Democrats gained control of the state without

---

[2] See John W. Caughey, *California*, 2nd ed. (Englewood Cliffs, N.J.: Prentice-Hall, Inc., 1953), pp. 275–288; Walton Bean, *California, an Interpretive History* (New York: McGraw-Hill Book Company, Inc., 1968), pp. 172–176; and Earl Pomeroy, "California, 1846–1860: Politics of a Representative Frontier State," *California Historical Society Quarterly*, XXXII (Dec. 1953), pp. 291–302.

actually forming a statewide organization. The California Democratic party was officially organized in March 1851, and the party continued to dominate the state until 1862, when Leland Stanford was elected the first Republican Governor of California.

Shortly after the California Democratic party was organized, the major issue that was to rend the nation as well as the state, slavery, began to cleave the party into two distinct factions. U.S. Senator William M. Gwin, who favored the position of the South on the question of slavery led one faction, and David C. Broderick, the boss of an incipient political machine in San Francisco, led the other faction. Senator Gwin, who had migrated to California from the South, sought support from the state legislature,[3] and Broderick, who fancied himself the boss of the legislature as well as of San Francisco, strongly opposed this move. Their personal struggle developed into an open conflict within the party during the 1854 gubernatorial campaign. The incumbent Democratic Governor, John Bigler, sided with Broderick. In spite of Senator Gwin's active and personal opposition, Governor Bigler was re-elected. The triumph of Bigler and Broderick did not, however, bring about unity in the Democratic party. The question of slavery and the personal animosity between Gwin and Broderick continued to plague the party.

The feud was renewed in the battle for California's two Senate seats in 1855. By this time Broderick exerted considerable influence in the state legislature, and blocked Senator Gwin's re-election until Gwin agreed to relinquish control of the dispensation of federal patronage in California. After both were elected to the U.S. Senate, Gwin reneged on his agreement and President James Buchanan dispensed patronage without consulting Broderick. Boss Broderick found himself ostracized by Democratic party leaders in Washington and he quickly lost his influence in the party and in the state's politics.

The embittered Broderick began a series of personal verbal attacks upon Gwin. He was challenged to a duel and killed by Gwin's long-time associate and friend, David S. Terry. This event caused a violent split within California's Democratic party, with most of Broderick's followers turning to the newly formed Republican party. The presidential candidacy of Stephen A. Douglas further widened the split in the Democratic party. Douglas and his abolitionist principles were unacceptable to many Californians who were sympathetic to the cause of the South. As a result, Abraham Lincoln carried the state and the stage was set for Leland Stanford's gubernatorial victory in 1862.

---

[3] U.S. Senators were elected by state legislatures until passage of the Seventeenth Amendment to the Constitution in 1912.

THE REPUBLICANS AND TWO-PARTY POLITICS[4]

The 1860 election left the California Democratic party split into three factions. The congressional delegation had supported John C. Breckenridge and the Southern Democratic ticket. Some of the state liberals had supported Douglas and the Northern Democratic slate. The remainder of the liberal and moderate Democrats had defected and supported the Republican victor, Lincoln. The party of Jackson was shattered in California and in the nation. The Republican party accommodated the renegade Democrats, and within a short time the state joined with the North to support the war effort under President Lincoln. Thus, the GOP became a major force in California politics.

A period of two-party rivalry began after the Civil War, with Democrats regaining some of their lost strength and alternating with Republicans in the control of the state's political fortunes. Between 1862 and the Republican sweep of 1898, thirteen men served as governor of California, seven of whom were Republicans, five were Democrats, and one was a member of the war-time Union party. This pattern of competition was paralleled in the state legislature during the same period. Republicans enjoyed an immediate postwar advantage, but Democrats soon successfully challenged Republican control in both the Senate and the Assembly. Although third parties actually held the balance of power in the legislature during the 1870s, two-party competition between Democrats and Republicans remained a stable pattern until the GOP established firm control of both houses in 1898.

The Republican party gained strength through its success in forming coalitions among interests that shared the moderate social and conservative economic ideologies of its leadership. The postwar renaissance of the Democratic party was built upon dissatisfaction with the economic policies fostered by Republican governors and legislators, who showed a distinct preference for the big business interests of the state. Mining, railroad building, and banking became allied with the Republican party, whereas workingmen, farmers, and smaller entrepreneurs supported the Democrats. The Democratic party, however, languished during the 1870s and 1880s when various radical movements drew away much of its natural support and the Southern Pacific Railroad[5] established the

---

[4] Caughey, loc. cit., and Bean, op. cit., pp. 176–181.
[5] The railroad was known as the Central Pacific until 1884; we shall always refer to it as the Southern Pacific to avoid confusion.

most powerful political machine in California history. The Democratic party could not withstand the economic power of the railroad and the vibrancy of the radicals, and it suffered a setback from which it did not fully recover until 1958.

THE WORKINGMEN'S PARTY[6]

Dennis Kearney led the most successful of the radical movements that developed in response to the depression of the 1870s. An articulate, roughneck Irish immigrant, Kearney mixed racism with antibusiness feeling to build the Workingmen's party. The Chinese, brought to California to work on the railroad, represented a threat to the other members of the state's work force. In 1871, open violence against the Chinese broke out in Los Angeles and several people were killed. This proved to be the first of a series of incidents involving Orientals, and overt anti-Chinese feeling swept over the state.

San Francisco, Kearney's home base, was the scene of failing businesses, mobs of unemployed workers milling the streets, and racial violence. Relying mainly upon street-corner oratory, the young Irishman gathered a large following. Aided by the antirailroad feeling in Los Angeles and Stockton, which had been fostered by discriminatory rates, Kearney and his followers organized a new political party in 1877. The Workingmen's party held its first convention in January 1878, and adopted a platform that, among other things, called for direct election of U.S. Senators, an eight-hour day, compulsory education, state regulation of banks, industry, and railroads, and a Chinese exclusion provision. This party, a strange mixture of racism and reformism, was moderately successful in state and local elections, but its major impact came during the state constitutional convention of 1879.

The Workingmen's party sent a well-organized minority delegation to the convention. These Kearneyites were able to secure the adoption of some of their reforms. Many of Kearney's followers, however, were bitterly disappointed at the failure of the party to fully gain the reforms they sought. A split began to develop in the party, which was at best a precarious coalition. In 1880 when Kearney failed in an effort to tie the Workingmen's party with the Greenback-Labor party, the wing of the organization that favored the Democratic party gained control and

---

[6] Bean, op. cit., pp. 233–243; James Bryce, *The American Commonwealth*, vol. II (New York: Commonwealth Publishing, 1908), pp. 439–464 and 833–836; and Ralph Kauer, "The Workingmen's Party of California," *Pacific Historical Review*, **XIII** (Sept. 1944), pp. 278–291.

dismissed the vitriolic leader. The power of the Workingmen's party quickly dissipated as its followers joined the ranks of one of the two major parties. A sad historical note is that the Kearneyites' two major reforms, the Board of Equalization and the Railroad Commission, fell under the corrupt control of the Southern Pacific Railroad soon after their creation.

THE RAILROAD MACHINE[7]

The political machine fashioned by the Southern Pacific Railroad stands as the most successful, if the most corrupt, political organization in the history of California politics. The political organization created and controlled by California's premier railroad literally ran the state's politics. The railroad, started in 1861 by Theodore D. Judah, Leland Stanford, Collis P. Huntington, Mark Hopkins, and Charles Crocker, was the single most important economic power in the state until the Progressive reforms after 1910. The Big Four, as Stanford, Huntington, Hopkins, and Crocker were known after Judah's death in 1863, entered politics to expand and protect their holdings. Their lobbyists in Washington, D.C. were able to secure a total subsidy for the railroad amounting to $27,855,000 in federal bonds and ten million acres in public lands, thereby making the Southern Pacific the richest business and the largest private landowner in the state. Furthermore, vast sums were wrested from local government and the state in the 1860s, and although such subsidies were ended in 1871, the Southern Pacific Railroad already owned 85 per cent of the state's railways and dominated land transport in California.

Local communities that refused to furnish the subsidies set by the Big Four were threatened with extinction by careful planning of the rail route to bypass them. Crocker, now famous for the art collection that bears his name, was even more famous for threatening the Los Angeles city council if they did not meet his demands; "If this be the spirit with which Los Angeles proposes to deal with the railroad upon which the town's very vitality must depend, I will make grass grow in the streets of your city."

The Southern Pacific had an agent in every town and village to

---

[7] Bean, op. cit., pp. 208–232 and 298–311; George E. Mowry, *The California Progressive*, paperback ed. (Chicago: Quadrangle, 1951, 1958), pp. 1–22; Franklin Hichborn, "California Politics, 1891–1939," vol. I, typed manuscript, UCLA library; and Frank Norris, *The Octopus, A Story of California* (Garden City, N.Y.: Doubleday & Company, Inc., 1901).

protect its interests. In time, both Los Angeles and San Francisco had resident political machines that were controlled by the railroad. Such machines were common throughout the nation, but the "Octopus," as the railroad was christened by novelist Frank Norris, was notorious in its open display of contempt for public morals and decency. It is not surprising that the Workingmen's party made the Southern Pacific a favorite target. Nor is it surprising to find that both the Democratic and Republican parties finally reacted to such blatant corruption. The federal government, not the state government, however, finally exposed the railroad machine. As a result of information brought out in a court case, Congress formed the Pacific Railway Commission in 1887 to examine federally subsidized railroads. Although Stanford and Crocker refused to cooperate, it became evident that considerable amounts of money were spent to influence federal and state legislation, and that the Southern Pacific dominated California politics through its business agents.

Even with the exposure provided by the federal investigations, state political leaders proved to be ineffectual in dealing with the "Octopus." The task of destroying the Southern Pacific machine fell to a group of political reformers and journalists. Led by John R. Haynes and Edward A. Dickson, an incipient organization was formed to battle the Los Angeles branch of the machine, and soon editors, writers, and professional people throughout the state were joining the movement. Despite the efforts of these reformers, the Southern Pacific Railroad faced the twentieth century still the number one force in California politics. Its demise was yet to come.

California's frontier politics had disappeared by 1900. The free and easy style of the early years gave way to a sophisticated and ruthless political machine. It made little difference which party was in power, the railroad still ruled. Politicians either played the game according to Southern Pacific rules or soon found themselves out of office. Obviously the power of the railroad's political machine could be checked only by an organization of comparable power. Before the end of World War I, reformers created such an organization; an organization that not only defeated the railroad, but also shaped California's political heritage for many years.

political reform and the progressives: 1900-1923

In 1900 the Republican party ran California and the Southern Pacific Railroad ran the Republican party. The Democratic party, which might have offered opposition to both the railroad and the GOP, proved impotent. A group of assorted muckrakers and local political reformers called "The Progressives," constituted the only effective opposition to the railroad. The Progressive Movement was not restricted to California, but was part of the general reformist groundswell that swept the nation in the 1890s and early 1900s. The Progressives, usually associated with the Republican party, actually drew strength from all of California's parties. Although it was eventually integrated into the regular Republican party, the Progressive Movement, at first, drew upon a wide spectrum of political support; political support united by its common disgust with the operations of the "Octopus" and local political machines.

CIVIC CORRUPTION AND CIVIC REFORM[8]

The most important of the civic reform movements took place in San Francisco, where muckraking newspapermen joined forces with business and professional groups to battle one of the most ruthless and graft-ridden city machines in the state. The Union Labor party, under the direction of Abraham Ruef, elected its own mayor, captured the police force, ran the franchise board as a private vending operation, and used utilities rates as a means of political payoff. After capturing city hall in 1901, Boss Ruef, through the mayor's office, began a five-year orgy of bribery, blackmail, and extortion. Reformers, thoroughly disgusted with party politics and stymied at the polls, turned to the courts. The ensuing graft prosecution, 1906–1909, provided the opponents of the San Francisco machine with the ammunition they needed to start a statewide campaign against political corruption.

Francis J. Heney, the special prosecutor whose tenacious work laid

---

[8] Bean, op. cit., pp. 312–325; Mowry, op. cit., pp. 23–56; Lincoln Steffens, *Autobiography* (New York: Harcourt, Brace & World, Inc., 1931), pp. 552–569; Walton Bean, *Boss Ruef of San Francisco* (Berkeley and Los Angeles: University of California Press, 1952); and ———, "Boss Ruef, the Union Labor Party and the Graft Prosecution in San Francisco, 1901–1911," *Pacific Historical Review,* **XVII** (Nov. 1948), pp. 443–455.

the foundation for the final collapse of the Ruef Machine, was seriously wounded by an assailant in the court room. While awaiting trial, Heney's attacker was murdered in his jail cell. Jurors were bribed with ease, and even though most were quickly exposed, bribery continued to be a major element in the proceedings throughout the four years of hearings and trials. Prosecutor Heney's talented young assistant, Hiram W. Johnson, was given the responsibility for conducting the trials when Heney withdrew because of his wounds. Johnson's work led to the conviction of Ruef and immediately made him the hero of the reform movement. He parlayed this popularity into political fortune and led the Progressive ticket to victory in the 1910 election.

Hiram Johnson was doubly lucky. He inherited the job of prosecuting the notorious Ruef and thereby established himself as the crusading leader of the reformers. He could not have intentionally chosen a better way to cast himself into the public light. Furthermore, he became the acclaimed leader of the well-organized antimachine groups. The anti-graft prosecutions in San Francisco had set off a chain of similar developments in Fresno, Stockton, Sacramento, and Los Angeles. The local reform groups had already formed a statewide organization, the Lincoln-Roosevelt League, by the time Hiram Johnson became the dragon slayer of California politics.

THE LINCOLN-ROOSEVELT LEAGUE[9]

The notoriety of the San Francisco trials accelerated the growth of a splinter group within the Republican party. Discontented with the machinations of the Southern Pacific, the group of rebels was incensed by the actions of the railroad during the 1905 state Republican convention. A popular and mildly progressive candidate, George C. Pardee, was pushed aside by the railroad bloc in favor of James N. Gillett. Edward H. Harriman, president of the Union Pacific Railway which had purchased the Southern Pacific in 1900, felt that Pardee was a distinct threat to the railroad interests and moved to prevent Pardee's nomination. A number of Republicans attempted to secure the nomination of a Democratic candidate attractive to GOP voters. The Democratic party responded by nominating Theodore A. Bell, whose reformist record might have drawn enough Republican support to win the election. The Democratic party, however, was itself split. William Randolph Hearst

---

[9] Mowry, op. cit., pp. 57–86 and Spencer C. Olin, Jr., *California's Prodigal Sons, Hiram Johnson and the Progressives*, 1911–1917 (Berkeley and Los Angeles: University of California Press, 1968), pp. 1–19.

formed the "Independence League," and Bell lost many Democratic and Republican votes to Hearst's candidate, W. H. Langdon.

After Gillett's election, the Republican rebels under the leadership of Edward A. Dickson, editor of the *Los Angeles Express,* and of Chester H. Rowell, editor of the *Fresno Republican,* attempted to form a state-wide reform party. Dickson sent letters to a number of other reformist newspapermen and Republican party leaders who opposed the railroad machine, inviting them to participate in a meeting to be held for the purpose of reforming the Republican party. The fifteen people who met in Los Angeles on May 21, 1907, decided to hold an organizational meeting later in the year. The Lincoln-Roosevelt League was officially formed at this second meeting held on August 1, in Oakland.

The main objectives of the Lincoln-Roosevelt League were to gain control of the Republican party and to mold it in the image of the National Progressives. The original members of the League supported the political aspirations of Theodore Roosevelt and the spirit of reform fostered by the Populists and the Progressives elsewhere in the United States. In 1908, this new organization was instrumental in securing the adoption by the voters of the state of a constitutional amendment permitting the direct primary. The argument of the Lincoln-Roosevelt League and its newspaper-editor members was simple and direct. Destroy the railroad machine; destroy the machine by taking nominations away from the parties; destroy the power of privilege and corruption by returning politics to the people. The League, with the aid of several Democratic as well as Republican legislators, was able to push through the legislature in 1909 a bill ending the convention system in California. This action broke railroad control of the Republican party through the convention and provided Hiram Johnson the means of becoming a candidate for Governor of the state.

THE PROGRESSIVE ERA[10]

The Lincoln-Roosevelt League designated Hiram Johnson as its candidate for Governor in 1910. He conducted a colorful campaign throughout the state, attacking the Southern Pacific, the conservative newspapers, the business community, and the political hacks who were under the control of the Republican regulars. Johnson easily defeated J. N. Gillett, the regular party organization's candidate. California's first gubernatorial direct primary heralded thirteen years of domination of California politics by the Progressives.

---

[10] Mowry, op. cit., pp. 105–273 and Olin, op. cit., pp. 20–103.

Johnson's opponent in the general election was Theodore A. Bell. California's voters were faced with an interesting choice in November 1910: two liberal-reformist candidates, each trying to outdo the other in his attacks upon the common enemy, the Southern Pacific Railroad. The campaign issues were so similar and the candidates so alike that Hiram Johnson, by far the best known of the two at the time of the primary election, won the governorship by only a narrow margin. Although the campaign did not clearly separate the two candidates in the minds of the voters, it did clearly demonstrate that the voters had had enough of corruption and that a thorough house cleaning was in order. The rascals had been thrown out.

Johnson's victory brought with it a Progressive majority in both houses of the state legislature, and the new Governor and his lieutenants went directly to work reforming California's elections code. A series of legislative bills, which have had far-reaching impact, were introduced and passed during the 1911 and 1913 sessions. The radicals, both Republican and Democratic, were able to establish the initiative, referendum, and recall procedures; the crossfiling system for which California was so famous; the home rule provisions, that made local government almost independent of legislative control; the enlargement of the civil service system; the revision of the State Railroad Commission to include all public utilities and to provide it with meaningful powers; the prohibition of child labor; the creation of a set of workmen's compensation laws; and the inauguration of a number of conservation projects within the state. The work of the first two sessions was hailed by Progressives throughout the nation, including Theodore Roosevelt. It was also uniformly attacked by conservative forces within the state as the work of political cranks. Nonetheless, the social and political reforms enacted during the first burst of power of the Progressives have constrained California politics ever since.

The attempts of the Progressives to enhance popular control of government were especially important, both for their impact in 1910 and 1912 and for their long-run influence. Over time, the establishment of non-partisan elections in local government, the gutting of the parties through crossfiling and the direct primary, and the initiative, referendum, and recall that invited direct citizen participation in decision making fostered the antiparty spirit of California politics. In the short run, the political reforms opened a breach in the Republican party that ultimately brought the downfall of the Progressives and the re-establishment of conservative control in the party.

Johnson's success brought forth anguished rejoinders from the conservative wing of the party. Conservatives were appalled by the prospects of popularization of government promised by the Progressive reforms.

Soon, however, conservatives saw that their attacks upon Johnson and the reformists would result only in animosity toward their cause. They attempted to make peace and close ranks, but were rudely rebuffed by Johnson. Conservatives then made the contest an intraparty struggle—one that in the end brought conservative victory.

The gulf between conservatives and liberals in the California Republican party was insurmountably widened by the national aspirations of Hiram Johnson. An ambitious man, Johnson leaped at the opportunity to be Theodore Roosevelt's running mate in the 1912 presidential election. This ticket split the Republican vote across the nation and Woodrow Wilson defeated both Roosevelt and William H. Taft. Although California supported the Progressive running mates, Johnson's defeat in national politics weakened his position within the California scene, even within the Progressive wing of the Republican party. The splintering effects of the national loss divided state Republicans into three or four camps, with the Progressives bolting the party in 1913 to form a completely independent organization. This experiment lasted only one year. Although Hiram Johnson was re-elected Governor in 1914, the California Progressive Movement was already beginning to lose its momentum. Conservative forces openly opposed Johnson during the 1915 session of the legislature. Increasingly frustrated and embittered by his lack of success within his own party, Johnson ran for the U.S. Senate and was elected in 1916.

Before his resignation Governor Johnson indicated that William Stephens was his successor. Stephens was duly elected in 1918, but immediately his administration began to suffer from the factionalism that had developed during Johnson's tenure. Stephens faced a legislature filled with members who had no strong party loyalty. The Progressives, anticipating the intraparty struggle and the formation of a third party for Progressives, had in 1913 amended the direct primary law to permit a candidate to run in the primary election of more than one party, a provision known as *crossfiling*. Thus, Progressives were able to run in both the Progressive and the Republican primaries. Few Republicans, however, changed parties for the 1914 election and the Progressives suffered a setback. The crossfiling device intended to serve Progressive candidates actually hurt them and Governor Stephens. Crossfiling confused party labels and party loyalty. In fact, it produced a basically nonpartisan legislature in 1918 in which individual legislators made their own deals independent of the party and its nominal leader. Under these circumstances, it is no wonder that the administration of Governor Stephens stands as a tribute to the influence of interest groups and to the failure of party leaders to hold the party line.

Conservative elements within the Republican party were quick to

take advantage of the ambivalence created by the nonpartisan character
of legislative politics and quickly forced the administrative leaders who
followed Stephens to mold their programs along conservative rather
than Progressive lines. The compromises worked out between liberal
governors and conservative leaders in the legislature further disenchanted
the Progressives within the Republican party, especially many of the
professionals and journalists who had founded the Lincoln-Roosevelt
League. They felt that their great dream had come to naught. Once
again, a disgust with party politics began to develop and slowly partisan
politics became the arena for those who enjoyed the low-level corruption
that characterizes a system devoted almost exclusively to interest group
politics.

In 1922, conservative leaders were able to dictate the nomination and
election of Friend W. Richardson as Governor. Although the Progressives made a small resurgence with the election of C. C. Young four
years later, 1923 marks the practical end of the Progressive era. From the
Richardson administration until Olson's election in 1938, conservatives
in both the Republican and Democratic parties successfully contained
liberal elements, and without meaningful opposition from the left, Republicans ruled California with an easy style often called *Republican
normalcy*.

normalcy and depression: 1924-1941

The economic well-being and political lethargy characteristic of much
of the United States during the 1920s were also predominant in California. The Progressives' spirit soon blended into the mainstream of
Republican conservatism. A series of undistinguished politicians were
elected to office and partisan politics became a game where powerful
interests negotiated among themselves for the distribution of public
benefits. The state's agricultural economy recovered from a postwar
slump and began to make a comeback. Extraction industries—lumber
and oil—began to boom. It appeared that everyone was making money
and the pressing economic and political problems that had fostered
radicalism in the 1890s and the Progressive movement in the early 1900s
were forgotten or masked behind a general feeling of prosperity.

The depression changed this picture throughout the nation. Even in
California, the great economic privations of the Thirties altered conventional political practices. In the Golden State, however, the political

impact of the depression and Franklin D. Roosevelt's New Deal did not bring the overthrow of the Republican party; instead, the Republicans continued to flourish.

CONSERVATIVE REPUBLICANISM[11]

Friend Richardson, who succeeded to the governorship in 1923 by defeating William Stephenson in the Republican primary, moved the GOP program several notches to the right. Although moderate and Progressive strength was sufficient to oust Richardson in the 1926 primary election, this was the last battle the Progressives would win. C. C. Young, the last of the Progressives to hold the governor's chair was replaced in the 1930 election by a do-nothing moderate James Rolph of San Francisco. Firmly entrenched, the conservative wing of the Republican party flourished under Rolph and his successor, Frank Merriam, who served California from the time of Rolph's death in 1934 to the election of the Democrat Culbert Olson in 1938. With the exception of Young, the governors who held office in the sixteen years of Republican normalcy were at best uninspiring. Young tried to pursue Progressive values, but he was able to accomplish little.

The administrations of Rolph and Merriam marked the end of the intraparty struggle among Republicans. Merriam was a hard-working conservative politician who had been Speaker of the Assembly and Lieutenant Governor. He proved the ideal candidate to defeat California's most famous socialist, Upton Sinclair, in his bid for Governor in 1934.

RADICALISM AND REACTION[12]

Upton Sinclair entered the Democratic gubernatorial primary in 1934. A socialist until the eve of his filing for nomination, Sinclair had written a book called *I, Governor of California, and How I Ended Poverty*, which appealed to hundreds of thousands of unemployed Americans. Much to the dismay of the Democratic regulars, Sinclair easily won the primary and went on to challenge Merriam. The utopian images aroused by Sinclair frightened both the left and the right, and Merriam's supporters

---

[11] Mowry, op. cit., pp. 274–301; Olin, op. cit., pp. 103–184; Bean, *California, an Interpretive History*, pp. 354–367.

[12] Arthur M. Schlesinger, Jr., *The Age of Roosevelt*, vol. III, *The Politics of Upheaval* (Cambridge, Mass.: Houghton Mifflin Company, 1960), pp. 109–124; Upton Sinclair, *Autobiography;* and Charles E. Larsen, "The Epic Campaign of 1934," *Pacific Historical Review*, XXVII (May 1958), pp. 127–148.

were able to translate these fears into a Red-Scare. The EPIC (End Poverty in California) program, based upon cooperatives and barter exchange, was characterized as "socialistic," "collectivistic," and "Bolshevistic" by opponents within both parties and the press. Republican conservatives had a field day and the utopian visionary was soundly defeated in the general election. This election widened the schisms in Democratic ranks and delayed by four years the party's return to political prominence in California.

DEPRESSION AND DEMOCRATIC FORTUNES[13]

A curious thing happened in California during the elections of the 1930s. It developed a bifurcated political culture. On national issues and in national elections, voters aligned with Democrats and the New Deal. On state issues and in state elections, voters generally supported Republicans and conservative platforms. Although the administration of Olson, 1938–1942, offered a brief Democratic interlude, Republicans continued to control the state, and a base of political operations was laid that allowed Republican dominance into the 1950s. Democrats secured support for FDR and Truman and elected a majority of California's members of Congress from 1932 to 1946, but they were not able to control both houses of the state legislature until 1958.

Roosevelt and the New Deal carried many state Democratic parties into power during the 1930s. What happened in California? Two things: the fateful 1934 election and the fitful administration of Olson. Sinclair not only split the Democratic party, but made it appear to the public that radicals had gained control of the party. Although the reaction in 1934 was clear, long-term effects were more severe. Some EPIC candidates, including Culbert L. Olson, were elected to legislative office in 1934 and enough additional Democrats were elected ot the Assembly two years later for the party to gain control of the lower house of the state legislature for the first time since 1894. This election and Olson's victory in 1938 seemed to indicate a possible Democratic resurgence in state politics. This hope was short lived.

Control of the Assembly for two sessions and the election of a governor did not mean control of the state's politics. Republicans remained the major force in the state and Olson's administration suffered one setback

---

[13] Bean, *California, An Interpretive History,* pp. 409–424 and Robert E. Burke, *Olson's New Deal for California* (Berkeley and Los Angeles: University of California Press, 1953).

after another. Olson, a reformer, came to the governorship when the tide was already turning against the reforms of the New Deal and against the radicalism fostered in California by the depression. He was frustrated not only by Republicans, who controlled the state Senate, and held the offices of Attorney General, Secretary of State, Controller, and Treasurer, but also by a conservative "economy bloc" within his own party.

The failure of Olson's administration and the general swing toward the right, particularly in southern California, contributed to the ascendancy of Earl Warren. Warren, who was Attorney General under Olson, used his office to snipe at the ineptness of Olson. He developed an image as a moderate who could protect California from the excesses of radicals within the Democratic party and who could provide strong leadership. Warren was an easy victor in the Republican primary of 1942 and was elected Governor. His election brought to an end the hopes of state Democratic regulars of riding the national party fortunes to power. It also marked the beginning of sixteen more years of uninterrupted Republican dominance of California politics.

the warren era: 1942-1954[14]

Earl Warren was an experienced and polished politician when he was elected Governor of California in 1942. He had held public office since 1919, and had served as district attorney of Alameda County from 1925 to 1938. He was also experienced in party politics and had served as chairman of the Republican State Central Committee. He had lived through the bitter decline of the Progressive wing of the Republican party and had seen personal and ideological clashes render the Democratic party impotent during the 1920s and 1930s. He was determined that his career was not going to be marred by the struggle between party factions. Warren adopted a style of politics characterized as independent and personal. In short, the new Governor held himself above intraparty struggles and interparty competition.

---

[14] Lloyd R. Henderson, "Earl Warren and California Politics," unpublished doctoral dissertation, Dept. of History, University of California, Berkeley, 1965; Richard B. Harvey, "The Political Approach of Earl Warren, Governor of California," unpublished doctoral dissertation, Dept. of Political Science, University of California, Los Angeles, 1959; and William Buchanan, Legislative Partisanship, the Deviant Case of California (Berkeley and Los Angeles: University of California Press, 1963).

INDEPENDENCE AND PERSONAL POLITICS

Earl Warren, in addition to being an experienced professional politician, was also one of the most popular candidates to seek public office in California. He had gained the nomination of the Republican, Democratic, and Progressive parties in his successful bid for Attorney General in 1938. Although he failed to gain the Democratic gubernatorial nomination in 1942, he received 57 per cent of the statewide vote in the general election, indicating a large number of registered Democrats voted for him. In 1946, via California's crossfiling system, he became the only Governor in the state's history to win the nomination of both major parties. Governor Warren won the 1950 election by a million votes, about the same margin the Democrats held in the total vote registration. He was the only candidate to be elected Governor three times. In all three of his victorious campaigns, his tremendous personal popularity was the key to victory, and he played upon this strength by emphasizing his individuality and independence from the other Republican office seekers and from the Republican slate.

"Personal accountability" is the phrase Warren used to describe his stand. Probably more than any other candidate, he stressed personal campaigning and shunned his party's organization and funds. He formed his own organization and tapped independent sources of funds. He rarely discussed issues as a partisan, even in private conversations. In a sense, Earl Warren invented personal campaigning as an adjunction to his overriding desire to remain politically "clean." His style of personal campaigning has been a fixture in California's politics since his first term in office.

NEO-PROGRESSIVISM UNDER WARREN

As Governor, Warren viewed himself as a Progressive. He was committed to the nonpartisanship and basic liberalism of the Progressive period and he successfully copied its political style.

Openly and purposefully nonpartisan, he refused to indicate his choices for leadership positions in either house of the state legislature. There was no overt Warren clique in the legislature. He sought the advice of leaders of both parties and allowed legislators to assist in the formation of his basic programs. He co-opted the leaders of the opposition party into his administration more successfully than any other California governor. Frequently, top administrative positions were filled after a nationwide search by a bipartisan advisory committee. The Governor made judicious use of advisory committees, usually non-partisan or bipartisan in nature, to assist in drafting proposed legislation and study of California's problems. It is easy to see why Warren is often characterized as the ideal Progressive. Above politics, he was able to deal with politicians, administrators, interest groups, and the public without regard to partisan bias and without any sense of making a deal.

Warren's style of politics was not only tailored to take advantage of the nonpartisan ethos inherited from the Progressive era, but his programs were designed to appeal to the liberal tradition in California. Joseph P. Harris, an admirer of Warren and a long-time student of California politics, has pointed out that as Governor, Warren received the continual support of the state's three largest conservative newspapers at the same time he espoused such liberal measures as old-age pensions, workmen's compensation, health insurance, prison reform, mental health programs, and welfare legislation. Warren's values and ideals were closer to the traditions of the Democratic party than those of the GOP. Therein lies the success of the Warren programs. A popular leader of the minority party, he was able to gain the support of the moderates and liberals of both parties. In effect, neo-Progressive politics under Warren cut away the natural strength of the Democratic party just as Progressivism under Johnson had done thirty years before. Warren's political style provided Republicans with an unimpeachable, middle-of-the-road leader who could and did beat Democrats at their own game.

REPUBLICAN FACTIONALISM

The very individualism and liberalism that endeared Warren to most Democrats and Republicans brought sharp criticism from more conservative elements. Many loyal Republicans viewed the Warren style and programs with suspicion. He appeared too similar to the dreaded Franklin Roosevelt and Harry Truman. The conservative wing of the GOP fought Warren's measures in the legislature. The fact that Warren was nominated as the favorite son candidate in 1948 and was Thomas E. Dewey's running mate in the presidential election did little to placate the fears of the conservatives in the Republican party. They viewed Dewey as an evil equal to Truman, and Senator Robert Taft of Ohio as the hero of true Republicanism.

After Warren's defeat as part of the national ticket, conservative hostility intensified. However, it was checked in 1950 when James Roosevelt was nominated by the Democratic party to oppose Warren for the governorship. Although conservatives were suspicious of Warren, they viewed Roosevelt as an outright threat. Republican leaders joined in a strong campaign against FDR's son. Warren won an unprecedented third term by a majority of more than a million votes. The Democratic party, as usual, was divided and demoralized, and its only successful candidate was incumbent Attorney General, Edmund G. Brown.

Republicans had hardly recovered from the 1950 primary and general elections when it became clear that Warren was going to run again as favorite son candidate in the 1952 presidential primary. This time conservatives refused to rally around the Governor and a separate slate of delegates was run in opposition to Warren. After a bitter campaign, the regular Republican slate under Warren was elected and the Governor went to the 1952 Republican convention as a dark horse candidate for the presidency, and many observers felt he had a good chance to repeat as the candidate for the vice-presidency. General Dwight Eisenhower and another Californian, Richard Nixon, won the nominations. Earl Warren returned to California once more, an unsuccessful aspirant to national office.

The beginning of the end of the Warren era came when President Eisenhower appointed Warren Chief Justice of the U.S. Supreme Court. Lieutenant Governor Goodwin Knight was able to unite the party behind him during his first year in office and during the 1954 election campaign. However, the coalition which Warren had built up over the years was beginning to crumble and Knight's leadership of the California Republican party was challenged from several quarters.

Vice-President Nixon lost no time in using his office as a base to secure political support in California and elsewhere. Nixon achieved success as a militant anticommunist in his campaigns for the House in 1946 and for the U.S. Senate in 1950, but he began to change his political image from conservative to moderate. Presidential ambition required that he develop the broadest possible support in California.

U.S. Senator William Knowland, known as one of the most able conservatives in Congress, also had presidential ambitions. He saw himself as the heir to Robert Taft's conservative bloc in the national Republican party. Knowland soon began to challenge Knight's leadership of the California Republican party and became the acknowledged leader of California conservatives. The other U.S. Senator, Thomas Kuchel, whom Warren had appointed to fill the seat vacated by Vice-President Nixon, made no overt claim to leadership in the state party at this time, even though much of the liberal membership of the Republican party identified with him as Warren's protegé.

Governor Knight found himself in the untidy position of having three potential claimants for his position as state party leader. He realized that if he was ever to become a serious candidate for national office, he must alter his image as a conservative and appeal to the more liberal elements in both parties. Although the GOP lost some seats in the state legislature in 1952, Knight was able to use both partisan and bipartisan appeals to secure support for the continuation of the Warren programs. Thus, the Governor was able to face the 1954 Republican primary with the expectation that he would be renominated and then re-elected. Both these expectations proved correct. However, disharmony soon struck the Republicans; disharmony that ultimately brought downfall.

democratic and republican rivalry: 1954·1969

Ironically, the California Democratic party was entering a period of revitalization just as the national party was suffering its worst hardships in decades. The overwhelming victory of General Eisenhower in 1952 marked the lowest point in the fortunes of the Democratic party since the days of Calvin Coolidge. This same campaign year marked the beginning of a resurgence in California politics for Democrats. A number of local Democratic clubs, primarily devoted to the candidacy of Adlai Stevenson, took an active part in the 1952 presidential campaign. and provided the root-stock of the California Democratic Council (CDC), which was formed in 1953. The local clubs, filled with enthusiastic amateurs, and the statewide Council provided the organizational muscle the Democrats had long needed at the grass roots level. Democratic fortunes began to rise from this time until the victory of Governor Brown in 1958, and there is little doubt that the clubs and the amateurs contributed mightily to the restoration of the Democratic party to power in California.

THE GENERAL ELECTION OF 1954

At first glance, the 1954 election would hardly seem to be a happy event for Democrats. Only one of their candidates for statewide office won—Edmund Brown, who ran for re-election as Attorney General. After one hundred years of costly fratricidal conflict, however, leaders of the Democratic party in California were united behind the party slate of candidates.

The Republican party, in contrast, was torn by dissension among its leaders. Goodwin Knight, the incumbent, was renominated and re-elected Governor, but the cost was high. Knight, who appeared to be a safe conservative at the time of his election as Lieutenant Governor in 1950, had turned out to be another Earl Warren when elevated to the Governor's chair. Seeking to secure the same broad-based support of his predecessor, he made overt appeals to organized labor, a traditional target of abuse from the right wing of his own party. Conservative leaders, already infuriated at the antics of Warren at the 1952 Republican National Convention and at the failure of their hero, Senator Robert Taft, were beside themselves at the spectacle of one of their own courting labor support.

Republican conservatives sought a more appropriate leader than this blossoming Progressive whom they viewed as a turncoat. U.S. Senator William Knowland became the active leader of conservative elements and even began to challenge Taft's leadership at the national level. Vice-President Richard Nixon found himself in the middle between Knight and Knowland, a role he cherished. Although the resulting broad-based support for Nixon was to pay off in the long run, for the time being the GOP was divided into three distinct factions. The Democrats could not have been happier. The factionalism of the Republican party which Governor Warren had so successfully managed was beginning to transform the party into a hopeless quagmire.

DEMOCRATIC LANDSLIDE IN 1958

Complete collapse of the Warren-inspired coalitions came with the elections of 1958. The Republicans, who had lost ground in the state despite the victory of Eisenhower and Nixon in 1956, suffered a ruinous conflict in the party primary, and a disastrous general election. The Democrats, who were unable to carry California for Stevenson in 1956, enjoyed a harmonious primary and achieved victory in the general election. The overwhelming majority that the Democratic party enjoyed in the voter registration finally paid off. The Democratic party gained full control of the state government for the first time since the 1890s. In this regard, the 1958 election probably may be regarded in the future as equally important as the 1910 election that swept the Progressives into office.

The 1956 California presidential preferential primary brought the ambitions of Nixon and Knight into clear and open conflict. The Vice-President, who wanted to head a favorite son delegation to the national convention, was unable to secure the necessary support among California

Republicans. Senator Knowland retained control of the conservative faction of the party, although he was willing to cooperate with Nixon in intraparty struggles. Governor Knight was hopeful of parlaying his substantial following within the party into a favorite son role for himself. A compromise was reached among the factions that provided that the seventy-member delegation be divided into three, twenty-three member groups.[15] Although a floor fight was expected by some observers, the three groups maintained harmony at the convention and throughout the 1956 campaign.

The tripartite split within the Republican party reappeared during the 1958 primary and the ensuing general election. Knowland, whose Senate seat was up for election in 1958, decided to run for Governor instead. Knight, the incumbent governor, naturally expected to run again and was understandably taken aback by Knowland's announced candidacy. A bitter contest in the Republican primary seemed inevitable, but Vice-President Nixon stepped in and persuaded Governor Knight to withdraw from the gubernatorial race and to seek Knowland's Senate seat instead. Liberals and moderates in the party were understandably upset at Knight's retreat and Knowland's heavy-handed tactics. Injured feelings and a sense of dismay ran high among the rank and file Republicans and the GOP was off to a rocky start.

The effects of the split within Republican ranks upon the election were compounded by an unfortunate choice of issues by Senator Knowland. Perhaps to strengthen his standing with conservatives, Knowland strongly endorsed a right-to-work iniative measure. According to Caspar Weinberger, an important GOP leader and a perceptive observer of Republican politics, Knowland's stand allowed Democrats to charge "extremism" during the campaign and solidify their labor support.[16] Weinberger argues that the issue of extremism had played a crucial role in the Republican victories in 1934, when Merriam defeated Sinclair, and in 1942, when Warren defeated Olson; and that in 1958, the tables were turned and Democrats reaped the benefits of the issue. Knowland, Knight, and the entire statewide Republican ticket, with the exception of Frank M. Jordan, the incumbent Secretary of State of California, were defeated at the polls.

Attorney General Edmund Brown, the only Democratic incumbent holding statewide office, was the party's logical choice for Governor. He was not only experienced in government and politics, but his appeal cut

---

[15] U.S. Senator Thomas Kuchel was the seventieth delegate.

[16] Caspar W. Weinberger, "Republican Politics," in *California Politics and Policies*, E. P. Dvorin and A. J. Misner, eds., (Reading, Mass.: Addison-Wesley, 1966), p. 57.

across factional lines in the Democratic party. Both party regulars and CDC amateurs supported Brown in the primary. After the primary, various factions of the party rallied behind him and the rest of the Democratic ticket.

The 1958 election brought such important Democratic leaders as Alan Cranston, Glenn Anderson, Clair Engle, and Stanley Mosk into office. In addition, sufficient numbers of Democrats were elected to the state legislature to give them control over both houses for the first time in the twentieth century. There is little doubt that the Democrats were riding a wave of reaction against the Republican party and things were looking rosy.

THE RETURN OF DEMOCRATIC FACTIONALISM

Many Democratic partisans had hoped that the tremendous victory of 1958 was the beginning of a period of Democratic dominance of California politics that would rival Republican control in the first half of the century. However, factionalism during the 1960 presidential campaign in California threatened to divide the Democratic coalition that had brought Brown to office only two years earlier.

In the face of dissension within the party, Governor Brown announced that he would be a favorite son candidate in the hope of maintaining party unity. Under Brown's leadership, a slate of delegates to the national convention, representative of all elements within the party, was selected. However, underlying hostility among factions broke into the open during the convention held in Los Angeles. Kennedy forces expected California to swing to their side; Stevenson supporters held firm for their candidate. The resulting vote, divided among Kennedy, Johnson, Stevenson, and others could have only pleased Republican onlookers.

California Democrats were, however, able to unite behind Brown and the national ticket during the campaign, and to run a strong campaign although Kennedy lost the state in the election. A sense of harmony prevailed after the presidential election and Governor Brown was able to secure the 1962 nomination for Governor with little trouble and he defeated Richard Nixon handily at the polls. Yet, things were not so smooth as it might seem. Some were looking beyond Brown's tenure and planning to gain control of gubernatorial succession. Independent bases of power were being developed within and without the party. Speaker Jesse Unruh was proving to be a strong and capable leader of the state Assembly. Alan Cranston was carefully building his own political organization. The CDC, crucial in both the 1958 and 1962 campaigns, was undergoing serious problems, some CDCers viewing their organization as mainly issue-oriented and others as mainly campaign-oriented. Factionalism was once more becoming apparent.

REVITALIZATION OF REPUBLICANISM

The Republican party reaped two unexpected dividends in the 1964 election—a U.S. Senator and a future candidate for the governorship. The presidential primary struggle between Senator Barry Goldwater and Governor Nelson Rockefeller provided strong indications of the depth of Conservative feeling in California. Conservatives had gained important positions in all Republican organizations since the Brown victory of 1958 and this organizational strength was put to good use in Goldwater's primary campaign. Among the nonpolitical luminaries who supported the Senator's candidacy was Ronald Reagan. Reagan's famous speech in support of Goldwater's candidacy made him a hero in conservative camps and started him on the way to the governorship in 1966. The Senator from Arizona defeated Rockefeller in the California primary and was selected as the GOP presidential candidate at San Francisco. At least, there seemed to be a "real choice": conservative Goldwater against liberal Johnson. President Johnson destroyed Goldwater in one of the most impressive state and national victories ever won in American politics. Yet, California Democrats had little cause for rejoicing. At the state level, they had suffered important losses, including the U.S. Senate seat which Clair Engle had held. Engle appeared to be a cinch candidate for re-election. The Senator, however, was incapacitated by what proved to be a terminal malignancy and the Democratic candidacy became an open question. Several Democratic hopefuls indicated an interest in the nomination, including State Attorney General Stanley Mosk, Controller Alan Cranston, and Congressman James Roosevelt. After Mosk's withdrawal, Roosevelt and Cranston both sought the preprimary endorsement of the CDC, with Cranston securing that endorsement. Cranston looked forward to the primary and the general election with some confidence— no CDC endorsed candidate for statewide office had ever lost in the primary. A surprise was coming. On the last day for filing nomination papers, Pierre Salinger flew in from Washington, D.C., and announced his candidacy.

Despite charges of carpetbagging and undue influence from the White House, Salinger won by over 100,000 votes. Democrats were uneasy, for fear the party would be divided in the general election, but Cranston attempted to close ranks by throwing his full support to the former presidential press secretary. Salinger's chances seemed to improve when Governor Brown appointed him to the U.S. Senate after Engle's death. Thus, Salinger approached the general election as the incumbent. The voters of California, however, were attracted to the less controversial George Murphy. Murphy, certainly much more conservative than Salinger, easily won despite President Johnson's overwhelming defeat of Goldwater.

Senator Murphy ran a most effective campaign, playing down his conservativism and avoiding involvement in Goldwater's cause. The carpetbagging issue continued to plague Salinger, even though he, in contrast to Murphy, is a native Californian. Equally important, however, was Salinger's opposition to the "antifair-housing initiative," Proposition 14. The initiative would have rescinded several pieces of legislation constraining the capacity of property owners to discriminate in the disposal of their holdings. Proposition 14 turned out to be one of the most controversial ever to be put before California voters, and Salinger's defeat was nearly by the same margin as the victory of the initiative proposal. Murphy, who took an ambiguous position on Proposition 14, stood out as the voice of moderation and the voters preferred this to the liberal stand of Salinger.

REPUBLICAN VICTORIES IN 1966 AND 1968

The Republicans faced 1966 with renewed hopes and improved organizational strength. The Democrats had reason for concern. The CDC was badly split. The regular party was divided on the question of Brown's possible third-term candidacy, and later on the question of who was to be the party state chairman. Public issues such as the race riots in Watts, continued controversy over fair-housing, demand for reform in mental health and welfare programs, and concern over increasing public spending and taxes plagued the Brown administration. The legislature, under Democratic control, bore the brunt of the controversy over reapportionment, an important sectional issue in California. All this indicated a difficult campaign for the Democrats in 1966, particularly if the Republicans could unite behind a strong candidate for Governor.

Many Democrats and Republicans expected that the GOP candidate would be a moderate or liberal; perhaps U.S. Senator Thomas Kuchel or George Christopher, former mayor of San Francisco. Most observers did not take the proposed candidacy of actor Ronald Reagan very seriously. Soon, however, it became clear that the Republican primary contest would be between Reagan and Christopher. Democratic strategists felt that Christopher would pose the stiffest threat to Brown's bid for a third term, and proceeded to try to knock him off in the primary. Perhaps Reagan did not need their help; he received twice as many votes as Christopher in the primary election.

Governor Brown, with the urging of many key Democratic leaders, had decided to enter his party's primary. Mayor Sam Yorty of Los Angeles, a renegade Democrat in a nonpartisan office, challenged Brown's candidacy and did very well. Yorty's impressive showing frightened Democratic leaders. How would Reagan do in the general election if Yorty had done so well in the primary?

The Democratic party failed to unite behind Brown, with some leaders lax in their efforts and others busily fighting for their own political lives. The campaign settled around a number of issues. The Democrats tried to capitalize on Reagan's lack of experience and his conservative ties. Reagan, in turn, attacked the idea that only professionals should run for office and attempted to make a virtue out of inexperience. The Governor pointed with pride to his record in office, and Republicans attacked it as being too expensive and wasteful. A major issue in the campaign was the University of California and in particular, the Berkeley campus where a series of student demonstrations had taken place since 1963. Reagan found his attacks upon the University and its administration a crowd pleaser in the campaign and Governor Brown was put on the defensive. Disorder in the streets, by now a stock issue with conservatives, was a rallying point for Reagan supporters. In all, the Republicans focused on the Brown record and the Democrats concentrated on personalities and the conservative connections of Ronald Reagan. The voters felt it was time for a change and Reagan scored an overwhelming victory at the polls.

Only one Democrat, Attorney General Thomas Lynch, was returned to office. Governor Brown, Lieutenant-Governor Glenn Anderson, Controller Cranston, and Treasurer Bert A. Betts were turned out of office. Governor Reagan, Lieutenant-Governor Robert Finch, Controller Houston Flournoy, and Treasurer Ivy Baker Priest joined incumbent Secretary of State Frank Jordan to make it a near Republican sweep in the executive branch. Equally impressive were the Republican gains in the state legislature. The 1967 Democratic majority in the Assembly was four seats and in the Senate it was two seats. The 1966 election was a foretaste of the future. Except for the election of Alan Cranston as U.S. Senator, the Democrats were even more rudely treated in 1968.

The 1968 election was a mixed victory for the Republicans. The incumbent U.S. Senator, Thomas Kuchel, was defeated in the primary by Superintendent of Public Instruction, Dr. Max Rafferty. In turn, Dr. Rafferty was defeated by Cranston in the Democrat's second attempt to be elected to the U.S. Senate. President Richard M. Nixon carried California in his second attempt for the nation's highest office. In the state elections, Republicans gained three seats in the Assembly and Robert Monagan, Republican from Tracy, was made Speaker in place of Jesse Unruh, who became the minority leader. The Senate, where the Republicans gained one seat in 1967,[17] retained its 20–20 split between the two parties until the death of George Miller a week before the 1969 session was to begin. When a Republican won this seat, the GOP gained a 21–19 edge.

The 1968 election must be considered a net gain for the Republican party, but the various campaigns took their toll. The bitterest primary campaign was between Dr. Rafferty, a conservative, and the liberal Kuchel. It demonstrated the wide split between the liberal and conservative appeals among Republican voters. Conservative Republicans had hoped to defeat Kuchel for some time and Rafferty criticized his opponent for being more liberal than the Democrats. A number of moderate and liberal Republicans appear to have been offended by Rafferty's tactics and voted for Cranston. The contest between Rafferty and Cranston in the general election brought forth many of the same issues as the primary—Vietnam, the Supreme Court, law and order, the grape strike, radicalism among ethnic minorities, student demonstrations —but with different results. Although Rafferty did well in the suburban areas, Cranston carried most of the counties where Kuchel had won, plus Los Angeles County, and won handily.

The presidential primary and general election was a serious organizational and personal blow to many California Democrats. Senator Robert F. Kennedy, who won the primary election from Senator Eugene McCarthy and from the regular Democratic slate, was murdered on the night of his victory. The Kennedy delegation, under the leadership of Jesse Unruh, was reconstituted after the Senator's death to include a number of McCarthy's supporters. Thus, it represented a liberal-moderate coalition that supported the peace plank of the national platform and opposed the nomination of Vice-President Hubert Humphrey.

In the Republican primary, Governor Reagan easily won as favorite son. He finally became an announced candidate the day the national convention began and seriously sought the presidential nomination. President Nixon defeated all challengers and carried California in the general election with the strong backing of Governor Reagan and the state Republican party.

Mr. Nixon won in California by 223,328 votes, about 3.6 per cent of the total votes cast for the candidates of the two major parties. Minor parties, however, were noticeable in this state for the first time since the 1930s. George Wallace and the American Independent Party received 487,270 votes in November 1968. The Peace and Freedom Party, a left-

---

[17] Senator Eugene McAteer, Democrat from San Francisco, died during the 1967 legislative session and his seat was won by Republican Milton Marks.

wing organization, had about 71,000 registered voters as compared with the more than 90,000 persons registered as members of the American Independent Party. Neither party did well in the general election although they each nominated several candidates for congressional and state contests. The fact that nearly 1 per cent of the voters would register for these radical parties and that Governor Wallace received about 6.6 per cent of the vote cast for presidential electors indicates that California's tradition of radical movements is still with us.

two-party competition in california

The 1958 election ended Republican dominance of California politics. The 1966 election ended dreams of Democratic domination of our politics. The 1968 election indicated that two-party competition is becoming an established pattern in the state. During the past two decades, it had become increasingly apparent that California politics was becoming more competitive, that both major parties would share in the direction of the state's government. The history of the past twenty years, however, also made it clear that factionalism and antipartyism will continue to plague both parties.

Established rivalries divided both parties. Republicans, in spite of the unity they displayed in 1966, have already lost a U.S. Senate seat largely because of splits along traditional lines. Since defeat in 1966, Alan Cranston, Jesse Unruh, Joseph Alioto, and Sam Yorty have been among those vying for leadership within the Democratic party. There is no question that intraparty factionalism will remain in California, as in so many states, a fixture with which future leaders will struggle.

California voters and political leaders have illustrated the nature of the state's antiparty tradition. Reagan ran, proudly, as a "citizen-politician" and charged Brown with the evil of professionalism. Brown ran as the heir to the "Progressive tradition of Hiram Johnson and Earl Warren." Max Rafferty, state Superintendent of Public Instruction, and Sam Yorty, Mayor of Los Angeles, both incumbents in nonpartisan positions, continue to seek partisan office, both stressing their independence from partisan loyalties.

Later chapters are devoted to closer examination of voting patterns, campaigning practices, parties, and partisanship in California. It is sufficient to observe at this point that the two major difficulties that have frustrated partisan politics in California still remain.

CHAPTER 3

voter registration
and primaries

oting in the United States is the fundamental act of self-
government. It provides the citizen in our free society
the right to make a judgment, to state a choice, to participate in the running of government—in the community,
the state, and the nation. The ballot box is the medium for
the expression of the consent of the governed." So concluded a commission created by President John F. Kennedy in 1963 to study the reasons for low voter turnout
in America.[1] The statement reaffirms a rather rudimentary
and hardly contestable notion regarding the process of
democracy. There are many modes of political participation, many ways in which a citizen may seek to affect the
actions of government and have his voice heard by those
who are the makers of public policy. But voting is that
mode of political action most familiar to most people:
Only a minority of our citizens fail to vote at one time or
another; and only an even smaller minority choose to

---

[1] *Report of the President's Commission on Registration and Voting
Participation*, Nov. 1963, p. 5.

adopt additional and less elementary modes of political participation.

The California citizen takes three discrete and deliberate steps to become a full voting participant in the state's political process: He registers to vote, thereby establishing his eligibility to take each of the other two steps; he votes in the primary election held on the first Tuesday after the first Monday in June of every even-numbered year; and he votes in the general election held on the first Tuesday after the first Monday in November of every even-numbered year.[2] At each step he must also decide which party or which candidates will receive his support. The present chapter deals with the first two steps of the voting process—registration and primary voting. The next chapter deals with the third step in the process—general election voting.

registration

To vote in California one must first register. That is, he must complete an "affidavit of registration" before the appropriate authority prior to a specified date in advance of the election in which he hopes to vote. (See Figure 3–1, an example of a registration affidavit used in California.) At the time of the 1968 general election, there were approximately eight and one-half million registered voters in California. But there were three and one-quarter million persons of voting age in the state who were *not* registered. Thus on election day in November over 25 per cent of the over-twenty-one population did not have even the option of voting for Richard Nixon or Hubert Humphrey, Alan Cranston or Max Rafferty. Between 20 and 30 per cent of California's voting-age population has been unregistered at the time of each general election since 1948.[3] (See Table 3–1.)[4]

---

[2] Local elections—nonpartisan in nature—are held at various times (e.g., municipal elections in general law cities occur in April of odd-numbered years). In addition, special elections to fill vacancies, to allow the electorate to vote on recall proposals, and the like may he held at any time.

[3] The percentage unregistered tends to be somewhat smaller in presidential election years, when public interest in politics is greater, than in nonpresidential, midterm election years.

[4] Most of the statistical data presented in the tables in this chapter and the next are derived from materials published by the Bureau of the Census (U.S. Department of Commerce), by the California Secretary of State in his periodic Reports of Registration and Statements of Vote, and by Eugene C. Lee in his *California Votes: 1928–1960*, (Berkeley: Institute of Governmental Studies, University of

66	67	68	69	70	71	72	73	74	75	76	77	78	79	80	81	82	83	84
85	86	87	88	89	90	91	92	93	94	95	96	97	98	99	100	101	102	103

OFFICE USE ONLY

Re-Registration_____Duplicate_____Death_____

Failure to Vote_____Affidavit of Cancellation_____

Cancelled_____, 19____

For reason indicated by √

W. T. PAASCH, County Clerk, By_____
Deputy

For transfer or Change of Name

I am registered under the name of

From _____

(or address) in this County, and I hereby authorize the cancellation of my last previous registration.

Precinct _____ Assembly District No. _____ No. _____

STATE OF CALIFORNIA
County of Contra Costa } ss.

AFFIDAVIT OF REGISTRATION

The undersigned affiant, being duly sworn, says: I will be at least 21 years of age at the time of the next succeeding election, a citizen of the United States 90 days prior thereto, and a resident of the State one year, of the County 90 days, and of the Precinct 54 days preceding next such election, and will be an elector of the County at the next succeeding election.

1. I am not now registered as a voter in this State.
   (If now registered in this county under this or another name, mark out word "not" and fill out transfer clause at top. If now registered in another county, mark out word "not" and execute a separate affidavit of cancellation before registering.)

2. My full name is_____
   (Including Christian or given name, and middle name or initial, and in case of women, the prefix Miss or Mrs.)

3. My residence is_____ Street
   (Do not write P. O. Box or R. F. D. Route above See Item 4.) Avenue

   between _____ and _____ Streets

4. Post-office address is_____
   (R. F. D. Route Box Number or Post Office Box Number)   (City or Town)   (Zip Code)

5. I intend to affiliate at the ensuing primary election with the _____ Party.
   (If affiliation is not given, write or stamp "Decline to State.")

6. My occupation is_____

7. My height is_____feet_____inches.

8. I was born in_____
   (State or Country)

9. I acquired citizenship by
   (Underline method of acquiring citizenship.)
   a. Decree of Court. Give date and place below.
   b. Father's naturalization. Mother's naturalization.
   c. Citizenship of father. Give name below.
   d. Marriage to a citizen. Fill in date, place and husband's name below.
   e. Naturalization of my husband. Fill in husband's name, date and place of nat. below.
   f. Act of Congress.   g. Treaty.

   (when) _____ _____ _____ (where) _____ _____ _____
         (month)   (day)   year)   (city)   (state)

   father's
   My husband's name is (was) _____
   mother's   (To be filled out when citizenship depends on citizenship or naturalization of parent or husband.)

10. I can_____reed the Constitution in the English language; I can_____write my name; I am entitled to vote by reason of having been on October 10, 1911, an elector.

    I can_____ mark my ballot by reason of_____
                                          (State physical disability, if any)

11. I am not disqualified to vote by reason of a felony conviction.

Subscribed and sworn to before me this

_____day of_____, 19____

W. T. PAASCH, County Clerk

By_____
           Deputy County Clerk.

AFFIANT SIGN HERE (including Christian or given name, and middle name or initial.)

_____
Print Name Here

RESIDENCE _____ (Street Address)

VOTING RECORD   For Use of County Clerk Only.

YEAR	1968	1970	1972	1974	1976	1978	1980	1982	1984	1986	1988	1990	1992
GENL.													

TRIPLICATE
50M H-85

FIGURE 3–1   REGISTRATION AFFIDAVIT

	Civilian Population 21 and Over (in thousands)	Registered Voters (in thousands)	Per Cent Registered
°1948	6,714	5,062	75.4
1950	7,212	5,245	72.7
°1952	7,571	5,998	79.0
1954	7,846	5,885	75.0
°1956	8,412	6,409	76.2
1958	8,716	6,752	77.5
°1960	9,549	7,465	78.2
1962	10,042	7,531	75.0
°1964	10,698	8,184	76.5
1966	11,262	8,341	74.1
°1968	11,840	8,588	72.5

° Presidential election year.

Note: The 1950 population estimate is for April; 1952, 1956, and 1958 estimates are for November. All others are for July.

Those who do not register to vote fail to do so for many reasons. Some are indifferent to election politics because they feel they lack the requisite informational background, because they are uncertain of their political convictions, or because they are contented with the social and political system and feel no need to take action. Others may have serious and rationally conceived grievances against their government but feel that the political system will be indifferent to them regardless of whether they vote or not.

For many persons, however, failure to register is a function of legal rather than psychological or attitudinal barriers. Under the United States Constitution the states are vested with the power to determine the qualifications for voting and to determine how the individual is to establish that he meets those qualifications. The states are obliged to observe certain prescribed limits in using this power, but within these limits they are left with a great deal of discretion.[5] This discretion

California, 1963). Although now somewhat out-of-date, Lee's work is an invaluable source of data on registration and voting in California.

[5] Among the limits is the requirement in Article I of the United States Constitution that anyone permitted to vote for "the most numerous branch of the state legislature" must also be permitted to vote in elections for seats in the U.S. House of Representatives. The Seventeenth Amendment extends the same principle of

**TABLE 3–2   WHO MAY REGISTER IN CALIFORNIA:
CONSTITUTIONAL REQUIREMENTS REGARDING
VOTER ELIGIBILITY**

By election day the voter must be

Twenty-one years old

A U.S. citizen for 90 days

Neither a convicted felon, nor an idiot, nor insane

A resident of the state for one year, of the county for 90 days, and of the precinct for 54 days

Able to read the California Constitution and sign his name

---

operates most directly through the laws pertaining to voter registration. In some states these laws better facilitate voting participation than in other states. Two aspects of the legal context of registration in California are of concern here. Both are treated in terms of the extent to which they do or do not facilitate voting participation. First is the question of voter eligibility (*who* may register), and second is the manner in which the state administers voter registration (*how* a person may register).

WHO MAY REGISTER AND HOW?

It is when registering that the individual is directly confronted with voter eligibility requirements established in the California Constitution. (See Table 3–2 for a summary of these requirements.) When completing his registration affidavit he must identify himself by giving his name, address, occupation, height, and place of birth, and he must state his party affiliation or be registered as a "decline to state." He must also affirm that he is qualified to vote or will be at the time of the next election. The U.S. Census Bureau estimates that 1,600,000 of the 3,250,000 voting age Californians unregistered in 1968 were not even in the run-

---

voter eligibility to the election of U.S. Senators. The Fourteenth Amendment provides that a state which denies the right to vote to twenty-one-year-old male citizens "except for participation in rebellion, or other crime" shall have the size of its delegation to the U.S. House of Representatives appropriately reduced. (The provision has never been invoked despite its obvious applicability to several states.) The Fifteenth Amendment prohibits the states from denying the right to vote on the basis of race, color, or previous condition of servitude, and federal legislation has also been passed to prevent racial discrimination in voting. The Nineteenth Amendment forbids the states to deny the right to vote on the basis of sex. The Twenty-fourth Amendment makes the payment of a poll tax unconstitutional as a prerequisite to voting in national elections.

ning—their failure to take this first step in the voting process resulted from the fact that they simply were not eligible under state law.

California's voting age requirement, twenty-one, itself excludes many persons who would otherwise be voting participants in the political process. In 1968 four states permitted persons under twenty-one to vote. Proposals to lower the voting age have long been under consideration in California. In 1939, for example, Assemblyman Sam Yorty (now mayor of Los Angeles) introduced a resolution into the state legislature to extend the suffrage to eighteen-year-olds. More recently—in 1969—the State Constitution Revision Commission endorsed lowering the voting age to nineteen, and agreed to submit the proposal to the legislature, probably in 1970, as part of its package of suggested modifications for the California constitution.

Similar attempts have been made regularly at the national level. In the Ninetieth Congress alone some fifty proposals came before Congress to let eighteen-year-olds vote, including a Constitutional Amendment to that effect proposed by President Lyndon Johnson.[6] However, it is doubtful that a reduction in the voting age would increase the *percentage* of voting age citizens who register to vote, as surveys of those already eligible indicate that the young are more likely to be nonvoters than their elders. That is, although lowering the voting age to eighteen at this time would extend the suffrage to about one million young persons in California,[7] it may well be that they would not register in proportions as great as those for persons over twenty-one. Nevertheless, it has been argued that extension of the franchise to younger persons is in order because today's young are better educated than their predecessors, because they assume so many of the burdens of the nation, because their lives can be so significantly affected by the action of government, and

---

[6] Said the President when sending the measure to Congress, "Under a government by and for the people, the right to vote is the most basic right of all. It is the right on which all others finally stand. Such a right is not to be idly conferred or blindly withheld. . . .

"We should now extend the right to vote to more than ten million citizens unjustly denied the right. They are the young men and women of America between the ages of 18 and 21. [They] are far more ready, far better qualified, far more able to discharge the highest duty of citizenship than any generation of the past. . . .

"America can only prosper from the infusion of youthful energy, initiative, vigor, and intelligence into our political processes. . . . The time has come to grant our youth what we ask of them but still deny to them—full and responsible participation in our American democracy."

[7] According to the U.S. Census Bureau, 1,054,000 Californians were in the eighteen- to twenty-one-year-old age group at the time of the 1968 presidential election.

because a greater and greater proportion of the total population is in the pre-twenty-one age bracket.

Like every other state, California requires that one be a United States citizen if he is to vote. Thus the approximately 660,000 aliens of voting age living in the state were prohibited from registering in 1968. Several tens of thousands of persons are also prohibited from registering because they have been previously convicted of a felony, are classified as idiots, or have been legally judged insane.[8] Here again California follows a pattern of selective eligibility found generally throughout the United States.

All states have residency requirements. California's, however, seem somewhat harsh and they become especially restrictive when put into the context of the high rate of migration into the state from elsewhere and the high rate of population mobility within the state. To register, the California citizen must affirm that at the time of the coming election he will have been a one-year resident of the state, a ninety-day resident of his county, and a fifty-four-day resident of his voting precinct.[9] The U.S. Census Bureau estimates that 827,000 Californians could not register to vote in 1968 because they failed to meet these requirements. Seventeen states had state residency requirements of *under* one year at the time of the last presidential election, with only one—Mississippi—requiring more than one year. Twenty-three states had county residency requirements less stringent than California and thirteen had more stringent requirements. Thirty-eight states had precinct residency requirements of less than California's fifty-four days—some having no such requirement at all—while eleven required longer residency in the precinct.[10] The 1963 President's Commission to study registration and voting participation cited at the beginning of this chapter recommended several measures regarding registration to increase voting participation. On residency they concluded; "State residence requirements should not exceed six months" and "local residence requirements should not exceed 30 days."[11] Thousands of Californians who would otherwise register to

---

[8] Some may even run afoul of the state constitutional provision that disfranchises persons who "shall fight in a duel with deadly weapons, or send or accept a challenge to fight a duel . . . or who shall act as a second, or knowingly aid or assist in any manner those thus offending."

[9] The state is divided into approximately 21,000 electoral units called precincts.

[10] For 1968 state residency requirements see U.S. Senate, Office of the Secretary, *Nomination and Election of the President and Vice President of the United States* (U.S. Government Printing Office: Jan. 1968). Corrected to Sept. 18, 1968.

[11] Op. cit., p. 34.

vote cannot because they have come into the state or moved about too recently.[12]

California was one of fourteen states in 1968 that still imposed some form of literacy test as a condition of registration, five of the other states being in the South where such tests have often been used to deprive Negro residents of their right to vote. Many Californians are deterred from taking the first step in the voting process because of the requirement that the citizen must affirm at the time of registration that he can sign his name and read the State Constitution in the English language (unless physically unable to do so.)[13] In 1960 charges were made by some Democratic leaders that Californians with Mexican-American surnames were being arbitrarily challenged on literacy grounds when they went to their polling places on election day. The purpose and the effect, it was charged, was to have those persons challenged return to their communities and describe to their neighbors the indignity to which they had been subjected. Other Mexican-Americans were thereby discouraged from even attempting to vote. The result of this controversy was that the legislature amended the Elections Code in 1961 so as to prohibit challenges on literacy grounds at the polls. *When registering to vote,* however, a person may still be asked to demonstrate that he is able to read the state Constitution in English. Undoubtedly literacy is rarely ascertained in this manner. The affirmation of literacy required in completing the Affidavit of Registration is ordinarily sufficient. In any event, with its literacy test, California once again fails to meet the recommendation of the 1963 President's Commission. The Commission concluded:

---

[12] Since 1960 a newcomer to California has been permitted to vote in a presidential election after residing in the state for only fifty-four days, so long as he was eligible to vote in the state of his previous residence and so long as he meets California's age and literacy requirements. He may not vote for any office other than President and Vice-President. As of 1966, California was one of nineteen states and as of 1968 it was one of twenty-nine states to make such a special allowance for new residents. In this respect it meets one of the standards recommended by the 1963 President's Commission. (Ibid., p. 35.)

It should be noted that if an already registered voter changes his residence after registration is closed, he may vote from his previous address at the next election. The barrier to voting posed by moving about within the state is therefore reduced. But returning to an old area of residency or voting absentee can be a burden many citizens are unwilling to assume.

[13] Although extent of formal education is not a clear indication of illiteracy, 1960 census data reveal that 164,000 Californians twenty-five years old and over had never had any schooling whatsoever, and an additional 760,000 had not gone beyond sixth grade. It has also been estimated that in 1960, 203,000 Californians over the age of fourteen were illiterate insofar as they were unable to read and write in English or any other language.

When noncitizens could vote, literacy requirements made some sense, but today only citizens may vote, and the process of naturalization involves a test for literacy, so the original reasons for the test as part of registration are gone. Many media are available other than the printed word to supply information to potential voters. The Commission is not impressed by the argument that only those who can read and write or have a sixth grade education should have a voice in determining their future. This is the right of every citizen no matter what his formal education or possession of material wealth. The Commission recommends that no literacy test interfere with the basic right of suffrage.[14]

The second area of concern regarding the legal context of registration in California involves the matter of administration. How well does the state facilitate registration among those who are constitutionally eligible to become registered? In some states and many western democracies the initiative for registering voters rests with the government rather than the citizen. That is, the responsibility for compiling a list of those eligible to vote and for keeping it up-to-date is assumed by public officials assigned the task. Idaho is a leading example of such a state. Its registrars —one in each voting precinct—are paid by the state to canvass door-to-door and to keep registration rolls current, thus assuring that the number of registered voters will approximate 100 per cent of those eligible. In some states, on the other hand, the entire burden is on the citizen. In order to register he must go on his own initiative and sometimes over great distances and possibly only during working hours to the county courthouse or some other designated place. The California practice falls between these two extremes. A person may complete his registration affidavit at the office of his County Clerk (or Registrar of Voters, as the chief election official is called in some counties). But the state Elections Code also authorizes and encourages the appointment of deputy registrars in each county to assist in registration, with these persons often being paid nominal fees for each person they register.[15] Further, it authorizes door-to-door canvassing to register voters. However, registrars in California are not charged with the responsibility, as they are in Idaho, for keeping registration rolls up-to-date and for canvassing a specified area to see that everyone is registered.

---

[14] Op. cit., p. 30.

[15] The Code states, "County Clerks, in order to promote and encourage voter registration, shall enlist the support and cooperation of interested citizens and organizations, and shall deputize as registrars qualified citizens in such a way as to cover most effectively every section of the county." A deputy registrar may register voters who reside outside of his own county during the last ten days prior to the close of registration.

Other provisions of the California Elections Code are not especially facilitative of voter registration. For example, registration rolls are closed fifty-four days prior to an election. In effect, this means that no one is permitted to register to vote in a forthcoming election at the very time election campaigns are in full swing and public interest in those campaigns is most likely to be at its peak. Only four other states closed registration as early as California in 1968. In Idaho just two days elapse between the close of registration and election day, a short time period made possible only because the state has assumed the burden of registering all voters.[16] Because Idaho's official registrars canvass continually, there is no last minute, preclosing rush to register on the part of the voters and hence no insurmountable problem to preparing final voter lists for precinct polling places on election day.) The 1963 President's Commission on Registration and Voting Participation recommended that "voter registration should extend as close to election day as possible and should not end more than three or four weeks before election day."[17] Once again, then, California falls short of the Commission's recommendations regarding voter registration.

Nearly all states, California among them, provide some form of permanent rather than periodic registration system so that the citizen need not reregister prior to each election. The California procedure is to have the registration of a voter continued as long as he votes at each general election, i.e., every two years, and as long as he keeps the same residence,[18] does not change his name, is not convicted of a felony crime or judged insane, or does not ask to be removed from the voter rolls. If a registered voter fails to vote in any general election, his registration is canceled and he must reregister prior to the next election if he intends to vote then.[19] Once again, California falls short of the registration

---

[16] It is interesting that Idaho has been among the nation's leading states in the percentage of its voting age population actually voting. In 1960, for example 80.7 per cent of voting age Idahoans voted in the presidential election—a percentage sufficient to rank the state first in voting turnout for the third presidential election in succession. As for California turnout, see Table 4-1.

[17] Op. cit., p. 35.

[18] If a registrant moves within his precinct, he may continue to vote without reregistering.

[19] When a registered California voter fails to vote in a general election he receives the following notice from his county clerk, "Your registration has been canceled this day because you did not vote at the last general election. Before you shall again be entitled to vote you will be required to register as provided by law. However, if you still reside and have not removed from the residence address stated in your affidavit of registration and you notify the county clerk of that fact either in person, in writing, or on the postcard attached, over your signature, within sixty days after date

procedures recommended by the President's Commission on Registration and Voting Participation. "No citizen's registration should be canceled for failure to vote in any period less than *four years*," says the Commission,[20] thereby endorsing the practice followed by such states as Delaware, Illinois, Iowa, Minnesota, Nebraska, New Jersey, New Mexico, Oklahoma, South Dakota, Tennessee, Washington, and West Virginia.

That the legal provisions concerning registration significantly affect the extent of political participation by the citizenry is suggested by California's experience with permanent registration. Prior to 1932 all Californians were required to register anew before each general election. In 1928, 43.6 per cent of the state's total population was registered. In 1930, a nonpresidential year, 39.5 per cent of the population was registered. After the introduction of permanent registration, the percentage increased to 52.2 per cent in 1934 and to 53.0 per cent in 1936. Between 1930 and 1936 the number of persons registered to vote had increased 44.9 per cent while the total population had increased only 8.4 per cent. In terms of voting age population, 58.1 per cent was registered in the year of the last decennial census prior to permanent registration (1930), whereas in the year of the next decennial census, 82.9 per cent of the voting age population was registered. It is impossible to determine what share of the California spurt in registration was attributable to the introduction of permanent registration. However, in California, as elsewhere, it has doubtlessly served to expand the number of registered voters on election day. And there can be little doubt that if California adopted the recommendations of the 1963 President's Commission on Registration and Voting Participation there would be another spurt in the percentage of voting age persons in the state who would be registered voters.

Many observers of American politics have remarked on and often lamented the relatively great number of our citizens who fail to vote, a failure particularly striking in light of our commitment to the centrality of the vote in the democratic process. But if in this respect we tend to "look bad" compared to some other western democracies, it is at least in part owing to the legal barriers to voting which we place before the citizen and which other nations do not. If we wish to expand the nation's voting population, we might well re-evaluate our laws regarding voter eligibility and the process of voter registration. California is one of those states where such an evaluation could be useful. In any event, to be fair

---

of mailing this notice, your affidavit of registration shall be restored to the file and shall remain permanent unless canceled for any other cause."

[20] Op. cit., p. 37. Emphasis added.

to ourselves, the legal context within which registration occurs deserves a share of the blame for nonvoting in this state.

THE POLITICS OF REGISTRATION: PARTISAN INPUTS

Writers about state politics have treated voter registration almost exclusively in terms of legal requirements. Certainly state provisions regarding the "who" and "how" of registration are indispensable items of information for the student of California politics and for anyone interested in assuming the voting responsibilities of citizenship. However, the nature of partisan efforts to encourage registration (partisan inputs) and the partisan configuration of registration figures (partisan outputs) are a significant part of "the real stuff of politics" and their neglect is both surprising and regrettable.

Most active deputy registrars—the men and women who actually sign up most of the voters—are not self-starters operating in isolation from partisan politics. Few are simply good samaritans motivated solely by a desire to maximize citizen participation in the democratic process. Further, few have been induced to serve as deputy registrars by the small remuneration they receive from their counties for each person they register.[21] More often than not, the active deputy registrar is primarily an agent of his political party. Each party has its "own" registrars who will engage in registering voters as part of a *partisan* effort. To a large extent, the registrar's partisan activities must be a labor of love. Registering voters is such a low level of political activity that it can hardly be expected to bring partisan rewards. This is especially true in a state where the number of partisan rewards available for distribution (e.g., patronage jobs) are so few to begin with. Moreover, although parties (like counties) are legally authorized to reimburse a deputy registrar for each person he registers, this is hardly a significant money-making enterprise, and, in fact, such a remuneration is usually not the practice.[22]

Although material incentives may be few, deputy registrars are found in election years assiduously seeking new voters of the same partisan persuasion as their own with increasing frenzy up until the closing of registration. Those imbued with California's antiparty tradition may find

[21] Counties may pay up to 25 cents to the deputy registrar for every voter he registers.

[22] In theory, parties may only reimburse registrars for expenses. In practice, they are paid on a head-count basis.

the practice offensive. Nevertheless, partisan efforts do serve to extend the suffrage to many who would otherwise remain nonvoters. And there are few persons whom one party or the other are not interested in reaching and would not reach if they had sufficient resources. Indeed, it is often those who register only upon the personal prodding of devoted partisans who have the most to gain from political participation and who are most in need of a government responsive to their needs.

The Democratic party, in particular, has played an active role in registering voters. Its appeal tends to be greater among lower socio-economic groups than that of the Republican party, and members of these groups tend to have characteristics associated with nonvoting. The potential Democratic registrant is more likely than his Republican counterpart to be unaware of election law specifics regarding the "who" and "how" of registration, to feel more left out of the political system, to find even the simple process of registration more ego-threatening, to be less imbued with the notion that political participation is a civic duty, to feel less secure about his political commitments, and to have less leisure time to act upon the commitments he does hold. Many Democrats have to be "dragged, kicking and screaming" into the election process, and that party has to make a special effort to do the dragging if it is to maximize its voting support. Moreover, nonpartisan registration drives, such as those mounted by the League of Women Voters, very often have an unintentional Republican bias: Being middle class themselves, the participants in these drives tend to gravitate toward middle-class areas and it is there that Republicans are disproportionately located. (See Table 4-6 for data on how different population groups line up behind the parties in California.)

Two general strategies are followed by an effective partisan registration drive. First, it will largely be concentrated in areas of highest potential support for the party organizing the drive—parties will tend to work their areas of strength and ignore their areas of weakness. The designation of these high priority areas—areas of good potential for the party—may depend on the answer to four questions.

What is the current partisan disposition of the registrants in the area? If existing registration figures indicate that a healthy majority of the residents favor the party organizing the drive, it is likely a good percentage of the unregistered citizens will also favor that party.

Is it an area in which party loyalty is high? An area favorable to a party in registration may not be favorable when it comes to voting. In such an area, a party registration drive may yield many registrants for the party without any payoff on election day, when it counts. It is better to concentrate in good registration areas that *also* have high party loyalty.[23]

Is it an area with a high purge rate? As indicated earlier, under the California Election Code persons who were registered but failed to vote in the last general election are dropped, or purged, from the registration rolls. In some areas significantly more persons are purged after an election than in others. Statewide, the numbers reach considerable proportions. After the 1968 general election, for example, approximately 1,250,-000 persons (or 15 per cent of those registered to vote) were dropped from the rolls because of their failure to vote. A high purge rate in an area suggests one or both of the following to the organizers of a partisan registration drive. First, many registered voters may have moved from the area before the election and there are newcomers in the vacated residences who need to be registered. Unless the area has undergone a drastic social or economic change, these newcomers are likely to have the same partisan preferences as those who left. Second, there may be many previously registered persons in the area who somehow failed to go to the polls on election day. They must be reregistered if they are to vote in the next general election. It should be noted that, in general, areas with high purge rates are likely to have a high Democratic potential because Democrats tend to have poorer voting habits than Republicans.

Has the area undergone a period of rapid population expansion so that there are newcomers needing to be registered? Of course, population expansion resulting from the construction of a high-income, apartment–town house complex is not likely to have the same kind of registration potential for a party as a subdivision built around a new, unionized automobile plant. The parties plan their registration drives accordingly.

On the basis of the foregoing then—to use a hypothetical situation— an area with 80 per cent Democratic registration, where Hubert Humphrey achieved 75 per cent of the vote in the 1968 presidential election (the 5 per cent difference between registration and vote reflecting high Democratic loyalty in that year), in which 25 per cent of the voters registered in November were dropped from the January registration rolls for failure to vote, and in which a new low-income apartment complex has been built—such an area would be an excellent place for a Democratic registration drive to swing into full motion.

---

[23] One method used by the parties in California to determine loyalty in an area is to divide the number of persons voting for the party's candidate by the number of persons registered with the party following the purging of the rolls. Applying such a formula, different areas may be ranked according to loyalty, and various campaign activities, including registration, are planned in light of the ranking.

The second general strategy pursued in an effective partisan registration drive is to register only those persons who will affiliate with the "correct" political party. That Democrats would like to register only Democrats and Republicans register only Republicans is only natural. But the successful pursuit of such a strategy requires some degree of ingenuity in the face of legal requirements regarding registration. Deputy registrars are not permitted to present themselves as partisans, to refuse to register any eligible voter, or to attempt to determine a person's party affiliation before agreeing to register him. There are three basic methods of pursuing the second general strategy while observing these legal constraints.

In high priority areas, the party sets up *registration tables* at central, high-traffic locations on the assumption that those who register will mirror in party preference the existing registration ratios in the area. A deputy registrar sitting at a table in front of a major supermarket in the middle of a predominantly Democratic area will most likely register a predominance of Democrats—and no public indication that this is a party-inspired enterprise is necessary. The major drawback of this method, of course, is that many persons favorable to the "wrong" political party will also step forward to be registered no matter how "correct" the general partisan disposition of the area may be.

A *telephone campaign* is undertaken. Party workers will telephone those persons who are found on lists of telephone subscribers in an area but who are not fonnd on the lists of those already registered to vote.[24] They will first ascertain in the conversation whether the person is a Democrat or Republican. If he identifies with the "correct" party, a deputy registrar may be dispatched to his home or he may be simply informed of the necessity to register by such-and-such a date and be given the address of the most convenient place at which he may register (e.g., the location of the nearest firehouse). If he identifies with the "wrong" party, however, the telephone conversation is terminated before the matter of registration is ever raised. The objective, as in other

---

[24] A list of telephone subscribers who are not registered voters can be developed in most areas by computer, with programmers comparing materials obtained from the telephone company to materials provided free by the county clerks. (Counties are obliged to provide registration lists at no cost to the political parties. In most counties information from the voter's registration affidavit is placed on magnetic tape suitable for computer use. Telephone companies also keep their subscriber's names and addresses on magnetic tape.) Alternatively, reverse telephone directories (where subscribers are listed by street order rather than alphabetically) may be purchased and used for manual, rather than computer comparison against lists of registered voters.

methods, is to avoid registering persons who favor the "wrong" political party.

Telephone campaigns suffer from several limitations. They are expensive; subscriber lists may be outdated; many persons who need to be registered have no phone; even where the person under whose name the phone is listed is registered there may be other family members who are not registered. Despite the drawbacks, however, a telephone campaign has only a slim chance of causing a person to register who is in the "wrong" party. And it is a method that can be effective in a low priority area, where other methods would be highly inefficient, as well as in a high priority area. Now that much of the preliminary work of telephone registration campaigns—the discovery of unregistered telephone subscribers—can be done on a mass basis by computer, such campaigns will more and more become a standard partisan approach to the problem. Moreover, the number of unregistered phone subscribers is not insignificant. In Los Angeles County alone, 671,000 phone subscribers were not registered to vote in the June 1966 primary elections. These were potential registrants whom each party could contact by telephone and, if "correct" party identifiers, could try to induce to take the first step in the voting process.

The preferred and older method of registering voters in a partisan campaign is by *door-to-door canvassing* in high priority areas. Because the deputy registrar must register everyone regardless of party, registration teams are used. In addition to a registrar, a team will include "bird dogs" or "bush beaters" whose task it is to proceed in an area door-by-door in advance of the registrar to identify the residents who favor the "correct" party and who need to be registered. As in the phone campaign, if a resident indicates he favors the "wrong" party, the matter of registration need never be raised by the bird dog. However, if a resident proves to be of friendly partisan persuasion and is unregistered, the bird dog advises the deputy registrar in his team, usually by marking the house in some manner. It is only to the homes of these persons that the registrars will go, well assured that the registration affidavits he completes will be for persons who will be added to the "correct" party's roll of registered voters. This is precisely what an effective party registration drive aims to do: many new registrants but few, if any, affiliated with the opposite party.

Technological developments—principally, the advent of television and the expanding usefulness of computer techniques—have significantly affected the campaign activities of political parties. The registering of voters in California is one of those traditional political party objectives which, while not totally unaffected by those technological developments, remains an unavoidable and arduous task for grass roots party workers. It continues to play a significant part in statewide election campaigns. For example, in 1966 a budget was submitted to the campaign managers of one of the parties in California that proposed the expenditure of $125,000 for a statewide preprimary registration drive. Although the investment of such a sum proved impossible, the way in which this "major effort budget" was broken down reveals something of the magnitude of partisan registration drives in California: $60,000 was budgeted for staff, one person to be hired in each of the eighty assembly districts in the state for the duration of the registration drive (February 1 to April 15); $10,000 was budgeted for the rental of registration campaign headquarters in each of eighty major cities or areas in the state; $20,000 was budgeted for the augmentation of the pay deputy registrars receive from their counties, the registrars participating in the drive to be "reimbursed for expenses" by being paid an additional 10 cents for every member of the party registered; $10,000 was budgeted for maps, data, registration kits, expenses for putting on training workshops, and staff expenses; and, finally, $25,000 was earmarked for telephone expenses.

THE POLITICS OF REGISTRATION: PARTISAN OUTPUTS

What is the result of all this effort to register voters—efforts of both the partisan variety we have been discussing and the nonpartisan? The California Secretary of State issues periodic reports of the party affiliations of those who register within various political subdivisions of the state as a whole. The data presented in these reports reveal much about the character of partisan politics in California. They indicate the outer limits of potential participation in partisan nominating primaries, inasmuch as all registered Democrats and only registered Democrats may vote in a Democratic primary, and all registered Republicans and only registered Republicans may vote in a Republican primary. The data also provide an index (although a very imperfect one, as we shall see) of the strength of each party in the state in terms of their vote-getting power in general elections. Party leaders may consider a significant fluctuation in registration ratios between the parties as a sign of things to come at election time. They consult registration ratios when deciding where to draw the lines of legislative districts and when deciding which candidates for legislative office should be considered hopeless and which hopeful in a general election. The following discussion is based on an analysis of the partisan breakdown of statewide registration over the past few decades. (See Figure 3-2 for a graphic presentation of registration by party in California since 1922.)

Two-party Oligopoly. Few persons who register in California fail to affiliate with either the Democratic or Republican party. In 1922, when statewide records were first collected and reported by the Secretary of State, 16 per cent of the registered voters had not affiliated with one of the two major parties. However, this percentage declined sharply during the ensuing decade. By 1932 it had dropped to 5.6 per cent. Since 1932 over 94 per cent of California's voters have been registered with one of the two major parties in every election year.

What of those who decline to affiliate with the Republican or Democratic parties? They may choose to affiliate with a minor party. California's minor parties have had occasional flurries of registration activity. In 1968 two minor parties—the American Independent party and the Peace and Freedom party—succeeded in achieving official status in this way. They thus became the first new parties to earn the right to hold their own nominating primary in twenty years. Approximately 105,000 persons were affiliated with each of them at the time of the state's January 1968 Statement of Registration—more than the 1 per cent of the number of voters in the previous gubernatorial election (66,059) required for party participation in the June primary election. Additionally, 38,000 Californians were affiliated with other minor parties —Constitution, Royalist, Prohibition, Socialist, Socialist Labor, and so on —but because none of these achieved the required 66,059 registrants they did not earn official status.

In the quarter of a century before the appearance of the American Independent and Peace and Freedom parties, only two minor parties enjoyed official status. The Independent Progressive party was organized on behalf of Henry Wallace's presidential candidacy in 1948 and achieved a total of 22,000 registrants in that year—less than 1 per cent of the registered voters in the state, but more than the required 1 per cent of the voters in the 1946 gubernatorial election. It struggled along until dropped from the ballot in 1956 for falling below the one tenth of 1 per cent of the registered voters then required to retain official status. The fate of the other minor party to enjoy official status since 1942—the Prohibition party—was sealed in a similar fashion in January 1964. The Prohibition party had been the state's most successful minor party in terms of registration since statewide registration records were first reported. But in the January 1964 Report of Registration its registration had dropped to 3,847—below the magic one fifteenth of 1 per cent of the total registration. (The one tenth of 1 per cent figures that had

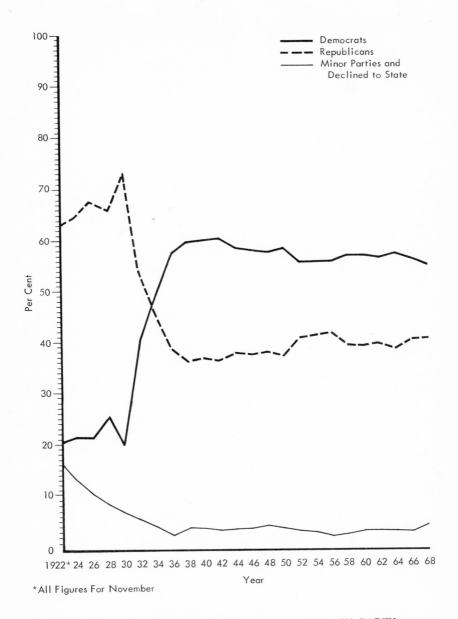

Per Cent

100

90

80

70

60

50

40

30

20

10

0

Democrats
Republicans
Minor Parties and
Declined to State

1922* 24 26 28 30 32 34 36 38 40 42 44 46 48 50 52 54 56 58 60 62 64 66 68

Year

*All Figures For November

FIGURE 3–2 CALIFORNIA REGISTRATION BY PARTY

applied to the Progressives in 1956 was changed to the present one fifteenth of 1 per cent in 1957 for the express purpose of saving the Prohibition party from extinction as an official party—a magnanimous but eventually fruitless gesture by the two major parties whose legislators passed the necessary legislation.)

It would not be unrealistic to expect that the demise of the Progressives and Prohibitionists will be repeated by the American Independent and Peace and Freedom parties in the not too distant future. For all the effort that underlay the success of these latter groups in achieving official status, their combined registration still amounted to only 2 per cent of the registered voters in the state at the time of the June 1968 primary and the November 1968 election. This was hardly a deep inroad into the registration position of California's two political behemoths, the Democratic and Republican parties. And even then each of the two new parties benefited from circumstances that are not likely to be present in future years. The American Independent party benefited from the presidential candidacy of George Wallace on behalf of which it was organized, i.e., it had a national personality around which to build its cause. The Peace and Freedom party benefited from dissatisfaction with America's Vietnam involvement, i.e., it had a critical issue that could serve to dramatize its cause.

Some voters refuse to register with any party, major or minor. Their party affiliation is recorded as "decline to state" on their registration affidavit.[25] As with those who register with the smaller, unofficial minor parties, those who "decline to state" have no nominating primary in which to participate. It is in part because of this exclusion from much of the political action in California—the politics of partisan primaries —that few citizens chose to "decline to state." The number has not exceeded 4.4 per cent of the state's total registration since 1932.

If experience is a guide—and it sometimes is not—the great majority of Californians will continue to register with the existing two major parties. All other parties will remain little more than interesting incidentals to the state's pattern of partisan registration.

The New Deal Revolution. The revival of the Democratic party nationally as a consequence of the Great Depression and of Franklin Roosevelt's New Deal in the 1930s is clearly reflected in California's pattern of registration. (Indeed, it is perhaps better reflected in these figures than in California election outcomes themselves inasmuch as

---

[25] Statements of registration have made it difficult to separate adequately the "decline to state" category from the category entitled "miscellaneous" on statements of Registration. Although those registered with minor parties that have not achieved official recognition are in the "miscellaneous" group, so too are persons who have registered as "nonpartisan" or "independent." These latter registrants would probably more appropriately belong in the "decline to state" group.

the state's Democrats had difficulty capitalizing on their new found registration majorities when it came to voting.)

In 1930 only 20.3 per cent of California's registered voters were affiliated with the Democratic Party. No major party before or since has fallen to such a low level in the entire history of registration record-keeping. The Republicans had maintained approximately a three-to-one margin over their major opposition since 1922, when the registration of the parties was first reported by the Secretary of State. By 1932 the Republican percentage of the state's total registration had dropped to 54.2. In 1934 it dropped below 50 per cent for the first time, and it continued to decline in successive election years until it reached a low of 35.9 per cent in 1942. It has never since that time approached 50 per cent.

Perhaps as striking as the Republican percentage decrease is the fact that during its sharp decline the party actually suffered a decline in the *number* of voters registered with it even though there was a significant increase in California's population. Between 1930 and 1936, while the Democrats were adding almost a million and one-half registrants (an increase of 313 per cent), the Republicans were losing approximately 400,000 registrants (a decrease of 24 per cent). Not until 1946 did the Republican party achieve as many registrants as it had in 1930 (in absolute number terms).

It seems safe to say that the sharp Democratic gain in the New Deal years was attributable to (a) Republican "drop-outs" who decided to change their registration, (b) the Democratic preference of newcomers to the state, many of whom came from the American South where identifying as a Republican was virtually unheard of, and many of whom were homeless victims of the Depression likely to vent their anguish against the party considered to be responsible, and (c) the Democratic preference of first-time voters—those coming of voting age in the period or those who previously had opted out of the voting process.

Moreover, the Democratic registration revival was statewide. It extended into rural as well as urban areas, and into both southern and northern California. In 1930, the Democrats had less than 40 per cent of the registered voters in every one of the fifty-eight counties in the state. In 1942, the Democratic high water mark, only three small counties in the north did not give them an edge over the Republicans. Ten of the twelve counties giving the Democrats a better than two-to-one margin over their opposition were in the rural Central Valley and mountain area extending from Shasta in the north to Kern in the south. A comparable area in most other states would have been the least likely to turn Democratic. More typically, California's two largest urban counties—Los Angeles and San Francisco—gave the Democrats 64.6 per cent and 66.7 per cent of the two-party registration, respectively.

One-Party Dominance? At the time of every general election beginning in 1936 and extending through 1966, the Democratic share of the total registration in California exceeded 55 per cent. (In 1968 it dropped a mere one half of 1 per cent below 55 per cent.) The Democrats have persistently maintained a margin of approximately three-to-two over the Republican party during this period. The stability of their margin is especially remarkable if one considers that California's great population growth since 1936 has produced an increase of over five million (or 160 per cent) in the number of registered voters in the state. However, for reasons to be discussed in the next chapter, the clear Democratic dominance in registration has not been translated into a corresponding dominance at election time.

Registration Figures as Barometers. The Democratic party's share of registered voters is clearly not a good index of the share of votes it will receive on election day. However, fluctuations in party registration may still be sensitive indicators of political dynamics in the state—even though they occur within the context of a persistent Democratic registration majority. Indeed, it is for this reason that skilled political professionals study the periodic Reports of Registration with care.

At the close of registration in September 1950, 61.2 per cent of those registered with one of the two major parties were affiliated with the Democratic party. Two years later—at the time of the 1952 general election—this percentage had fallen sharply to 57.4 per cent, the lowest for the party since 1934. The election-to-election decline was the most pronounced for any party since the Republican 1932–1934 slide and the sharpest for the Democrats since 1928–1930. It proved to be a harbinger of things to come: Dwight Eisenhower became the first Republican presidential candidate to carry California since 1928.

Between 1956 and 1958, 300,000 registrants were added to the Democratic rolls—ten times the number added by the Republicans. The Democratic share of two-party registration increased from 57.5 per cent to 59.2 per cent, the largest percentage increase for that party since 1936–1938. Again, the relatively sharp change in registration ratios was reflected in the ensuing election: The Democrats swept into state office in 1958, most notably by electing the second Democratic governor of the Twentieth Century.

Between 1962 and 1964 the Democratic party increased its registration by 419,000—the greatest two-year increase it had ever enjoyed and surpassed only by the 1950–1952 Republican increase. The Democratic share of the two-party registration in 1964 was the highest since before Eisenhower's 1952 candidacy. In the 1964 general election, President Lyndon Johnson easily carried California—the first success for a Democratic presidential candidate in the state since 1948.

Between 1964 and 1966, 180,000 more Republicans than Democrats were added to the registration rolls, a larger Republican margin than in all other two-year periods since the beginning of the New Deal. The Democratic share of two-party registration declined from 59.8 per cent to 58.5 per cent. Only twice since 1928 (1942–1944 and 1950–1952) had the Democrats suffered a greater setback. At election time, the Republican candidate, Ronald Reagan, wrested the governorship away from two-term Democrat, Edmund Brown, and the Republicans made significant inroads into Democratic legislative majorities.

When registration was closed in September 1968, the Democratic registration margin in percentage terms over the Republicans had eroded away to its smallest since it became California's majority party in 1936. And for the first time since 1934 less than 55 per cent of the registered voters were affiliated with the Democratic party. The 1966–1968 percentage decline for the Democrats was the largest since 1950–1952. In the presidential election, Richard Nixon returned the state to the Republicans, and his party captured control of the state Assembly.

Fluctuations in the party preferences of California's registrants seem to be barometers of election outcomes, even though the majority of those registrants continue to affiliate with the Democratic party.

primaries

The second major step to becoming a full voting participant in California's political process is taken on the first Tuesday after the first Monday in June of every election (even-numbered) year. This is primary day in California.[26] On this day the voters in the state's direct partisan

---

[26] The date of the primary was moved from August to June in 1964. It comes rather early in the year compared to other primaries across the nation. Of the forty-five states in 1968 using primaries to nominate candidates for statewide office, only ten held theirs before California's. Four others held theirs on the same day. The five-month interval between primary and general election is considered by many to be too long. Electoral campaigns, it is charged, become too tedious and too expensive. On the other hand, some observers maintain Californians need this time span to move beyond a mere "image" acquaintance with major candidates.

primary nominate candidates for partisan public office. A nonpartisan primary is held simultaneously, with candidates being nominated for county offices, for state superior court judgeships, and for one statewide executive position (the nonpartisan Superintendent of Public Instruction). Primary voters also select the members of their party's county central committees. And every fourth year, presidential primaries are held in which delegates are chosen to the national conventions of the major parties. Finally, the primary voter may be called upon to consider initiative and referendum measures, attempts to recall public officials, or special election matters if the Governor of the state chooses to use primary day for these purposes.

The major business of the voter on primary day is to nominate candidates for partisan public office. One of the chief functions of a political party system is to "simplify the alternatives" facing the voters on election day. And one of the ways parties fulfill this function is through the nominating process, for here they reduce the number of candidates for different public offices to manageable size. Thus, for example, the California voter normally chooses between only two principal candidates for Governor on election day in November—one nominated by each of the major parties—rather than choosing between the untold number of citizens who might feel the urge to serve and who might believe they are capable of performing the responsibilities of the office.

At one time party conventions were the nation's principal means of nominating candidates for elective office—as they still are when it comes to nominating candidates for the presidency and vice-presidency of the United States. In every state in the nation, however, conventions have been either supplemented or supplanted by primaries. This means that rank-and-file voters are now permitted to play a role in the nominating process. No longer is the decision as to who shall represent one's party on the election day ballot left exclusively to a select group of its leaders.

California was the first state to adopt a primary law. In 1866 the state legislature authorized parties to hold nominating primaries if they wished. The party leaders, however, did not so wish. It was almost a half-century later when the flames of antipartyism and "progressivism" in California—fed by charges that the conventions had become instruments of corrupt party "bosses" and the powerful Southern Pacific Railway—finally destroyed the convention system. In 1908 California voters passed a constitutional amendment making primaries mandatory and the legislature proceeded to pass the necessary legislation. Amended many times, this 1909 legislation is the basis of today's primary system.

One of the central characteristics of California's partisan primaries is that they are "closed"—just as they are in most other states. That is, registered voters are permitted to vote only for persons entered in the primary of the party with which they are affiliated. On primary day the registered Democrat receives a ballot at the polling place that lists the Democratic but not Republican contenders for the various partisan offices to be filled in the November general election.[27] He votes for one candidate per office, and the candidate receiving the most votes for that office becomes the Democratic candidate in the general election. (Only an election plurality is necessary rather than 50 per cent plus.) Similarly, of course, the Republican primary voter is permitted to vote only for those seeking the Republican nomination. Thus voters affiliated with one party are prevented from interfering with the nomination of candidates by the other party.

In "open" primary states, on the other hand, it is possible for members of one party to "raid" the primary of the other party.[28] They may deliberately "cross over" to the other party to help nominate a weaker candidate and thus to place their own party in a more advantageous position on election day.[29] They may cross over to help nominate candi-

---

[27] Elections for state partisan executive office (Governor, Lieutenant Governor, Attorney-General, Controller, Secretary of State, Treasurer, and State Board of Equalization) take place in even-numbered, nonpresidential years. (This is also true of the Superintendent of Public Instruction, a nonpartisan state executive.) State senators have four-year terms, just like the state's elected executives. However, half of the forty senators are elected in even-numbered nonpresidential years and half in even-numbered presidential years. All of the eighty state assemblymen and thirty-eight U.S. Congressmen are elected every even-numbered year. United States Senators have six-year terms, with the term of one California Senator next expiring in 1970 and the other in 1974.

[28] Eight states use the open primary. Here the voter is permitted to choose the party primary in which he will vote at the time he goes to the polls; he retains the option of voting in either party's primary until the very last moment. One of the eight states, Washington, uses a "blanket" or "wide open" primary system in which the voter may actually vote in more than one party's primary. He is given a single ballot on which are listed the candidates of all parties for each office and is permitted to vote for one candidate per office regardless of party, possibly moving back and forth between parties as he proceeds down the ballot.

[29] It has been alleged that in 1946 Democrats crossed over in Wisconsin's open primary to vote for Senate candidate Joseph McCarthy in the expectation that he would be the easiest Republican to defeat in the general election. McCarthy did in fact win the Republican nomination. However, he went on to win the election and to fashion a stormy career in the U.S. Senate.

Similar charges were made regarding the 1956 Minnesota presidential primary, with Republicans allegedly crossing over to vote for Estes Kefauver over Adlai Stevenson.

Duane Lockard reports that "in 1962 Texas Republicans by public advertisement openly encouraged their members to raid the Democratic gubernatorial primary and vote for the liberal candidate, hoping thereby to improve Republican chances in November," *The Politics of State and Local Government* (New York: The Macmillan Company, 1963), p. 193.

dates with whom they are in general ideological agreement. The result in such an instance may be that the programmatic differences between the parties, already considered by many as inadequate, are further reduced. A party that loses control of its own nominations can hardly be expected to maintain much ideological cohesion among those carrying the party's standard on election day and into the governmental arena.[30]

In California's closed primary system, those who have declined to state a party affiliation when registering and those registered with a minor party lacking official status are left with no party primary in which to vote. On primary day they are limited to observing the contests within the major parties, contests that effectively determine the only real alternatives they are likely to have on general election day in November. Nor can they vote in the state's presidential primaries or in the election of members of party county central committees, because in each case participation is also limited to members of the major parties. To avoid being thus left out of the real action in California's party primaries is one reason the great majority of the state's registrants affiliate with one of the two major parties. Persons failing to register with one of the major parties may, however, join with the others to vote in California's non-partisan primaries and for any measures that appear on the primary ballot; they are entitled to vote on primary day, but their ballot is considerably shorter, inasmuch as it excludes candidates for partisan public office and for party office.

Primaries are very much like general elections. The stakes are different, of course, for primaries are basically designed to nominate candidates rather than to elect them. But, like general elections, they are regulated in California by the state Elections Code. One must be registered at least fifty-four days prior to primary day to vote in the primary election, just as he must be registered fifty-four days prior to the general election to vote in November. County governments hire, pay, and direct the officials who administer the primaries just as they do those who administer general elections. Ballots in both primaries and general elections are printed at public expense. In both cases the California Secretary of State issues certificates indicating the victorious candidates in the various races and publishes the results of these races in a pamphlet entitled *Statement*

---

[30] Mayor Samuel Yorty of Los Angeles, a maverick Democrat of generally conservative leanings, feels that an open primary would have enhanced his chances against incumbent Governor Edmund Brown in the 1966 Democratic gubernatorial primary. Advocating the open primary in California, Yorty concluded, "If the moderate Republicans who were for me could have crossed party lines as voters are permitted to do in Washington and some other states, I am certain we would have won."

of Vote. When contests for a nomination are lively—and they often are in California—primary campaigns are often filled with the same sort of political drama as a general election campaign, and they may be just as difficult for the contestants and just as expensive.[31] Moreover, there have been circumstances, which will be indicated shortly, in which primaries in California have actually served as the final election. Finally, voting in a primary—like voting in a general election—is an indispensable step in the process of political participation for the Californian who takes his citizenship responsibilities seriously.

In fact, although all states have adopted primaries to one extent or in one form or another, no primaries outside of the one-party South have been so important in the state's political scheme of things as California's. Let us examine the factors giving them such importance.

THE ABSENCE OF PARTY NOMINATING CONVENTIONS

The role of the primary in California is complete when it comes to nominating candidates for partisan public office. All but one of the seven statewide executive officers of the state are nominated by party primary. (The other is a nonpartisan official who is nominated by non-partisan primary.) So, too, are all members of the state legislature, the state's two U.S. Senators, and the thirty-eight members of its contingent to the U.S. House of Representatives. Everyone running over the label of a major party in California's November general election has been nominated by primary.[32]

About a dozen states still use party conventions for nominating purposes. In some—New York and Indiana, for example—candidates for the most significant government positions are nominated by convention, with primaries reserved for less significant positions. In some states—Massachusetts and Colorado, for example—party conventions are held to officially endorse candidates for nomination prior to the primary, such

---

[31] For example, in 1964 one prominent Democrat—then-Attorney General Stanley Mosk—took himself out of the race for the Democratic U.S. Senate nomination, citing the high cost of campaigning as his reason. Mosk estimated it would cost $628,000 for the primary battle alone.

[32] An exception occurs if a person nominated in a partisan primary dies before the general election. The resulting vacancy on the general election ballot is filled by the appropriate central committee(s) of the party whose candidate has died. The specifics as to who fills vacancies differ from office to office and are spelled out in the state Elections Code. In the case of the death of a person nominated in a nonpartisan primary, the candidacy is filled by that candidate in the primary who received the next highest number of votes.

endorsements serving to indicate to the voters the official recommendations of the state's party leaders.[33] In Connecticut—which in 1955 became
the last of the states to adopt a primary system—a "challenge" primary
is used: Party conventions nominate candidates for statewide office and
a primary contest occurs only if a defeated contender at the convention
achieved 20 per cent or more of the convention vote and wishes to challenge the convention decision. In South Dakota, if for any office no
candidate receives at least 35 per cent of the votes in the primary a
convention of party leaders is held to do the actual nominating. Some
states holding conventions also hold indirect primaries in which delegates
to the nominating conventions are selected.

California has no party nominating conventions. All party nominations
are made by primary, pure and simple. Official state party conventions
are held periodically but are not permitted to play a part in the nominating process. The state central committees and county central committees
of the parties are likewise forbidden to take a position on forthcoming
primary races. The responsibility for nominating candidates for partisan
public office is left to those registered party members who care to exercise
it by voting in the June primary of their party.

THE IMPORTANCE OF PRESIDENTIAL PRIMARIES

Every fourth year, for two weeks in the summer, the attention of
America focusses on the national conventions of our two major parties.
They are condemned by some as the most monstrous of political institutions and extolled by others as the most ingenious of American political
inventions. But, good or bad, out of the tumult and confusion of one
of these quadrennial extravaganzas emerges the man who will serve as
the nation's president and as one of the world's most powerful leaders
for the succeeding four years. Those who actually nominate the presidential candidates and participate in the other deliberations of a national convention—the delegates from the various states—bear a heavy
responsibility indeed.

In most states these delegates are chosen by party leaders meeting
in convention or in committee and they carry out their responsibility
without formal reference to the opinions of rank-and-file party members.

---

[33] Normally only one candidate per office will receive the official party endorsement. In Colorado, however, any candidate who receives 20 per cent or more of the
convention vote for an office receives the endorsement. Here, as in other states with
preprimary endorsing conventions, the fact that a candidate has been officially endorsed by the party organization is indicated on the primary ballot.

However, almost a third of the states—California among them—hold presidential primaries. Although these are all designed to give some voice to ordinary party members in the process of nominating a presidential candidate, no two presidential primary systems are identical. In some of these primary states the voter may well feel that his voice will be virtually inaudible in the presidential nominating process. The Californian, on the other hand, may reasonably conclude that his state's presidential primaries are among the most important in the nation. Why?

No state has so many delegate votes at stake in its presidential primary as California. Although the precise formula for allotting convention votes to the various states may vary from party to party and year to year, that formula is always based in large part on population. As a result, only New York was allotted more delegate votes than California at the two 1968 National Conventions, probably the last time New York will enjoy such primacy. But the number of New York delegates actually selected by primary was considerably smaller than the number selected by primary in California.

All California delegates to a national convention are selected in the state's presidential primary.[34] Only eight of the nation's seventeen presidential primary systems involve such a total commitment to the primary method of delegate selection. Among the primary states in which a significant number of delegates are selected by party convention rather than by primary voters are the three which, in addition to California, had the largest convention delegations in 1968—New York, Pennsylvania, and Illinois.

In the California presidential primary the voters choose between slates of would-be delegates that may be and almost always have been officially pledged and committed to a particular presidential candidate.[35] This commitment is indicated on the primary ballot. In fact, since 1944

---

[34] At the 1968 Democratic National Convention, party National Committeemen and Committeewomen served automatically on the state's delegation to their party's national convention and they are not selected in the presidential primary.

[35] A person serving on a slate of delegates entered in the primary and pledged to a particular candidate must file an affidavit with the state Secretary of State stating, "I personally prefer _____ as nominee of my political party for President of the United States, and hereby declare to the voters of my party in the state of California that if elected as delegate to their national party convention, I shall to the best of my judgment and ability, support _____ as nominee of my party for President of the United States."

Though there are no explicit legal requirements, the pledged delegate, if elected, is expected to continue supporting his candidate until released by him.

A candidate for delegate on an unpledged slate files an affidavit with the statement, "I express no preference for a particular candidate. The chairman of my group is _____."

the primary ballot has not listed the individuals seeking to serve as
delegates but instead identifies a delegation slate only by the presidential
aspirant to whom it is committed or, when not committed, by the
chairman of the delegation slate.[36] (See Figure 3–3.)

Prior to the last two presidential election campaigns, all delegate slates
entered in the California primary were required by law to be formally
pledged to a presidential candidate. As a result of a 1961 Elections Code
change, unpledged delegations are now permitted. Republicans have
not taken advantage of the change: The slates entered in the 1964 and
1968 GOP presidential primaries have all been pledged. In the 1964
Democratic primary two unpledged slates confronted each other—one
headed by Governor Edmund Brown and the other by Mayor Sam Yorty.
Both, however, were unofficially committed to the renomination of President Lyndon Johnson, who declined to permit his name to be used. In
the 1968 Democratic presidential primary another unpledged slate was
entered, presumably favorable to Johnson and—after Johnson's decision
not to seek re-election—to Vice President Hubert Humphrey, with State
Attorney General Thomas Lynch as its chairman. However, the two other
slates entered in the primary—one pledged to Senator Robert Kennedy
and the other to Senator Eugene McCarthy—received most of the attention and the great majority of the primary votes.

The fact that the Californian may ordinarily vote for one or more presidential candidates in his party's presidential primary adds importance
to that vote. He is permitted to vote for convention delegates while,
with the same vote, being permitted to express a candidate preference.
Voters in other primary states are not all so privileged. In New York
and Illinois in 1968, for example, primary voters could vote only for
delegates whose presidential preferences, if any, were not indicated
on the ballot or otherwise officially transmitted.

On the other hand, voters in several presidential primary states vote
in a presidential preference poll but not for the delegates themselves,
the latter being selected by party convention or committee. In these
states it is sometimes possible for delegates to the national conventions
to be personally opposed to the candidate whom the preference poll
in their state binds them to support, a situation that applied to members
of the Massachusetts delegation to the 1968 Democratic National Convention. The delegates in these instances hardly make persuasive advocates at the convention for the candidate preferred by their state's

---

[36] A list of the members of each delegation slate entered in the primary of one's
party is received by each registered voter prior to primary day along with his sample
ballot.

FOR DELEGATES TO NATIONAL CONVENTION	Vote for One Group Only
Candidates Preferring EUGENE J. MC CARTHY	
Candidates Expressing No Preferrence THOMAS C. LYNCH (Chairman)	
Candidate Preferring ROBERT F. KENNEDY	

FIGURE 3–3 PRESIDENTIAL PRIMARY BALLOT

primary voters. Moreover, such delegates are usually required to vote for the preference poll winner for only a single ballot at the convention.

The California primary is the last major presidential primary in the nation prior to the national conventions. As a result, the success or failure of a presidential candidate in that primary is likely to have an especially dramatic effect on convention deliberations.

Delegates are selected in the California primary as a slate on a state-wide, winner-take-all basis, rather than individually at the district level or proportionate to voter preferences.[37] For the presidential aspirant this ordinarily means it is "all or nothing" when it comes to California's large bloc of votes at the national convention: If he wins or if he loses the state's presidential primary by only a single vote, he generally wins or loses the support of the entire California contingent to his party's national convention. In 1964 a slate pledged to Senator Barry Goldwater defeated one pledged to Governor Nelson Rockefeller by only 68,000 out of a total of almost 2,200,000 votes. Goldwater received all of California's delegate votes at the Republican National Convention. In 1968 Robert Kennedy's slate of delegates won the California Democratic primary with less than 50 per cent of the votes in its three-way race with the McCarthy-pledged and the Lynch-headed slates. Had he not been assassinated, Kennedy would have received all of California's 172 delegate votes at the national convention, the largest bloc of votes going to any single candidate when the roll of states was called. The method of selecting the New York delegation—the only delegation larger than California's—made it unavoidable that its members would be divided as to presidential preference.

---

[37] It is true, however, that slates must be geographically balanced in composition. The Elections Code provides that each congressional district is entitled to approximately equal representation.

Less than half of the presidential primary states adhere to a system that assures the type of delegation unity behind a candidate comparable to the unity found on a California delegation that has run on a pledged basis. Some of these states, as indicated, hold presidential preference polls that bind the entire delegation even though the delegates do not themselves necessarily favor the preference poll winner.[38]

The winner-take-all nature of the California primary, added to its timing and the size of the state's convention delegations, makes it very difficult for a candidate actively involved in a contest for his party's presidential nomination to refuse entering a delegation slate in the California sweepstakes. For this the primary voter may be thankful. He is not so fortunate, however, as his neighbor in Oregon, whose system guarantees that the full array of active candidates for the presidency will be entered in their respective party primaries. All presidential candidates, excluding late entries, appear on the primary ballot whether they wish to or not.

In 1968 the California legislature passed a bill designed to duplicate the Oregon system by providing that candidates on the presidential primary ballot would be those found by the state's Secretary of State to be nationally recognized candidates for the office of President. Any such person could withdraw by filing an affidavit that he or she is not a candidate. A presidential aspirant omitted by the Secretary of State could achieve a ballot position by petition. The state's delegates to a national convention—chosen by nonprimary means—would be obligated to vote for the preference poll winner. Governor Reagan vetoed the measure. He argued, in part, that the bill "limits the people's responsibility by placing the responsibility for putting names on the California presidential ballot on the shoulders of one man. This is considerably less desirable than California's present open primary method which requires a significant number of persons to show an interest in a man's candidacy before his name is placed on the ballot." The California Elections Code provides that before a slate of delegates may appear on the primary ballot a nominating petition for that slate must be signed generally by registered party members numbering between 0.5 per cent and 2.0 per cent of the vote cast for the party's candidate in the last gubernatorial election.[39] Moreover, the Code provides that a

---

[38] In some cases presidential polls are held that are nonbinding on the delegates. In the 1968 New Hampshire Democratic primary, for example, President Johnson won the preference poll but 20 of the 24 Democratic district-level delegate elections were won by McCarthy-pledged delegates.

[39] At times, achieving the necessary number of signatures is relatively easy, especially when the candidate is supported by an army of zealous followers. In 1964

candidate, unlike in Oregon, must agree beforehand to have a delegate slate entered in the primary on his behalf.

In sum, the Oregon system, like that proposed by the state legislature in 1968, goes one step further than California's present system in terms of maximizing the meaning of the presidential primary for the voter. Recent experience suggests that despite all the reasons for entering the California race, some active presidential aspirants decline to enter. At times, a candidate's strategy calls for avoiding primaries in general, hoping—like Nelson Rockefeller in 1968—that lightning will strike at the national convention itself. At other times, a front-runner for his party's nomination may choose to avoid the risk of an embarrassing defeat in such an important state as California. Humphrey, because of President Johnson's late withdrawal from the race, became a candidate in 1968 after the closing date for entering delegate slates in the California Democratic primary. However, as the front-runner with sufficient delegate votes in hand to assure his nomination, Humphrey would probably not have entered that primary even if time permitted.

Most significantly, a candidate may be deterred from entering the California primary by the prior entry of a slate pledged to a favorite son candidate or of an unpledged unity slate broadly representative of all factions in the state's party. There are several reasons for entering such slates. By forestalling a primary fight, party unity in California may be maintained. By not being pledged to any bona fide candidate, California's maneuverability at the national convention may be enlarged to the point where it can play a king-maker role. In the process, it may reap rewards for the state and its leaders resulting from bargains struck with the candidate whom it makes king. Finally, the favorite son may entertain presidential ambitions of his own and may wish to use the large California delegation as the base for a drive to his party's presidential nomination. Governor Earl Warren's favorite son candidacy in 1952 and Governor Reagan's favorite son candidacy in 1968 were widely

---

Barry Goldwater's slate of delegates had to submit 14,000 valid signatures to the Secretary of State to get on the ballot. Several times that number were on hand after the first day on which it was permitted to gather signatures, thanks largely to the work of 9,500 volunteers in Los Angeles county alone. Goldwater's success was matched on the Democratic side four years later by the volunteer effort on behalf of a slate pledged to Eugene McCarthy.

At other times, the task is not an easy one. Often firms specializing in signature gathering are employed, with the cost approximating 50 cents per valid signature.

Even this strategy may prove unavailing. In 1964 Harold Stassen, former Minnesota Governor and perennial presidential aspirant, sought to run in the California Republican primary. He hired Joseph Robinson and Co., a signature-gathering firm, paying a reported $19,000 for the required 14,000 valid signatures. The Robinson firm failed.

regarded as covers for full-fledged designs on the Republican presidential nomination. A California Governor, coming as he does from a large and doubtful state, must always be considered a possibility for his party's nomination.

Once the formation of a favorite son or unpledged unity slate has been announced, bona fide presidential candidates find it difficult to enter the California race. Richard Nixon and other presidential aspirants did not challenge the Reagan slate in the 1968 Republican primary. Similarly, in 1960 Senator John Kennedy and other aspirants for the Democratic presidential nomination decided not to enter the California primary in the face of Governor Edmund Brown's favorite son candidacy. In cases such as these, it seemed to be the better part of wisdom not to risk alienating party leadership in the state or damaging party unity, perhaps beyond repair, just prior to a general election campaign.

Even though bona fide candidates may be frightened out of entering the California presidential primary, as often as not favorite son or unity slates are challenged by dissident party factions within the state. Thus in 1952, a slate pledged to a conservative Republican, Thomas Werdel, was entered in the Republican primary against the favorite son slate pledged to Governor Warren. In 1960 a slate of party unknowns pledged to old-age pensioner George McClain was entered in the Democratic primary against the unity slate pledged to favorite son Edmund Brown, then in the midst of one of his periodic plummets into unpopularity. And in 1964, the unity slate headed by Governor Brown was challenged by a slate headed by Los Angeles Mayor Sam Yorty. In each case, the party rank-and-file was able to register their dissatisfaction with their Governor in the presidential primary—and hundreds of thousands did. In 1968, a last minute attempt to enter an opposition slate in the Republican primary against Governor Reagan's slate failed to achieve the necessary number of signatures on the nominating petition. California Republicans who were unhappy with Reagan's performance in office or with his apparent designs on the presidency could only register their disapproval by not voting in the presidential primary. Indeed, approximately 700,000 Republicans who voted for party Senatorial aspirants Thomas Kuchel or Max Rafferty in the 1968 primary refused to vote for the unchallenged Reagan slate entered in the presidential primary.

The importance for the voter of primary day in California is enhanced by the importance of the state's presidential primary in the nation's complex system of nominating presidential candidates. In the absence of the entry of a favorite son or unity slate, Californians are likely to be treated to a direct confrontation between delegate slates pledged to the principal rivals for their party's presidential nomination. The Kennedy-

McCarthy confrontation in 1968, the Goldwater-Rockefeller confrontation in 1964, the Stevenson-Kefauver confrontation in 1956 serve as the most recent examples of such confrontations. In each instance one could argue that because of the nature of the California primary the confrontation was decisive in terms of convention outcome, or, in the 1968 instance, would have been decisive had Kennedy lived. And even when bona fide candidates are not entered and the California presidential primary thus has little effect on national convention decision making, the voters are still often given an opportunity to express their dissatisfaction with state party leadership through the entry of dissident factions.

"PRIMARIES" THAT ELECT

Primary day in California may be the day on which a candidate for nonpartisan office is elected rather than only nominated. When any such candidate receives more than 50 per cent of the primary vote he is deemed elected without having to run in the general election. Thus in 1966, State Superintendent of Public Instruction, Dr. Max Rafferty, running for re-election received more votes in the June primary than his three opponents combined and thereby was declared elected. The citizen who missed voting in the primary election missed his only opportunity to participate in the selection of the state's only elected educational officer. If no candidate for a nonpartisan office receives a majority of votes in the primary, the two candidates with the most votes for that office face each other in the general election.

Members of the county central committees of each party are also elected—not nominated—on primary day. These are the only elected party positions in California, unless one also includes the delegates to the national party conventions who are similarly elected on primary day. Whereas in the case of the Superintendent of Public Instruction, all registered voters may vote for any candidate, elections to official positions in a given political party are open only to persons registered with that party.

Additionally, a recall election (wherein an incumbent is forced to stand for re-election before the expiration of his term of office as a result of a petition signed by a specified number of voters) may be held on primary day. So too may a special election to fill a vacancy in an elective office resulting from death or resignation, and an initiative or referendum election wherein the citizens vote on issues of public policy. If the Governor decides to schedule a recall, special, initiative, or referendum election on primary day, any registered voter may participate and the results are final.

CROSSFILING

Voting in California's primaries achieved special importance during the period from 1913 to 1959 when the curious and controversial system of crossfiling was in effect. One of the major monuments to antipartyism in the state, crossfiling permitted a candidate for a partisan public office to seek and to gain the nomination of more than one party on primary day.[40] An individual going through the process of seeking his own party's nomination needed only to duplicate the process in the opposite party to run in its primary: He had to file his "declaration of candidacy," pay a nominal filing fee, and submit a petition bearing a specified but always small number of signatures of persons registered with that party. If he received a plurality of votes in both primaries, he became the candidate of both parties. The label "Republican-Democrat" or "Democrat-Republican" would appear after his name on the November election ballot, and he was virtually assured of election.[41] In effect, the primary in such a situation served as the final election—just as it still does in the instances cited earlier.[42]

It was not unusual for a candidate to win the nomination of both major parties by successfully crossfiling. For example, between 1940 and 1952, 84 per cent of the state Senate races and 72 per cent of the state Assembly races were decided in the primary in this way. In 1940 a record 55 per cent of California's congressional seats were won in the primary through successful crossfiling. In 1944, no less than 90 per cent of California's state Senate races and 80 per cent of its Assembly races were decided in the primary. Earl Warren won the nomination of both parties in the 1946 gubernatorial primary. Hiram Johnson in 1934 and in

---

[40] Crossfiling was originally adopted so that members of the newly founded Progressive party could win not only the Progressive nominations but the more important Republican nominations.

[41] If a candidate failed to win his own party's primary he was disqualified from becoming the other party's nominee. Examples of disqualifications of this sort were not unusual. In 1932, for example, fifteen candidates for legislative office—state or congressional—failed to carry their own party's primary even though they were successful in the other party's primary. In such instances, the responsibility for selecting the other party's candidate in the general election rested with party officials serving on the appropriate county committee(s) or, if statewide office, on the party's state central committee.

[42] To successfully crossfile did not necessarily preclude some opposition in the general election. Minor parties could have candidates. Write-in campaigns could have been conducted. "Independent" candidates could achieve a place on the ballot by filing a petition bearing the signatures of 5 per cent of the registered voters in the district.

1940, and William Knowland in 1952 successfully crossfiled for the U.S. Senate in the primaries of those years. In 1950 Goodwin Knight and in 1954 Edmund Brown successfully crossfiled for the offices of Lieutenant Governor and Attorney General, respectively. Anyone who missed voting in the party primaries of those years found on election day in November that the decision in the foregoing races had already been made for him and there was no real contest for the offices in question.

In 1952 the electorate approved a change in the Elections Code that served to reduce the incidence of successful crossfiling. Prior to the change, candidates in primaries did not have their party affiliation listed on the ballot. They were identified only by their occupation. In the absence of party labels, many voters did not know when their party primary was being "raided" by a candidate from the opposition party. Often they would vote for the candidate whose name was most familiar or most euphonious or whose occupation was most prestigious. In general, incumbents had an advantage in efforts to capture the nomination of both parties. The 1952 change provided that the party affiliation of candidates would appear on the primary ballot. A voter in the Democratic primary, for example, would know which candidates seeking his party's nomination were of his own party and which were Republicans.[43] The effect of the change was felt immediately. Whereas in 1952, seventy-nine of the one hundred state legislative seats up for election were filled in the primary by crossfiling, in 1954 the number had dwindled to thirty-three.

Crossfiling was finally abolished in 1959. As a result, to become a candidate in a party primary, a person must now not only meet the legal qualifications for the office he seeks and file a declaration of candidacy accompanied by a nominal filing fee and a petition signed by a specified number of voters registered as party members. He must also have been a registered member of the party whose nomination he seeks for at least three months prior to primary day and he must not have been a member of any other party within the year prior to filing for nomination. Thus, no independent or opposition party member may run in a party's nominating primary.

By reducing the likelihood that primaries would serve as final elections, the abolition of crossfiling has made voting on primary day somewhat

---

[43] The Elections Code change provided that the names of the political party could be abbreviated on the ballot by including no less than the first three letters of the party name. Some Democratic officials objected on the grounds that the voters may conclude that "Rep." on the ballot meant "Representative." In Los Angeles county, the Registrar of Voters responded to the objection by spelling out the party names in their entirety.

less important. On the other hand, abolition has increased intraparty competition in primaries. The danger of an opposition party member seeking a nomination had placed severe constraints on each party to present only a single candidate of its own in the primary. With the danger removed, intraparty contests in primaries have increased.[44] Moreover, a double nomination is still possible if a candidate can carry the opposite party's primary by write-in vote. (In 1960, for example, six candidates for legislative office—all incumbents—were able to win the nomination of both parties by successful write-in campaigns.)

"SAFE" SEATS

Another factor making California's primaries especially important to the voter is the number of legislative districts in the state that are "safe" or noncompetitive in character. The effect of safe districts is much the same as that of crossfiling: They reduce the importance of the general election and elevate the importance of the primary. The candidate in such a district who receives the nomination of the dominant party is virtually assured of success in November. If there is a real contest for the seat it is within the majority party's primary. Such contests are especially likely when there is no incumbent seeking re-election—when he has retired, run for another office, or dies, or when the district has been newly created by the state legislature as a result of reapportionment or redistricting. (See Chapter 8 for further discussion of noncompetitiveness in legislative districts.)

INTRAPARTY FACTIONALISM

A final factor making California's primary especially important is the extent to which party factionalism and the wide-open character of the state's politics produces primary contests. Each party is afflicted with persistent ideological divisions and with organizations too weak to suppress or contain internal conflicts before they are carried to the rank-and-file voters.

From 1960 through 1968 approximately 45 per cent of the nominations for seats in the state Assembly, state Senate, and U.S. Congress were contested at the primary, most of the contests occurring within the Democratic or majority party. (See Table 3–3.) Primary voters have also been regularly treated to dramatic and bitter clashes for party

---

[44] See Eugene C. Lee and James Buchanan, "The 1960 Election in California," *Western Political Quarterly* (March 1961), p. 311.

TABLE 3–3 CONTESTED PRIMARY ELECTIONS IN CALIFORNIA,
1958–1968: STATE ASSEMBLY, STATE SENATE,
U.S. HOUSE OF REPRESENTATIVES

Year	Democratic		Republican		Total	
	Number	Per Cent	Number	Per Cent	Number	Per Cent
1958	32	25	23	18	55	21
1960	50	38	32	25	82	32
1962	81	62	65	47	146	53
1964	53	38	56	41	109	39
1966	93	59	81	51	174	55
1968	64	46	60	43	124	45

nominations to statewide office and to the U.S. Senate. In 1964 Pierre Salinger, a national personality by virtue of his role as press secretary to Presidents John Kennedy and Lyndon Johnson, returned to California to challenge Alan Cranston for the Democratic nomination to the Senate. Despite the support Cranston received from most of the state's Democratic leaders and from the California Democratic Council, Salinger's whirlwind campaign brought him the nomination. The drama of the vote-getting phase of the campaign extended into the vote-counting stage: Salinger's margin of victory over Cranston was a scant 140,000 out of 2,260,000 primary votes. Ronald Reagan and George Christopher were the principal candidates for the Republican gubernatorial nomination in 1966, in many ways repeating the hard-fought contest between the Goldwater and Rockefeller forces in California's 1964 Republican presidential primary. Reagan won with 65 per cent of the Republican vote. In 1968 the conservative-moderate division within the Republican party once again erupted in a primary contest. Veteran Senator Thomas Kuchel, assistant Republican leader in the Senate and party moderate was challenged in his attempt to gain renomination by Dr. Max Rafferty, state Superintendent of Public Instruction. Rafferty carried the primary with only 52 per cent of the two-candidate vote.

One of the factors making the incidence of primary conflicts especially important is the impact they seem to have on general election outcomes. Gladwin Hill concludes that there is "an axiom of California politics" which finds that "the party with a primary fight is almost certain to lose the general election."[45] A bitter primary clash often seems to result in a party turnover in the office being contested. The heated 1964 Salinger-

---

[45] *Dancing Bear: an Inside Look at California Politics* (Cleveland: World, 1968), p. 86.

Cranston contest for the Senate seat held by retiring Democrat Clair
Engle was followed by Republican George Murphy's victory in the
general election. The Kuchel-Rafferty contest similarly led to a party
turnover, with Democrat Cranston subsequently defeating Rafferty
in the general election. Nor are these relatively contemporary examples,
the only ones in recent times to illustrate Hill's axiom. In 1950, for
example, the Democrats lost the Senate seat held by retiring Sheridan
Downey when young congressman Richard Nixon defeated Congress-
woman Helen Gahagan Douglas.[46] The general election had been pre-
ceded by a vigorous Democratic primary contest between Mrs. Douglas
and Manchester Boddy, and Nixon proceeded to pick up where Boddy
left off in running hard against Mrs. Douglas' alleged "pink" (i.e., left
wing) voting record in Congress. Concludes Hill; "Mrs. Douglas ended
up in the large gallery of California candidates who have survived
primaries only to emerge so battered as to be unpalatable to an electorate
favoring unmessed nominees."[47]

Primary contests would not be so critical in affecting the outcome of
the general elections that follow if party loyalty among voters were
strong in California and party labels important. But they are not. Hill
concludes that the state's "voters are so loosely oriented to party lines
that they recoil from a nominee who has been involved in a blood bath
and in November they will vote for a less disheveled nominee."[48]

One way to mitigate the damaging effects which a primary contest may
have on party fortunes in the general election is to conduct it so that
candidates do not direct their oratory at each other but rather at the
probable opponent in the general election. It was in order to avoid taking his party into a general election campaign in a state of disarray
that Republican state Chairman Gaylord Parkinson issued his "Eleventh
Commandment" prior to the 1966 primary, "Thou shall not speak ill of
any other Republican." The obeisance of Ronald Reagan and George
Christopher to the commandment in the 1966 gubernatorial primary
probably diminished Christopher's chances—as he argued—but it enhanced Reagan's position once the primary election was over.

California's primaries, then, are a critical part of the election process.
What is the level of voter participation in these primaries? In general,
approximately one half of the voting-age population or two thirds of

---

[46] Mrs. Douglas was an actress, the first of her profession to seek high public
office in California. Interestingly, her candidacy was warmly supported by another
actor who later became the most illustrious member of the profession to seek and
to win high office, Ronald Reagan. Reagan was then a liberal Democrat.

[47] Op. cit., p. 168.

[48] Ibid., p. 115.

Year	Gubernatorial Primary		Senatorial Primary		Presidential Primary		Total Vote in Primary as Per Cent of Total Registered
	Dem.	Rep.	Dem.	Rep.	Dem.	Rep.	
1942	44	50	—	—	—	—	47
1944	—	—	47	56	39	46	56
1946	48	56	44	52	—	—	51
1948	—	—	—	—	30	44	55
1950	61	68	55	63	—	—	64
1952	—	—	58	70	55	71	68
1954	55	57	51	54	—	—	56
1956	—	—	62	65	60	60	67
1958	65	65	61	63	—	—	66
1960	—	—	—	—	54	60	63
1962	51	73	51	64	—	—	64
1964	—	—	66	72	62	75	72
1966	57	70	—	—	—	—	65
1968	—	—	66	70	73	48	72

those registered to vote do in fact vote in this state's primaries. (See Table 3–4.)

In most years, Republican registrants vote in greater percentages than Democratic registrants, a difference related to the general propensity of Republican-oriented higher socioeconomic groups to participate in politics.[49] The data available from other states suggest, however, that significantly higher percentages of California registrants, regardless of party, vote in primaries than their counterparts elsewhere. Given the importance which the aforementioned factors give to California's primaries it is little wonder.

[49] In 1968 the normal pattern was reversed. For the first time in recent years, a smaller percentage of Republicans than Democrats went to the polls on primary day. Apparently many moderate Republicans resented the fact that they had no choice in the presidential primary, with only one slate pledged to favorite son Ronald Reagan entered. The victim of lower Republican turnout may well have been Senator Thomas Kuchel.

voting: general elections

he California citizen's final step toward becoming a full voting participant in the political process is taken on general election day, the first Tuesday after the first Monday in November of every even-numbered year.[1] For

---

[1] Absentee voters take the step somewhat earlier. A registered voter who expects to be absent from his precinct or physically unable to go to the polls on election day may cast an absentee ballot. He must apply to his county clerk for such a ballot at least seven days but no more than twenty-nine days prior to an election, and his ballot must be completed and returned to the county clerk no later than 5 P.M. on the day before the election.

Absentee ballots must be counted on election day, a 1963 requirement resulting from the 1960 election cliff-hanger. John Kennedy seemed to have carried California when the polls closed on election day in that year; but when the counting of absentee ballots was finally completed days later, Richard Nixon had turned defeat in the state into a 36,000-vote victory margin. The loss of California, however, was not quite enough to deny Kennedy a majority of the nation's electoral votes and the presidency.

Republicans typically cast a disproportionate share of absentee votes as persons of higher socioeconomic status are more likely than others to be on business trips or on vacation on any given day, to be aware of state provisions regarding absentee voting and to be interested in acting upon them, to be willing to use the absentee voter alternative as a means of avoiding the possible inconvenience

TABLE 4-1 CALIFORNIA VOTING TURNOUT

Year	Number of Californians Voting (Thousands)	Number Voting as Per Cent of Those Registered on Election Day
1936	2,712	83.4
1938	2,696	74.6
1940	3,302	81.4
1942	2,264	59.3
1944	3,567	86.1
1946	2,760	62.9
1948	4,077	80.5
1950	3,864	73.3
1952	5,210	86.9
1954	4,102	69.7
1956	5,548	86.6
1958	5,366	79.5
1960	6,593	88.3
1962	5,930	78.7
1964	7,233	88.4
1966	6,606	79.2
1968	7,341	85.5

hundreds of candidates and thousands of their supporters, election day is the moment of truth following the long political countdown of an arduous campaign; it is pay day for some, doomsday for others. As for the average voter, it is the day on which he fulfills a high civic responsibility and exercises a right of precious importance in the history of modern political institutions and to the concept of self-government. His personal fortunes and even those of the state, the nation, perhaps the world, may be affected by an election outcome.

voter turnout

On November 5, 1968, 7,341,000 Californians voted—a new election high. This was two thirds of the approximately 11,850,000 persons who

---

of waiting in line at a polling place, and to have secretaries to remind them of deadlines and carry out application details.

In 1966 approximately 218,000 Californians voted absentee. And whereas Republican Ronald Reagan received 58 per cent of the two-candidate total vote in defeating Democrat Edmund Brown, among absentees his percentage was 65 per cent.

comprised the voting-age population and 85.5 per cent of the state's 8,588,000 registered voters. Although this latter percentage was the lowest for a presidential election since 1948, it was less than one half of 1 per cent from the average for such elections from 1936 through 1964. (See Table 4–1.)

In general, approximately 10–15 per cent of California's registered voters fail to vote in a presidential election year either through disinterest, oversight, personal imponderables, or inaccuracies in registration lists owing to deaths or persons who have moved but remain on the registration rolls of their old precincts.

The turnout pattern of Californians is not very different from that of the citizens of most other states. An average of 59.2 per cent of civilians of voting age have voted nationally in presidential elections from 1936 through 1964. The California average for the same elections is somewhat higher—64.2 per cent. But California has ranked only about thirtieth among the states in each of the eight contests and it has generally had a lower turnout than the other large states. (See Table 4–2).

TABLE 4–2 TURNOUT IN PRESIDENTIAL ELECTIONS: 1936–1968

Vote as Per Cent of Civilian Population of Voting Age for U.S., California, and the Five Other Largest States

	1936	1940	1944	1948	1952	1956	1960	1964	1968
CALIFORNIA	59.6	66.9	62.9	58.9	68.0	63.8	67.4	66.2	60.2
Illinois	76.3	78.4	79.4	68.1	76.0	73.2	75.7	74.1	70.2
New York	61.7	67.4	74.1	60.8	68.3	66.0	67.0	63.7	59.1
Ohio	67.7	72.4	69.5	55.8	70.0	65.0	71.3	66.6	63.5
Pennsylvania	68.3	64.2	64.1	54.6	66.3	65.7	70.5	68.2	65.6
Texas	23.4	27.0	30.5	24.7	42.3	37.9	41.8	45.4	49.0
UNITED STATES	57.5	59.7	56.3	51.5	62.0	60.1	63.8	63.0	61.0
CALIF. RANK AMONG STATES*	32	26	30	26	28	30	30	30	30

* Forty-eight states until 1960; fifty in 1960–1968.
Sources: Lester Milbrath, "Political Participation in the States," in Herbert Jacob and Kenneth Vines, eds., *Politics in the American States* (Boston: Little, Brown and Company, 1965), pp. 38–39 (for data on 1936–1960 elections). U.S. Bureau of the Census, *Statistical Abstract of the U.S.: 1967* (for 1964 data). The 1968 figures are found in *The 1968 Elections: A Summary Report with Supporting Tables* (Research Division, Republican National Committee, 1969). In this case, the percentages are based on the total voting age population in each state according to the U.S. census.

TURNOUT BY TYPE OF ELECTION: PRESIDENTIAL VERSUS OFF-YEAR

Since 1936 an average of approximately 13 per cent more registered voters in California have voted in presidential elections than in off-year elections. The percentage voting in a presidential election year ranged from a low of 80.5 in 1948 to a high of 88.4 in 1936. The percentage voting in the off-year elections ranged from 59.3 in 1942 to 79.5 in 1958. This pattern is similar to the national "midterm drop off" in voting turnout, a familiar phenomenon in American politics. For example, in 1964 61.8 per cent of voting age Americans went to the polls, whereas only 50.1 per cent voted in nonpresidential year 1966. Apparently greater public interest in national issues and candidates, more intense efforts by presidential campaign organizations, and other factors produce greater electoral turnout in presidential than gubernatorial years.

TURNOUT BY PARTY

As previously indicated, Democrats tend to have poorer voting habits than Republicans. They are less likely to register to vote and less likely to vote in primary elections. By the same token, among those who are registered, Democrats are less likely than Republicans to turn out on election day.

Persons who are registered to vote but fail to go to the polls are purged (dropped) from the registration rolls following each election. Over the last several years, the Secretary of State has been issuing post-election Reports of Registration enumerating the persons in each party who remain registered after purging. By consulting these reports and comparing them to pre-election reports one may arrive at a reasonably accurate picture of the extent of nonvoting among each party's registrants in California. Such a comparison is made in Table 4–3. It indicates that proportionately more Democrats than Republicans have failed to vote in every one of the last five elections. Consider 1966, when party differences in turnout were especially marked: Of the 4.7 million Democrats registered to vote in the general election, 1.1 million—23 out of every 100—did not go to the polls and were consequently purged; of the 2.8 million registered Republicans, 0.5 million—18 out of every 100 —did not go to the polls and were purged.

TABLE 4–3 *VOTER TURNOUT BY PARTY: REGISTRATION BEFORE AND AFTER PURGING OF THE ROLLS*

	Democratic			Republican		
	Registered to Vote in Nov.	Registered After Purge	Per Cent Voted	Registered to Vote in Nov.	Registered After Purge	Per Cent Voted
1960	4,295,330	3,758,555	87.3	2,926,408	2,642,604	90.3
1962	4,289,997	3,331,260	77.7	3,002,038	2,460,224	82.0
1964	4,737,886	4,168,989	88.0	3,181,272	2,835,485	89.1
1966	4,720,597	3,629,153	76.9	3,350,990	2,808,304	83.8
1968	4,682,661	3,967,558	84.7	3,462,131	3,036,605	87.7
		Average:	82.9		Average:	86.6

"TURNOUT" BY OFFICE

Many persons who vote on election day cast only partially completed ballots, turning out to vote for some offices or issues but "turned off" by the prospect of voting for others. In 1964, 175,000 Californians who went to the polls failed to vote for either of the two presidential candidates— Lyndon Johnson and Barry Goldwater—listed on the ballot. In 1966, 102,000 voters failed to vote for Governor. Typically, the number of persons voting decreases as one moves from the more important or more publicized to the less important offices and issues on the ballot. This "drop-off" phenomenon is illustrated by the figures for 1966, indicated in Table 4–4.

TABLE 4–4 *VOTER "TURNOUT" BY OFFICE, 1966*

Total vote cast in California	6,605,866	(100.0)
Vote cast for Governor	6,503,445	(98.4)
Vote cast for Lieutenant Governor	6,417,414	(97.1)
Vote cast for Congressional candidates	6,278,601	(95.0)
Vote cast for state Senate candidates*	6,184,098	(93.6)
Vote cast for state Assembly candidates	6,131,098	(92.8)
Vote cast on antiobscenity initiative (proposition 16)†	5,805,229	(87.9)

* Ordinarily only one half of California's state Senate seats are up for election in an election year. In 1966, however, owing to court-ordered reapportionment, all seats were voted on.

† Proposition 16 was the most controversial of the sixteen statewide measures on the 1966 ballot and the one on which the most votes were cast.

TURNING OUT THE VOTE:
A PARTISAN EFFORT

"Getting out the vote" on election day—like registering voters earlier —is a major organizational activity of California's political parties and their candidates. Despite various nonpartisan efforts to encourage people to vote, parties still find it profitable to "work" the precincts, telephoning and ringing doorbells, on election day. As a partisan activity, the object of a GOV drive is to maximize voting turnout among potentially "friendly" voters and to ignore those who are likely to vote for the opposing party's candidates.

Typically, three kinds of information are used in conducting such a drive. First, high priority areas are designated where election day efforts are likely to reap the greatest dividends to scarce manpower resources. For the Democrats, these are likely to be low-income areas, where friendly partisans are most highly concentrated, but where voting turnout is traditionally low. Second is a list of persons in a high priority area who are likely to be "friendly" to the party's candidates. Such a list is compiled from the official roll of registered voters and usually is comprised of all persons registered with the "correct" party. (Registration roll information is sometimes supplemented by information gleaned from pre-election day canvasses of the area by campaign workers.) If the GOV drive is to be conducted on a door-to-door basis rather than by telephone, the list of potentially friendly voters is usually arranged in "walking" order, and on 3 × 5 cards. That is, whereas official precinct registration lists are arranged alphabetically, an efficient door-to-door operation requires that the names of "friendly" voters be arranged on a street-by-street basis by house number. The third item of information used in a GOV drive are the names of those potentially "friendly" voters who, as election day progresses, have still not voted. From time to time on election day, election board officials mark off the names of those who have voted from copies of precinct registration lists posted outside each precinct polling place. It is ordinarily impossible to contact all presumed supporters in a given area early on election day to encourage them to vote. But toward the end of the day—between 5 P.M. and the closing of the polls at 8 P.M.—an effective GOV drive will reach those friendly registrants who have still not voted according to the lists posted at the polling place. Contact will be made either by phone or preferably, by door-to-door canvassing. A ride to the polls and babysitting may be provided by a party's GOV committee when necessary.

election ballot

Two characteristics of the California election ballot deserve notice. (See Figure 4-1, a reproduction of a sample ballot.) By making the voting process somewhat more onerous for the citizens, both characteristics serve in some measure to discourage voting in the state, especially as one moves from the top of the ballot to the less significant or less publicized contests. Both reflect the state's Progressive antiparty tradition, with its "theme that 'the man is the thing,' that party considerations too often intrude and interfere with a direct relationship between the citizen and his elected representative."[2]

OFFICE BLOCK BALLOT

Candidates for partisan office are grouped on the California ballot by the office they seek rather than by party. Under the heading "Governor," for example, is found the name of each candidate for that office, along with his party identification and occupation. Many states use a party column type ballot instead of this office block type. So did California until a Progressive-sponsored election code change in 1911. The party column ballot lists Democratic and Republican candidates for all offices in separate columns. That is, under the heading "Democratic," for example, would appear the names of the Democratic candidate for Governor, Lieutenant Governor, Secretary of State, and so on down through the other partisan offices. Each person's name is followed by the title of the office he seeks. In another column would appear all the Republican candidates for the various offices being contested.

California's office block ballot discourages straight-ticket voting and encourages split-ticket voting, making it more difficult to vote for all the candidates of a single party than the party column ballot. In some party column states (including pre-1911 California), a circle is even provided at the head of the column (or a single lever on a voting machine), which may be marked (or pulled in the case of a voting machine lever) if one wishes to vote for all of the candidates of a single party.

Clearly, the California ballot form complicates the job of the voter, and raises the importance of a candidate's personality as a factor affecting

---

[2] Eugene C. Lee, ed., *The California Governmental Process* (Boston: Little, Brown and Company, 1966), p. 46.

(This number shall be torn off by Inspector and handed to the voter.)

No. 00000

I Have Voted— Have You?

SAMPLE BALLOT

STAMP A MARK (●) ON BALLOT **ONLY WITH BALLOT MARKING DEVICE;** NEVER WITH PEN OR PENCIL.

(ABSENTEE BALLOTS MAY BE MARKED WITH BALLOT MARKING DEVICE, PEN AND INK OR PENCIL.)

SAMPLE BALLOT

40

(Fold ballot to this perforated line, leaving top margin exposed.)

GENERAL BALLOT — ALAMEDA COUNTY — TUESDAY, NOVEMBER 5, 1968

INSTRUCTIONS TO VOTERS:

To vote for a candidate of your selection, stamp a mark (●) in the voting square next to the right of the name of that candidate. Where two or more candidates for the same office are to be elected, stamp a mark (●) after the names of all the candidates for that office for whom you desire to vote, not to exceed, however, the number of candidates who are to be elected. To vote for all of the electors of a party, stamp a mark (●) in the voting square opposite the names of the Presidential and Vice Presidential candidates of that party.

A mark (●) stamped in the square opposite the name of a party and its presidential and vice presidential candidate, is a vote for all of the electors of that party, but for no other candidates. To vote for those electors who have pledged themselves to vote for a candidate for President and Vice President of any party not qualified to participate in the election write in the names and party of those presidential and vice presidential candidates in the blank space provided for that purpose and stamp a mark (●) in the voting square opposite such names. To vote for a person not on the ballot write his name under the title of the office in the blank space provided

for that purpose and stamp a mark (●) in the voting square opposite the name of that person. **No write-in vote will be counted unless the marking device is used in marking the ballot when writing in a candidate's name.** To vote on any measure, stamp a mark (●) in the voting square after the word "Yes" or after the word "No". All distinguishing marks or erasures are forbidden and make the ballot void. If you wrongly stamp, tear or deface this ballot, return it to the inspector of election and obtain another. On absent voter ballots stamp a mark (●) with ballot marking device or mark a cross (+) with pen or pencil.

PRESIDENTIAL ELECTORS

Vote for One Party

GEORGE C. WALLACE, for President — American
MARVIN GRIFFIN, for Vice President — Independent

PEGGY TERRY, for President — Peace and
— for Vice President — Freedom

HUBERT H. HUMPHREY, for President — Democratic
EDMUND S. MUSKIE, for Vice President

RICHARD M. NIXON, for President — Republican
SPIRO T. AGNEW, for Vice President

CONGRESSIONAL

United States Senator   Vote for One

MAX RAFFERTY, Republican
State Superintendent of Public Instruction

ALAN CRANSTON, Democratic
Writer

PAUL JACOBS, Peace & Freedom
Writer

**Representative in Congress
7th District   Vote for One**

JEFFERY COHELAN, Democratic
United States Congressman

HUEY P. NEWTON, Peace & Freedom

BARNEY E. HILBURN, Republican
Oakland School Board Director

STATE LEGISLATURE

**State Senator
11th District   Vote for One**

NICHOLAS C. PETRIS, Democratic
Incumbent, State Senator, 11th
District, California Legislature

ROBERT E. HANNON, Republican
Member of the Board of Supervisors
of Alameda County

MARIO SAVIO, Peace & Freedom
Writer

**Member of the Assembly
15th District   Vote for One**

MARCH K. FONG, Democratic
Incumbent, Member of the State Assembly,
15th District, California Legislature

ROBERT M. CHEFSKY, Republican
Attorney

DISTRICT

East Bay Regional Park District

Director,
Ward No. 4   Vote for One

JOHN A. MACDONALD
Incumbent

**Alameda-Contra Costa
Transit District**

Director,
At Large   Vote for One

RAY H. RINEHART
Incumbent

J. HOWARD ARNOLD
Industrial Process Planner

RICHARD KARL WINDRICH
Merchant

WILLIE WITT, JR.
Government Employee

**East Bay Municipal
Utility District**

Director,
Ward No. 1   Vote for One

W. D. McNEVIN
Incumbent

Director,
Ward No. 4   Vote for One

G. HOWARD ROBINSON
Incumbent

Director,
Ward No. 5   Vote for One

A. C. CARRINGTON
Incumbent

MEASURES SUBMITTED TO VOTE OF VOTERS

STATE

1-a	HOMEOWNERS' PROPERTY TAX EXEMPTION. Provides minimum tax exemption for owner occupied dwelling. Provides for grants to local government for lost revenue. Legislature may establish maximum tax rates and bonding limitations for local government.	YES
		NO
1	CONSTITUTIONAL REVISION. Repeals, amends, and revises various provisions of Constitution relating to schools, cities and counties, public utilities, and other matters.	YES
		NO
2	TAXATION OF PUBLICLY OWNED PROPERTY. Provides that after 1968 publicly owned property located outside boundaries shall be assessed according to prescribed formula and specified conditions.	YES
		NO
3	BONDS TO PROVIDE STATE COLLEGE, UNIVERSITY, AND URBAN SCHOOL FACILITIES. (This act provides for a bond issue of two hundred fifty million dollars ($250,000,000).)	FOR
		AGAINST
4	PERSONAL INCOME TAXES. Legislature may provide for reporting and collecting California personal income taxes by reference to laws of the United States. Prohibits change in state rates based on future federal rates.	YES
		NO
5	HOSPITAL LOANS. Authorizes Legislature to insure or guarantee loans for construction, improvement, or repair and for purchase of original equipment of specified hospital and other facilities.	YES
		NO
6	INSURANCE COMPANIES: GROSS PREMIUM TAX. Permits Legislature to exclude from base of gross premium tax premiums paid on specified contracts providing retirement benefits.	YES
		NO
7	STATE FUNDS. Legislature may provide that money allocated from the State General Fund to any county, city and county, or city may be used for local purposes.	YES
		NO
8	APPORTIONMENT OF LOCAL SALES AND USE TAX. Legislature may authorize contracts between local entities to apportion sales and use tax revenue collected for them by state, if approved by voters.	YES
		NO
9	TAXATION. LIMITATIONS ON PROPERTY TAX RATE. Provides formula limiting total ad valorem tax burden on all property after July 1, 1969.	YES
		NO

COUNTY

PROPOSED AMENDMENTS TO THE CHARTER OF THE COUNTY OF ALAMEDA

A	Shall the Charter of the County of Alameda be amended to provide that the County Clerk-Recorder shall be an appointive officer in the classified civil service subject to a probationary period of not less than twelve months, instead of an elective officer, and that the person occupying such office on the date this amendment becomes effective shall have the right to be appointed to such office with regular civil service tenure at the expiration of his present term of office, by amending Section 15 and Section 17 of the Charter and adding Section 17.1 to the Charter.	YES
		NO
B	Shall the Charter of the County of Alameda be amended to provide that the Treasurer-Tax Collector shall be an appointive officer in the classified civil service subject to a probationary period of not less than twelve months, instead of an elective officer, and that the person occupying such office on the date this amendment becomes effective shall have the right to be appointed to such office with regular civil service tenure at the expiration of his present term of office, by amending Section 15 and Section 17 of the Charter and adding Section 17.1 to the Charter.	YES
		NO

CITY

PROPOSED NEW CHARTER OF THE CITY OF OAKLAND AND ALTERNATIVE PROPOSITIONS

J	PROPOSITION (J). Shall the proposed new Charter of the City of Oakland be adopted?	YES
		NO
K	PROPOSITION (K). Shall the proposed alternative to Section 303 of the proposed new Charter of the City of Oakland, which alternative provides for the appointment of the City Auditor by the City Council, be adopted?	YES
		NO
L	PROPOSITION (L). Shall the proposed alternative to Section 218 of the proposed new Charter of the City of Oakland, which alternative provides that the Mayor shall receive an annual salary equal in amount to the annual salary from time to time paid to a Judge of the Alameda County Superior Court, be adopted?	YES
		NO
M	PROPOSITION (M). Shall the proposed alternative to Section 203 of the proposed new Charter of the City of Oakland, which alternative provides that seven Councilmen shall be nominated from districts, that each shall be elected by the qualified electors of the district from which he was nominated, and that one Councilman shall be elected by the qualified electors at large, be adopted?	YES
		NO

election outcome while reducing the importance of his party affiliation. By making straight-ticket voting more difficult, the office block ballot increases the possibility of divided control of the state's executive branch and of a Governor facing a hostile legislature.

LONG BALLOT

If California's antipartyism is reflected in the form of its election ballot, it is also reflected in its length. Eleven state executive officers are elected by the voters every fourth year.[3] This is a sharp contrast to our national system in which the President and Vice-President are the only elected executive officers and even they are chosen as a single indivisible ticket. Here again is reflected the great faith California places in "personal" government and the voters' ability to pick the right man for the right job, and the little faith it has in party government and the ability of party leaders to fill executive positions by appointment. And here again, one result is a greater likelihood of divided partisan control of the executive branch of state government. Indeed, the six major partisan offices have been simultaneously held by a single party during only four years since 1942.

In addition to the eleven executive officers and to legislative positions, Californians also vote for superior court justices and county executive officers on election day. Moreover, state and local ballot propositions are added to the ballot. In 1968 ten state level measures of this kind had to be decided upon. Usually there are more. From 1912, when Californians were first called upon to consider initiative and referendum measures, through 1968, 635 propositions of various kinds and of various degrees of complexity—often defying intelligent analysis by anyone but an expert —have been put to the vote. Thus an average of over twenty such propositions have appeared on the ballot at every general election. In total, a voter must make approximately fifty separate decisions in the average election, fifty marks he must place on his ballot.[4] Many persons, of course,

---

[3] These include six statewide executive officers elected on a partisan basis (Governor, Lieutenant Governor, Secretary of State, Controller, Treasurer, and Attorney General), four members of the partisan State Board of Equalization elected on a district rather than a statewide basis, and the nonpartisan Superintendent of Public Instruction.

[4] Prior to 1940 the California presidential year ballot even included the names of all candidates for presidential elector (nominated, as they are now, at state party conventions). Numbering the equivalent of California's delegation to the U.S. House of Representatives and Senate, the citizen voted for each elector separately. In all

FIGURE 4–1   SAMPLE ELECTION BALLOT

stop trying as they move into the more obscure recesses of the printed page, thereby causing the considerable drop-off mentioned earlier.

Frank Sorauf reaches this conclusion concerning lengthy ballots and American elections:

> The one observable effect of the long ballot, especially in the office block form, has been a noticeable voter fatigue. Many voters, either tiring or despairing, do not vote in contests at the bottom of the ballot. Partial voting [drop-off] of this sort can be as high as 20 or 30 per cent of the voters at a given election.[5]

The burden on the California voter is eased somewhat by mailing him beforehand, a sample ballot—distributed by his county clerk—and a pamphlet prepared by the Secretary of State including the pros and cons on each of the ballot positions. Many people complete their sample ballot in the privacy of their homes, often with the aid of the pamphlet, and even bring it to the polls for assistance. Additionally, the parties often seek to activate the partisanship of their respective registrants by mailing "slate mailers" to them immediately before election day. These are rough facsimiles of the election ballot, with marks conveniently placed beside the names of the party's candidates in the hope that the voter will mark his own ballot in an identical manner. Many do.

tides of electoral fortune

What major conclusions can be reached regarding the behavior of Californians in general elections? Later in the chapter we shall consider how particular segments of the electorate vote—members of different social groups, residents of different regions in the state, persons distinguished by their formal party affiliations. For now let us consider some

---

but four elections, however, a single party's entire slate of electors was chosen by the voters. Today this "presidential long ballot" has been replaced by one in which only the names of the presidential and vice-presidential candidates appear—in addition, of course, to state and local candidates and propositions. A vote for a presidential ticket is counted as a vote for the state's entire slate of presidential electors supporting that ticket. The victorious elector slate travels to Sacramento, the state capital, on the first Monday after the second Wednesday in December, as provided by Act of Congress, to officially cast the state Electoral College votes for the winning ticket.

[5] *Party Politics in America* (Boston: Little, Brown and Company, 1968), p. 227.

general historical patterns of electoral behavior of Californians in the aggregate.

BAROMETER IN PRESIDENTIAL ELECTIONS

Californians have often heard that they have peculiar political habits. Yet the state's voters have behaved remarkably like the national electorate in presidential elections; the tides of party fortune in presidential elections have ebbed and flowed in California as in the nation as a whole. For example, like the nation as a whole, Californians turned their backs on the Republican candidates in 1912 and 1916 after contributing to successive party victories beginning in 1896. They returned to the Republican fold with the nation beginning in the 1920 presidential election, not only voting for a new series of winning GOP presidential candidates but electing Republicans to a majority of the state's congressional seats and giving them both U.S. Senate seats from 1920 to 1936. California participated in the national repudiation of the Republicans with the Great Depression and in the elevation of the Democrats to hegemony nationally. They supported Franklin Roosevelt in 1932 and in each of his successful campaigns for re-election and voted for Harry Truman in 1948. Like the nation as a whole, they sent a majority of Democrats to the House of Representatives from 1932 to the 1946 election. In five elections for the U.S. Senate in that period, Democratic candidates won each of the three that were contested, with progressive Republican Hiram Johnson successfully crossfiling in the primaries in the other two cases. The nation returned to the Republicans with Dwight Eisenhower in 1952 and 1956 and with Richard Nixon in 1968 and California joined in electing both. Both U.S. Senate seats were in Republican hands from 1951 to 1959. There is, in sum, nothing very peculiar about the way Californians judge national candidates unless it is their uncanny ability to "pick a winner." California voters have been marching to the same drummer as the national electorate when it comes to presidential preferences.

Indeed, in the twenty-nine contests for the presidency since 1856 Californians have preferred the losing candidate only four times. Of the forty-six states that have had statehood since the turn of the century, only Illinois can boast a voting-with-the-winner percentage equal to California's. Two of the aberrant four elections were in the twentieth century. In 1912 the presence of a native son—Hiram Johnson—on the Progressive party ticket with Theodore Roosevelt doubtlessly contributed to its narrow 1,000-vote victory margin in California (out of 678,000 cast) over national winner Woodrow Wilson. In 1960, John Kennedy lost the state to a ticket headed by another native son, Richard Nixon, but the margin of defeat was only 35,000 votes or less than one half of 1 per cent of those cast, and Kennedy's percentage of the vote in California (49.6 per cent) deviated by only one tenth of 1 per cent from his national vote percentage.[6]

That the California electorate is but a miniaturized version of the national electorate in presidential contests is well reflected in the fact that in the six such contests since World War II the percentage of the state's vote going to the Democratic candidate has never deviated by more than 2.3 per cent from his national vote percentage. Of the large states, once again it is only Illinois that has followed the nation more closely. (See Table 4–5.)

TABLE 4–5   DEMOCRATIC PERCENTAGE OF VOTE IN PRESIDENTIAL ELECTIONS: 1936–1968

	1936	1940	1944	1948	1952	1956	1960	1964	1968
CALIFORNIA	67.0	57.4	56.5	47.6	42.7	44.3	49.6	59.1	44.7
Illinois	57.7	51.0	51.5	50.1	44.9	40.3	50.0	59.5	44.2
New York	58.8	51.6	52.3	45.0	43.6	38.7	52.5	68.6	48.5
Ohio	58.0	52.2	49.8	49.5	43.2	38.9	46.7	62.9	42.9
Pennsylvania	56.9	53.2	51.1	46.9	46.9	43.3	51.1	64.9	47.6
Texas	87.1	80.9	71.4	66.0	46.7	44.0	50.5	63.3	41.2
UNITED STATES	60.8	54.8	53.5	49.5	44.4	42.0	49.5	61.1	42.6
CALIF. PER CENT MINUS U.S. PER CENT	+6.2	+2.6	+3.0	−1.9	−1.7	+2.3	+0.1	−2.0	+2.1

TWO-PARTY DOMINANCE

The two major parties have dominated partisan elections in California in much the same way as they have dominated voter registration rolls.

---

[6] The Roosevelt-Wilson and Kennedy-Nixon contests were not the only cliff-hangers to which Californians have treated election-watchers. Grant carried the state in 1868 by only 500 votes. Grover Cleveland's margin over his Republican opponent in 1892 was a mere 124 votes. In 1916 a different vote decision by approximately 1,500 Californians would have cost Wilson the state's electoral votes and, with them, the presidency. More recently, in 1948, a shift of a mere 9,000 California voters (two tenths of 1 per cent of the total) would have given Thomas Dewey rather than Harry Truman the state.

One must look back to 1944 (and before that to 1934) to find a winning candidate for partisan office who was not a Democrat or Republican. (Ralph Beal of Los Angeles won a seat in the state Assembly running as an Independent in 1944.) And one must look back a good deal farther —to the second decade of the century—to find a third party that had substantial influence at the state capital: In 1914 the Progressive party elected nine state Senators and twenty-eight Assemblymen.[7]

There have been occasional bursts of enthusiasm for third-party candidates in statewide elections during the last fifty years, but none of these candidates has scored a victory. In those instances where their votes have been significant—in 1932, 1936, 1940, and 1952—it was a result of the peculiarities of the particular election situation and not because of long-term third-party inroads into major party support. Thus in 1932 the proposed repeal of the eighteenth amendment to the U.S. Constitution (the "Prohibition" amendment banning the sale, manufacture, and transportation of intoxicating liquour) aroused voters across the nation. In California, a "dry" state, the Prohibition party candidates for the U.S. Senate was able to capitalize on concern over the threatened repeal and managed to receive 560,000 votes, or 25 per cent of those cast and enough to deprive the winning candidate of a clear electoral majority. No third-party candidate has done so well since.

In 1934 Raymond Haight ran as the gubernatorial candidate of the Commonwealth and Progressive parties, receiving 302,000 votes, or 13 per cent of those cast and again depriving the winning candidate of a majority. Haight was no "radical" and in fact was located ideologically between the two major candidates, somewhere in the political center— an unusual place for third-party candidates who come normally from the outer fringes of the ideological spectrum. The Republican candidate, Frank Merriam, was too conservative for many Republicans, whereas Upton Sinclair, his Democratic opponent, was too liberal for an even greater number of Democratic voters. (Haight attempted to persuade Sinclair to withdraw from the race on the grounds that his radicalism made him unelectable. Had Sinclair succumbed to the persuasion,

---

[7] As indicated in Chapter 2, the Progressives—originating as a dissident wing within the Republican party—had captured the GOP gubernatorial nomination with Hiram Johnson in 1910. Johnson went on to win the general election. In 1912 Johnson and his followers turned their backs on the Republican presidential nominee, William Howard Taft, and supported the "Bull Moose" candidacy of Theodore Roosevelt, with Johnson as Roosevelt's running mate on the national ticket. In 1913 the Progressives bolted the state GOP to officially establish themselves as the Progressive party of California. They scored their significant legislative victories the next year. But by 1920 the third party effort had collapsed and the Progressives had returned to the Republican fold where they fought their political battles with intermittent success in the years that followed.

Haight might well have been elected Governor and thus become the only third-party Governor in California since the Civil War.)

On two ocasions since 1932 third-party candidates for the U.S. Senate did exceptionally well only because the Republican aspirant had managed to capture the Democratic nomination as well as that of his own party by crossfiling in the primary. In 1940 the Prohibition party candidate received 366,000 votes (15 per cent of those cast) against the otherwise unopposed William Knowland. In 1952 the Senate candidate of the Independent Progressive party received a half-million votes (12 per cent of those cast) against the otherwise unopposed William Knowland.[8]

Circumstances in 1968 held out the prospect of a banner year for third parties in California and nationally. Former Alabama Governor, George Wallace ran for the presidency under the American Independent Party banner, seeking to capitalize on resentment over domestic disorder. Enough A.I.P. supporters were registered to qualify the party for a place on the California ballot. Even though the Wallace effort was better organized, better financed, and better publicized than most third-party movements, the ticket received only 7 per cent of the California vote. The Peace and Freedom party also earned a place on the 1968 ballot, hoping to capitalize on disatisfaction with Vietnam policy and black resentment. The party received less than one half of 1 per cent of the presidential vote, however, and its Senate candidate received less than 2 per cent of the vote.[9]

In general, one may say that third parties have fared a little better with California voters than with voters elsewhere in the nation, a reflection of the California voters' independent character, relatively weak party loyalties, and perennial attraction to quixotic and extravagant political schemes of various sorts. However, to do better is not to do well, and third parties in the state have suffered much the same fate as third parties nationally. Their candidates have typically been smothered under an avalanche of votes for the two major parties. The obstacles faced have proved to be virtually insurmountable. Some are institutional or legal in nature—most prominently the presidential system (in contrast to the parliamentary system used in most other democracies), the system

---

[8] The I.P.P. had been organized in 1948 on behalf of Henry Wallace's presidential candidacy. Wallace received 190,000 votes in California. Although his percentage of the state vote was twice what he received nationally, it still only amounted to 5 per cent of the total. In 1952 the same party nominated a Californian—Vincent Hallinan—for the presidency but he emerged with only 24,000 votes in the state.

[9] Contributing to the poor Peace and Freedom showing in the presidential race was the fact that only the party's vice-presidential candidate appeared on the ballot. Its presidential nominee, black militant Eldridge Cleaver, was denied a place on the ballot because he was under thirty-five years of age, the minimum age for a President established by the Constitution.

of single ballot/plurality elections in single member districts by which we select legislators, and state Elections Code restrictions.

Part of the explanation for third-party failure rests with the attitudes of the voters themselves. Jess Unruh once said in another context that "winning may not be everything, but losing is nothing whatsoever." Many voters tend to behave accordingly, preferring to vote for candidates who have a reasonable chance of winning and for parties with a reasonable chance of electing legislative majorities. It takes little acquaintance with election history and election machinery to know that a third-party vote is almost tantamount to a "throw-away" vote.

Moreover, we have been a people united on basic principles of government, with our politics serving as an arena in which means rather than ends are in dispute. On the one hand, this has meant that parties have been flexible and pragmatic in their approach to issues rather than ideological and rigid. They have been able to adjust quickly to any rising chorus of dissent that under other circumstances might result in powerful new party movements. On the other hand, consensus on fundamentals has meant that voter opinions on issues are not intensely held. Fairly well satisfied with his world, the voter finds accommodation to existing party programs rather easy. Radical politics, which is usually the form taken by third-party politics, has not found a receptive audience among a basically moderate American electorate.

Finally, there is the force of tradition. Clarence A. Berdahl writes that "the two-party system is so much a part of our governmental and political structure that it need not be argued, nor explained, nor even understood; it is . . . something we accept as a matter of course."[10] For most people the notion of supporting a third party is unthinkable. Moreover, for most people a party affiliation is very much like a religious affiliation. That is, they are "born" into their party—inheriting their allegiance from their parents—and usually go through life feeling a sense of attachment to it. Upton Sinclair perceived the problem for third parties well. He ran for Governor twice—in 1926 and in 1930—as the Socialist candidate, each time receiving approximately 50,000 votes. On the eve of the 1934 election he switched his affiliation to Democratic and proceeded to win the gubernatorial nomination of his new-found party. He explained his maneuver by noting "that to get anywhere [in American politics], it is necessary to have a party which has grandfathers." As a Democrat, Sinclair received 880,000 votes in the general election.[11]

---

[10] *Our Two-Party System* (University: University of Mississippi, 1951), p. 1.

[11] The Sinclair episode reflected the way in which radical movements may find accommodation within the rather malleable major parties. Although Sinclair and his

REPUBLICAN DOMINANCE AND DEMOCRATIC REVIVAL IN STATE ELECTIONS

If two-partyism has had an enemy in California it has not been the third party but the threat of one-party domination. Legislative seats are often "safe" in character for one party or the other. But more to the point has been the long period during which the Republican party has been virtually unbeatable in statewide elections.

One of the marked characteristics of the voting behavior of Californians is their separation of national from state politics. If national trends in presidential elections have been duplicated in California, as indicated, they have not always intruded into elections for state office. In registration, as we have seen earlier, and in presidential voting, Californians embraced the Democratic party during its national renaissance in the 1930s and 1940s. However, the California habit of voting for Republican gubernatorial candidates, which extended back to 1894, was broken only once before 1958. Democrat Culbert Olson captured the governorship in 1936 for a brief four-year interlude. Earl Warren won it back for the Republicans in 1942 and proceeded on to a second and third term in the statehouse, to be followed by his Republican Lieutenant Governor, Goodwin Knight, who won the 1954 election. With the exception of three elections—1936, 1938, and 1940—Republicans elected majorities to the state Assembly from 1894 to 1958. As for the state Senate, which Republicans had controlled since 1890, the Democrats failed to elect a majority in that house throughout the New Deal-Fair Deal period and until 1958. It is little wonder that the late V. O. Key, Jr., a most distinguished political scientist, concluded in the 1958 edition of his basic text on political parties in America that California was a "strong Republican state"—along with ten other GOP stalwarts including Iowa, Kansas, Maine, South Dakota, Vermont.[12] The partisan revolution of

---

End Poverty in California enthusiasts lost the 1934 general election, they captured the official Democratic party organization, writing an EPIC platform and electing Culbert Olson state chairman. Olson subsequently went on to be the party gubernatorial nominee in 1938 and this time the Democrats were not to be denied. Sheridan Downey, the Democratic-EPIC Lieutenant Governor nominee in 1934, went on to the U.S. Senate in 1938, first defeating the regular Democratic incumbent, William Gibbs McAdoo, in the senatorial primary.

[12] *Politics, Parties, and Pressure Groups*, 4th ed. (New York: Thomas Y. Crowell Company, 1958), p. 313. Others came to similar conclusions. For example, under the classificatory scheme developed by Joseph Schlesinger, California is characterized as "One-Party Predominant" (Republican). ("A Two-Dimensional Scheme for Classi-

the thirties and forties, which marked the resurgence of the Democratic Party in many states, had little impact on state elections in California.

The 1958 election may well have ushered in a new era in terms of interparty competition for state office. The story of Democratic party revival and its 1966 setback was recounted in a previous chapter. It is, of course, too early for a definitive characterization of the present nature of interparty competition in the state. The Brown victories may have represented merely a brief hiatus in the continuing Republican domination of state politics. Conversely, Reagan's success may represent only a brief setback for the Democrats on the road to dominance in state politics. Or the state may be in the midst of an era comparable to the 1867–1894 period during which a Republican Governor was always succeeded by a Democrat and vice versa, and legislative majorities shifted regularly between the two parties.

TICKET-SPLITTING

In at least two major respects, California's voters are a highly independent lot. The failure of many registered Democrats to vote for their party's candidates, even during the New Deal-Fair Deal period is one measure of that independence and will be considered hereafter. A related phenomenon is the willingness of the Californian to be a split-ticket voter, with a decision to vote for a given party's candidate for one office a rather imperfect index of how he will vote on other offices. In 1962 Richard Nixon lost his race for the governorship to incumbent Edmund Brown by 300,000 votes. But at the same time his fellow Republican, Thomas Kuchel, won re-election to the U.S. Senate by no less than 700,000 votes. In 1964 Pierre Salinger lost the Senate race to George Murphy by 200,000 votes while, simultaneously, fellow Democrat Lyndon Johnson was carrying California in the presidential race by 1.3 million votes. In 1968 Richard Nixon more than compensated for his 1962 gubernatorial defeat by carrying California in his successful bid for the presidency. But even though he topped Humphrey by over 200,000 votes in the state, Max Rafferty, the candidate for the U.S. Senate on the same Republican ticket, was being defeated by Alan Cranston by more than 300,000 votes.

When one party has swept into the governorship, more often than

fying States According to Degree of Inter-Party Competition," *American Political Science Review*, 49 [1955], pp. 1120–1128.) Coleman Ransome likewise considered California to be a Republican state, *The Office of Governor in The United States* (University, Ala.: University of Alabama, 1956).

not the other party has retained at least one statewide elective office. Democrat Thomas Lynch was elected as Attorney General while Reagan was enjoying his overwhelming victory in the 1966 gubernatorial election. Republican Frank Jordan survived as Secretary of State while Edmund Brown was being elected and re-elected Governor. Brown himself was elected to two terms as Attorney General under Republican Governors Warren and Knight. Another Democrat, Robert Kenney also was elected Attorney General under Warren. Kenney's predecessor was the same Earl Warren, elected to serve as Attorney General under Democratic Governor Culbert Olson. Party labels, it seems, have only limited meaning to the California electorate. Candidates are required to make their own way with the voters.

CANDIDATES' BACKGROUND AND ASPIRATIONS

If the party identification of candidates is not always an important determinant of how the Californian will vote, what candidate characteristics do play a role? First, Californians seem to have a fondness for candidates, who like themselves, are politically independent and "above" party politics. Hiram Johnson and Earl Warren were, of course, the greatest expositors of the nonpartisan tradition and the state's most successful vote-getters. Thomas Kuchel probably added to his considerable popularity with the general electorate by establishing his independence from the Republican party and failing to endorse fellow Republicans—Richard Nixon for the governorship in 1962, Barry Goldwater for the presidency in 1964, and Ronald Reagan in 1966—a failure that incensed many Republicans enough to vote against Kuchel in the 1968 GOP primary and to cut short his career in the U.S. Senate. Republican Ronald Reagan called himself a "citizen-politician" and was not ashamed of the fact that he earlier had been an active Democrat when he waged his antipolitician campaign against former Republican, Edmund Brown, in the 1966 gubernatorial race. Of course, Republicans may feel—and correctly so—that separating themselves from their party is politically wise in a state in which Democrats enjoy such a large registration majority. But Democrats, too, often play the same nonpartisan theme in attracting votes. "I want to make it very clear," said Edmund Brown, the most successful Democratic vote-getter in recent years when he ran for Governor in 1958, "that I intend to guide our state in the great tradition of Earl Warren and Hiram Johnson." The intrepid Mayor of Los Angeles, Sam Yorty, seems to have added rather than detracted from his appeal as a candidate by displaying almost impeccable credentials as a party maverick, having opposed John Kennedy's presidential candidacy in 1960 and having engaged in a running feud with Governor Brown and the Democratic "establishment."

Second, Californians seem to be attracted in gubernatorial elections to candidates with previous experience in public office. The election of Reagan in 1966 seems to suggest otherwise, as he had never before served in government. However, Reagan is an exception among California's Governors. When party labels have relatively little meaning to voters, "name familiarity" becomes important. Some may gain such name familiarity outside of the political arena—as a motion picture or television actor, for example. For most, however, holding public office is the most effective way to become sufficiently well known among the electorate to carry out a successful campaign. The average prior experience in elective office of California Governors elected in this century has been eleven and one-half years.[13] (The election advantages of incumbency are discussed later.)

Third, California voters seem to resent candidates whose dedication to serving the state's interests seems less than perfect and their dedication to feeding their own ambition more than ample. Thus, they reject "carpetbaggers" who descend on the state's political scene from far-off expecting instant success. Persons elected to serve the state in the nation's capital who proceed to lose touch with the state and its problems are also treated badly. And so, too, are those who seem to be running for office in California only as a means of achieving a spot on a presidential ticket at some later date. "Time and again," says Gladwin Hill, "California voters have shown they resent anyone's assumption that he can convert alien structure into political legal tender in California. . . . And they

---

[13] A brief look at the careers of the last nine Governors elected before Reagan reveals that all of them had considerable governmental experience prior to their governorships.
1. William Stephens (1917–1923): Mayor of Los Angeles; Congressman; Lieutenant Governor
2. Friend Richardson (1923–1927): long-time state Treasurer
3. Clement Young (1927–1931): long-time Assemblyman; Assembly Speaker; Lieutenant Governor
4. James Rolph (1931–1934): Mayor of San Francisco for twenty years
5. Frank Merriam (1934–1939): Assemblyman; Lieutenant Governor (as well as a public officeholder in Iowa)
6. Culbert Olson (1938–1943): state Senator (in Utah, as well as California)
7. Earl Warren (1943–1953): District Attorney of Alameda County for twelve years; state Attorney General
8. Goodwin Knight (1953–1958): Superior Court Judge and Lieutenant Governor under Warren
9. Edmund Brown (1959–1967): District Attorney of San Francisco County for seven years; state Attorney General for two terms.

resent any implication that California office is merely being used as a
steppingstone to a better position elsewhere."[14]

In the 1958 gubernatorial race Brown scored campaign points by
charging his opponent, William Knowland, with really being a "Washington politician" whose long service as U.S. Senator had put him out of
touch with state issues, and who was really seeking the governorship as
a steppingstone to a presidential candidacy. Neither charge was effectively countered by Knowland in the campaign. In 1962 Brown levelled
almost identical charges—again with success—against his new opponent,
Richard Nixon, who had served two terms as Vice-President and had
just earlier lost a presidential race against John Kennedy. In 1964 White
House Press Secretary Pierre Salinger announced his candidacy for the
U.S. Senate and was subsequently haunted by the carpetbagger charge,
embarrassingly evidenced by the fact that he had become a Viriginia
resident while serving under Presidents Kennedy and Johnson and was
not even eligible to vote in California for his own candidacy. And
Thomas Kuchel was severely lambasted in the 1968 Republican senatorial
primary for failing to keep "in touch" with his California constituents
while serving in the Senate. As the *New York Times'* Tom Wicker has
said, "Absence from the state [of California], no matter what the mission,
does not make the voter's heart grow fonder."

who votes how?

Studies of American voting behavior have multiplied during the last
quarter century, particularly as survey research and polling methods
have become more sophisticated. The social attributes of the supporters
of the two major parties have been explored in detail. Each party, it is
true, has avoided explicit links to any single social class or other social
group. To do otherwise would be to risk alienating too many voters
and perhaps to sacrifice hopes of electoral success. And America's tremendous diversity has made impossible the development of clear and
unambiguous relationships between the party preferences and social
attributes of the voters as most persons fall into several politically
relevant social categories.

Nevertheless, the parties do differ in the coalition of supporters on
which they are based. Although these coalitions shimmy and shake some-

14 *Dancing Bear* (Cleveland: World, 1968), p. 147.

what from election to election, they have been remarkably durable. In general, to know a man's economic status or religion or race tells us a great deal about his politics. There is much to the statement in one of the pioneer studies of American voting behavior that "a person thinks, politically, as he is socially."[15]

SOCIAL BASES OF PARTY SUPPORT

Table 4–6 presents poll data on the social characteristics of the supporters of candidates for major office in California in 1966 and 1968. The two *California Polls* analyzed in the table were taken shortly before election day, in October of each year. They were based on general population samples selected by established methods of assuring that such samples would be microcosms of the universe being studied, in this case California's voters.[16] The poll data reveal that in the 1966 gubernatorial contest between Edmund Brown and Ronald Reagan the Democratic candidate drew his support much more heavily from persons of lower socioeconomic status and the "working class" than the Republican candidate. Thirty-one per cent of the Brown supporters were from the lower and lower middle economic groups, whereas only 15 per cent were from the upper and upper middle economic groups. The percentages were reversed for the Reagan supporters, with 28 per cent being in the upper and upper middle and 13 per cent in the lower and lower middle economic groups. Family income figures conformed with this pattern. The median income for the respondents favoring Brown was approximately $6,600, or almost two thousand dollars under that of the Reagan respondents. In terms of education, a variable highly related to economic status, Reagan again had greater appeal among the higher achievement groups: 47 per cent of his supporters compared to 35 per cent of Brown's supporters had more than a high school education. Eminent historian Charles Beard said a half-century ago that "the center of gravity of

---

15 Paul Lazarsfeld, Bernard Berelson, and Hazel Gaudet, *The People's Choice* (New York: Columbia University Press, 1944), p. 27.

16 Some of the interviewees did not indicate a preference for either of the two major candidates in the election considered. These persons, of course, are not considered in the table. Moreover, some of the interviewees supporting each candidate did not respond to all of the questions asked of them. Thus, for example, only 430 of the 442 Brown supporters in 1966 gave their income. The percentages in these instances are based on the number of persons answering the question.

We are grateful to the Field Research Corporation, originators of the *California Poll*, for making this data available. The *California Poll* and the other major poll in the state, the *State Poll*, are among the most highly respected state polls in the nation.

TABLE 4–6 SOCIAL CHARACTERISTICS OF CALIFORNIA VOTERS

	1966 Gubernatorial		1968 Senatorial	
	Brown (D) (N: 442) (Per Cent)	Reagan (R) (N: 515) (Per Cent)	Cranston (D) (N: 572) (Per Cent)	Rafferty (R) (N: 419) (Per Cent)
Income				
Under $3,000	17	11	9	10
$3,000–5,000	15	9	9	8
$5,000–7,000	22	16	12	11
$7,000–10,000	20	26	26	18
$10,000–15,000	19	25	24	30
$15,000 and over	7	13	20	23
Economic Level				
Lower	4	2	5	5
Lower middle	27	11	17	14
Middle	54	59	58	60
Upper middle	14	26	18	19
Upper	1	2	2	2
Extent of Education				
11th grade or less	34	22	24	23
High school graduate	31	31	30	33
1–4 years of college or equivalent	27	41	36	38
Graduate study beyond college	8	6	10	6
Union Membership				
Respondent and/or spouse is member	35	23	34	23
Neither is a member	65	77	66	77
Religion				
Protestant	53	73	54	70
Catholic	28	20	26	19
Jewish	12	1	7	1
Other	3	3	6	6
None	4	3	7	4
Race				
White	87	98	91	98
Negro	10	1	7	1
Other	3	1	2	1
Age				
21–29	12	11	20	17
30–39	20	18	23	18
40–49	24	21	24	21
50–59	17	20	16	15
60–69	13	17	10	16
70 and over	14	13	7	13

wealth [in America] is on the Republican side while the center of gravity of poverty is on the Democratic side." His conclusion, it would seem, is not inapplicable to California in 1966.

In 1968, the class difference in the coalition of voters supporting the candidates of the two parties is somewhat more ambiguous. The median income for the Democratic voters ($9,300) was $1,200 below that of the Rafferty voters. But in economic level and education, the supporters of the two candidates were almost identical.

That Democratic candidates rely more heavily than Republican candidates on working class support is suggested by the fact that approximately one third of both Brown's and Cranston's supporters were members of or married to members of a trade union, whereas less than one quarter of the Reagan and Rafferty supporters came from such families.

In terms of race and religion, the Democratic supporters in both years prove to be a more diverse group and include among their number a greater percentage of minority—nonwhite and non-Protestant—members. The approximately 10 per cent of the Democratic supporters who are nonwhite in each year is five times the percentage of nonwhites among Republican supporters. Jewish voters make up a similarly disproportionate share of the Democratic supporters in both years. Catholics account for over one quarter of the Cranston and Brown supporters, whereas they comprise only one fifth of the Reagan and Rafferty supporters.

Finally, the supporters of the Democratic candidate in both years tend to be a younger group than their Republican counterparts. Whereas in 1966 44 per cent of the Brown supporters were over fifty years of age, 50 per cent of the Reagan group fell into this age bracket. Similarly, 33 per cent of the Cranston supporters as contrasted to 44 per cent of the Rafferty backers were over fifty in 1968.

What can we make, in a general way, of these data? First, the candidates of both parties appear to have highly heterogeneous support and to enjoy appeals that extend into all the social groups considered. However, the Republican appeal among nonwhite and Jewish groups seems to have reached an irreducible minimum. Second, although both parties have broad appeals there are still differences in the patterns of support for their candidates. In general, Democratic candidates tend to rely for their support more heavily on those of lower socioeconomic and educational achievement, on trade union members, on racial and religious minorities, and on the young. The Republican candidates, contrariwise, have greater appeal among the economically and educationally successful, the white Protestant community, and those who are older. Third, the groups upon which the Democrats rely more heavily are the very groups which various studies show are least likely to vote on election day. Fourth, comparing these data with the plentiful evidence gathered over the past generation about the social bases of party support nationally, it would appear that the California voters divide in party preference in very much the same way as voters elsewhere in America. If "a person thinks, politically, as he is socially," he apparently does so in California in much the same way as he does in other parts of the nation. Fifth, the way in which the party's candidates tend to rely more heavily on some social groups than on others appears to be related, probably in some reciprocal way, to the party posture on issues of public policy over the years. The Democratic party has generally been considered more responsive to lower class needs and more receptive to change in its policy orientation than the Republicans. It is not incomprehensible, then, that it has drawn much of its support from "outsiders" in the economic and social fabric of the society, those who are least likely to be satisfied with things the way they are. And their presence, in turn, has no doubt helped to perpetuate the unique policy orientations of the party. The Republican party, on the other hand, has greater appeal among the "haves" in the society. It is not surprising that it is considered to be the more conservative of the two parties and that its policy orientation has generally been characterized as status quo-oriented and resistant to change, i.e., appropriate for those likely to be satisfied with their position in society and who feel little need for governmental assistance. Sixth, the social bases of support for each party's candidates do not appear to be fixed and immobile from election to election. For example, the advantage enjoyed by Reagan in 1966 with the upper class was largely lost to his fellow Republican, Rafferty, two years later. The personality and issue posture of individual candidates may have their own impact on the nature of their support. More significantly, perhaps, is the possibility that old, long-term coalitions of support for a party may begin to erode at some point in time. The differences in the nature of Brown's support in 1966 and Cranston's in 1968 may be a reflection of a long-term breakdown of the class basis of party support that has been so pronounced since the New Deal; the virtual indistinguishability between Rafferty and Cranston supporters in terms of certain measures of economic class may signal a major realigning trend among the voters extending over several elections.[17]

---

[17] Totten Anderson and Eugene Lee suggest such a trend in California in their study of the 1966 election. "An analysis of *California Poll* reports over the past eight years," they note, "suggests that basic realignments may be taking place within the Democratic Party, despite the relative constancy of its 2–1 share of registrants. The

GEOGRAPHY OF ELECTION OUTCOMES

One persistently interesting and convenient way of analyzing the pattern of support for the two major parties and election outcomes generally is by considering the geographic distribution of the vote. How do voters living in different geographic components of the nation behave at election time? Do urban and nonurban areas have contrasting partisan dispositions? Are there sectional or regional divisions in voter preferences? These kinds of questions are traditionally applied to national election returns. They are also applicable when considering the behavior of the California electorate.

Table 4–7 presents the over-all partisan performance of each of California's fifty-eight counties in the sixteen contested presidential and gubernatorial elections from 1936 through 1968. (It serves as the basis for the map appearing on the inside cover of the book.) Although the counties range incredibly in size—from tiny Alpine, with a population of 400 to overblown Los Angeles, with a population of seven million and over one third of the state's inhabitants—and although they have lost most of their importance as governmental entities, they are still basic political units in California and are to the state very much what the states are to the nation.[18] The table ranks the counties by the number of elections since 1936 in which the Democratic candidate for President or Governor outpolled his Republican opponent. Each party carried the state eight times and carried each county at least once in the elections considered. Only in the case of President Franklin Roosevelt's 1936 campaign for re-election and of Governor Earl Warren's 1950 campaign for re-election did a candidate carry every county.[19] Seventeen counties are listed as "Democratic," each having been carried by Democratic

---

data indicate that Governor Brown suffered substantial losses in support among the white working people, especially union members, and among lower income and educational groups which had been his chief source of strength in 1958, and, to a lesser degree, in 1962." ("The 1966 Election in California," *Western Political Quarterly*, **XX**, 2 [June 1967], pp. 547, 550.)

[18] Parties are officially organized below the state level only at the county level, and statewide election campaigns are organized at the county level. Until 1967, counties served as units of representation in the state Senate. The Secretary of State presents the results of all statewide election contests only on a county-by-county basis. Finally, unlike such election units as the Assembly district, the county has boundary lines that do not change with time.

[19] During the 1936–1968 period one U.S. senatorial candidate, Republican incumbent Thomas Kuchel in 1962, carried every county. Earlier, Republican Hiram Johnson in 1928 and James Rolph in 1930 carried every county in their bids for re-election to the U.S. Senate and to the governorship, respectively.

TABLE 4–7 PARTISAN PERFORMANCE BY CALIFORNIA'S COUNTIES IN ELECTIONS FOR PRESIDENT AND GOVERNOR: 1936–1968*

Counties Ranked by Number of Elections Carried by Democratic Candidate

17 Democratic Counties	24 Inconsistent Counties	17 Republican Counties
15 of 16	*10 of 16*	*5 of 16*
Plumas (−)	Stanislaus	Del Norte
		Glenn
		Marin (+)(M)
13 of 16	*9 of 16*	Monterey (M)
Fresno (M)	El Dorado	SAN DIEGO (+)(M)
Kings	LOS ANGELES (+)(M)	
Lassen (−)	Siskiyou (−)	
Madera	Tuolumne	*4 of 16*
SACRAMENTO (+)(M)	Ventura (M)	Imperial
Solano	Yuba	Inyo (−)
		San Benito
12 of 16	*8 of 16*	Santa Barbara (M)
ALAMEDA (+)(M)	Humbolt	
Amador	Kern (M)	
Merced	Modoc (−)	*3 of 16*
Placer (M)		Lake
Shasta	[CALIFORNIA: 8 of 16]	Riverside (M)
		Santa Cruz
		Sonoma (M)
11 of 16	*7 of 16*	Sutter
CONTRA COSTA (+)	Colusa	
(M)	Mendocino	
SAN FRANCISCO (+)	Napa (M)	*2 of 16*
(M)	Nevada	Mono (−)
Sierra (−)	SAN BERNARDINO	
Trinity (−)	(M)	
Yolo (M)	San Joaquin (M)	*1 of 16*
	SAN MATEO (+)(M)	Alpine (−)
	SANTA CLARA (+)(M)	ORANGE (+)(M)
	Tulare	
	6 of 16	
	Butte	
	Calaveras	
	Mariposa (−)	
	San Luis Obispo	
	Tehama	

* The 1946 gubernatorial election is excluded because Governor Warren successfully crossfiled in the primary and consequently became the nominee of both parties in the general election.

Note: The names of the ten most populous counties appear in capital letters. Counties whose names are followed by (M) are the 22 counties included in California's 14 Standard Metropolitan Statistical Areas. Counties whose names are followed by (+) are the ten most densely populated in the state. Those followed by (−) are the ten least densely populated.

candidates more than twice as often as Republican candidates. A like number of counties are classified as "Republican," each having been carried by Republican candidates more than twice as often as Democratic candidates. Twenty-four counties are classified as "Inconsistent" in their partisan dispositions. The ten largest counties (appearing in capital letters)—in which three quarters of the state's inhabitants reside —are dispersed among the three categories, and neither party claims a majority of these under its heading.[20]

It is interesting that the performance of the counties does not support the persistent conclusion of American voting studies that the Democratic party's appeal outside the South is predominantly urban whereas the Republican appeal is strongly small-town and rural. Twenty-two counties are included in the state's 14 Standard Metropolitan Statistical Areas, a U.S. Census Bureau term applying to highly urbanized areas. Eight are among the seventeen counties listed in Table 4–7 as Democratic and seven are among the seventeen Republican counties. Similarly, of the ten counties with the highest population density in the state—population density being another index of urbanization—four are among the Democratic and three among the Republican counties. And four of the ten counties with the lowest population density in the state are Democratic, three Republican. The urban Bay area counties of San Francisco, Contra Costa, and Alameda are Democratic counties. But so too are the Sacramento Valley counties of Fresno, Kings, Madera, and Merced, and the sparsely settled mountain counties of Amador, Lassen, Plumas, and Sierra. In fact, Plumas is the state's most Democratic county, although two other low density mountain counties— Alpine and Mono are among the three most Republican in the state. High density, metropolitan Orange county shares with Alpine the distinction of having voted Republican in all but one of the 16 elections covered in Table 4–7.

But if we extend the analysis below the county level, the urban-nonurban differences in partisan preferences found nationally also appear in California. Table 4–8 presents the 1966 vote for the two major

---

[20] One of the disadvantages to using a time period of 22 years for analysis is that recent shifts in county voting patterns may be concealed. Suggestive of the extent of partisan stability among the citizens of the counties is the fact that of the 17 Democratic counties in Table 4-7 only tiny Trinity gave Democrat Hubert Humphrey a smaller percentage of the vote than he garnered statewide in the 1968 presidential election. All of the 17 Republican counties preferred Richard Nixon in that race to a greater extent than he was preferred statewide. Of the top 10 Humphrey counties (in terms of percentage of vote), nine classify as "Democratic" in the Table and of the top 10 Nixon counties, seven are classified as "Republican."

TABLE 4–8 VOTE FOR GOVERNOR, 1966: TEN LARGEST COUNTIES AND THEIR LARGEST CITIES

	Brown Vote		Reagan Vote		Brown Per Cent	Reagan Per Cent
County: Alameda	190,968		189,055		50.2	49.8
City: Oakland		78,670		61,603	56.1	43.9
County: Contra Costa	87,525		107,543		44.9	55.1
City: Richmond		16,889		10,950	60.7	39.3
County: Los Angeles	1,037,663		1,389,995		42.8	57.2
City: Los Angeles		503,389		449,146	52.8	47.2
County: Orange	113,275		293,413		27.8	72.2
City: Anaheim		14,058		34,516	28.9	71.1
County: Sacramento	105,861		108,801		49.3	50.7
City: Sacramento		51,656		42,167	55.1	44.9
County: San Bernardino	74,120		121,916		37.8	62.2
City: San Bernardino		15,684		17,073	47.9	52.1
County: San Diego	142,890		252,070		36.2	63.8
City: San Diego		82,629		127,886	39.2	60.8
County: San Francisco	164,435		114,796		58.9	41.1
City: San Francisco*		164,435		114,796	58.9	41.1
County: San Mateo	92,654		107,498		46.3	53.7
City: San Mateo		13,741		16,520	45.4	54.6
County: Santa Clara	132,793		164,970		44.6	55.4
City: San Jose		48,560		58,224	45.5	54.5
Ten County Total	2,142,184		2,850,057		42.9	57.1
Ten City Total		989,711		932,881	51.5	48.5
California	2,799,174		3,742,913		42.3	57.7

* The County of San Francisco and the city of San Francisco are identical.

gubernatorial candidates in each of the ten most populous counties and the vote in the largest cities within those counties. Only in one case—the city of San Mateo within the county of San Mateo—was Democrat Edmund Brown's vote percentage in the city smaller than in the county. Indeed, while his Republican opponent, Ronald Reagan, outpolled Brown in the ten counties by approximately 700,000 votes, he lost their major cities by over 50,000. If the gubernatorial election had been held in only these ten of the state's fifty-eight counties, the outcome would have almost been identical in percentage terms to what it actually was. If it had been held in the cities considered, however, Edmund Brown would have been elected to a third term.

What of regional or sectional differences in voting behavior? California, much like the nation, is much noted for its persistent north-south cleavage.[21] In part, such cleavage is generated by different regional interests regarding issues of public policy, e.g., over apportionment of legislative districts, the allocation of state highway funds, conservation programs, the disposition of state water resources. But the cleavage is also a function of the fact that northerners and southerners differ in political predispositions. Election returns reveal the difference quite clearly.[22] In general, southern Californians are more Republican, more conservative, and more to the political "right."[23] Thus, of the eight California counties south of the Tehachapi mountains, traditionally considered the north-south dividing line in the state, five are listed as Republican in Table 4–7 and none as Democratic. Of the ten most populous counties considered in Table 4–8, four are in southern Cali-

[21] It was less than a decade after the achievement of statehood that the legislature passed, and the Governor signed, a measure to divide the state in two. The necessary federal ratification was not then forthcoming. But there have been periodic proposals to achieve such a division ever since—all fruitless but nevertheless suggesting the persistency of regional conflict in California.

[22] Eugene Lee's analysis of California voting behavior has led him to conclude that "there are two worlds of California politics." (Eugene Lee, "The Two Arenas and the Two Worlds of California Politics," in Lee, ed., The California Governmental Process, pp. 51–53.) Michael Rogin, another political scientist, concludes from a study of voting patterns in the state that "the electoral choices of southern California form a historically, symbolically coherent regional pattern." ("Southern California: Political Symbols and Right-Wing Behavior," June 1967, unpublished manuscript, p. 5.)

[23] It is a common observation that southern California is a breeding ground for a wide variety of right-wing causes and organizations. The John Birch Society, for example, has found a receptive audience in the southern part of the state. (See Seymour Martin Lipset, "Three Decades of the Radical Right: Coughlinites, McCarthyites and Birchers—1962," in Daniel Bell, ed., The Radical Right [Garden City, N.Y.: Doubleday, 1963, 1964].) Indeed, two Birch Society members were elected to the U.S. Congress from the region—the only congressmen to claim such an affiliation—and one has been elected to the state Senate. In 1964, the Society claimed to have more than 50 members serving on the 260-man Republican County Central Committee in Los Angeles.

So-called superpatriotic organizations proliferate in southern California as nowhere else in the nation. (See Richard Schmuck and Mark Chesler, "On Super-Patriotism: A Definition and Analysis," Journal of Social Issues, XIX, 1963.) Participants in radical right letter writing campaigns seem to be heavily located in southern California. (See James McEvoy, "Letters from the Right: Content Analysis of a Letter Writing Campaign" [Ann Arbor: University of Michigan Institute for Social Research, 1966].) Concludes Michael Rogin, "For more than half a century, southern California has been the home of right-wing extremism. . . . Like the deep South, it is peculiarly susceptible to right-wing appeals." Op. cit., pp. 5, 23.

TABLE 4–9   REGIONAL SUPPORT FOR REPUBLICAN CANDIDATES

Region	GOP Per Cent of Two-Party Vote for Governor and President (1958–1968)					
	1958	1960	1962	1964	1966	1968
Northern California						
San Francisco Bay Area	35	48	43	34	51	45
Other	36	49	45	37	57	51
Total	36	48	44	35	54	47
Southern California						
Los Angeles County	42	50	47	42	57	51
Other	48	56	55	49	66	61
Total	44	52	50	45	60	55
California	40	50	47	41	58	52

Note: Bay area counties in this table and the two that follow include Alameda, Contra Costa, Marin, Napa, San Francisco, San Mateo, Santa Clara, Solano, and Sonoma. Southern counties outside of Los Angeles include Imperial, Orange, Riverside, San Bernardino, San Diego, Santa Barbara, and Ventura.

The 1958–1966 figures are based on material presented in Totton Anderson and Eugene Lee, "The 1966 Election in California," *Western Political Quarterly*, **XVIII**, 2 (June 1967), p. 547.

fornia and they awarded Reagan higher vote percentages than any of the other six. Table 4–9 presents the regional distribution of the vote in six elections from 1958 through 1968 and in each case Republican candidates fared better in the south than the north. In 1960 and again in 1968 only a Republican majority in the south kept the Democratic presidential candidate (John Kennedy in 1960 and Hubert Humphrey in 1968) from carrying the state against Richard Nixon.[24] Generally it is felt by political pundits that a Democratic candidate for major office must carry northern California by at least 200,000 votes to compensate for the losses he can anticipate in the south.

North-south differences along left-right, conservative-liberal lines are equally if not more pronounced when the party label is absent from

[24] In the 1964 race for the U.S. Senate a similar situation developed. Republican candidate George Murphy won in the southern counties by 350,000 votes and thereby carried the state, while losing to his Democratic opponent Pierre Salinger by 150,000 votes in the north.

In that same year, presidential candidate Barry Goldwater broke even in the southern counties outside of Los Angeles—a remarkable feat given his overwhelming defeat almost everywhere else in the state.

the ballot and cannot serve as a guide for the voter. Three ballot measures considered by the electorate in recent years have generated a clear and dramatic clash of political ideologies. These included a 1962 "antisubversive" initiative (the so-called Francis amendment) listed on the ballot as Proposition 24; a 1964 "antifair housing" initiative, Proposition 14, designed to nullify and prevent legislation banning discrimination in the sale and rental of housing; and, a 1966 "antiobscenity" measure, Proposition 16. In each case, serious questions were raised as to a possible violation of the U.S. Constitution's protection of civil liberties if the measure was to pass. (Actually, only Proposition 14 in 1964 passed, and it was subsequently declared unconstitutional by the state Supreme Court.) In each case, the proposed measure was condemned by most religious, labor, liberal, and civil liberties groups. In each case right-wing or ultraconservative elements tended to comprise the most ardent advocates of the measure; left-wing elements were adamantly opposed. And in each case, as indicated in Table 4–10, southern California voters proved significantly more favorable to the conservative (or affirmative) position than the north.

Finally, southern conservatism has also been dramatically revealed in primary election returns. The Democrats have not suffered from a

TABLE 4–10 CONSERVATIVE SENTIMENT ON STATEWIDE PROPOSITIONS: PER CENT VOTING YES ON THREE RECENT INITIATIVE MEASURES

Region	Proposition 24 (1962) "Antisubversive"	Proposition 14 (1964) "Anti-Fair Housing"	Proposition 16 (1966) "Antiobscenity"
Northern California			
San Francisco Bay Area	31	58	36
Other	34	63	41
Total	32	60	38
Southern California			
Los Angeles County	48	67	47
Other	44	72	48
Total	46	69	47
California	40	65	44

clear liberal-conservative primary clash in recent years. But the Republican Party has been afflicted with three contests for nomination to major office with powerful liberal-conservative overtones—one presidential, one gubernatorial, and one senatorial. In each instance, GOP voters in the eight southern counties were significantly more favorable to the conservative candidate. (See Table 4–11.) In the 1964 presidential primary, Nelson Rockefeller carried the north with ease, but not sufficiently to overcome the overwhelming 240,000-vote margin by which his conservative opponent, Barry Goldwater, carried the south. In 1966 gubernatorial aspirant George Christopher carried the Bay area and lost the north by only 48,000 votes out of 862,000 cast. But his more conservative opponent, Ronald Reagan, carried the south by 694,000 votes

TABLE 4–11   CONSERVATIVE SENTIMENT IN REPUBLICAN PRIMARIES

Region	Goldwater Per Cent (v. Rockefeller) 1964	Reagan Per Cent (v. Christopher) 1966	Rafferty Per Cent (v. Kuchel) 1968
Northern California			
San Francisco Bay Area	38	45	40
Other	42	62	43
Total	40	53	41
Southern California			
Los Angeles County	60	79	59
Other	58	77	58
Total	59	78	59
California	52	68	52

out of 1,231,000 cast. In the 1968 senatorial primary, as in the 1964 presidential primary, the more liberal candidate, Thomas Kuchel, carried the north handily—by 135,000 votes. But he lost his bid for renomination by falling 224,000 votes behind conservative Max Rafferty in southern California.

In all of these instances, then—contests for major public office, Republican party primaries, and voting on statewide propositions—there are substantial regional differences in the behavior of the electorate.

Moreover, the differences are more complex than merely north versus south. The San Francisco Bay area electorate is clearly more liberal or left in the various elections covered than the rest of the northern part of the state; not once in the twelve instances did the Bay area fail to add to the liberal/left coloration of its region. At the same time, even the northern part of the state outside of the Bay area is consistently more liberal than the southern part of the state. In the south, Los Angeles County voters have been less favorable to Republican candidates than other southern voters in each of the six elections considered. However, when the party label is not present—in primaries and in voting on propositions—Los Angeles' difference from the rest of the south tends to break down.

Los Angeles, of course, should be given special consideration in analyzing California voting patterns. It is not only the largest county in the state—indeed, in the nation—it is a veritable supercolossus. More than one third of the state's voters reside in the county. In view of the dominant size, it is hardly surprising that Los Angeles tends to vote in elections for major partisan office very much like the state as a whole. In fact, the county percentage of the two-party vote going to Democratic candidates for Governor or President from 1948 through 1968 has never deviated by more than 2 per cent from the statewide Democratic vote, and only once in the eleven elections in that period was the deviation in excess of 1 per cent.[25]

How can California's north-south differences in voting behavior be explained? First, it might be hypothesized that northern and southern Californians differ significantly in terms of the demographic variables considered earlier when we discussed the social bases of the Democratic and Republican parties in California. However, the two regions are actually quite similar in age, education, income, and racial makeup of their citizens. Most of the groups that are inclined toward the Democratic party, for example, comprise no smaller a percentage of the voters in the southern than in the northern part of the state.[26]

---

[25] Eugene Lee concludes from an analysis of election returns from 1948 to 1960 that "by virtue of its dominant size, Los Angeles almost always approximates the voting pattern for the state as a whole." *California Votes*, p. 69.

Peculiarly, little Modoc County was second to Los Angeles in Lee's analysis as the county deviating the least from the statewide two-party vote in the period considered. Moreover, Lee found that Modoc had the distinction of being the only county in the state that voted for the winner in every presidential, gubernatorial and senatorial election from 1936 through 1960. It still has not "gone wrong." As Lee concluded, "On the basis of the evidence of the past quarter-century, the cry might well be raised: 'As Modoc goes, so goes California.' " Ibid.

[26] Raymond Wolfinger and Fred Greenstein, "The Repeal of Fair Housing in California: An Analysis of Referendum Voting," *American Political Science Review*, LXII (Sept. 1968), p. 762.

A second factor that may contribute to regional differences in the political predispositions of California's voters is the extent to which the southern economy relies on defense-related enterprises. Fred Cook suggests one aspect of what the relationship between a defense-oriented economy and right-wing political beliefs may be

> California is the number one state in the nation in the manufacture of missiles, warplanes, all the intricate paraphernalia of potential nuclear annihilation. For these creative endeavors, it receives an annual bounty. . . . from a grateful federal government; and on this bounty, it has been estimated, depend the livelihood of at least half of the residents of the Los Angeles area and, in great measure the prosperity of the entire state. Such dependence upon federal munitions contracts has given California a vested interest in the Menace—the perpetuation of the cold war and the intensification of international tensions to the point where they become almost explosively hot. And so, perhaps, it is no accident that it is in this premier state of the Golden West that one finds the voice of the cuckoo shrilling loudest in all the land.[27]

A third factor that may contribute to California regionalism involves place-of-origin differences among the people living in northern and southern California. Each region has drawn in different ways on different sections of the nation as a whole for their populations. Southern or border state migrants comprise a larger share of southern than northern California's population.[28] Often these persons are Democratic in terms of party affiliation—an affiliation likely to be inherited and to be maintained out of habit. But their political inclinations are more conservative than this party affiliation would suggest, for the Democratic party has a different meaning in California than in these other states. And when the opportunity arises—especially on ballot matters unconnected with a party label—they will vote accordingly. Similarly, southern Californians are more likely to have the relatively agrarian and conservative Midwest as their place of origin. Michael Rogin concludes that "Southern California was settled by respectable Protestants from the small towns and cities of the Midwest. . . . [They] remain overwhelmingly white, Anglo-Saxon Protestants of native American stock."[29] In this sense, the southern part of the state differs considerably from the San Francisco Bay area and from metropolitan areas elsewhere in the nation, where

---

[27] "The Ultras," *Nation* (June 30, 1962), p. 571.

[28] For example, persons from the South or border states comprised 22 per cent of the persons who moved into southern California from 1955–1960; whereas they only comprised 16 per cent of those moving into the Bay area.

[29] Op. cit.

Catholic and European immigrant stock have contributed richly to the
left and liberal orientations of their communities. Writing of the Great
Migration to California from the Middle West between 1916 and 1930,
Gladwin Hill observes,

> A great many of the newcomers were farmers from Iowa and environs who
> for years had been reading glowing accounts of California as an agricultural
> paradise, where you could sit in the sun, in retirement or half-retirement,
> counting the dollars that poured in from your automatically growing
> orange groves, and from rising land values. They founded dozens of southern
> California communities, or gravitated to one that predecessors of their own
> kind had founded—on the outskirts of Los Angeles and in adjacent Orange,
> Riverside, and San Diego counties—tincturing the region with a strain of
> conservatism so iron-jawed and doctrinaire that it was still exerting a strong
> political influence 40 years later.[30]

A fourth factor that may contribute to north-south voting differences
—one related to the last—involves regional differences in the magnitude
of in-migration. There are more newcomers in the southern part of the
state.[31] Raymond Wolfinger and Fred Greenstein explain this hypothesis
(which they challenge) as follows: "Having left communities in which
they had roots, unable to establish meaningful new social contacts,
frustrated by the absence of familiar institutions, they turn in their
trauma to the certainties of patriotism and political fundamentalism. In
this view it is the newcomers whose votes and activity give Los Angeles
its conservative cast."[32]

---

[30] *Dancing Bear*, p. 73. See also Daniel J. Elazar, *American Federalism: a View
from the States* (New York: Thomas Y. Crowell Company, 1966), pp. 104–5.

[31] The greater amount of in-migration to the south is suggested by figures on
regional population growth: Between 1930 and 1960, northern California increased
its population from 2.7 to 6.7 million while the population of southern California
increased from 2.9 to 9.0 million. As Rogin points out "since newcomers continuously
pour into the area, native Californians have always been scarcer in the south than
in the north. In 1960 one half to two thirds of the population in each southern
county had been born outside the state." Op. cit.

[32] "Comparing Political Regions: The Case of California," *American Political
Science Review*, LXIII (Mar. 1969), p. 77. Paul Seabury relies on population instability to account for the general ideological content of politics in southern California:
"In the newer developing urban areas of the south, for example, where stable communities are unheard of, ideological carpetbaggers arrive bringing with them their
own preconceptions of national and international problems. . . . Knowing little or
nothing about the special political and governmental problems of the place, [new-
comers] tend to fit local issues into a Procrustean bed of long-familiar great issues;
to engage in abstract, rather than empirical, thought about politics; to take positions
—whether of the Right or Left—on peace and communism, recognition or non-
recognition of Red China, abolition or strengthening of the House Un-American
Activities Committee, medicare vs. free enterprise." ("The Antics of California Politics," *Harper's Magazine* [June 1965], p. 86.)

A fifth factor that may contribute to regional voting differences in California is an extension of the fourth. Conservatism in the south may be a product of its fantastically rapid economic growth, only one manifestation of which is the region's high rate of in-migration. Growth may affect everyone, regardless of length of residence. Old-timers in the region, for example, react to rapid change in their environment by an exaggerated commitment to the old ways which they now find threatened or destroyed.[33] Many in an area of rapid growth climb the economic ladder quickly and the *nouveaux riches* "find it difficult to modify their acquisitiveness with social conscience and are likely to see any political disagreement as a threat to their status and a prelude to revolution."[34] Sociologist Seymour Lipset suggests that in economically stable northern California wealth is "old" wealth, with the well-to-do coming from families having enjoyed upper class status for generations. In the south, on the other hand, wealth

> is almost exclusively *nouveaux riches,* and the well-to-do there possess the attitudes toward politics and economics characteristic of this stratum. They are more likely to back the rightist groups that oppose the welfare state, the income tax, and trade unions, and, lacking political and cultural sophistication, are more prone to accept conspiracy interpretations of the strength behind liberal or welfare measures.[35]

Finally, it might be suggested that once having established a reputation for having a particular political climate, say of conservatism, selective migration may serve to perpetuate and even increase the distinctiveness of that style. Orange County, for example, is nationally reputed to be a conservative oasis and persons of like political persuasion who are on the move may choose to make it their home.

---

[33] Wolfinger and Greenstein describe this notion that the old-timers, "resent not only the physical dislocations produced by expanding population, new traffic patterns, and changing land use, but also the social adjustments resulting from an influx of people of different cultural tastes, economic status, and, perhaps, ethnicity." ("Comparing Political Regions," p. 78.)

[34] Ibid., pp. 79–80.

[35] "Three Decades of the Radical Right: Coughlinites, McCarthyites, and Birchers —1962," in Daniel Bell, ed., *The Radical Right*, p. 437.

Wolfinger and Greenstein question the accuracy of the notion that the southern *nouveaux riches* are the source of regional differences as well as throwing doubt on a number of other suggested contributing factors. They do find, however, that these political differences are most pronounced at the elite level of the society and that upper-income, highly educated groups contribute disproportionately to the regional liberal-conservative division. And the elites, by their control of "the environment of communication and persuasion"—the mass media, organizational leadership posts, and so on—may well set the political tone of their respective regions.

CASE OF THE DISAPPEARING DEMOCRATS

As we have seen, Democrats have enjoyed a comfortable—approximately three-to-two—registration margin over their Republican opponents since 1934. Yet when the votes have been counted on election day, more often than not Republicans have emerged as victors. They even managed to maintain their place of dominance in state politics during the New Deal-Fair Deal era of Democratic renaissance nationally. The message is clear: Registration figures are a very poor index of vote power in California; a significant number of registered Democrats—usually numbering in the hundreds of thousands—disappear on the way to the polls only to reappear emerging from the election booth having just voted Republican.[36] At times the desertion rate is not large enough to cause Democratic election defeat; often it is. In any event, it is ordinarily quite substantial, and almost never is canceled out by Republican desertion to Democratic candidates.[37] In fact, in only two of the twenty-seven presidential, senatorial, and gubernatorial elections from 1934 through 1968 have Democratic candidates received a greater percentage of the two-party vote than the Democratic percentage of two-party registration.[38] On the average, the vote percentage for the Democratic

---

[36] In the 1966 gubernatorial election, for example, Edmund Brown's 2,700,000 votes were 900,000 short of the number of Democrats who actually went to the polls. He lost to Ronald Reagan even though his party enjoyed a 17 per cent registration margin over the Republicans. Spencer Williams—Republican candidate for Attorney General and the only candidate of his party running for statewide office who lost in 1966—received 250,000 more votes than his own party's turnout. Even the roundly defeated Barry Goldwater ran ahead of Republican registration in California in 1964.

[37] Desertion is not confined to Democrats, of course. Many Republicans at each election vote Democratic. For example, pre-election polls suggest that in both the 1964 senatorial and 1966 gubernatorial races—won by GOPers—approximately 15 per cent of the Republicans in the state intended to vote for the Democratic candidate. However, in those same races one quarter to one third of the Democrats polled intended to vote Republican.

"Yellow dog Democrats," as some have called them—those who would vote for a yellow dog running for important office as long as he were a Democrat—probably comprise about two thirds of the Democratic registrants in the state or 40 per cent of the vote. (No Democratic candidate for President, Governor, or Senator since 1934 has received less than 41 per cent of the California vote.) "Yellow dog Republicans," on the other hand, probably comprise about 75 per cent of the Republican registration or 30 per cent of those who vote. (Polls suggested that 25 per cent of the state's Republicans intended to vote for Lyndon Johnson rather than Barry Goldwater in the 1964 presidential election.)

[38] One of the exceptions was President Roosevelt's race for re-election in 1936; the other was Edmund Brown's race for the governorship in 1958.

candidate for President, Governor, or Senator has been 10 per cent below his party's registration percentage. (See Table 4–12.)

A similar Democratic cross-over occurs in legislative races. The vote in California's eighty state Assembly contests in 1966 shows dramatically how Democratic registration margins tend to disappear at election time. (See Table 4–13.) In only four of the eighty contests was the Democratic candidate's share of the vote greater than the Democratic share of registration in the district, and in each instance the difference was small. On the average, the Democratic candidate's share of the vote was 9.9 per cent less than his party's share of registration.

How do the Democrats repeatedly fail to translate a registration advantage over the last thirty-five years into election victories? How does a three-to-two registration margin evaporate so easily? A number of factors are likely to be involved, some more significant than others and some operating for a different part of the period in question than others.

The Democratic registration margin is reduced on election day by different *rates of turnout* among partisans, with registered Democrats less likely to vote than registered Republicans. (This phenomenon was considered earlier.)

California, like most other states, holds its *gubernatorial elections in the off-year,* i.e., they occur in the middle of the presidential term. The lower rate of turnout among Democrats is especially marked in off-year elections. Moreover, the off-year election system serves to insulate state politics from the tides of presidential politics. Thus, Democratic gubernatorial candidates could never benefit from Franklin Roosevelt's political coattails in the 1930s and 1940s. At the same time, these candidates probably were hurt at the polls by the midterm "slump" in popularity that usually afflicts parties in power nationally. On the other hand, Democratic gubernatorial candidates did not have to appear on the same ballot with Dwight Eisenhower in 1952 and 1956, and a Democrat captured the governorship in 1958 at the time of a midterm slump in GOP popularity nationally. Reagan won the governorship back for the Republicans in the middle of Lyndon Johnson's administration and no doubt benefited from a Democratic midterm slump. Democrats tended to do well in presidential elections in the 1934–1968 period—winning seven of the ten contests—but the off-year election system in California prevented the state party from reaping the full rewards of these successes.

California's system of *permanent registration* may conceal shifts in actual voter preferences toward the Republican party. Many persons improve their economic position with time and all grow older. Often such changes lead to a more conservative political outlook. As a result, persons who have registered Democratic in an earlier day may find

TABLE 4–12 DEMOCRATIC REGISTRATION AND DEMOCRATIC VOTE FOR PRESIDENT, GOVERNOR, AND SENATOR: 1934–1968*

Year	Office	Democratic Percentage of Two-Party Registration	Democratic Percentage of Two-Party Vote	Percentage Registration/Vote Difference
1934	Governor	52.1	43.6	8.5
1936	President	60.2	67.9	−7.7
1938	Governor	62.4	54.3	8.1
1938	Senator	62.4	54.9	7.5
1940	President	62.4	58.1	4.3
1942	Governor	62.7	42.3	20.4
1944	President	61.0	56.8	4.2
1944	Senator	61.0	52.3	8.7
1946	Senator	60.8	45.0	15.8
1948	President	60.3	50.2	10.1
1950	Governor	61.2	35.1	26.1
1950	Senator	61.2	40.8	20.4
1952	President	57.4	43.1	14.3
1954	Governor	57.5	43.2	14.3
1954	Senator	57.5	46.1	11.4
1956	President	57.5	44.4	13.1
1956	Senator	57.5	45.8	11.7
1958	Governor	59.2	59.8	−0.6
1958	Senator	59.2	57.0	2.2
1960	President	59.5	49.7	9.8
1962	Governor	58.8	52.5	6.3
1962	Senator	58.8	43.5	15.3
1964	President	59.8	59.2	0.6
1964	Senator	59.8	48.5	11.3
1966	Governor	58.5	42.3	16.2
1968	President	57.5	48.3	9.2
1968	Senator	57.5	52.5	5.0

* In the 1946 gubernatorial election and the senatorial elections of 1934, 1940, and 1952, the Republican incumbent was not opposed by a major candidate as a result of successfully crossfiling in the primary. These elections are thus not included in the table.

Registration and Vote figures through 1962 appear in Lee's *California Votes*.

Republican candidates more and more attractive. However, they may not bother to reregister and change their party affiliation to conform with their new political dispositions.

Public opinion polls taken during the 1966 and 1968 elections in California suggest that the issues of race, "law and order," our Vietnam

135

TABLE 4–13

Democratic Percentage of Registration Minus Democratic Percentage of Vote	Number of Assembly Races
25.0 or more	6
20.0 to 25.0	3
15.0 to 20.0	7
10.0 to 15.0	17
5.0 to 10.0	23
0.0 to 5.0	20
−0.1 to −5.0	4
	80

involvement, and student rebellion tended to deflect many persons who identify themselves as Democratic to Republican candidates Reagan and Nixon. Permanent registration is one factor preventing such changes of heart from being accurately reflected in statements of registration.

Many of California's Democrats have *states of origin* where the Democratic party's posture on issues of public policy is and was significantly more conservative than it is in California. Persons from southern states, for example, may retain their traditional Democratic registration out of habit but on election day may feel more comfortable voting for candidates of the more conservative Republican party. By comparison, few California Republicans formed their party allegiance in states where the Republican party was more liberal than it has been in California over the past three decades. Writing about Democrats who voted for Ronald Reagan in 1966, Gladwin Hill concluded; "There is not much mystery about who these pseudo-Democrats are. Many are immigrants from 'one-party' Democratic states and conservative Democratic areas who have maintained misleading registration out of habit."[39]

Incumbency is a campaign advantage which the Republicans, as the party in power, used effectively during most of the post-1934 period. In politics, as elsewhere, "nothing succeeds like success," and the GOP's hold on most of the offices in the state helped it to perpetuate its dominance even after the dramatic shift in registration to the Democrats in the 1930s. Power-holders are more likely to be familiar to the voters than power-seekers; the incumbents' names are more likely to be recognized on the ballot than those of their challengers. And familiarity may not breed contempt for the average voter as much as it breeds a sense of security and trust.

---

[39] "Ronald Reagan and the Million Frogs," *Frontier,* **XVIII** (Dec. 1966), p. 6.

Similarly, money and other campaign resources are more likely to gravitate to one who is tried, tested, and a proven vote-getter than to a newcomer. Additionally, incumbents tend to be more familiar with the intricacies of public policy issues and to display a degree of political expertise which many challengers cannot match. Moreover, an incumbent in California has the advantage of having his name listed first on the election ballot, with the word *incumbent* or the title of his office beneath it. (See Figure 4–1.) Often the eye of the voter never moves beyond the first name listed among the candidates for a given office, particularly if the ballot informs him that the name belongs to one already serving in that office. Further, an incumbent more easily gains access to the media of mass communication—and thus to the voters—than a candidate without an office. Finally, California's weak partisan spirit contributes to the incumbent's advantages. As David Leuthold concludes from his study of congressional elections in California; "The partisan independence of California voters, compared to the voters of other states, would also contribute to increased ticket splitting and thus frequently to a greater advantage for incumbents."[40] Many persons could vote for Franklin Roosevelt for President in the 1930s and 1940s in California but turn around as they went down the ballot (already designed so as not to encourage straight-ticket voting) and vote for incumbent Republican legislators.

The extent of the discrepancy in state Assembly races between Democratic registration in a district and Democratic vote was indicated earlier. Some measure of the advantages of incumbency is provided by asking if the discrepancy differs when the Democratic candidate is an incumbent from when he is a nonincumbent facing a Republican incumbent or from when neither he nor his opponent is an incumbent. The average Democratic registration/Democratic vote difference in the eighty Assembly districts in 1966, was found to be 9.9 per cent. (That is, on the average, Democratic Assembly candidates ran 9.9 per cent behind Democratic registration in their districts.) For those races in which Democratic incumbents faced nonincumbent Republicans, however, the average difference was only 6.2 per cent. That is, the Democrat's vote percentage was closer to his party's registration when he was running as an incumbent Assemblyman. When there was an incumbent Republican running, the vote for the Democratic candidate, on the average, fell 18.8 per cent behind his party's registration. When neither candidate was an incumbent, the Democratic candidate's vote was, on

---

[40] *Electioneering in a Democracy* (New York: John Wiley & Sons, Inc., 1968), p. 127, passim.

the average, 7.6 per cent behind his party's registration. Clearly, Assemblymen running for re-election in 1966 did better relative to their party's registration than candidates who were not incumbents. Incumbency, it seems, does make a difference and Republicans have been most likely to benefit from it during the past thirty-five years as they have held most of the elective offices.

Nor are the advantages of incumbency absent in races for statewide office. At least California's voters, when given the opportunity, have not been unkind to those who seek re-election. No U.S. Senator since 1928 has been defeated for re-election; all turnovers have been due to the incumbent's death (Hiram Johnson in 1945), illness (Clair Engle in 1964), primary defeat (Kuchel in 1968), or decision not to stand for re-election (Knowland in 1958). The same factors have resulted in a high turnover among California's Governors since statehood was gained.[41] But only one man in the twentieth century—Culbert Olson in 1942—has come before California's electorate as an incumbent Governor without being returned to office. (Brown was re-elected once before his defeat by Reagan in 1966.)

Crossfiling served to aid the Republicans in their long-successful efforts to withstand the tide of Democratic registration. Alan Cranston explains the partisan impact of this "grotesque device" by which a candidate could enter and win both parties' nominating primaries without revealing his own party affiliation:

> Typically, a candidate, particularly an incumbent, campaigned without revealing his partisan identity. His literature usually described his political beliefs in safe generalities, extolled his professional abilities, listed his community affiliations, displayed his family (especially if attractive), and neatly avoided references to his party. When the unsophisticated voter went to the polls at primary time, he assumed that all the candidates on his party ballot were members of his own party. He tended to vote for the most familiar name for each office, or the one on top of the list, or the one with the most impressive title. This benefited the incumbent, and usually the incumbent was a Republican.[42]

The change in the crossfiling system, which went into effect in the 1954 election, providing that the partisan affiliation of a crossfiling candidate be indicated on the ballot, lessened the Republicans' advantage. The

---

[41] There have been thirty-four gubernatorial elections in California through 1966 and no fewer than thirty-three different Governors. In the last one hundred years only two persons have served two full terms or more as Governor.

[42] "Democratic Politics," in Eugene P. Dvorin and Arthur Misner, eds., *California Politics and Policies* (Reading, Mass.: Addison-Wesley, 1966), p. 33.

Democrats proceeded to abolish the system entirely, effective in the 1960 election. It had, after all, given the advantage to incumbents generally and Republicans specifically.

A candidate's political party is an important campaign resource. The party label next to his name on the election ballot and on his campaign literature cues voters of the same partisan persuasion that the candidate is "one of us." A candidate's party is often a more important determinant of how a voter will vote than what he believes, how he looks and talks, or what his experience has been. Moreover, the parties engage in various organizational enterprises benefiting their candidates—registering voters, distributing literature, getting-out-the-vote, and so on.

But there are also *nonparty campaign resources* which candidates try to call upon and which can be translated into votes on election day. These resources—such as newspaper support and campaign funds— are important anywhere. But they assume special significance in California. With high population mobility and so many newcomers, many voters need quick guidance regarding candidates for public office but do not fully believe that the party affiliation they brought with them from elsewhere is a perfect guide to the best man in their new locale. The candidate who can reach into their homes via paid advertisements or newspaper endorsements may also reach into their hearts. This is especially true where party organizations are relatively weak—as in California—and thus provide nonparty media of communication little competition in the "marketing" of candidates. The whole political ethos of nonpartisanship in California helps "well-merchandised" candidates overcome the liability of a minority party label. And during the period when crossfiling produced free-for-all primaries with labelless ballots, candidates could win elections at the primary stage by relying entirely on nonparty campaign resources.

In general, these nonparty resources have been more readily available to Republican than Democratic candidates in California, as they have been elsewhere. Campaign money—"the mother's milk of politics" as Jesse Unruh has called it—has usually flowed more freely to Republicans. The support of California's newspapers has usually gone the same way. (Campaign resources are considered in detail in Chapter 5.)

These power sources have no doubt contributed to the ability of Republicans to win elections even after the Democrats gained their majority in voter registration. The late Clair Engle, Democratic U.S. Senator, once put it this way; "The GOP press and money [in California] can make a four-minute miler out of a political corpse."[43]

---

[43] Quoted in Ronnie Dugger, "Politics in California," *New Republic* (June 23, 1968), p. 11.

California has *nonpartisan local elections*. The party affiliation of candidates for local office has not appeared on the election ballot since antiparty reformers at the state capital succeeded in enacting the appropriate legislation in the second decade of this century.[44]

Nonpartisan local elections, however, have had a partisan bias. In general, Republicans have won elections to local office well out of proportion to their voter registration percentage. There are several explanations. Nonparty campaign resources are obviously crucial when party guidance and support is not available to candidates, and, as indicated, Republicans are more likely than Democrats to have these resources available. Moreover, voter turnout is relatively low in local elections generally and especially when they are nonpartisan. By and large, the smaller the turnout percentage in an election the greater the percentage of Republicans among those voting. Further, when a party is outnumbered among registrants by a three-to-two margin, as the Republicans in California have been since 1934, anything that serves to blunt, blur, or erase party identification as a factor in elections would tend to operate to that party's advantage.[45]

However one explains it, Republicans have been better able to win local elections than Democrats. Eugene Lee found from his comprehensive study of nonpartisan elections in California that (a) in a half-dozen representative cities studied over a 25-year period, the percentage of voters registered Democratic was twice the percentage of city councilmen registered Democratic; (b) in the same six cities during the same period, approximately one half of the mayoralty and city council candidates were Democrats but less than one third of those elected were so registered; and (c) in 1955 and again in 1959, the persons holding approximately 3,000 important offices in the cities and counties of California "tend to be Republicans by a three to two margin, almost the direct reverse of the distribution of the state's registered voters."[46]

But the partisan implications of local nonpartisanship extend beyond the question of who holds local office. They extend into the battle for

---

[44] In 1915 a bill was even passed by the state legislature making all state positions nonpartisan. Delayed by a referendum, the measure was defeated by the voters later in the year. In 1955, the state Senate passed a bill making state legislative positions nonpartisan but it was defeated in the state Assembly.

[45] See Willis Hawley, *The Partisan Bias of Nonpartisanship* (Berkeley: Institute of Governmental Studies, University of California, Berkeley, forthcoming).

[46] Eugene C. Lee, *The Politics of Nonpartisanship: a Study of California City Elections* (Berkeley: University of California Press, 1960), pp. 55–59. The quote appears on p. 56. (See also Chapter Seven of Lee's book regarding the limited organizational activity by the political parties in local elections in California.)

ballots in partisan elections as well. Local nonpartisanship makes it difficult for the Democratic party in California to develop the kind of political organization built upon city politics, local patronage, and so on, which contributed so much to Democratic power at the state level in other states. Moreover, Democrats are less successful than Republicans in finding candidates for partisan office whose names are recognized easily in their communities and who have previous governmental experience to their credit as a result of service in public office at the local level.

It is hardly surprising that a 1962 survey by the state Assembly of 1,600 party leaders in California found Democrats much more favorable than Republicans to making local elections partisan. (See Table 4–14.)

TABLE 4–14   PARTY LEADERS AND LOCAL NONPARTISANSHIP

Office to Be Made Partisan	Per Cent Favoring Party Nomination for Various Local Offices or Designation of Candidate's Party Affiliation on Local Election Ballot	
	Republicans	Democrats
County supervisors	28 per cent	84 per cent
City councils	25	80
School boards	16	48
Special district boards	16	51
Elective administrative officers of county	28	71
Elective administrative officers of city	22	64

Source: Adapted from California, Assembly Interim Committee on Elections and Reapportionment, *Political Party Organization* (Sacramento: Assembly of the State of California, 1963), pp. 32–33.

Finally, the *Republican party has been better organized* than the Democratic party during much of the 1934–1968 period and thus better able to avoid debilitating internal conflicts. The Republicans were the first to devise an effective procedure for endorsing candidates prior to nominating primaries without running afoul of legal prohibitions imposed on the official party organizations. (See Chapter 6.) Thus they were able to settle on and unite behind a single candidate for each office at an earlier stage in the election process than the Democrats. Indeed, under crossfiling the earlier primary stage was often the final stage, and Republican candidates frequently captured both party nominations while the Democrats were busy feuding among themselves. Says Mary Ellen Leary regarding GOP organizational innovations; "It was a smart way to keep ahead of the more fractious Democrats, and it paid off. Through the Democratic decades, Republicans stayed in office in California."[47]

In the mid-fifties, the Democrats finally adopted Republican techniques for controlling internal conflict. For a brief period, election successes resulted. More recently, the Republican party—particularly under the leadership of state party chairman, Gaylord Parkinson—has once again proved more successful than the Democrats in keeping its house in order and has thus been able to profit from renewed Democratic intraparty conflict.

---

[47] "The Two-Party System Comes to California," *The Reporter,* XVI (Feb. 7, 1957), pp. 33–36.

CHAPTER 5

candidates and campaigning

political campaign is the process by which political parties compete for popular support in order to elect candidates to governmental office. But a campaign achieves more than the election or defeat of officeseekers. The dialogue between candidates educates voters and helps clarify public differences on policy issues. The campaign sublimates violence by settling peaceably conflicts over governmental policies and leadership. It also relates people to government because it is the one occasion when an entire electorate acts in a free expression of will. It is clear, then, that democracy requires free and vigorous campaigning that is a reflection of genuine competition among parties and candidates.[1]

Despite the fact that contemporary campaigns are relatively free from corruption, people seem dissatisfied with the character of American campaigning. Critics charge

---

[1] Alexander Heard, *The Costs of Democracy* (Chapel Hill: University of North Carolina Press, 1960), pp. 426–28.

that political campaigns are too frequently noisy spectacles, full of buncombe and nonsense, designed to deceive rather than inform the voter. Moreover, advertising men and public relations experts have adapted their manipulative skills to campaigns, packaging and selling candidates like commercial products to the public. Rationality is sacrificed by reducing issues and candidates to their lowest common denominators in an attempt to reach the masses of voters.

As disturbing as these accusations are, some political scientists point out that many of these developments may be inherent in the nature of the campaign. Any realistic appraisal of campaign practices, they argue, must take account of the fact that campaigns are chiefly designed to elect candidates to office. Candidates base their campaigns on what is required to win and on their perception of the character of the American voter. Studies indicate that the average voter has only a transient interest in government and political issues.[2] Presented with this situation, candidates utilize every campaign technique that will effectively appeal to this kind of voter. Obviously there is a conflict between actual campaign practices in our society and the theoretical requisites of a campaign (rational voters, reasoned dialogue, and so on) as prescribed by democratic theory.

Campaigning in California perhaps reflects this conflict more clearly than in other states. A California campaign is a colorful, noisy, sometimes vulgar and always expensive spectacle, aimed at capturing the attention of a restless and distinterested electorate. Admittedly, elections occasionally occur at times when the electorate is truly concerned with political issues. But more frequently voters are influenced by a candidate's manner, style, and appearance rather than his message. The chief task of a California campaign is to "sell" the candidate to the people, and extensive use is made of political public relations men. Through the media of mass communications these professionals attempt to create an attractive and winning image of their candidate. Television, radio, and newspapers are used to present simple name identification, tied to a noncontroversial and even nonpartisan appeal. Firms have developed in the state that specialize in political campaign management and employ all the techniques of public relations, advertising, and mass communications. California-style campaigns obviously require great financial resources and consequently they are undoubtedly the most expensive in the nation.

---

2 Angus Campbell et al., *The American Voter* (New York: John Wiley and Sons, Inc., 1960), passim. Bernard Berelson, Paul Lazarsfeld, and William McPhee, *Voting* (Chicago: University of Chicago Press, 1954), passim.

Outsiders are baffled by California campaigns; they view them as aberrations. But a careful examination of campaigns in California illustrates in bold relief trends in political campaigning throughout modern urban America. In fact, it might be argued that the rest of the nation is moving toward the California pattern of political campaigning.

This chapter deals with partisan campaigns in California; it focuses primarily on statewide races for executive office. The following discussion is organized according to the four major stages of a campaign. The first stage involves strategy and planning, which includes the process of evaluating issues and developing a campaign theme, and the planning, timing, and execution of publicity. Next the candidate forges a campaign organization through the recruitment, management, and coordination of the various individuals and groups comprising his organization. The third phase deals with communications, the means of presenting the candidate and issues to the electorate. The last stage concerns the problems of campaign finance or the raising and spending of money for these various activities.

campaign strategy

A successful statewide campaign is a complex and costly undertaking that demands careful and comprehensive planning. In an abstract sense, strategy implies an ordering of preferences (ends) within a framework of available resources (means) in order to facilitate rational assessment of tactical opportunities. The candidate's ultimate goal is to win public office, and in a democracy this requires that he gain the support of a plurality (often a majority) of the electorate. His ability to influence the electorate depends on an intelligent use of campaign resources at his command. A candidate needs a strategy because his resources are limited; he must decide among alternative courses of action. A strategy enables the candidate to made discriminating decisions. Of course, strategies vary with candidates and campaigns. In general, however, a strategic plan must consider (1) campaign theme and issues, (2) candidate's appeal and voter reactions, (3) campaign timing and momentum, (4) group targets and appeals, (5) media campaign and costs, and (6) campaign organization and finance. The planning may be contained in a thoughtfully drafted document based on considerable research or it may involve only ideas in the mind of the candidate or his advisers.

Regardless of the details of a plan, it must be sufficiently flexible to adjust to the shifting circumstances of the campaign.

Candidates increasingly utilize more sophisticated and scientific techniques to develop campaign strategies. The practical judgments of professional politicians are often supplemented by information gathered through sample surveys conducted by commercial pollsters. An opinion survey helps chart the course of the campaign by testing voter reactions to the candidate and his opponent, uncovering public concerns and helping define campaign issues, and analyzing the political sentiments of target groups (e.g., racial, ethnic).[3] Indeed, few candidates for major office in California would chance a campaign without the benefit of at least one political poll. Depending on the size of the sample and the number of questions asked, a confidential statewide poll costs between $10,000 and $15,000. But survey findings are never an infallible guide to campaign strategy; only the candidate and his advisers can make the subjective judgments that determine the outcome of campaigns.

Candidates must consider an infinite number of factors when planning a campaign. These factors together constitute what one textbook calls the "strategic environment" of the campaign—that is, the political context within which the candidates make their strategic calculations.[4] Some elements constituting this environment are relatively stable and enduring features of the state's political scene and are not, therefore, easily manipulated. These are political facts of life, which every candidate must face by either turning them to his advantage or compensating for them in some way. Other elements grow out of the immediate environment of a particular campaign, and are more easily controlled by a candidate. The relatively stable conditions of California politics include the ingrained political disposition of the voters, the nature of the political parties and the institutional factors of the electoral system, and the influence of the state's interest groups and voting blocs.

Although candidates must make decisions within this broad framework, campaign strategies are also dependent upon distinctive factors directly related to the particular campaign. Each candidate needs certain vital resources to conduct a successful campaign. Such assets, or lack of them, significantly affect his strategic calculations. Among the most important are the candidate's image and issues appeal and his campaign organizing and financing.

---

[3] Louis Harris, "Polls and Politics in the United States," *Public Opinion Quarterly,* XXVII (Spring 1963), pp. 3–8.

[4] Nelson W. Polsby and Aaron B. Wildavsky, *Presidential Elections,* 2nd ed. (New York: Charles Scribner's Sons, 1968), chap. 1.

GUBERNATORIAL STRATEGY: REAGAN

The goal of the realistic candidate in California is never a mass conversion of voters to his cause; he seeks simply to activate existing predispositions. He will try through partisan appeals to hold the party regulars in line and turn them out in large numbers. He will seek the support of independents, and undecided and disinterested voters. He will emphasize issues that will hold the support of the faithful, but also concentrate on issues particularly appealing to groups temporarily disaffected with the opposition. An analysis of the strategies of Ronald Reagan and Edmund G. ("Pat") Brown in the last gubernatorial campaign illustrates how many of these factors influenced the candidates' thinking.

Two political facts dominated Ronald Reagan's strategic thinking in 1966; he was a minority party candidate, and he was challenging an eight-year incumbent. Reagan faced a three-to-two Democratic registration advantage, and this required not only that he maintain the support of Republicans, but also win over at least 20 per cent of the Democratic voters. This Democratic registration advantage was undercut to some extent simply because a greater percentage of Republicans than Democrats make their way to the polls in an election. Reagan calculated that he needed more than an 80 per cent turnout of Republican voters, and about 20 per cent of the vote of a relatively light Democratic turnout.

Reagan's first campaign objective, then, was to forge a united Republican party voting in large numbers for a united Republican slate. But he faced a party traditionally torn by factional disputes, and a primary challenge from moderate George Christopher, former San Francisco Mayor. He was greatly benefited, however, by the "Eleventh Commandment" of Party Chairman Gaylord Parkinson: "Thou shalt not speak ill of any Republican." Reagan followed this dictum closely, rarely aiming political attacks on Christopher. An intense primary battle which Reagan won by more than one million votes caused no harmful schisms within the Republican party. With the possible exception of an incumbent Secretary of State candidate, the other successful Republican candidates recognized that victory in the general election would come on the coattails of Ronald Reagan. When the primary battles ended, Republicans enjoyed a unified party flushed with the taste of victory and optimistic about success in the November election. In fact, a poll taken immediately after the primary showed that Reagan enjoyed an 11 per cent lead over the incumbent Brown.

As a minority candidate, Reagan clearly needed to win the support of large numbers of Democratic voters. Therefore, he was forced to play down his Republican affiliation and pursue an obviously nonpartisan campaign. This particular approach to California voters has been a Republican tradition since the Progressive era. From the beginning, Reagan played down "party" and instead emphasized image, personality, and nonpartisanship. Reagan continually referred to himself as a "citizen-politician" in an attempt to disassociate himself from politics and political alignments. But incumbents are usually far better known by the electorate than challengers, and under normal circumstances Governor Brown would have benefited greatly from this political fact. However, Reagan was probably as well known—if not better known—as the incumbent governor. This, of course, was because of his career as an actor in both movies and television. Moreover, his image was positive and favorable. Throughout his acting career he played "good guys" who were charming, unassuming, and much like "the boy next door." He was viewed by the public as a pleasant, well-meaning nonprofessional who made "good speeches." Moreover, an additional advantage of Reagan's playing the "citizen-politician" role was that it offered a defense against the charge of inexperience. Not being a politician, he was not expected to know as much about government as Brown.

A potential threat to Reagan's political image was his association with the disastrous presidential campaign of Barry Goldwater; he had been cochairman of Goldwater's California campaign and had spoken on television as a Goldwater advocate. Goldwater's defeat made it clear to Reagan that a strong, ideologically conservative appeal could not attract sufficient independent and Democratic votes for victory. Reagan's appeal was dependent on moderation and nonpartisanship. Senator Goldwater, usually an active Republican campaigner, did not once appear in California during the campaign. In fact, in an effort to emphasize his identification with moderate Republicanism, Reagan made a pilgrimage to Gettysburg and received the blessings of former President Dwight D. Eisenhower.

Reagan followed a two-fold strategy in dealing with the issues of the campaign. First, as the candidate of the party out of power, Reagan could easily attack the eight-year record of the Brown administration. After two terms in office, any administration in California suffers from accumulated problems and disaffection from large segments of the electorate. Moreover, no Governor with the exception of Earl Warren had ever been elected to office for a third term.

Reagan's principal appeal was "it's time for a change." He concentrated on the past frustrations and errors of the incumbent administration. Throughout the campaign Reagan accused the Brown administration of lacking leadership and imagination. He criticized the growing welfare rolls and high taxes; he claimed Brown had turned California into a federal fiefdom; he decried the breakdown of "law and order," and he promised to clean up the "mess" at the University of California. He in turn pledged himself to building a "Creative Society" where private citizens solve their own problems with a minimum of government involvement and dependency.

Secondly, Reagan stressed political issues that would appeal to dissident Democratic groups. He sought the votes of discontented farmers who felt they had suffered under policies of the Brown administration. Particularly he criticized Governor Brown's farm labor policy, including the Governor's failure to prevent the federal termination of the bracero program. Perhaps the most effective means of cutting across party loyalty in the 1966 campaign was the race issue and its corollary, "white backlash."[5] Reagan never directly appealed to racial prejudice; still, his stand on several civil rights issues appealed to white discontent. This nationwide discontent was punctuated in California by the bitter controversy over the Rumford Fair Housing Law and Negro rioting in Watts. "I've had enough of this," said one voter. "These people (Negroes) burn and loot and get people killed in their riots, and we turn around and give them money. I'm voting for Reagan. Brown has coddled these people too much."[6]

In 1963 a Democratically controlled legislature with Governor Brown's support enacted a fair housing law that outlawed racial discrimination in the sale and rental of housing. However, the California real estate lobby in 1964 conducted a successful battle for an initiative measure repealing the Rumford law. Rumford advocates then appealed the constitutionality of the initiative before the California Supreme Court; the court declared it illegal because it violated the Fourteenth Amendment of the United States Constitution. Reagan gained wide support by arguing that the defeat of the Rumford law by two thirds of the electorate justified its

---

[5] Some evidence of this backlash effect can be seen in the 1966 election results. In defeating Brown for governor, Regan won 64 per cent of the white vote, compared with the 52 per cent that went to Richard M. Nixon in 1962. Moreover, Governor Brown received 96 per cent of the Negro vote, three points more than in 1962. (*Sacramento Bee,* November 9, 1966.) According to Eugene C. Lee and Totton J. Anderson, "Analysis of *California Poll* reports . . . indicates that Governor Brown suffered substantial losses in support among white working people, especially union members, and among lower income and educational groups. . . . Whether this decline was at least substantially attributable to white backlash could not be conclusively demonstrated, but the high relationship between opposition to California's fair housing act and support for GOP candidate Reagan gives credence to the supposition." "The 1966 Election in California," *The Western Political Quarterly,* XX, No. 2, Part 2 (June 1967), pp. 547–550.

[6] *Sacramento Bee,* September 11, 1966.

repeal. Although Reagan was a Republican, his views on this issue appealed strongly to some normally Democratic voters, particularly in lower income groups and organized labor.

BROWN'S STRATEGY

Democratic strategy during the primary campaign planted the seeds of defeat for the party in the November general election. As an incumbent Pat Brown expected no difficulty in winning the Democratic nomination; consequently he failed to consider seriously the challenge of maverick Sam Yorty. Instead, he concentrated his campaign efforts on the defeat of Republican George Christopher, whom he perceived as the strongest possible challenger. Democratic strategists assumed that conservative Ronald Reagan could not successfully appeal to moderate Democrats and independents. But this judgment was a serious miscalculation.

In order to defeat Christopher, members of Brown's campaign staff launched an attack on the Republican candidate's personal reputation. They leaked to columnist Drew Pearson information about a 28-year old "scandal" involving Christopher and his milk company and a misdemeanor conviction for price law violation. Although Christopher's defeat cannot be wholly attributed to this incident, polls taken immediately after the publicity demonstrated that Christopher's popularity had severely declined. Although Democrats may have succeeded in influencing some voters against Christopher, they paid dearly by alienating moderate Republicans who otherwise might have voted for Brown in the general election. Moreover, the Democratic strategy against Christopher helped Reagan to a momentous primary victory without inflicting party wounds by Republican infighting.

Democratic strategy was further complicated by the failure of party leaders to recognize the challenge of Los Angeles Mayor Sam Yorty. Yorty captured 42 per cent of the votes in the Democratic primary despite a modest campaign. Yorty's phenomenal success surprised the Brown organization and demonstrated a significant and threatening Democratic dissatisfaction with Governor Brown. A poll taken immediately following the primary showed a majority of Yorty's supporters favoring Reagan.

The first task facing Democrats in the general campaign was regaining the support of disaffected party members. A poll taken by the Democratic organization indicated that much of the dissatisfaction could be traced to the race issue, and Brown adjusted his strategy accordingly. First, he attempted to placate Yorty by endorsing the Mayor's proposal for stricter "antiriot" legislation. Brown also began to equivocate on the open housing law; in fact, he appointed a special commission to study the Rumford law and recommended modifications. Another move probably designed to gain conservative support was the firing of the state's welfare director, who had supported the use of state funds for organizing a welfare recipient lobby.

Brown's strategy also called for discrediting the moderate image Reagan attempted to develop in order to attract Democratic support. The Governor's campaign criticized Reagan for his association with Barry Goldwater and his refusal to disavow the support of John Birch Society members. In most campaigns an incumbent would not provide publicity for his opponent by referring to him directly. But in the 1966 campaign, this tactic would have little effect because of Reagan's extensive previous public exposure. Instead, Democrats concentrated directly on Reagan's political philosophy and attempted to hang on him the label of "right-wing extremist." They accused Reagan of hiding his "extremist" views in order to gain the support of a majority of California voters. Finally they warned the electorate against trusting California government to a rank amateur with virtually no previous political experience.

Brown selected quite naturally a "good times" slogan as the theme of his campaign. Californians, he proclaimed, "never had it so good," and he attributed their prosperity to the accomplishments of the Brown administration. Emphasizing the achievements of his eight-year record, he stressed the particular benefits derived from these programs by individuals and groups, and warned that these benefits might be lost if the voters turned over the reins of government to a "right-wing amateur." A Democratic campaigner summarized Brown's appeal in these words, "California is on a winning streak. We have the finest highways, a massive water program and irrigation projects. Luck has nothing to do with this. It takes a man—a strong and able governor. I am not going to gamble on the future. I'll stick with Governor Brown."[7] The Governor himself stated his case more succinctly, "I've made decisions that will help you, now I need your help."

The 1966 gubernatorial election demonstrates sharply that candidates of either party, operating with a proper strategy and supported by volatile issues, can be elected to statewide office. An overwhelming Democratic superiority in registration is deceptive because of the ticket-splitting proclivities of the California voter (see Chapter 4). Recent history shows that these voters are regularly willing to support attractive and personable candidates of either party who are politically astute enough to hold the party faithful while exploiting through nonpartisan appeals

---

[7] *Sacramento Bee,* October 25, 1966.

the discontent of voters in the other party. Reagan was enormously successful in pursuing this strategy. He played down the notion of "party" and labeled himself a "citizen-politician"; he avoided intraparty conflict; he had a winning image and a famous name; and he cleverly capitalized on the electorate's frustration with the eight-year administration. Brown's strategists, on the other hand, committed a series of serious miscalculations. They took for granted the loyalty of the rank-and-file Democrats; they alienated moderate Republicans by attacking George Christopher; they underestimated the popular appeal of conservative Reagan; and their appeals failed to hold the support of disaffected Democratic conservatives.

campaign organization

A statewide campaign requires a complex formal organization. The task of organization is obviously more difficult and time consuming than strategic planning, as the former involves the identification of jobs, recruitment of workers to perform the jobs, and the construction of the machinery to handle the "work load." Few corporation bureaucrats would approve of the haphazard structure of most campaign organizations; they are poorly designed, makeshift structures, lacking any semblance of hierarchy. Tasks are poorly performed, jobs are often duplicated, and little coordination exists between various organizational levels. In short, campaign organizations are loose-knit and relatively inefficient units.

The inefficiency of campaign organizations is understandable. They lack a solid continuing base because they are *ad hoc* structures designed to conduct a single campaign during a relatively short period of time. And they are essentially nonprofessional, manned almost exclusively by party volunteers, the vast majority of whom contribute their services without material reward.

The organizational problem is more confused in California than in many other states, where candidates for statewide office build their campaigns on the existing party machinery. In California, however, the party organization is traditionally weak and ineffective, and consequently few candidates depend on the central party unit for campaign support. Each candidate develops a personal organization and operates a separate campaign. The development of personalized campaigns, combined with an intense competition among candidates for scarce resources, has resulted in an increasing reliance on professional public relations firms for the operation of campaigns.

Campaign organizations vary considerably, depending on whether the candidate is an incumbent, the amount and kinds of resources available to him, the office he seeks, the degree to which he uses professionals, and a number of other factors. Moreover, despite carefully prepared and well-publicized formal "organizations," campaigns frequently are conducted in an informal manner that totally disregards any organizational chart. A number of shared characteristics, however, are typical of most state-wide campaign organizations. Governor Brown's 1966 campaign organization illustrates some of these characteristics. (See Figure 5-1)

TYPICAL ORGANIZATION

Nominal leadership of a campaign rests with a number of statewide cochairmen, chosen by the candidate. Although not political figures themselves, these people are generally successful businessmen or professionals whose names command public attention and respect. Supposedly their names attached to press releases assure a wide audience and enhance the credibility of political appeals. But these are only figurehead leaders; they are much too busy with their own affairs to assume the responsibility for the day-to-day operations of a campaign. For example, a statewide cochairman of Brown's campaign was Dan Kimball, who was then chairman of the board of a major national aerospace firm, Aero-Jet General Corporation.

Candidates split their campaign organizations, designating San Francisco as the headquarters of the northern region, and Los Angeles as headquarters of the southern region. Each region has its own autonomous organization, headed by cochairmen who technically control activities in their area. This organizational independence frequently leads to duplication of effort, and coordination of north-south activities is a serious problem in most campaigns. The Los Angeles headquarters is much larger than its San Francisco counterpart and often serves as a statewide headquarters. In 1966 both Reagan and Brown operated their campaigns from headquarters in Los Angeles, located only a few blocks from each other along the "miracle mile" on Wilshire Boulevard. The preferred position of the Los Angeles headquarters is understandable in view of the fact that almost 60 per cent of the electorate resides in the southern region of the state. Attached to each regional organization is a finance committee charged with the responsibility of raising campaign funds. Finance committees are only nominally connected with the rest

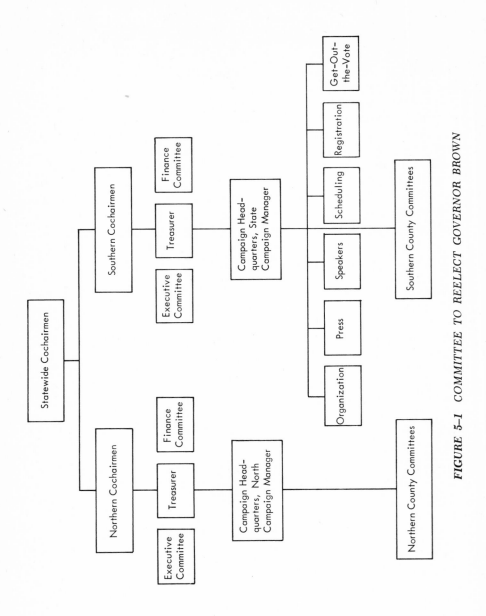

FIGURE 5-1 COMMITTEE TO REELECT GOVERNOR BROWN

of the campaign organization; they operate under their own cochairmen and a separate staff.

Responsibility for the day-to-day operation of campaigns normally rests in the hands of three campaign managers—one each for the north and south and a statewide manager. A talented and effective manager is crucial to the success of any campaign. As chief administrator he develops the budget and determines expenditures; he influences strategy and plans organization; he oversees the production and distribution of campaign literature and materials; and he is responsible for scheduling candidates' appearance and providing transportation. In sum, his hand touches all phases of the campaign. A man with the abilities to perform these tasks well is difficult to find. He must be thoroughly versed in the political traditions, character, and nuances of the state; he must be an expert in voting behavior; he must possess the skills necessary to effectively utilize mass media; and most importantly, he must hold the confidence and trust of his candidate.

Don Bradley, Governor Brown's chief campaign manager, exemplified this kind of political personality. Bradley's service to the California Democratic party stretched over two decades. Despite his relative anonymity, Bradley had been a key figure in numerous Democratic campaign successes. He had served as manager for congressional, senatorial, and statewide races, including Brown's 1962 and 1966 campaigns. When not actually running a campaign, Bradley was still intimately involved in party affairs, usually serving in one of the few paid posts of the state central committee. Much of his value to the party lay in his organizational skills. He could mobilize competent and influential people, an expert in the use of media, he could devise budgets for expenditures, allocate funds for the highest returns, and serve as an intermediary between the campaign and public relations agencies that make arrangements for television and radio time. Most importantly, he had direct lines to the party's largest campaign contributors and could raise large sums of money with relative ease.

North and south headquarters are organized according to major campaign activities. Figure 5–1 illustrates the division of labor into a number of organizational units: press, speakers' bureau, scheduling, organization, registration, and get-out-the-vote units. The working core of these divisions consists of a paid professional staff, including publicity men, organizers, media experts, speech writers, and so on. Brown's Los Angeles headquarters in 1966, for example, employed a staff of fifty or more paid employees. Totally involved in the details of running a campaign the staff employees operate in a hectic, frenzied atmosphere, working daily to meet press deadlines, and reacting to the latest polls. They provide professional direction at the local level—where campaigns are won or lost. Working side-by-side with the paid workers are hordes of volunteers, recruited to stuff envelopes, answer telephones, run mimeograph machines, and perform the myriad tiresome tasks required of all campaigns.

The largest and most important organizational unit is the press section. These people prepare and reproduce reams of press releases and distribute them to newspapers, sustaining the war of words that engulfs the voter throughout the campaign. The press section cooperates with the candidate's hired advertising agency. The speakers' bureau reviews requests for speakers, locates appropriate party officials for assignments, and assists in writing laudatory speeches designed to benefit the candidate's cause. The scheduling unit is responsible for outlining the candididate's intinerary in the area, coordinating arrivals and departures, providing transportation, and serving as a liaison between the candidate in the field and the campaign headquarters. The organization unit provides advice and assistance in establishing organizations at the county and local level; it serves as a link between the regional and state headquarters, and these local units. It also works closely with ethnic, racial, religious, and occupational organizations and all other groups representing special interests. The registration and get-out-the-vote units organize these drives and direct the crucial grass roots activities.

In a state as physically large as California, the only face-to-face contact with the average voter is through the work of the county and local campaign organizations. The most effective campaign demands widespread organizational decentralization; in California the county serves as the principal organizational unit at the local level. Los Angeles tends to be organized along state and federal legislative district lines. County committees headed by appointed cochairmen, and organized along the same lines as the regional headquarters, operate the county campaign, raise the necessary funds, arrange for candidates' appearances in the county, and manage publicity in local newspapers. Although the least populated counties often have only "paper organizations," committees in the larger urban counties are especially important to the campaign, and usually employ a paid professional to oversee campaign activities. The county and its organizational subunits at the grass roots level are aided by large vólunteer forces that register voters, canvass neighborhoods, and turn out the voters on election day.

In addition to the regular campaign organization, a number of volunteer "nonparty" groups play a vital role in most campaigns. Among these groups are the California Democratic Council (CDC), the California Republican Assembly (CRA), Young Republicans and Democrats, party women's organizations and a host of quasi-party groups (see Chapter 6). Such groups provide the manpower for the precinct level aspect of the campaign. In Brown's 1966 campaign, for example, the CDC was principally responsible for organizing neighborhood campaign units. Organized labor in California operates with relative autonomy from the regular party organizations, but nonetheless is deeply involved in partisan politics. AFL-CIO's Council on Political Education (COPE) raises funds for the candidates it endorses, circulates literature among rank-and-file labor, supports candidates in its own publications, and conducts registration and get-out-the-vote drives among its own members.

An inevitable fixture of every campaign is a variety of citizen or volunteer groups. Appearing during the 1966 gubernatorial campaign were such organizations as "Citizens for Reagan," "Democrats for Reagan," "Mexican-Americans for Brown," "Professors for Brown," and so on. There groups give the illusion of independence and are intended to appeal to the nonpartisan voter. But in truth they are carefully organized by the regular organization and are generally nothing more than facades. However, citizens groups are especially important to the Republican candidates who must attract large numbers of independent and nonpartisan voters. For example, Reagan's "Citizens for Reagan" organization assumed a central role in his campaign and was much more than a front organization.

CAMPAIGN MANAGEMENT FIRMS

The use of campaign management firms developed first in California, and although the practice has spread to other states, candidates in the Golden State continue to make greater use of these firms than candidates elsewhere. A distinction should be made, however, between public relations agencies often hired to handle the candidate's advertising and a campaign management firm hired to direct all aspects of the campaign. Every statewide campaign requires some professional assistance in the production of publicity materials, preparation of television "spots," and in the purchasing of network time for political broadcasting. Management firms, however, take complete charge of a campaign, including campaign strategy, fund raising, speech preparation, press relations, and general media publicity. These professional firms take the place of the regular party organization, and substitute for the politician the public relations expert who handles the candidate's campaign as any other client's account.[8]

---

[8] A general treatment of professional public relations and campaigning is found in Stanley Kelley, Jr., *Professional Public Relations and Political Power* (Baltimore: Johns Hopkins Press, 1956). For an account of campaign management firms in California, see Robert J. Pitchell, "Influence of Professional Campaign Management Firms in Partisan Elections in California," *Western Political Quarterly*, Vol. II (June 1958), pp. 278–300, Irwin Ross, "The Supersalesmen of California Politics: Whitaker and Baxter," *Harper's Magazine*, Vol. 219 (July 1959), pp. 55–61; and Herbert M. Baus and William B. Ross, *Politics Battle Plan* (New York: The Macmillan Company, 1968).

Probably the most famous of California's numerous campaign management firms was the husband and wife team of Whitaker and Baxter of San Francisco. Beginning in the early 1930s, Whitaker and Baxter were pioneers in the development of the application of public relations techniques to the campaign process. They eventually formed "Campaigns Inc." and by 1959 they had managed eighty major campaigns. Their operations served as a model for the rapidly growing business of campaign management. Harry Lerner, who began his career with Whitaker and Baxter, managed numerous campaigns for Democratic candidates and ballot propositions supported by liberal-labor elements. Herbert Baus, who heads the firm of Baus and Ross, is another alumnus of Whitaker and Baxter. His Los Angeles based agency managed the highly successful primary campaign of Barry Goldwater in 1964.

The hottest property in campaign management today is the firm of Spencer-Roberts & Associates, located in Los Angeles. "Stu" Spencer and William Roberts joined forces in 1960 after serving together as officials in the Los Angeles County Young Republicans. Spencer-Roberts ran liberal Republican Thomas Kuchel's 1962 re-election campaign and worked for him again in 1968, and also Nelson Rockefeller's 1964 presidential primary campaign. Ronald Reagan's campaign organization hired the firm for an estimated $150,000 to engineer his overwhelming victory in the 1966 gubernatorial contest.[9] It is apparent that Spencer-Roberts, although accepting only Republican "accounts," has no binding ideological coloration. In fact, much of the material Spencer-Roberts prepared for use in the Rockefeller primary against Senator Barry Goldwater was employed by the Brown forces against the conservative Ronald Reagan. Ideology is not a crucial factor in the thinking of these "pros"; most candidates, regardless of party or platform, and possessing sufficient resources, can hire expert firms to conduct campaigns.

A number of factors contribute to the phenomenal growth and success of campaign management firms in California. Perhaps the most important reason is the traditionally weak political parties and the lack of permanent and active precinct organizations that provide the best base for a strong campaign. The size and geography of the state and a mushrooming, mobile population force candidates to conduct the bulk of their campaigns via mass media. Candidates inevitably become more dependent on experts in media, who in turn rise to positions of dominance within the campaign. In addition, the frequent use of direct legislation through the referendum and initiative requires expensive statewide campaigns that are not the responsibility of the political parties. Instead, special interests that favor the various proposals have turned to campaign management outfits to run the propaganda campaigns necessary to gain the approval of the electorate.

Although no two campaign management firms operate alike, they all follow a basic "public relations" approach, which requires a saturation appeal to the voter via the mass media. This approach is premised on certain assumptions about the nature of the voter and how he makes political decisions. "The average American," Whitaker once informed a public relations audience, "doesn't want to be educated, he doesn't want to improve his mind, he doesn't even want to work conscientiously at being a good citizen. But there are two ways you can interest him in a campaign . . . you can interest him if you put on a fight . . . if you can't fight, PUT ON A SHOW!"[10]

Television and radio time account for the greatest single expenditure in professional campaigns. Public relations men recognize, however, that saturation coverage in the mass media is not always effective in gaining the attention of every voter, because a significant portion of the electorate is naturally suspicious of direct political appeals. Consequently, PR men expend considerable effort in placing indirect appeals in local newspapers and popular magazines. One firm, for example, was particularly successful at planting "boilerplate" material favoring its candidate in the columns of small town newspapers. In addition, some PR men make an effort to organize special interest associations behind their candidates, and to direct registration and get-out-the-vote drives. Spencer-Roberts emphasizes this organizational approach, and during the Reagan campaign employed seventy-five people throughout the state to undertake these tasks. The PR men in effect replace regular party leadership in the direction and control of grass roots volunteers who provide the manpower for precinct operations.

The management firms believe that success requires full control of all aspects of the campaign. They insist "that every worker must be under their control, that every issue must be formulated by them, every check must be signed by them, and speeches, posters, radio and TV spots, and other mass media paraphernalia must be written by the firm."[11] Hal Evry a Los Angeles based political publicity specialist, has carried this view to the extreme. He claims the ability to elect any candidate to high office through the manipulative use of simple slogans. "Before I take a client," he declares, "I ask them to agree that they will deliver no speeches, make no public appearances, and never get into a discussion of the issues. All I want them to do is stay out of sight."[12]

---

[10] Irwin Ross, op. cit., p. 59.
[11] Pitchell, op. cit., p. 289.
[12] *San Francisco Chronicle*, December 3, 1965.

Some campaign management firms have impressive performance records. Whitaker and Baxter, for instance, ran eighty campaigns over a period of two decades and won seventy-four. Spencer-Roberts reports success in thirty-four out of forty races. These firms represent, however, two of the most successful operators in the field. Other agencies with less enviable records choose not to make them public. Although complete data are unavailable on the performance records of all campaign management firms, limited information indicates that the better-known firms have won far more campaigns than they have lost.[13] This does not prove, however, that a campaign management firm, even of the caliber of Spencer-Roberts, is the crucial element that assures victory in a campaign. The candidate may very well have won without the assistance of the agency, and many of the firms take only clients having a good chance of winning. Clearly, these firms have not discovered a push-button technique guaranteeing the election of any candidate to office. Many factors, a great many of them beyond the control of a PR expert, influence the outcome of a political race.

campaigning and communications

Campaigning can be viewed as a communication process—an attempt to transmit to voters appeals that will persuade them to support candidates. The process by which these persuasive messages are tranmitted—their perception or misperception by the voter and their effect on the voter's behavior—is highly complex. Technological innovations in communications significantly influence campaign styles. For example, during most of the nineteenth century, speeches by presidential candidates were not reported until weeks later in many parts of the nation. But the invention of the telegraph permitted the instantaneous transmission of speeches and greatly altered the character of campaign dialogue. Alexander Heard identifies five broad periods of campaigning in American history, each basically related to changing communication techniques.[14] The first period, 1789 to the beginning of the Jacksonian era, was distinguished by an absence of active campaigning. During the "torchlight era" from Jackson to the 1880s, campaigns were localized, with an emphasis on organization and face-to-face appeals to the voters. Technologi-

---

[13] Pitchell, op. cit., pp. 282–83.
[14] Heard, op. cit., pp. 401–03.

cal advances in printing and publication led to an era of campaign literature from the 1880s to 1920. The radio determined the style of campaigning
from 1924 to 1952. The electronic revolution in the past two decades has
made television an effective and popular means of communicating political appeals. Television has added the visual dimension to radio, exposing
candidates' faces to millions of voters. In 1960, an estimated seventy-five
million people watched the first television debates between presidential
candidates John Kennedy and Richard Nixon. Kennedy believed, in fact,
that the TV debates "turned the tide" in his favor.

TELEVISION

Since 1952, television has dominated national political campaigning
in the United States; TV directly reaches more people faster and for
relatively less cost than any other medium. Richard Nixon estimated that
in 1960 he saw ten million people on his grueling fifty-state campaign
tour; but by appearing on one national television debate he was viewed
by seventy-five million Americans. A rough notion of the growing importance of television in campaigning is illustrated by sizes of audiences
for the principal media. V. O. Key, Jr. reports the following figures:[15]

	1952	1956
Read about the campaign in newspapers	79 per cent	69 per cent
Listened to radio speeches or discussions	69	45
Watched campaign programs on television	49	74
Read about the campaign in magazines	40	31

It is obvious that television is the major source of political news for
most voters, and that it now overshadows the newspapers. Moreover,
studies show that most voters accept television as a highly credible
source of information. Another indication of the influence of TV is that
it accounts for the greatest single expenditure of campaign funds. However, candidates running for lesser offices tend to use television less extensively than statewide or national candidates. The chief reason, of
course, is the great expense of the medium. The cost of television campaigning in most legislative districts is based upon the total audience of
the TV station, and the candidate's constituency usually constitutes only
a small portion of that expensive audience.

A number of trends have distinguished the use of television broad-

---

[15] V. O. Key, Jr., *Public Opinion and American Democracy* (New York: Alfred
A. Knopf, Inc., 1961), p. 346.

casting in political campaigning in the United States. When television was first introduced to the American society in the early 1950s, politicians were dazzled by its possibilities for reaching millions of American voters. At the outset, politicians firmly believed that the candidate who purchased the most television time would benefit the most at the polls. They quickly adopted the technique of saturating the airways with political appeals. Half-hour to hour long campaign programs filled the airways during prime viewing time. Because television turned out to be the most expensive "per-unit" method of campaigning, campaign costs skyrocketed.[16] But by pre-empting the most popular entertainment programs, the politicians earned the hostility of myriad voters. In 1952, Adlai Stevenson received the following telegram after pre-empting a popular show, "I like Ike and I love Lucy. Drop dead."

The expense of the medium, as well as the high "turn-off" rate, forced politicians to reappraise their use of television in campaigns. They restricted the number of long programs to avoid voter hostility caused by pre-emption; they realized that in order to gain and hold the attention of large audiences it was necessary to turn the traditional political rally into an entertainment "spectacular." Major entertainment personalities were long denied by their studio bosses the right to publicly engage in controversial political activities. However, with the breakup of the largest movie studios, stars gained new freedom in their personal and political lives. This new freedom had an especially significant effect in California politics because of the parties' access to the entertainment industry based in Los Angeles. Edmund Brown's campaign, for example, offered a "night of the stars" featuring such luminaries as Frank Sinatra, Gregory Peck, Henry Fonda, and Sammy Davis, Jr. Against these stars Reagan pitted his stable of famous Republicans, including Ray Bolger, Pat Boone, Chuck Connors, and Andy Devine. Such shows are obviously an attempt to hold an audience by providing entertainment, only occasionally interrupted with political appeals. A variation on the entertainment show is the television "telethon," which allows the viewer to phone in a question and in the process enjoy intimate contact with the famous star who answers the phone, and the candidate who answers the question. Perhaps the irony of this style of campaigning is when the star himself becomes the candidate.

But the greatest amount of television expenditures is poured into short five-minute programs, or ten- to sixty-second spot announcements. These

---

[16] Television surpasses all other media in terms of absolute cost; however, in terms of the number of voters reached, it is a relatively inexpensive means of campaign communication.

spots are usually inserted as "trailers" after entertainment shows, catching the large audiences who have not yet turned off their TV sets. In 1962 combined primary and general election expenditures for all candidates in California showed five times as much money was spent for announcements ($1.9 million) as for programs of five minutes or more ($400,000).[17] The short announcements are not attempts to present to the voters issues or rational appeals; rather, they permit only momentary exposure of the candidate's name and face.

Efforts have been made in California to use the television debate format patterned after the 1960 Kennedy-Nixon debates. In the 1964 Democartic senatorial primary, Pierre Salinger and Alan Cranston participated in such an exchange. Cranston, however, refused to debate Max Rafferty in the 1968 U.S. Senate race. Brown and Reagan agreed to participate in a televised debate, but despite extensive negotiations concerning format, the event never took place. Candidates also try to appear on a nationally televised press program. Brown and Reagan both appeared on "Meet the Press" but they faced the cameras in different studios. Debates and press programs are important not only because they reach large audiences but also because they offer the candidates long periods of free television time.

In the early days of television politicians believed that the medium would be a powerful force in molding and radically changing voting behavior. This hope was not realized. The individual's decision to vote, as well as his partisan choices, are basically influenced by the attitudes he holds toward the personal attributes of the candidates, the issues of domestic and foreign policy, the comparative record of the two parties as managers of government, and his perception of the interest of groups with which he identifies.[18] Although these attitudes are shaped by elements of the campaign, they are directly related to partisan affiliation and are stable and not easily altered by persuasion through the mass media. In fact, the most potent effect of the medium is to reinforce the predispositions of the voter, rather than significantly change them.

Television, however, does influence the electorate to some degree. During campaigns, most voters are exposed to some medium. For example, one study reported that only one person in twenty said that the

[17] Herbert E. Alexander, "Broadcasting and Politics," in M. Kent Jennings and L. Harmon Zeigler, eds., The Electoral Process (Englewood Cliffs, N.J.: Prentice-Hall, Inc., 1966), p. 87. An indication of the high cost of television spot announcements is gained from the following rates for the main NBC stations in Los Angeles and San Francisco: twenty second spot—prime time—network—KNBC (L.A.), $2,300; KRON (S.F.), $1,000.

[18] Campbell, op. cit., pp. 64–88.

campaign failed to reach him through any of the major media of communications.[19] But the audience that receives political information via television is far from representative of the entire electorate. Studies show that the audience for political broadcasting consists primarily of voters who are already involved in politics and hold strong political convictions. Voters with no real commitment to any particular candidate are least likely to be among this audience.[20] Moreover, viewers of political programs are highly selective in what they watch, with Democrats and Republicans paying more attention to the appeals of their respective parties. Two leading experts on the medium conclude, "Perhaps the most important generalization in this area—at least as far as an understanding of the process of effective persuasion is concerned—is that those groups which are most hopefully regarded as the target of communications are often least likely to be in the audience."[21]

Although campaign programs on television do not radically change firm convictions, they can influence the outcome of an election by causing marginal changes; television can significantly affect voter turnout by reinforcing partisan allegiances and stimulating interest. Moreover, television seems to have some effect on the voter's perception of the personal qualities of the candidate. Television personalizes the electorate's relationship with the candidate; indeed, the politician's face and personality are projected directly into the voter's home on the television screen. In the 1966 gubernatorial election, few denied the force of the Reagan "image" and personality. Finally, television is an effective means of developing opinions toward new issues that arise during a campaign.

No one doubts that television has had a significant impact on the style of California campaigning. But whether this impact is totally salutary will continue to be debated. Certainly, television's impact on elections has never met the wild optimism of its most enthusiastic supporters. Television news pioneer Sig Michelson, in summing up the case for the medium, observed, "Television . . . has brought a juxtaposition of conflicting ideas in a form that encourages the voter to make his own judgments. . . . It has made politics more honest, politicians more responsible. Most importantly, it has made democracy more effective."[22] Arthur Schlesinger, Jr., on the other hand, takes issue with this lofty statement. He writes, ". . . the effect of television has been to cheapen

---

[19] *Ibid.*, p. 92.

[20] Key, op. cit., p. 357.

[21] Elihu Katz and Paul F. Lazarsfeld, *Personal Influence* (New York: The Free Press, 1955), pp. 21–2.

[22] Walter Cronkite, "'Television and the News," *The Eighth Art*, ed. Robert L. Shayon (New York: Holt, Rinehart & Winston, Inc., 1962), p. 240.

political discourse, steadily reducing its length, its substance and its rationality."[23] An accurate evaluation of the effects of television probably lies somewhere between these two extreme comments. Television has not been a revolutionary medium elevating the political discourse in campaigning; nor has it developed into the master persuader. But it has provided candidates with an effective means of cultivating the political predisposition of large masses of voters; it enables an attractive, personable candidate to project his best qualities. Though television has not greatly elevated the level of political discussion, chances are it has not significantly lowered it. And although television has indeed resulted in substantial increases in campaign costs, it is only another weapon in the candidate's arsenal. Above all, any evaluation of the worth of television as a medium in politics must consider that it is a commercial enterprise, not a public service institution. Television networks are principally involved in the business of entertaining the masses in order to sell the products of its advertisers. The politicians themselves must accept the greatest responsibility for putting television to intelligent uses.

RADIO, NEWSPAPERS, MAILERS

Although the importance of television is undeniable, the medium has supplemented, not replaced, the more traditional methods of political persuasion. "A campaign is a mixture," as one party professional commented, "of speeches, bumper strips, mailings, billboards, buttons, brochures, radio, television, precinct work, volunteers, meetings, committees, endorsements, news releases, charges and counter charges—cooked over a hot fire of $100 bills." The hardest task of the campaign manager is to find the *proper* mixture of these various media to ensure his candidate's victory.

Radio continues to be used extensively by candidates in local and legislative races. In fact, radio may be more effective than television in reaching the candidate's constituency because the boundaries of the radio audience often correspond more closely with the boundaries of the political district. Moreover, lower rates for radio advertising make it more accessible than television to many candidates. Not only is radio time available for purchase, but the prolific news broadcasting of the medium provides an important outlet for campaign news and information. Through the radio, the working man driving to and from his job and the housewife washing her dishes receive a sizable portion of their daily news. No candidate should overlook this medium when distribut-

---

[23] Arthur Schlesinger, Jr., *T.V. Guide* (Oct. 22, 1966), p. 9.

ing his campaign press releases. Radio is much more flexible than television in the scheduling of political broadcasting. Ten- to 60-second spot announcements, the chief vehicle of political advertising on both radio and television, can be easily inserted into the radio program format.

"Crusading" newspapers helped shape much of California's early history; in fact, many of the founders of California progressivism were working newspapermen. During the Progressive era a number of important newspapers conducted sustained attacks on the corrupt influences of the railroads and powerful political machines. For example, *San Francisco Bulletin* editor Fremont Older used his newspaper to expose the criminal activities of Abe Ruef's political machine in San Francisco. The famous California muckraker, Lincoln Steffens, began his career as a news reporter in California with an attack on the monopolistic power of the Southern Pacific Railroad. James McClatchy, founder of the Central Valley's chain of *Bee* newspapers, championed the cause of the valley farmers against oppressive land monopolies owned by the Southern Pacific.

The state's newspapers continue to play an important role in California campaigns. Political advertising, especially by legislative candidates, is an important vehicle for campaign publicity. Also, the teams of news reporters who follow statewide candidates on the campaign trail provide a major source of public information on the candidates and the issues. Furthermore, candidates on all levels eagerly seek endorsements of their candidacies by influential newspapers.

There are approximately 125 daily newspapers in California. The state also supports numerous weekly, semiweekly, and suburban shopping papers that carry a measureable amount of political news; in Los Angeles County alone there are more than 60 newspapers. By far the largest and undoubtedly the most influential urban newspaper is the Chandler family's *Los Angeles Times* with a circulation of 830,000. Other important papers include the *San Francisco Chronicle* and the *San Francisco Examiner;* the *Oakland Tribune,* owned by former Republican Senate leader William Knowland; the *Sacramento Bee,* located in the state's capital and owned by the McClatchy family; and the two Copley owned dailies in San Diego.

The days of blatant affiliation of newspapers with political parties are gone; modern newspapers are fiercely competitive businesses that cannot jeopardize their economic position by obvious political partisanship. Nearly four fifths of California's 125 dailies claim political independence. Of those who list affiliation, twenty-six are Republican and six are Democratic. Despite the fact that most of California's newspapers indicate political independence, a majority of them do endorse candidates for public office. James E. Gregg reported that 90 per cent of the state's papers have consistent endorsement records, and that the overwhelming majority of these (80 per cent) are very perceptibly Republican. Gregg writes, "It is reasonable to conclude that 80 per cent [of the California papers] are Republican in orientation, 10 per cent are Democratic in orientation and 10 per cent are either truly independent, or are papers which do not make political endorsements."[24] Politicians continue to believe that newspaper endorsements exert an overwhelming influence on the decision of the voters, and this is especially true in a state like California where many newcomers are unfamiliar with names on the ballots. Moreover, candidates are traditionally suspicious of slanted news coverage, and consequently feel that endorsement by the paper will guarantee them an advantage in coverage over their opponents.[25] However, Gregg found in his study of eleven major dailies over a fourteen-year period that endorsements were most influential when there were few other determinants affecting the voter's decision. Thus, voters were more willing to follow newspaper endorsements of local nonpartisan candidates and ballot propositions than they were to accept the newspaper's advice on presidential, gubernatorial, or senatorial elections.[26]

Because political developments in California are important to the rest of the nation, national news magazines must be considered along with newspapers as a principal source of information to some California voters. A cover story by *Time* magazine on a gubernatorial or senatorial candidate can influence the course of political events in California. *Life, Look, Newsweek,* and *Time* are primarily objective news sources; they are not subject to direct manipulation by candidates. Yet all these journals have a particular political viewpoint that conceivably could affect a candidate's political fortune. Magazine readers, however, constitute only a small part of the total electorate; they are generally political activists with strong partisan convictions. Therefore, the impact of these

---

[24] James E. Gregg, "Newspaper Editorial Endorsements and California Elections, 1948–62," *Journalism Quarterly,* Vol. 42, No. 4 (1965), p. 533.

[25] President Richard M. Nixon made perhaps one of the most acrimonious indictments of campaign press coverage in his famous post-election press conference in Los Angeles in 1962. "And as I leave the press, all I can say is this: For 16 years, ever since the Hiss case, you've had a lot of fun—a lot of fun—that you've had an opportunity to attack me and I think I've given as good as I've taken. . . . I believe in reading what my opponents say and I hope that what I have said today will at least make television, radio, and the press first recognize the great responsibility they have to report all the news and, second, recognize that they have a right and a responsibility, if they're against a candidate, to give him the shaft, but also recognize if they give him the shaft, put one lonely reporter on the campaign who will report what the candidate says now and then." Transcript of news conference.

[26] Gregg, op. cit., p. 535.

magazines on their political views is probably limited. Yet these readers constitute an elite group of opinion leaders who are in a position to influence a much broader audience.

Although a mailer can be anything from a newsletter to a postcard almost every candidate sends out at least one piece of political literature during a campaign emphasizing his name and some simple message. Candidates seem to feel that the advantage of a mailer is that it gets into the hands of the voter—if only between the mailbox and the garbage can. California's post offices would handle approximately twenty-five million pieces of literature assuming that every Republican and Democratic candidate for state and national office sent out at least one mailing during a campaign. The work involved in preparing a mailer has caused many candidates to turn to professional firms that perform the tedious tasks of addressing, stuffing, stamping, and mailing. Ken Ross and Co. of Los Angeles County provides this kind of service. This firm has the particular advantage of an exclusive contract with Los Angeles County to maintain a duplicate of the Great Register of Voters on IBM data processing equipment, thereby allowing it to handle rapidly large volumes of mail. In the 1966 primary election the firm addressed more than sixteen million pieces of campaign literature to registered voters of both parties in Los Angeles County alone. Ross estimated at the time that the cost of a mailing, including printing and third-class postage, average five cents per piece. Of course, this cost has increased since then. The price could go much higher if the candidate sent his mailers via first class. First-class mail has priority in postal handling, thus enabling the candidate to time its arrival in the voter's home on the strategic day before the election. One device used by some candidates is a first-class mailer arriving on Monday before the election, which includes with the political message the polling place of the individual voter.[27]

A staple diet of all campaigns consists of billboards, posters, bumper strips, brochures, tabloids, and throw-aways. These devices all offer quick publicity for and name-identification of the candidate. Their value to a campaign is difficult to assess; to what extent they actually persuade the voter is not measurable. However, no candidate is willing to eliminate entirely this potpourri of colorful political appeals. One significant factor is their expense. A billboard, depending on its location, size, and other factors, can cost a candidate as much as $100 or more a month. Widely

---

[27] The use of electronic data processing (EDP) equipment in campaigns is creating a new technology that campaign managers must understand. EDP can be used to analyze political data, write letters, maintain lists of contributors, simulate elections, and many other tasks. For a discussion of these developments, see James M. Perry, *The New Politics* (New York: C. N. Potter, 1968), pp. 139ff.

distributed bumper strips represent a considerable outlay of campaign funds, especially in local campaigns.

campaign finance

Alexander Heard observed, "the giving, receiving, and handling of political money is a unique and especially important form of political action . . . it ranks next to voting itself in deserving study."[28] The present system of campaign finance represents a serious threat to the process of democratic elections. High campaign costs, boosted in recent years by the increased use and continually rising cost of expensive media, have placed on all potential candidates the heavy burden of raising enormous sums of money to finance their campaigns. Herbert E. Alexander estimates that the costs of all national, state, and local campaigns in 1964 amounted to about $200 million.[29] Although this figure is indeed large, it is not an exorbitant price to pay for the right to choose freely the nation's political leaders. Certainly a nation that spends for advertising cigarettes $250 million anually can afford this price for election campaigns. The real problem of campaign finance is not high cost per se; rather, it is the danger inherent in a system that forces candidates to raise necessary funds from a limited number of private interests.

CAMPAIGN COSTS

As the most populous state in the Union, with more than 8,000,000 registered voters spread over 160,000 square miles, it is obvious that political campaigns for statewide office are unusually expensive. It is difficult to determine the over-all cost of political campaigns in California; the law requires no exact accounting of income and expenditures. Any attempt to summarize campaign costs involves a great deal of guessing and estimating. The principal source of information on campaign costs are the financial reports required of candidates and committees by the California Elections Code. These statements of expenditures contain a summary of the money raised and spent, with a listing of individuals who contributed the money and an itemized breakdown of expenditures.

---

[28] Heard, op. cit., p. 3.
[29] Herbert E. Alexander, *Financing the 1964 Election* (Princeton: Citizens Research Foundation, 1966), p. 13.

These reports, though useful, provide only a partial picture of all the costs of a campaign. One shortcoming of the reports arises from inadequate enforcement of reporting procedures. Although the law requires all candidates and committees for statewide offices to file finance statements with the Secretary of State, no serious efforts are made to ensure compliance. In fact, many local committees operating for statewide candidates never file reports. Moreover, the reports reveal only direct monetary expenditures; many services and facilities donated to campaigns are not included in finance statements, but, if included, would add appreciably to the over-all expense. Nevertheless, this is the best available source for estimating the costs of campaigning in California.

Table 5–1 summerizes the information contained in finance reports filed in the office of the Secretary of State for all primary and general elections in 1966.

The data in the table show that the candidates of both parties for

TABLE 5–1   TOTAL REPORTED EXPENDITURES, PRIMARY
AND GENERAL ELECTIONS, 1966

Office	Primary* Expenditures	General† Expenditures	Total
Governor	$2,643,329.	$ 4,755,561.	$ 7,398,890.
Lieutenant Governor	569,553.	393,177.	962,730.
Attorney General	328,617.	291,918.	620,535.
Secretary of State	186,658.	40,675.‡	227,333.
Controller	129,119.	299,061.	428,180.
Treasurer	66,321.	150,294.	216,615.
Board of Equalization	15,247.	66,435.	81,682.
Subtotal	3,938,844.	5,997,121.	9,935,965.
State Senators**	1,523,872.	1,396,803.	2,920,675.
Assemblymen	1,494,093.	1,633,298.	3,127,391.
Subtotal	3,017,965.	3,030,101.	6,048,066.
Congressional	881,175.	1,739,417.	2,620,592.
Grand Total	$7,837,984.	$10,766,639.	$18,604,623.

* Based on tabulations compiled by Martin Salditch, *Riverside Press Enterprise,* on file in Secretary of State's Office.
† Based on public reports filed with California Secretary of State, and *Sacramento Bee,* Dec. 16, 1966.
‡ No report filed by Democratic candidate for Secretary of State.
** Because of reapportionment, all forty Senate seats were at stake.

statewide, legislative, and congressional offices spent $7,837,984 in the primary, and $10,766,639 in the general election, for a total reported campaign expenditure of $18,604,623. This latter figure is the minimal cost of all partisan elections in 1966. A maximum figure, based upon more comprehensive reporting, would probably raise the total by at least $2 million. The significance of these figures, however, can be realized only by developing some comparative measure of costs. Campaign costs in California, measured in gross expenses, have increased significantly since 1952. Professor Heard estimated that the total cost of all campaigns in California in 1952 was $10.5 million, indicating a cost increase of nearly 80 per cent in the past fourteen years.[30] Gross comparisons, however, are somewhat deceptive. A more accurate comparison can be derived by comparing relative expenditures per voter (divide total expenditures by total votes cast). Such a comparison shows that per voter expenditures since 1952 have increased from $2.04 to $2.82, not as overwhelming a figure as the gross increase. This increase can be explained, in part, by the effects of normal inflation. Actual increases can be attributed primarily to a wider use of television since 1952. Another way of placing California campaign costs in perspective is to compare the state's cost per voter to figures for the nation as a whole. In 1964 the national cost per voter was $2.83, almost the same as the cost in California.

An analysis of Table 5–1 reveals expenditures for the primary election in 1966 accounted for 42 per cent of total campaign costs. This figure represents a sizable chunk of over-all costs, and indicates that primary expenses should not be overlooked, as they often are, in computing campaign costs.

Not surprisingly, the most money (40 per cent) was spent in the primary and general gubernatorial campaigns. Highly competitive primaries in both parties provide some explanation for this large expenditure. A further breakdown of campaign expenses by office, excluding governor, show candidates for that office accounting for 14 per cent of the total; state legislative races, 32 per cent; and congressional races, 14 per cent.[31]

Table 5–2 presents general election expenditures for Republican and Democratic candidates by office. It shows that Republican candidates, accounting for 55 per cent of the expenditures, outspent the Democratic candidates. The largest percentage of the total sum went for the guberna-

---

[30] Heard, op. cit., p. 372.

[31] Elections were held for all legislative seats for both houses in 1966 because of reapportionment. This fact probably accounts for a higher than normal cost for legislative campaigning.

TABLE 5–2 TOTAL REPORTED EXPENDITURES BY PARTY, GENERAL ELECTION, 1966*

Office	Republican	Democratic	Total
Governor†	$2,674,193.	$2,081,368.	$ 4,755,561.
Lieutenant Governor	257,317.	135,860.	393,177.
Attorney General	122,921.	168,997.	291,918.
Secretary of State	40,675.	‡	40,675.
Controller	73,965.	225,096.	299,061.
Treasurer	73,861.	76,433.	150,294.
Board of Equalization	12,231.	54,204.	66,435.
Subtotal	3,255,163.	2,741,958.	5,997,121.
State Senators	771,211.	625,592.	1,396,803.
Assemblymen	901,247.	732,051.	1,633,298.
Subtotal	1,672,458.	1,357,643.	3,030,101.
Congressional	1,008,049.	731,368.	1,739,417.
Grand Total	$5,935,670.	$4,830,969.	$10,766,639.

* Based on public reports filed with California Secretary of State and *Sacramento Bee*, Dec. 12, 1966.

† Figure represents only the expenditures of Brown's statewide committee; expenditures of some of the committees in the larger counties were integrated into the statewide report. Reagan's figure includes all local committees reporting.

‡ No report filed by Democratic candidate for Secretary of State.

torial race between Ronald Reagan and Pat Brown.[32] Some indication of the increasing cost of major statewide races can be seen by comparing reported expenses for both Republican and Democratic candidates in the past three gubernatorial elections: 1958, $1,705,800; 1962, $3,091,-900; 1966, $4,755,500. Although these comparisons of gross figures may exaggerate differences, the trend is obviously toward more expensive campaigns. Table 5–2 presents no information on expenditures for U.S. senatorial campaigns because none were scheduled in 1966. However, a competitive senatorial race can cost almost as much as a gubernatorial campaign. In the 1964 senatorial campaign, expenditures in the primary and general election were $3,600,000.[33] The Rafferty-Cranston senatorial

---

[32] Brown's reported expenditures are not entirely accurate because only a few of Brown's local committees reported to the Secretary of State. These included, however, most of the larger counties. Reagan's local committees filed finance statements reporting expenditures of approximately $400,000.

[33] John R. Owens, *Money and Politics in California: Democratic Senatorial Primary, 1964* (Princeton: Citizens Research Foundation, 1966), pp. 32–7. The

race in 1968 cost both candidates in the primary and general election $4,427,400.

Costs of legislative campaigns, both state and federal, vary considerably, depending on the size and location of the districts, and the degree of political competition. An analysis of individual races for the state Senate and Assembly in 1966 shows that costs range from the minimum expense of a filing fee ($160) to the most expensive Senate race, $98,653 (24th District—Ventura-Santa Barbara County) and the most expensive Assembly race, $59,962 (69th District—Orange County).

CAMPAIGN EXPENDITURES

An examination of the ways candidates spend such large sums of money provides further insight into the general question of campaign finance. Candidates, of course, allocate varying sums for various campaign activities, depending on the office, the candidate, the degree of competition, and so on. But expenditures can be analyzed according to three general categories: publicity, personnel, and provisions. Candidates are required to record in state finance reports a breakdown of expenditures, according to the "purpose and specific nature" of each item of expense. Although accounting procedures are far from uniform, an analysis of these reports reveals, at least, a rough pattern of the distribution of political funds according to the foregoing categories.

Some indication of the proportional allocation of money according to purpose in the highly competitive 1966 gubernatorial campaign is presented in Table 5–3. The accuracy of this table, however, is limited because it contains only a partial report of the statewide expenditures of Ronald Reagan.[34] Campaign costs, as presented in Table 5–3, are broken down into three main categories (publicity, personnel, and provisions) and into eight subcategories (radio and television, direct mail, newspapers, billboards, salaries, travel, headquarters, and supplies).

The table demonstrates broad similarities in the allocation of funds by both committees. Approximately the same percentage of the total funds was spent for the three major categories: publicity— Brown, 58 per cent, Reagan 63 per cent; personnel—Brown 24 per cent, Reagan, 24 per cent; provisions—Brown, 18 per cent, Reagan, 12 per cent. It is not surprising

---

authors have drawn on this study in preparing this section on campaign finance. Permission granted by the publisher.

[34] Reagan's southern committee reported expenditures on a day-to-day accounting basis instead of reporting costs according to the "purpose" categories as defined by the Elections Code, making it virtually impossible to summarize expenditures by our categories.

TABLE 5–3 CAMPAIGN EXPENDITURES BY PURPOSE, GENERAL ELECTION, GOVERNOR, 1966*

Purpose	Brown— Statewide	Percentage	Reagan— No. Calif.	Percentage
Radio and T.V.	$ 796,035.	38.28	$222,540.	47.31
Direct Mail	147,967.	7.12	34,718.	7.38
Newspapers	127,190.	6.12	37,242.	7.93
Billboards	128,555.	6.18	149.	†
Publicity	1,199,747.	57.70	294,649.	62.62
Salaries	367,780.	17.69	58,631.	12.48
Travel	131,309.	6.31	54,157.	11.52
Personnel	499,089.	24.00	112,788.	24.00
Headquarters	217,060.	10.43	50,549.	10.75
Supplies	148,803.	7.16	7,075.	1.51
Provisions	365,863.	17.59	57,624.	12.26
Miscellaneous	14,792.	.71	5,289.	1.12
Total	$2,079,491.	100.00	$470,350.	100.00

* Based on public reports filed with California Secretary of State.
† Less than one tenth of 1 per cent. All expenditures for billboards probably were handled by Reagan's southern committee.

that nearly two thirds of the total expenditures were for campaign publicity. Moreover, the overwhelming share of publicity money was spent for radio and television; Reagan's northern committee spent 47 per cent of the total funds on this item and Brown's state committee spent 38 per cent. This figure appears significantly higher than comparative spending by national level committees, which reported expenditures in the 1964 presidential elections of about one third of their total funds for political broadcasting.[35]

California's dependence on political broadcasting becomes even more apparent when examining the reports of the Federal Communications Commission. These data, required of all television and radio stations by federal law, provide an accurate statement of funds spent for media time in the primary and general elections in California during 1964.

All candidates in California (presidential and state) spent on radio

---

[35] Herbert E. Alexander, "The High Costs of T.V. Campaigns," *Television Quarterly*, Vol. V, No. 1 (Winter 1966), p. 48.

and television publicity $3,251,171 or approximately 10 per cent of the national total.[36] Of this total approximately 75 per cent went for television. Republicans outspent Democrats for political broadcasting, accounting for 59 per cent of the total expenditures. As noted earlier, the largest percentage of the broadcasting funds paid for spot announcements and short five-minute trailer programs. Interestingly, a large part of gross television expenditures by political candidates goes for costs other than time charges. Gross television expenses included agency fees averaging about 15 per cent, and production costs that ranged from 10 to 20 per cent of the total figure.

Publicity funds, other than radio and television, went for the purchase of newspaper advertising, direct mailings, and billboards. An average of between 6 and 7 per cent of the total funds was spent by each candidate for each of these items. Although the newer media have not entirely replaced these more traditional methods of political propaganda, the latter are accounting for smaller percentages of the total campaign budget. This phenomenon is apparent in comparing an estimated budget in 1953 with the 1966 figures in Table 5–3. In 1953, when political television was just introduced, funds for TV comprised approximately 7.5 per cent of the total campaign expenditures. Other publicity expenditures in 1953 included 36 per cent for direct mailings and pamplets; outdoor advertising, 19 per cent; newspaper advertising, 8.7 per cent; and radio, 6.5 per cent.[37] Money is obviously being reallocated from the areas of outdoor advertising and direct mailings to television as a means of campaign publicity. Of course, there has been a very large increase in television time costs since 1953.

Approximately 25 per cent of the total funds went for personnel expenditures, including salaries and travel. This is a fairly important item of expenditure: It covers the costs of professional assistance in the form of campaign managers, pressmen, publicity and media experts, field representatives, and speech writers. The high costs of travel during California campaigns is a significant factor in campaign expenditures. All in the same day, a candidate may attend a breakfast meeting in Sacramento, a midmorning press conference in San Francisco, a barbecue luncheon in the East Bay, a fund raising dinner in San Diego, and an evening television appearance in Los Angeles. Remaining expenditures

---

[36] *Survey of Political Broadcasting, Primary and General Election Campaign of 1964* (Federal Communications Commission, July 1965), Table 2, pp. unnumbered.

[37] Harry Lerner, campaign management specialist, gave these estimates in "Why It Costs So Much to Run for Political Office," *The Commonwealth*, Vol. XXIX, No. 1 (Jan. 5, 1953), pp. 3–4.

(accounting for approximately 15 per cent) were designated for provisions, maintaining headquarters and the purchase of supplies.

In most campaigns the largest percentage of funds is spent in Los Angeles County, which has more than 40 per cent of the voters. A program on the major Los Angeles television station can be viewed by as many as 74 per cent of California's voters. A rough indication of the allocation of funds between north and south can be gained from an analysis of the division of Reagan's expenditures. Reagan's southern committee reported spending approximately three times as much money as its northern counterpart.

RAISING THE FUNDS

Some of the more intriguing questions concerning campaign finance relate to sources of funds. Who gives to political campaigns? Why do they contribute? How do candidates organize to raise money? What techniques are used to obtain funds? Knowledge of these matters is scattered and tinged with sensationalism, often leading to simplified or false conclusions. People contribute for diverse reasons involving complicated human motivations that are difficult to explain or categorize. Information about who contributes to California campaigns is available in official reports, but the law does not require candidates to reveal the sum contributed by each individual nor his full name or address. Consequently, the reports are merely pages of names without any indication of who gave as much as $10,000 or as little as $1.

Further evidence of the weakness of California's political parties is their failure to provide adequate funds to their candidates for the running of campaigns. In recent years both parties have sought to improve their fund raising capacities, but only the Republican party has achieved some success. Individual candidates continue to raise most of their campaign funds, and contributors still prefer to donate to the candidate directly rather than to the political party.

The major parties have finance committees attached to their state central committees, charged with the responsibility of raising money for party operations. These finance committees raise money from individuals by direct solicitation and fund raising dinners; they also collect funds from county and other local party committees by assessment. It appears, however, that the bulk of these funds are used for regular party activities, rather than the specific campaign costs. In addition to these regular fund raising functions, both parties have attempted to establish centralized systems of campaign fund raising; only the Republicans have had any amount of continuing success. In 1948, the Republican party pioneered a centralized system of fund raising, establishing permanent finance committees in the north and south to raise money through a united appeal patterned after the Community Chest drives. Republican-oriented businessmen organized the United Republican Finance Committee to collect money primarily from the business community for the party. The performance of the United Republican drive varies, depending on their leadership and other political conditions.

Methods of raising campaign funds vary from direct personal solicitation to indirect public appeal. The approach seems to be related to the size of the contribution; the $1,000 giver is approached directly, but the $10 giver can be approached through a mailer or a television appeal. The task of direct personal solicitation of funds from large givers is handled by a finance committee set up by the candidate. Of the thousands of individuals involved in a campaign, none surpasses in importance these key fund raisers who are the "middle men in influence." They perform the crucial service of providing access to people of wealth. Large amounts of money are sought from wealthy, politically oriented individuals much in the same manner as fund raising for charity. Key fund raisers call their friends and business associates to a small luncheon or cocktail party during which a "political pitch" is presented. The virtues of the candidate are extolled and the importance of his election to those present is made clear. An appeal for funds is made, and someone who has possibly been prompted to do so will start the ball rolling with his contribution. Hopefully others will follow. The donor is expected to fulfill his pledge personally or, at least, raise the money from his friends and associates Such "middle men in influence" were active for both Reagan and Brown in the 1966 campaign. Reagan's finance committee included Henry Salvatori, a Los Angeles oil developer; Holmes Tuttle, an automobile distributor; and the late A. C. Rubel of the Union Oil Company. Salvatori, for example, was Reagan's finance co-chairman, and having been a successful fund raiser for Senator Goldwater was able to open the vaults of conservative Republicans who wanted California under the leadership of Ronald Reagan. Pat Brown relied on men like Cyril Magnin, a San Francisco merchant; Eugene Wyman, former Democratic National Committeeman; Lewis Wasserman, President of the Music Corporation of America; and Dan Kimball, an Aerojet-General Corporation executive. These men served as intermediaries between Brown and the wealthy Democratic contributors. In the 1966 election the Democratic party benefited from another technique for raising large sums of money from wealthy Californians; Governor Brown established the "Golden Bear Club," patterned after the "President's Club," which solicited contributions of $1,000 or more in return for more direct access to the

Governor. The members could, for instance, meet the Governor or dine with him, or even call his office directly to discuss personal matters.[38]

An equally lucrative technique is the fund raising dinner. Both parties, and candidates at all levels, make extensive use of these general subscription dinners. Major candidates usually charge $100-a-plate, of which approximately $75 is net profit. These profits are augmented by predinner cocktail parties attended by an even more select group of individuals who kick in additional money for this event. Prior to 1966, perhaps the largest profit came from advertisements sold for the dinner's souvenir program, with a single page selling for as much as $5,000. These programs had been a phenomenal success, mainly because businessmen could write off part of the cost as a tax deduction. However, in March 1966, the Federal Internal Revenue Service ruled that businessmen could no longer deduct such contributions. The ruling ended the souvenir program as a lucrative source of funds.

The ways money can be raised are limitless. Ronald Reagan was successful in promoting hundreds of barbecues throughout the state. Receptions, lawn parties, cocktail parties, and coffee klatches each provide income for major and minor candidates. Office seekers deluge the voters with appeals for funds through radio and television, newspaper advertisements, and door-to-door solicitation. Most of these efforts, however, are directed at the small contributor. Some candidates, usually those without access to large contributors, turn to professional fund raisers who, for a percentage fee, promise to deliver the money the candidate needs for his campaign. Max Rafferty employed Richard A. Viguerie, a Washington, D.C. professional fund raiser, in his 1968 U.S. senatorial campaign. Reportedly, Viguerie raised $800,000 for the primary simply by using a direct mail appeal to a specially prepared list of contributors to conservative causes throughout the nation. Rafferty claimed that 75,000 people contributed to his campaign.[39]

Analysis of campaign fund sources is a difficult job, largely because of the problems encountered in attempting to determine the sizes of individual contributions. Most of the funds for major campaigns, however, come from contributors who give $500 or more. Candidates for lesser offices also depend on a few large contributors, even though the amounts of single donations are smaller in the minor campaigns.

Individuals contribute to campaigns for a variety of reasons.[40] Some

---

[38] The President's Club was introduced by John F. Kennedy in 1962, and continued by President Lyndon Johnson. The members bought, in effect, some amount of personal attention from the President for a minimum $1,000 contribution. California and New York had the largest President's Club membership.

[39] *Sacramento Bee*, October 10, 1968; July 10, 1969.

[40] For a classification of contributor motives, see Heard, op. cit., pp. 71–72.

give out of a sense of civic duty; they feel obligated to give financial support to our system of free elections. Others give because it somehow enhances their prestige or elevates their status; by giving they can mingle with the powerful, with a President, a Governor, or a Senator. Certainly one of the most important incentives for many large contributors and for most groups is access to government; giving usually opens doors, results in an official's willingness to listen, and provides a chance to plead a cause. Access does not mean that there is necessarily a consideration for every contribution. Every act of giving does not involve a *quid pro quo* between the candidate and a contributor. Access does not guarantee a favorable decision; it mainly provides the opportunity to be heard, something which in theory is available to all citizens. But if the individuals and groups giving the most money to campaigns are those having large economic stakes in government, then the notion of access may imply special hearing and special consideration for special interests.

There are few clear-cut examples in California of total identification of economic interests with either political party. This is true because the basic motive for monetary contributions by individuals identified with these interests is the achievement of favorable public policy. Therefore, most major interests tend to contribute to either the incumbent candidate or party, or the candidate with the best chances of victory. And the groups most involved in California campaigns are naturally those most regulated by state legislation; included in this category are the public utilities, savings and loan associations and banks, labor unions, agribusiness, oil industry, defense contractors, liquor wholesalers and retailers, race track operators, and building and highway contractors. Several of these groups are by nature more consistently identified with one party. For example, the Democratic party has in recent years received the lion's share of labor unions' funds, but Republican Governors Earl Warren and Goodwin Knight also received financial support from some AFL unions. One source of political income peculiar to California is the entertainment industry based in Hollywood. Wealthy businessmen in this industry have traditionally supported the Republican party; but in recent years, as the movie and television performers have become active politically, many with liberal beliefs have contributed handsomely to Democratic coffers.

REGULATION OF PARTY FINANCE

In 1893 California became one of the first states in the nation to enact legislation regulating campaign finance. Present laws require all candidates for statewide office to file reports that include the names of contributors, the names of all persons to whom money was paid or loaned, and the purposes of all expenditures. Candidates must file these reports within thirty-five days after the election. Since 1955 candidates are required to file separate reports for the general and primary campaigns. Although national legislation and laws in some states place various limitations on the total amounts spent by candidates and committees, and on the sizes of individual contributions, California laws since 1949 contain no such restrictions.

General agreement exists concerning the inadequacy of California's legislation in this area. Moreover, the enforcement of the admittedly inadequate law is obviously ineffective. Although the Secretary of State is responsible for the administration of the law and is empowered to withhold a certificate of nomination or election from any candidate failing to file a report, there is no guarantee that all candidates and committees will report, nor does the Secretary attempt to verify the accuracy of information contained in reports.[41] The legislature in 1965 enacted a law that prohibits defeated candidates from running for office again without filing the delinquent campaign reports. This law also states that failure to file financial reports is a misdemeanor punishable by fine, but the Secretary of State has ruled that criminal suits must be initiated by voters. Such a suit has never been filed against a candidate.

Even though the reports are open to public inspection, they in fact receive little attention or publicity. The justification of finance regulation is that the voter should know which individuals are financing the candidate's campaign, and the manner in which the funds are spent. But as the reports are filed more than a month after the primary or general election, this information is worthless to the voter in making political choices. The goals of the law are further undermined by the fact that amounts of money contributed by individuals are not revealed by the reports.

This situation can probably be considerably improved in two ways. First, the legislature could enact laws to provide some kind of assistance or subsidy for candidates and parties for legitimate campaign expenditures. This aid could take the form of a direct subsidy to underwrite some of the costs of radio and television, or it could go directly to the major political parties to be channeled to candidates for certain types of campaign expenditures. California could also improve its present system of tax incentives aimed at encouraging small campaign contributions from large numbers of givers. Laws now permit taxpayers to deduct up to $100 for political donations.

---

[41] In 1966 Secretary of State Frank Jordan refused to certify the elections of three congressmen who failed to report, and instructed them to seek permission from the Superior Court to file late reports. See Elections Code, sections 11500–11629.

Secondly, current laws regulating campaign finance could be strengthened by the legislature. It could require individual candidates to appoint a single treasurer or agent responsible for handling and accounting for all campaign income. This system would facilitate complete disclosure of funds by a responsible political agent. The law could require periodic reports during a campaign instead of a single report following the election. The Secretary of State's office could be granted more enforcement powers and not serve, as it does now, merely as a depository of records. Candidates could be required to report explicitly the names and addresses of givers, along with the exact amounts of contributions. Finally, the legislature could consider imposing some restrictions on the sizes of individual contributions and, perhaps, prohibit contributions from specific sources such as corporations and labor unions.[42]

Despite the blatant shortcomings of state regulation of campaign finance, the California legislature has to date failed to enact any significant reforms of the present law. Legislators regularly submit bills for change and reform, but none of them have received serious consideration by legislative committees. A partial explanation for this failure to act is the reluctance of leaders in both houses to fully support serious moves for reform. This reluctance reflects the politicians' realistic attitudes toward campaign finance. Campaigns are expensive, and this expense is continually increasing; the responsibility for fund raising rests almost entirely with the individual candidate, and he must depend heavily on the bank accounts of wealthy men seeking the support of public policies. The hope for campaigns financed by larger numbers of small donors has never been realized.

---

[42] For comprehensive discussion of recent reform proposals, see Herbert E. Alexander and Laura L. Denny, *Regulation of Political Finance* (Berkeley: Institute of Governmental Studies, 1966).

CHAPTER 6

party organization and leaders

he success of a political party depends a great deal upon how well it is organized and how effectively it is led. The political party is a large-scale organization, a system of human activities ordered by some specialization of function. It has all the characteristics of a formal organization: A collective identity, a set of common goals, a membership with differentiated roles, and a system of dividing authority and duties.[1] The formal structure of the party is defined in state law and party rules and regulations. It consists of an intricate network of committees, conventions, and officers. Because the party is primarily interested in influencing the election of public officials and the policies they make, the organization is built around the electoral divisions of the state.

But the party, particularly in California, includes more than the official or statutory units. A number of groups that play a vital role in the life of the party are tech-

---

[1] Samuel J. Eldersveld, *Political Parties: a Behavioral Analysis* (Chicago: Rand McNally and Co., 1964), chapter 1.

nically speaking not part of the legal organization. Yet these groups such as the California Democratic Council and the California Republican Assembly carry on important party functions and in fact are organizationally associated with the party. Although this association is extralegal, it makes these groups a part of the informal structure of this party.

official party organization

Legally speaking, what is a political party? This is not an easy question to answer because numerous groups operating in California call themselves political parties. The federal and state constitutions guarantee the right of political association to all citizens and any group of people can join together, nominate candidates, and campaign for votes in elections. For example, a survey made a few years ago of Los Angeles County's registration rolls uncovered more than forty political parties. In addition to the Republican and Democratic parties, registrants reported membership in the Vegetarian, Christian Nationalist, Monarchy, Independent, Independent Progressive, Progressive Independent, Independent Republican, and many other parties. The confusion results, of course, from the fact that these groups are not legal political parties because they have no official place on the California election ballot.

PARTY IN LAW

The state's Elections Code defines a legal political party as an "organization which has qualified for participation in any primary election."[2] The Code then specifies three ways that a group can qualify for a place on the primary ballot. First, a political group may qualify if in the last preceding gubernatorial election at least one of its candidates for statewide office received 2 per cent of the total votes cast (132,118 votes as of 1969). Secondly, a group can qualify by enrolling members equal to 1 per cent of the state vote in the preceding gubernatorial election (66,059 registrants as of 1969). Finally, a group may obtain a place on the ballot by circulating petitions and obtaining a number of signatures equal to 10 per cent of the preceding state vote (660,590 signatures as of 1969).

Once a minor party has achieved official status in California, it must maintain a registration of at least one fifteenth of 1 per cent of the total registration in the state if it is to retain a place on the ballot. If it falls

---

[2] Elections Code, sec. 39.

below that in any statewide Statement of Registration (now issued in January of each year, and in April and October of each election year), the Elections Code provides that it "shall be deemed to have been abandoned by the voters, since the expense of printing ballots and holding a primary election would be an unjustifiable expense and burden to the State for so small a group."[3]

Since the Progressive era only eleven political parties have qualified for a place on the California ballot. Besides the Republican and Democratic parties, nine minor parties have been officially recognized for various periods of time; these include the following: Socialist, Liberty, Prohibition, Commonwealth, Independent Progressive, Communist, Townsend, Peace and Freedom, and American Independent. Of these parties, the Prohibition party remained the longest on the ballot, appearing first in 1875. Its membership, however, declined after the repeal of prohibition and although the legislature reduced the number of members needed to continue as a legal party, the Prohibition party lost its official status after the 1962 election.

During the 1968 campaign two new parties obtained a position on the California ballot. Supporters of George Wallace for President successfully gathered over 100,000 registrations to win official recognition for the American Independent party; the Peace and Freedom party qualified by getting slightly more than the legal minimum. The American Independent party gives every indication that it intends to remain as an official party. It has established a statewide organization and announced that it plans to run candidates in coming elections. The future of the Peace and Freedom party is uncertain. When the party met in Sacramento in January 1969, to form a permanent organization, a dispute broke out among its members over the status of the party. According to one newspaper account, "a majority of the 35 or 40 members of the Peace and Freedom state central committee indicated that they liked their organization better as a movement than as a political party."[4]

California's statutory provisions regulating the recognition of parties are fairly stringent when compared with statutes in other states. The fact that so few minor parties have qualified for a place on the ballot bears witness to the strictness of these requirements. A group must have considerable resources to support a drive for recognition. According to one newspaper report, George Wallace's 1968 registration campaign cost anywhere from $500,000 to $2,000,000.[5] The California Supreme Court,

---

[3] Elections Code, sec. 6430.
[4] *Sacramento Bee*, Jan. 1, 1969.
[5] *San Diego Union*, Dec. 28, 1967.

however, has supported the right of the legislature to regulate the ballot in this manner. The Peace and Freedom party challenged these provisions, asking the court to strike them from the Code, but the court dismissed the suit in December, 1967.

Although most experts agree that some regulations are needed to discourage frivolous candidates and keep a reasonably short ballot, overly strict regulations can have undesirable consequences. The great danger is that these requirements make it difficult, if not impossible, for minority opinion to be expressed in elections. The voters' real choice is between one or the other of the major parties, but in a state the size of California there is always a sizable number of voters who feel neither major party adequately represents them. What choice does the ballot offer them? These people might easily become alienated and reject the politics of the ballot box for the politics of the street. Furthermore, any change in the present regulations must be made by the major parties who doubtlessly are not interested in increasing their political competition.

The official organization of the political party is prescribed in the California Elections Code and in party rules and regulations. The Progressives were the architects of the present party organization, completely revamping the party structure in the years 1910–1912. Motivated by their deep distrust of partisanship and parties, the Progressives left nothing to chance; they enacted detailed regulations controlling the structure, procedures, and powers of the party organization. Statutory controls are so complete that the parties have practically no discretion in how they organize themselves or conduct their affairs. The Code even specifies the exact time and place for the meeting of the party convention, and the exact hour the party must issue its platform. Such regulations have tended to create a fairly rigid organization incapable of adjusting and responding to changing conditions.

STATE CONVENTION

The party's official organization consists of four parts: A state convention, a state central committee, central committees in each of the fifty-eight counties, and the national committee representatives. (See Figure 6–1 for a diagram of the official party organization.) There are now only slight differences in the way the two major parties organize, but in 1967 a technical change in the law opened the door for more drastic differences in the future. The legislature reorganized the Elections Code and split the provisions affecting the major parties into parts so that there are now separate sections for the Republican and Democratic

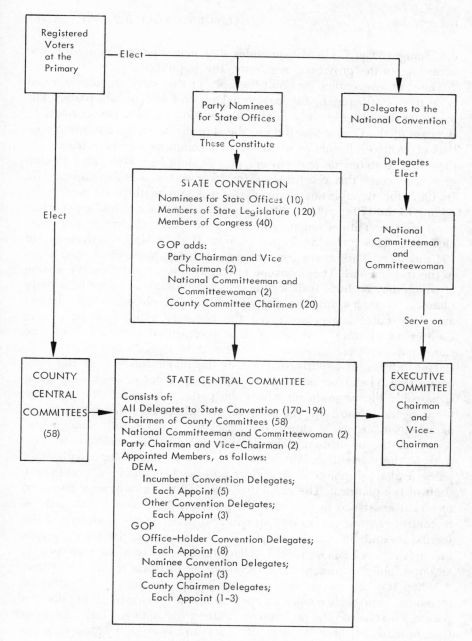

FIGURE 6-1 OFFICIAL PARTY ORGANIZATION

parties. The two major parties can thus make changes in their individual organizations without having to convince each other to go along with

187

the changes. The Code also provides that minor parties must organize according to the provisions regulating the Republican party.

The state convention stands at the apex of the party organization and is, in theory at least, the top policy-making unit of the state party.[6] The major parties differ slightly in the composition of their conventions. In the case of the Democrats, the membership of the state convention consists of elective officials or of the party's nominees for these offices. As there are 10 statewide partisan offices, 120 state legislative, and 40 congressional seats, this constitutes a total convention membership of 170. In 1967, the Republicans changed the make-up of their convention by adding to the 170 members, 20 county chairmen, the national committeeman and committeewoman, and the state party chairman and vice-chairman. This gave the Republicans a slightly larger convention of 194 members. Both party conventions meet only once every two years in the state capital. They convene in August for a short two-day session at which they perform their legally prescribed duties of adopting a party platform and choosing the party's presidential electors. The electors are party faithful who are given the honorary assignment of casting California's electoral vote when their presidential candidate wins the state's popular vote.

The drafting of a party platform is the major function of the state convention. The object of the platform is to spell out in as glowing terms as possible the program on which the party will contest the gubernatorial election. Naturally, the platform lavishly praises the party's record of achievement, while caustically attacking the "woefully inadequate" record of the opposition. Considerable work on the platform is done prior to the convention. The state chairman, in consultation with other party leaders, appoints a special committee to prepare a preliminary draft of the platform. The committee uses interest groups as a source of technical assistance in preparing its program draft, and if the party is in control of state government, it can also draw on the resources of the legislature and the state agencies. The Democrats in 1962 held public hearings in San Francisco and Los Angeles in order to allow more people an opportunity to present their views on the platform to the committee.

When the convention meets, a Resolutions Committee consisting of members from each county is appointed; the chairman is usually the person who chaired the preliminary drafting committee. The Resolutions Committee holds brief hearings at which any interested group may appear and give testimony. Candidates and representatives of the state's major interest groups are the most frequent witnesses. Following the

---

[6] Elections Code, secs. 8000–8028.

hearings, the committee prepares the platform and presents it to the full convention. Usually, the convention passes the platform with little debate, routinely endorsing the work of the Resolutions Committee.

The platform is not a carefully reasoned or judiciously phrased statement of party doctrine; it is a polemic, a campaign document with which the party hopes to win an election. Nonetheless, contrary to popular belief, the platforms of the major parties frequently differ in important ways. They reflect, not in black and white terms but more subtly, the broad policy differences between the major parties. Democratic platforms in recent years have called for more positive government and advocated action in the areas of social welfare, civil rights, business regulation, and natural resources; the Republican platforms, on the other hand, have stressed the need for less government and more private and business initiative, reduced taxes, less economic controls (except in the case of labor), and more efficient administration of existing governmental programs.

There are deep factional divisions within both parties that constantly threaten to tear them apart. It is necessary, therefore, for the sake of party unity to paper over these differences by wording certain issues in general or even ambiguous terms. Sometimes it is easier for the governmental party to handle these policy conflicts because the Governor is able to provide some leadership in the platform deliberations. The minority party, however, often handles the problem by simply omitting the issue from the platform. In 1966, for example, Governor Brown urged the Democratic convention to draft a "strong, vital, and specific" platform, and the convention in deference to his wishes promulgated a long and detailed platform filled with flattering references to the achievements of the Brown administration. In comparison, the 1966 Republican platform was short, lacked specific details, and contained mostly general statements of party principles. Thinking of victory, candidate Reagan and his strategists wanted a broad umbrella under which all the feuding interests of the Republican party could unite.

Despite all the work that goes into the preparation of the platform, its impact on the election is probably quite small. Only a handful of candidates pay much attention to it in the course of their campaigns; in fact, it probably serves more as a target for the opposition than as a program on which the party runs. Most voters never see the platform, much less read it, and if they were to see it, they would probably discount much of what they read as propaganda. Finally, platforms are electioneering documents, and few successful candidates feel an ironbound obligation to fulfill platform promises.

Clearly, the convention is not a very important body in the life of the party. Besides drafting the platform the convention has few other important duties. At one time it performed the important function of nominating statewide officers, but with the enactment of the mandatory direct primary, this duty passed to the rank-and-file voters. Although few politicians advocate the end of the direct primary, in some states the party convention is allowed an official role in nominations through the means of preprimary endorsements. In California, however, preprimary endorsements are not made by the official party but by unofficial party groups. Until recently, there was some legal confusion as to whether the official party did have the right to make preprimary endorsements. Conflicting legal interpretations of the Code by the Attorney General and Legislative Counsel led to this confusion. A few county committees did in fact make preprimary endorsements. The legislature, however, ended this confusion by specifically outlawing in 1963 preprimary endorsements by the state convention, state central committee, or county committees.

Even if the convention did have more important responsibilities, it is doubtful whether it could ever develop into an effective instrument of party policy. Its present composition prevents it from becoming representative of all elements of the party. With the exception of the twenty Republican county chairmen, the conventions of both parties consist exclusively of elective officials or nominees. Not only does the convention represent the elective elements of the party, but it also is dominated by state legislators or nominees, who constitute 70 per cent of the membership of the Democratic convention and 62 per cent of the Republican. Through some distorted logic, the Progressives believed that because the party's candidates ultimately would have the responsibility for enacting the party platform into law, they should dominate the convention. But of course, the platform is never really intended to be a blueprint for governmental policy. Rather it is a campaign document that serves as a rally point for the party. Certainly a broadly representative party group should have responsibility for drafting it. More importantly, however, an unrepresentative convention has an even deeper effect on the California parties because it is the unit on which the state central committee is built.

STATE CENTRAL COMMITTEE

Legal responsibility for the management of party affairs rests with the state central committee.[7] In the "Alice in Wonderland" world of

---

[7] Elections Code, secs. 8200–8262.

California parties, the committee, consisting of approximately 1,000 members, is much larger than the convention. According to the Elections Code its principal duties are to elect a state party chairman, vice-chairman, and executive committee and to conduct the general election campaign for the party in behalf of its candidates. However, because the committee is such a large and unwieldy body, it meets infrequently and leaves the management of the party in the hands of its officers. The Republicans organize their central committee in January following the general election; whereas the Democrats continue to meet immediately following the state convention in August. The Republicans feel this arrangement gives them a certain continuity in party leadership and allows a seasoned and experienced leadership to be responsible for the campaign.

The membership of the state central committee consists of all delegates to the state party convention, the party chairman and vice-chairman, the national committeeman and committeewoman, the chairmen of the fifty-eight county central committees and appointed members. The bulk of the committee consists of appointed members; thus, the state convention delegates who are empowered to make these appointments control the committee. For many years each delegate appointed three committee members, but currently each party has its own complex formula for the selection of appointive members. In 1961, a distinction was made between officeholder delegates to the convention and nominees; the former were allowed to appoint five members to the state committee whereas the latter continued to appoint three. The Republicans went a step further in 1964 and gave officeholder delegates eight appointments to the committee; in addition, they allowed county chairmen delegates for the first time to make appointments to the committee. Depending upon the number of Assembly districts in a county, the chairman can appoint anywhere from one to three committee members.

Ostensibly, these changes were made to broaden the representative make-up of the committee, and in fact, an increase in county committee appointees does permit greater grass root participation in Republican committee affairs. Yet the real effect was to strengthen even further the control of officeholders, particularly legislators, over the party organization. The changes made by the Republicans in 1964 were clearly for these reasons. The Republican organization was threatened at that time by a "right-wing" take-over, engineered by the Goldwater forces led by ex-Senator William Knowland. The Goldwater faction sought to control the party by running candidates for congressional and legislative seats in hopelessly one-party Democratic constituencies. These candidates did not expect to win, but, as party nominees, they could then appoint members of their persuasion to the state central committee.

Although the meetings of the state central committee are infrequent and brief, they are of symbolic importance. Because the convention consists almost entirely of officeseekers, the state committee more clearly represents the whole party. The meetings of the committee are the only occasions when a large and fairly representative gathering of the statewide party takes place; these meetings provide the best opportunity for the party to act as a unit. They serve to rally the party. By praising the party's performance with party oratory and resolutions, they stimulate the faithful, improve their morale, and stir them to greater activity.

Obviously, a state committee of over 1,000 members is unable to guide party affairs on a regular basis. Thus, the Code authorizes the selection of an executive committee to which the state committee may delegate all or a portion of its powers. Both major parties have established executive committees, which meet at the call of the chairman on an average of four times a year to handle party affairs. They consist of over 100 members, chosen to represent all elements of the party, including the extralegal groups.

By far the most significant duty of the state committee is the election of the party officers: A chairman, vice-chairman, woman's chairman, secretary, and treasurer. The chairman is the top executive of the party. His principal task is to advance the fortunes of the party—which in practical terms means having the party candidates win as many offices as possible. He must make sure that the party is in fighting shape, and that it has the necessary organization and resources to succeed. The only qualification the Code sets for the job is that it must alternate between the north and south every biennium; thus the chairman serves for a two-year term and can not succeed himself.

The chairmanship is a part-time job paying no compensation other than expenses. It is not a post to which an aspiring politician points his whole career and, in fact, the backgrounds of past chairmen are quite varied. Because the post demands some prior experience in practical politics, officeholders and especially legislators are natural candidates. Moreover, given the power of legislators in the committee, it is not surprising to find one acting as chairman. In the last two decades, roughly one third of the chairmen of both parties served concurrently as legislators. Other chairmen have come from backgrounds of party service on county committees in the larger urban areas, and some have cut their political eyeteeth on the affairs of the volunteer groups. Lawyers, naturally, are the dominant professional group represented among the chairmen, although the Republicans have frequently turned to businessmen, and one of the most successful of the recent chairmen was a doctor.

Periodically, fierce factional battles are fought over the chairmanship, or to be more precise, over the vice-chairmanship. This is so because the Republicans, and to a lesser degree the Democrats, have adopted the practice of routinely elevating the vice-chairman to the top post. The dispute over the chairmanship can involve a battle between conservatives and liberals, north and south, legislators and other officeholders, state incumbents and representatives of the grass roots, or volunteers and party regulars. If the party is commanded by a dominant faction, which is frequently the case, when it controls the governorship, the chairman may be hand picked by this group. When the factions are more evenly balanced in the party, the chairman may be a compromise choice, a neutral that all factions can agree on.

The appointment of Charles Warren as Democratic chairman and Putnam Livermore as Republican vice-chairman are two recent examples of factional conflict over the post. In August 1966, after a bitter interparty wrangle, Warren defeated Mrs. Carmen Warschaw's bid to become the party's first woman chairman. Having served for two years as southern vice-chairman, Mrs. Warschaw felt she was the logical successor to the retiring northern chairman. She was the choice of the powerful Speaker of the Assembly, Jesse Unruh, the majority of the state legislators, and many of the members of the congressional delegation. Governor Brown gave her a rather lukewarm endorsement. However, most of Governor Brown's supporters as well as the leaders of the California Democratic Council who disagreed with Unruh, backed Warren, a Los Angeles state legislator.

More recently, in January 1969, the Republicans experienced a similar conflict over the vice-chairmanship. The battle was between the self-designated moderates and the conservatives, the former backing Putnam Livermore, Chairman of the San Francicso county committee, and the latter supporting Frank P. Adams, a Piedmont attorney. The moderates represented the pragmatic, less ideological wing of the party that felt that the issues, especially those dividing the party, should be played down. The conservatives, representing primarily the volunteer groups within the party, seemed more concerned to have a leadership that was "right" on the issues. The battle was a classic conflict between the ideologists and those elements of the party interested in winning office.

It is difficult to generalize about the role of the party chairman because in so many ways the man makes the job. There are no well-defined duties and some chairmen are mere time-servers, whereas others seek to provide leadership to the party. Perhaps the first obligation of the chairman is to be an articulate and effective spokesman for the party.

He must be an expert in the art of public relations, a man capable of projecting a favorable image of the party through the mass media. As party spokesman, he acts mainly as a critic of the opposition. He is expected to be a dedicated partisan; a hatchet man who attacks, attacks, attacks. Although he speaks for the party, he does not make party policy. He must be an "image-maker without being a policy-maker."

Secondly, the chairman should be an effective money-raiser. If the state committee is to maintain any kind of permanent organization or engage in any meaningful activity, it must have money to do the job. Raising money can be a difficult task in a state where individuals tend to contribute to candidates instead of to the political party. Although the chairman does not have to be wealthy himself, he must have access to some of the party's more generous contributors. His job is probably made easier if his party controls the governorship, because the Governor can help raise money for the organization. Moreover, any member of the state central committee can be expected to be assessed for contributions. Apparently, the Republicans have always been more successful in raising party money than the Democrats. Reportedly, Governor Reagan is a very effective fund raiser for the state committee.

In addition to raising funds, the chairman should be a talented administrator capable of organizing the party apparatus and directing its activities. Each party maintains permanent central committee headquarters, usually with regional offices in San Francisco and Los Angeles. The size of the headquarter's staff varies widely depending on the resources available to the chairman and whether a campaign is being waged. The Democratic organization fluctuates more than the Republican because the Democrats always have less money to keep their operation going. This is particularly true in the interim between elections. Usually, the staff is headed by an executive secretary or director, a paid employee; the staff includes people responsible for press relations, publicity materials, registration and get-out-the-vote drives, organizational activities, and fund raising. Many of the people are volunteers or part-time employees, particularly during the campaign.

The Republicans run a much more integrated statewide organization than the Democrats; the Republicans do not sharply divide the organization between the north and south. The chairman and vice-chairman, though they come from different regions, direct the affairs of the party statewide. In 1969, the Republicans maintained committee offices in Sacramento, Newport Beach (home of the chairman), San Francisco, Fresno, Los Angeles, Santa Barbara, and San Diego; they employed 27 full-time staff people and had a budget of $980,000 for a two-year period for all committee operations, including candidate contributions. On the other hand, the Democrats have almost two organizations, one in the south and one in the north. The chairman runs the affairs of the party in his area, and the vice-chairman manages the party's business in the other. In 1969, the Democratic committee organization consisted of a skeletal staff in San Francisco (the residence of the chairman) and in Los Angeles.

A few party chairmen stand out and will be remembered for their innovative party leadership. George Miller, Jr., Democratic chairman (1952–1954), must be credited with revitalizing the party and setting it on the road to victory in 1958. He was the individual principally responsible for calling the famous conference at Asilomar in January 1953, which led to the founding of the California Democratic Council. More recently, Dr. Gaylord Parkinson, Republican chairman (1964–1967), proved to be an outstanding leader. He rebuilt the state organization, increased and reorganized the staff of the central committee. He established a field staff consisting of six to twelve people operating in various parts of the state doing organization work but reporting directly to him. He set up the "Cal Plan," a program designed to elect Republicans in crucial legislative districts. He forced all factions of the party to accept the "eleventh commandment." He was a technician interested in rebuilding the party so it could win office; he refused to be drawn into the ideological conflicts within the party.

COUNTY CENTRAL COMMITTEES

The fifty-eight county central committees constitute the lowest layer of the official party organization; they are the only party units with members elected directly by rank and file party members. The legal organization ends abruptly at the county level; there are no precinct, ward, or city party units in California. The Progressives made no provisions for these units because of the existence of the nonpartisan ballot at the local level. Because only state elections would be partisan, they reasoned that the county was the proper unit for the organization of local parties. Considering the Progressives' interest in democratizing the party, it seems odd that they established a party organization lacking locally based units close to the people. Not only do the county committees lack a base in the local community, they also lack any clearly defined relationship to the state central committees. In fact, the county and state central committees originally had no organic connection with each other. The Progressives did not establish a single party hierarchy with the county committees at the bottom and the state committee consisting of delegates from the county at the top. They set up two distinct and unrelated levels of party organization. Not until the 1930s was the law amended to allow chairmen of the county committees to be members of the party state central committee. And it was only in 1964 that the Republicans went one step further by giving twenty county chairmen places in the state party convention. The Elections Code says very little about the relationship of the county committees to the state central committee; it provides only that the county committees "shall have charge of the party campaign under general direction of the state central committee. . . ."

Party voters in the June primary elect county committee members by Supervisor or Assembly districts for two-year terms, except in Los Angeles where the term is four years. Membership on the committee varies from twenty-one to thirty members depending on the size of the county, again with the exception of Los Angeles, which has a committee of 263 members as of 1969. The Code establishes the following formula for committee size: Counties with less than five Assembly districts, a minimum of twenty-one members, with the actual number set in proportion to the party's vote cast in the district; counties with five to twenty Assembly districts, six members elected from each Assembly district; counties with more than twenty Assembly districts, seven members elected from each Assembly district. State legislative nominees and incumbents are ex-officio members of the committee in the county where they reside; the Republicans also have added nominees and incumbents for statewide and congressional offices.[8] Although both parties elect committee members in the June primary, the Democrats organize their committees in July, whereas the Republicans wait until the following January, thus allowing them an experienced committee during the general election.

Despite the intentions of the Progressives, the election of county committee members has not inevitably led to popularly controlled local party organizations. In most counties there is little competition for county committee posts, and where there is a choice it is frequently made on the most capricious criteria. A study of county committee elections in thirty-two counties done by an Assembly committee reported that "candidates exceeded vacancies in only 27 per cent of the district races . . . and in 46 per cent of the total, there were fewer candidates than vacancies."[9] In fact, the competition for county committee seats was so limited that the law was recently changed to provide that if there

---

[8] Elections Code, secs. 8400–8475.
[9] California Assembly, *Interim Committee on Elections and Reapportionment* (Jan. 1963), pp. 9–10.

were fewer candidates than seats the candidates would be declared elected without appearing on the ballot. Why clutter up the ballot with meaningless races? In some of the smaller counties where there appears to be the least interest, membership on the committee is frequently brought up to full complement by appointment rather than election.

Some of the larger counties, however, occasionally have some intense competition for county committee posts. Whether this competition has any meaning is subject to doubt, because the election often takes on the aspect of a lottery. It appears that the contest is not decided on the basis of the candidate's qualifications or on any questions of policy. Rather the selection of committeemen is based on such things as ballot position, incumbency, and occupational designation appearing on the ballot. The Assembly committee reported that in a study of 125 contested races there was a significant correlation between ballot position and winning. Seventy-two per cent of the candidates with number one position on the ballot were elected as opposed to 30 per cent of those in the last position. Moreover, the report noted that less than 10 per cent of the incumbents were defeated. Obviously voters either lack any real interest in these races or find it difficult to make a decision on reasonable criteria. There is little newspaper coverage of these elections, and the candidates do not actually campaign for the jobs. At most they might pay for an ad in a local paper.[10]

True to form the Code briefly and vaguely outlines the duties of the county committee. It merely notes that "the committee shall perform such other duties and services for their political party as seems to be for the benefit of the party." (Another duty, but one seldom exercised, authorizes the committee to appoint a legislative candidate when the duly nominated one dies between the primary and the general election.) What the committees do in actual practice depends on the committee, the time, and the place. In some of the smaller, more rural counties, the committee probably does little more than hold an organizational meeting as required by law at which it elects a chairman and other officers, and adopts a set of rules and bylaws. It may not meet again unless at campaign time it receives an urgent message for aid from a local candidate or directives for action from the state central committee.

Still the picture is not always so dismal. In the larger counties, e.g., San Francisco, Los Angeles, Orange, and San Diego, the committees may operate on a year-round basis. They have local committee offices, sometimes combined with the state central committee office, manned by a small part-time and volunteer staff. On the whole, Republicans

---

[10] *Ibid.*, pp. 10–11.

are better organized than Democrats. These committees engage in a full range of partisan activities, but they naturally are most active during a campaign. They raise funds to support their organization and make modest contributions to candidates; these activities run the whole gamut of cocktail parties, dinners, raffles, and personal solicitation. They set up party headquarters during the campaign, recruit party workers to canvass, hand out political literature, put up signs, and organize get-out-the-vote drives. It is hard to assess how effective all of this is. Obviously a lot of time is wasted on trivial electioneering. At times the organization is bad, and the volunteer labor is not very reliable, but this is probably true of most other volunteer organizations.

Over the years proposals have been made for strengthening the county committees and making them more active in the life of the party. Legislation has been introduced to extend the term of committee members to four years, to establish grass roots units at the precinct level, to provide space in local government buildings for permanent offices, and many other suggestions. None have been enacted. Moreover, many office-holders don't want a stronger party organization; they want only a personal organization consisting of people committed to them rather than to the party.

NATIONAL COMMITTEEMAN

The national committeeman and committeewoman serve as the link between the state and national party organizations. The national committee consists of one man and woman from each state, and in the case of the Republican committee, the state party chairman is made a member if the party carried the state in the previous presidential election or controls the governorship or a majority of the congressional delegation. In California the delegates to the national party convention select the national committeeman and committeewoman, a method that has not always led to the appointment of politically effective people in the office. The national convention delegation is merely an *ad hoc* assortment of partisans usually identified with a particular presidential candidate. If the presidential hopeful loses his bid for the party nomination, the committeeman and committeewoman may not represent any real power in the state party. For example, in 1952 the regular Democratic party delegation was defeated by a Kefauver slate of delegates, and after Stevenson's nomination, the group failed to represent any power in party.

Although the national committeeman and committeewoman are members of the state's official party units, their role in state party affairs may be quite insignificant. During a presidential campaign the national committeeman serves as a liaison between the state and national campaigns. The national committeeman and committeewoman are also consulted on most federal patronage appointments, but this power has become less important as the number of patronage positions has decreased. Because of California's importance in national politics, some committeemen can play an important role in national party affairs. Paul Ziffren, Democratic committeeman in the early 1950s, was instrumental in establishing the Democratic Advisory Council. He was one of the most influential backers of National Chairman Paul Butler.

From this discussion we see that the official parties in California are weak and ineffective organizations, lacking dynamic and forceful leadership, and only marginally meeting their responsibilies. The legal parties suffer from three major weaknesses: (1) they lack an effective statewide organization; (2) they lack significant and meaningful duties; (3) they lack representativeness. Despite what organization charts show neither the Republican nor Democratic parties are hierarchically organized units joined into a single statewide party. Instead they are highly decentralized organizations, consisting of a number of semiautonomous units, only loosely associated with each other. Leadership is not centralized and there is no chain of command from the top of the party to its lowest levels. Normally, in such a highly decentralized structure, power would be at the base of the organization. In California, however, the official party organization does not even exist at the grass roots level. Therefore, where we might expect the most effective and powerful party units to exist, we find no party organization at all. In their zealous efforts to destroy corrupt party machines, the Progressives shattered the party organizations into many pieces.

Not only are California's parties weak organizationally, but they also lack significant functions. Although the Elections Code is long and detailed, it says practically nothing about party activities. The Code establishes a party organization, proceeds for pages detailing all kinds of regulatory controls over the organization, and then fails to provide it with any meaningful duties. The most detailed discussion of duties in the Code is a section that in fact prohibits the party from acting, the section outlawing preprimary endorsements by the party. Whereas the party organization many years ago lost the right to nominate for public office, it is today even denied any participatory role in the endorsing of candidates for nomination. Oddly enough, any group, except the party, may endorse individuals for partisan nominations.

The Code does assign to the party responsibility for the management of campaigns. Yet the party organization actually plays only a nominal role in most candidates' campaigns. The candidates raise most of their own funds, establish their own organizations, and campaign independently of their party. Moreover, both parties are woefully unprepared to carry on any useful political activities at the local level because they lack any organizational roots in the community.

Finally, the political parties are not very representative institutions. The state convention and state central committee are dominated by elective officers who receive their appointments indirectly; in a sense they are all ex-officio because they are not elected to a party office but serve by virtue of their other appointment. Moreover, because there are more legislators than other elective officers the party is in their hands. And though county committee members are elected, they have little connection with or control over the upper echelons of the party organization. In addition, the results of the election system leave some doubt as to how popularly based most county committees really are. The fact that the party organization is not of the people raises the serious problem as to whether it should have the power to act in their name.

We hasten to add, however, that official party units are weak and relatively inefficient organizations just about everywhere.[11] California is not unique in this regard, although the condition may be more advanced. Monolithic statewide organizations, tightly managed by party leaders are becoming more the exception than the rule. Moreover, local party machines have not only declined in number but probably are a passing phenomenon of American life. Perhaps the bureaucratic model of a party organized into a tightly knit hierarchy is not the right one against which to judge contemporary party organizations. This type of organization depends heavily upon some form of material incentives and political parties no longer have many jobs or public benefits to dispense. Possibly the party should be viewed more in terms of a mass association, largely voluntary in character, performing semipublic functions.

Our discussion so far has dealt only with the official party. To stop here would be to neglect an important part of the party organization. We must consider the actual or the working organization which encompasses in California a host of extralegal and unofficial party units. To a large extent these units have developed to fill the vacuum of power created by the ineffective official units.

---

[11] See Austin R. Ranney, "Parties in State Politics," in Herbert Jacob and Kenneth N. Vines, eds., *Politics in the American States* (Boston: Little, Brown and Company, 1965), pp. 61–99, and especially pp. 93–94.

unofficial party organizations: republican assembly and democratic council

In March 1934, a convention of California Republicans concerned about the future of their party was held in Fresno to organize the California Republican Assembly. The state GOP had suffered a serious defeat in the 1932 election, with Democratic presidential candidate Franklin Roosevelt carrying the state, with the Democrats gaining a majority of the state's delegation to Congress for the first time in the century, and with heavy Democratic inroads being made into the Republican majority in the state Assembly. The handwriting seemed to be on the wall as far as the future of the party was concerned. Only an infusion of new blood, new ideas, and new vitality could stem the party's slide into public disfavor.

To its organizers, the California Republican Assembly—the first organization of its kind in the nation—was to be the vehicle for such an infusion. The moving force behind its creation was a group of "Young Turks"—among them, Alameda County District Attorney Earl Warren—who were convinced that the official party leadership was inadequate to the task. Not only was that leadership considered to be "old guard," too conservative, and unresponsive in its approach, but it also had to operate within a legal strait jacket. The CRA—as an unofficial, extralegal, mass membership organization of local assemblies presumably dominated by political progressives—would suffer from neither of these liabilities. Most importantly, it could freely take part in the process of nominating Republicans to public office, endorsing and supporting candidates of its liking, and using its political muscle to head off the entry of other candidates into the party's primaries. Elections Code provisions and tradition prevented the official parties from engaging in these activities.

The CRA proved to be a success. By stimulating the rise of local assemblies it provided a place where party enthusiasts could participate. It sustained and strengthened the progressive element in the party. And it contributed mightily to halting the Republican slide with the voters. Bitter intraparty primary contests that could weaken the party were avoided. Moreover, California's peculiar system of crossfiling made the CRA preprimary maneuvering on behalf of particular GOP candidates especially important. The Democratic party had no machinery like the CRA for narrowing its field of candidates entered in a primary. Whereas several Democrats would fight each other for their party's nomination to a given office, the CRA-endorsed Republican candidate could crossfile in the Democratic primary and walk off with that party's nomination with a plurality of votes.

The Democrats were somewhat slow to profit from the Republican example. There were some localized efforts to create effective preprimary endorsing procedures through unofficial, extralegal party groups as early as 1939 and a countywide structure was created in Los Angeles in 1942. But these organizational efforts were largely on behalf of individual candidates. Finally, in 1953 a statewide Democratic organization—the California Democratic Council—was created to parallel the CRA. It was largely the product of "Young Turks" who wanted a greater role in their party, just as the CRA had been two decades earlier. And like the CRA, the CDC was born in election defeat. After improving their position in the 1930s, the Democrats lost the governorship and their Assembly majority in 1942 and lost their majority on the California delegation to Congress in 1944. In the 1952 presidential race, the Republicans carried the state for the first time since 1928. They dealt a particularly cruel blow to the Democrats when Republican incumbent William Knowland successfully crossfiled in the U.S. senatorial primary of 1952—a dramatic example of the failure of the Democrats to control their own nominations.

The setting for the origin of the CDC differed from that of the CRA in two ways. First, the CDC had the CRA to emulate, and there was little question that the CRA had given the Republicans the kind of new direction and new vitality which the Democrats sorely needed. Second, the Democrats in 1952 had a presidential candidate whose campaign generated so much enthusiasm among a new breed of Democratic activists that it proved to be the catalyst needed for an organizational breakthrough. Although Adlai Stevenson lost the presidential election to Dwight Eisenhower, he awakened to political activity in California hundreds upon hundreds of young, educated, issue-conscious men and women committed to the liberal orthodoxy of New Dealism, internationalism, civil liberties, and social consciousness. These "amateur Democrats," as they have been called, created scores of new neighborhood Democratic clubs, many calling themselves Stevenson clubs, and swelled the membership rolls of clubs already in existence.

Forward-looking party leaders were quick to recognize the potential of the blossoming club movement for needed organizational rejuvenation. The new insurgent chairman of the Democratic state central committee, George Miller, called a general conference of concerned Democrats at Asilomar on the Monterey Peninsula in January 1953. The five hundred party regulars and club people in attendance agreed to the creation of an organization that would re-establish Democratic party control of its own nominations by endorsing candidates prior to the primaries. And they agreed that the local clubs would serve as the basis for such an organization. With the encouragement of Miller and under the leadership of a newcomer to California politics—Alan Cranston—plans for the organization proceeded apace and in November 1953, an organizing convention of some five hundred delegates from the various clubs throughout the state was held in Fresno. A constitution for the California Democratic Council was approved, and statewide officers were elected, with Cranston chosen as president. Each party now had an extralegal, mass membership, statewide organization built upon a broad local base that could engage in the preprimary endorsement of candidates. Each had moved to fill the political vacuum left by ineffective and weak official parties. And, just as the CRA seemed to breathe new life into the GOP in the 1930s and 1940s, the development of the CDC coincided with Democratic revival at the polls in the late 1950s and 1960s.[12]

ORGANIZATION

The CRA and CDC have quite similar organizational structures. The basic units are local Republican Assemblies and Democratic clubs. These are usually comprised of from twenty to one hundred members, are open to any party member willing to pay the nominal dues required for membership, hold regular meetings, and support only candidates of their party for public office. These local units send representatives to district assemblies or councils in proportion to their membership. The district organizations coordinate the campaign activities of the local units, endorse or call conventions to endorse candidates for public office within their jurisdiction, and select members to serve on a state CRA or CDC Board of Directors. At the top of the CDC and CRA structures are their annual state conventions, which are close approximations of national party conventions. The delegates are treated to the impassioned oratory of a series of party notables, participate in credential fights, consider a host of policy statements on a variety of political issues, engage in campaigning for candidates running for organization office or seeking the organization's endorsement in forthcoming primaries, and generally

---

[12] For a lucid account of the early development of the CDC see Francis Carney, *The Rise of the Democratic Clubs in California,* Eagleton Foundation Case Study in Practical Politics (New York: Henry Holt, 1958).

partake in the wheeling and dealing and the late night high jinks characteristic of political conventions everywhere. Most of the delegates and
alternates are representatives of the local clubs or assemblies, which
suggests that the different levels of the unofficial organizations are integrated in a way in which the different levels of the official party are
not. Each club or assembly sends delegates in proportion to its membership. In even-numbered years, the convention is primarily concerned
with endorsing candidates for statewide public office. In odd-numbered
years it selects its own officers and considers current issues of public
policy. CDC conventions have been particularly well attended, reflecting
the fact its membership has been substantially larger than that of the
CRA.[13]

It would be an oversimplification to see the unofficial and official party
groups as organizationally discrete and hostilely confronting each other
across a structural chasm. The two organizational components of each
party have been inextricably intertwined and have worked in close
cooperation. Many of the same persons are active in both segments.
The Democratic state chairman was instrumental in the formation of
the CDC and the official party was quite cooperative in its development. For example, the Los Angeles County Democratic central committee once had a full-time employee assigned the task of organizing
new clubs. Until recently, the state central committee and the CDC in
the northern part of the state shared the same offices and facilities in
San Francisco. Moreover, local assemblies and clubs are chartered by
the county central committee in their area and the state CDC and CRA
recognizes only clubs that are so chartered. The state Elections Code
requires that assemblies and clubs receive permission from official party
committees to solicit money from the public for political campaigns. As
a rule, such permission is freely given. Persons holding various official
party positions and the party's public officeholders are automatically
CRA or CDC members and often appear at its club or district-level
meetings and state conventions. The unofficial party organizations were
not created to replace the official machinery but to assume a role that
official parties had been unable to assume.

One major organizational difference between the CDC and CRA has

---

[13] CDC conventions are usually attended by well over one thousand delegates and
a similar number of alternates. Conventions held in nonelection years are designated
as Issues Conferences and provide the best vehicle for the organization to establish
its ideological identity. They are not poorly attended affairs. In 1963, for example,
there were close to 6,000 at the Bakersfield convention, of whom 2,300 were registered delegates. CRA conventions normally have been attended by 500–700
delegates.

been the method used to endorse primary candidates. In terms of endorsements for statewide office, the president of the CRA names a number of prominent members of the organization to serve on a Candidates and Fact Finding Committee. When there are several statewide offices to be contested in the election, the committee divides itself into subcommittees assigned to each office. These subcommittees (or the full committee when there are no subcommittees) interview, and review the backgrounds of, those seeking the organization's endorsement. Public opinion is normally sounded out, as well as the sentiments of various leadership groups within the party. The subcommittee will then recommend one candidate to the full committee and the full committee will, in turn, recommend candidates for each office to the convention for its formal endorsement. A similar procedure for the screening of candidates is carried out at the district level. Candidates and Fact Finding Committees may actually seek out qualified candidates if none come forward of their own volition.

Usually, the candidate for an office recommended by the subcommittee is approved by the full committee and then by the convention. There have been exceptions, however. In 1950, for example, a subcommittee on U.S. Senate candidates recommended that the CRA endorse Judge Frederick Houser over young Congressman Richard Nixon, but the full committee reversed the decision by a 13–12 vote and the convention proceeded to endorse Nixon. In 1964, the subcommittee on the party's presidential nomination recommended the endorsement of Barry Goldwater over Nelson Rockefeller. The full committee overruled the subcommittee by proposing that the convention make no endorsement in the California presidential primary. The convention, however, endorsed Goldwater. In 1966, the subcommittee on gubernatorial candidates endorsed William Penn Patrick, right-wing cosmetics manufacturer, over Ronald Reagan, by a 6–2 vote. But the full committee overturned the decision and their recommendation was sustained on the floor of the convention. Normally, however, subcommittee and committee decisions are respected. Leonard Rowe concludes that "the single most important feature of the CRA endorsing procedure is the Candidates Fact Finding Committees. Being small, they can perform the candidate-sifting or promoting function more efficiently than a large body. The price for this efficiency is, however, the concentration of the endorsement decision in a relatively few hands. In this respect the CRA differs radically—at least from a structural standpoint—from the California Democratic Council."[14]

---

[14] *Preprimary Endorsements in California Politics* (Berkeley: Bureau of Public Administration, University of California, 1961), pp. 41–42.

The Democrats appoint no screening committees and make no formal evaluation of the candidates prior to their endorsing conventions. Rather they pursue the practice followed by the national conventions of the two parties. Appeals for the CDC endorsement are made directly to the convention delegates—in speeches to the convention, meetings with district caucuses, and the buttonholing of individual delegates. A similar procedure is followed at the local level, although there have been "Candidate Development Committees" appointed in some areas to seek out possible candidates.

FUNCTIONS: PRIMARY ENDORSEMENTS

Historically, the chief function of the two major unofficial party organizations in California has been to endorse candidates for party nomination prior to the primaries. This was especially important under crossfiling for reasons that should be clear.

The CRA came upon their preprimary endorsing function rather slowly. The organizing convention in 1934 agreed to forego the endorsement of candidates in that year's GOP primary. In 1936 they voted to support a presidential primary slate headed by favorite son Earl Warren, then state party chairman, over one headed by conservative Governor Frank Merriam and pledged to Alfred Landon, the eventual nominee of the party. The decision reflected the progressive inclination of the organization and the Warren slate went on to win the primary. In 1938 the CRA convention elected to avoid a bitter clash in its ranks by agreeing to endorse neither Frank Merriam, seeking re-election as Governor, nor his primary opponent. In 1940 Senator Hiram Johnson received an endorsement for renomination to his Senate seat, but he had no opposition. Thus, it was not until 1942 that the CRA went into state-level preprimary endorsements in a big way. They endorsed candidates for all but one statewide office and against opposition in each case. All CRA-endorsed candidates won nomination in the primary and went on to win the general election in November. The one office for which the CRA made no endorsement—Attorney General—was won by the Democratic candidate in the general election.

The CDC, for its part, wasted no time in embarking on a preprimary endorsement course, endorsing a full slate of candidates in the 1954 Democratic primary at its first regular convention. Party leaders generally rejoiced over the ensuing success. For the first time since the beginning of crossfiling, no primary contest between Democratic candidates for any statewide office occurred except for Governor, where only one insignificant candidate challenged the CDC candidate, and no Republican candidate successfully crossfiled. In fact, the CDC-endorsed candidate for Attorney General entered and won the Republican primary as well as his own. Although the Republicans won election to all but one state-wide office in November, the Democrats had at least controlled their own primary and party unity had been achieved. How much of this success was attributable to the CDC endorsing procedure and how much to the change in the crossfiling law, which for the first time saw a candidate's party affiliation designated on the election ballot, is problematical.

For many years the preprimary endorsement function of the CRA and CDC was pursued with considerable success. Often a candidate who sought the endorsement would withdraw his candidacy if it was not forthcoming. The endorsed candidate would then have an open field in the primary—exactly what the preprimary endorsement procedure was designed to achieve. When Nixon defeated Houser for the 1950 CRA senatorial endorsement, Houser withdrew from the primary race. At the first CDC endorsing convention, the Reverend Laurence Cross, Berkeley Mayor, was defeated by Richard Graves in his bid for the organization's gubernatorial endorsement and Cross immediately withdrew his candidacy. In 1964, after the abolition of crossfiling made it less important that a party avoid multiple candidacies in its primary, James Roosevelt withdrew from the U.S. Senate primary race once the CDC endorsed Alan Cranston.

Moreover, most serious candidates for statewide office have shown their respect for the CRA or CDC by seeking their endorsement. There have been a few exceptions, but usually their fate has not been good. In 1956 Sam Yorty concluded that he could not receive the CDC sena-torial endorsement as he had two years earlier and withdrew his name from convention consideration. The CDC convention, he told the dele-gates, "is packed, stacked, rigged, and wired" and he intended to take his case directly to the primary voters. The endorsed candidate, Los Angeles state Senator Richard Richards, went on to defeat Yorty by a three-to-one margin in the June Democratic primary. Two years later San Francisco state Senator Robert McCarthy did not seek CDC endorse-ment of his candidacy for Attorney General, condemning "the phony so-called endorsing antics of the hot rod set of the Democratic party" as violating the spirit of the primary system. But like Yorty before him, the challenge failed and the CDC-endorsed candidate, Los Angeles Superior Court Judge Stanley Mosk, carried the Democratic June pri-mary. In 1958 Congressman Pat Hillings did not officially seek the CRA endorsement before running against CRA-endorsed Casper Weinberger for the Republican nomination for Attorney General. Hillings won the primary but lost the general election to the Democratic candidate.

Actually, whenever a CRA or CDC endorsement failed to forestall a primary contest, it was almost always the case that the endorsed candidate defeated his challenger. The first primary loss for a CRA-endorsed candidate for statewide office did not occur until 1954, when its endorsee for the Republican nomination to Lieutenant Governor, James Silliman, Speaker of the Assembly, was easily defeated by Harold Powers, President pro tempore of the state Senate. The CDC's first loss was in 1964, when Pierre Salinger entered the U.S. Senate race after the CDC endorsing convention and defeated the endorsed candidate, Alan Cranston.

Salinger's 1964 primary victory could not help but raise doubts about the effectiveness of preprimary endorsements, especially by the CDC. Perhaps the earlier success of CDC-endorsed candidates for statewide office was not so much because of the political clout that the organization brought to bear on behalf of its endorsees, but because of the wisdom of convention delegates in endorsing candidates who were so effective that they could have won with or without that endorsement. Often the CRA or CDC endorsement has gone to incumbents, who probably would have won their primary in any event. In 1966 the CDC endorsed William Bennett over an incumbent Democrat, Attorney General Thomas Lynch. Lynch overwhelmingly defeated Bennett in the primary.

Moreover, Salinger's victory seemed to usher in a new and unhappy era for CDC endorsements. Several candidates who have sought but not received such endorsement decided to carry on a primary campaign anyway. They have not all returned empty handed. In 1966, for example, the CDC-endorsed candidate for Secretary of State was defeated, as was Bennett in his race against Lynch. In 1968 Alan Cranston—out of favor with the organization that was largely his creation—defeated a CDC-endorsed candidate for the U.S. senatorial nomination. And in the 1968 presidential primary campaign, the CDC helped form, endorsed, and vigorously supported the delegation slate pledged to Eugene McCarthy, only to have that slate defeated in a close contest by a late entry pledged to Robert Kennedy. As for the CRA, although its endorsed candidate in the 1966 gubernatorial primary, Ronald Reagan, defeated George Christopher, it was not successful with all of its other endorsed candidates for statewide office.[15]

---

[15] We know little about the record of local endorsing councils. James Wilson provides data on Democratic legislative and congressional primaries in 1960. He reports that there were thirty-four contests for the party's nomination at this level in which no incumbent was running. "Of these thirty-four open races," he concluded, "CDC made endorsements in thirty and their candidates won in twenty-two." Moreover, all but three of the twenty-two were defeated by their Republican opponents in the November general election, whereas four of the twelve non-CDC Democratic primary winners defeated their Republican opponents. *The Amateur Democrat* (Chicago: University of Chicago Press, 1962), pp. 324–325.

In recent years, the question has frequently been raised as to whether a CDC endorsement is really an asset to a candidate at all. Has the organization been so discredited that the endorsement is actually a liability? In mid-1966 California (Field) Poll interviewers asked a state-wide sample of California voters what their reaction would be, "If a Democratic candidate for Governor were endorsed by the CDC?" The following results were obtained

	Democrats (Per Cent)	Republicans (Per Cent)	All Voters (Per Cent)
Would be more likely to vote for him	35	10	25
Would be less likely to vote for him	5	25	13
Would make no difference	45	52	47
Don't know	15	13	15

These figures reveal that among Democrats a CDC endorsement was still an asset in 1966, whereas it was a liability among Republican voters; helpful in the primary election, it might be harmful in the general election.

OTHER FUNCTIONS

California's major unofficial party organizations do more than endorse candidates in primaries. To a great extent, they have been the work horses of their respective parties. The responsibility for much of the nitty-gritty work of politics—the door-to-door canvassing, the solicitation of small money contributions, the addressing of envelopes, the telephoning, the typing of letters—has been assumed by local CRA assemblies and CDC clubs. In many communities in California, a newcomer who wishes to come to the aid of his party could only be directed to his local CDC or CRA unit. A seeker of public office has normally been less interested in what a CRA or CDC endorsement might mean in terms of publicity or of winning the votes of the organizational members as in what it may mean in terms of the contribution of labor and effort by local activists on his behalf.

There are also social functions served by the two organizations. The social interaction and conviviality provided in many local assemblies and clubs can be very satisfying for the participant. Through participation in the CDC, wrote Seyom Brown, "Fun Can Be Politics." He concluded that "the primary motive power behind the California Democratic clubs

is social not political."[16] Along a similar vein, Bernard Crick attributed
the success of the Democratic club movement to "the quest for community and recognition amid the loneliness and rootlessness of the
suburbs."[17]

Of course, old-fashioned political machines also fulfill campaign work-
horse and social functions. But one of the features of the CRA and CDC
that most distinguishes them from such machines has been their function as forums for the discussion of issues of public policy. The Democratic club movement, in particular, has been able to sustain itself by
providing an opportunity to its members to express themselves on such
policy issues, to pass resolutions, to hear panel discussions, and to engage
in heated debate on timely subjects, often of a global variety. Many club
people are willing to serve their party leaders through campaign work
and effort but also expect that between campaigns those leaders will
listen and respond to their ideas; if they are to inform the voters of the
principles of their party they want a voice in framing and developing
those principles.

In many states, grass roots party activists have been motivated by a
desire to attain or retain an appointed government position; they expect
to have their campaign work rewarded in a very material way.[18] Under
such circumstances, these activists are likely to confine themselves to
working toward election victory and to avoid taking controversial stands
on issues. In California, however, there are few material rewards for
grass roots activity. For all intents and purposes, patronage is nonexistent
in the state: With nonpartisanship at the local level and a long tradition
of civil service reform at all levels, few jobs are available to the faithful.[19]

---

16 "Fun Can Be Politics," *The Reporter*, XXI (Nov. 12, 1959), pp. 27–28.

17 "California's Democratic Clubs: A Revolt in the Suburbs," *The Reporter*,
XVIII (May 31, 1956), pp. 35–39.

18 Sonya Forthal points out, for example, that 80 per cent of the 1950 ward
committeemen she interviewed for a study of local party activists derived their
livelihood from patronage positions. (*Cogwheels of Democracy*. [New York: William-
Frederick, 1946], pp. 36–41.) In a study of political activity in King County, Washington, Hugh Bone found that approximately one eighth of local party leaders holding
party positions at the ward or precinct levels held patronage appointments in
government. (*Grassroots Party Leadership* [Seattle: University of Washington, 1952],
mimeo.) The authors of *Voting* emphasize the importance of patronage expectations
among those engaged in campaign work during a presidential campaign in Elmira,
New York. For example, among the Republican party workers interviewed for the
study, fully a third held local government posts whereas "many of the others had patronage incentives of one kind or another." (Bernard Berelson et al., *Voting* [Chicago:
University of Chicago Press, 1952], p. 164.)

19 The Governor of California has only about 600 partisan appointments to make,
a sharp contrast to the situation in such states as Pennsylvania, where the Governor
has had in the neighborhood of 40,000 partisan appointments, and Illinois where

Those active in California's unofficial grass roots parties are thus less likely to be victory-oriented and more likely to be issue-oriented than party activists elsewhere.

Generally, one of the most important functions of the CRA and CDC has been that they have served to enlarge the Californian's opportunity for meaningful political participation on a continuing basis. Everyone is invited to become a member and thousands have—whether to contribute their time and energy out of a sense of commitment to their political party, or to enjoy the social interaction which organizational participation provides, or to listen and contribute to a public dialogue on political issues. In an age of increasingly large government, impersonal bureaucracies, specialized competencies, and techniques of mass persuasion, the CRA and CDC have made no small contribution to the democratic process.

PROBLEMS

In recent years the two major unofficial party organizations in California have fallen into decline. There has always been some opposition to preprimary endorsements on the grounds that, by allowing a small group of party activists responsible to no one to reduce the alternatives open to the voters, the spirit of the primary system is violated. A *Sacramento Bee* editorial put the argument this way:

> [Preprimary endorsements] never had any usefulness and they never had any justification. . . . The purpose of the primary system is to give party members a free and open choice of candidates. For would-be bosses to try to insure their candidate's nomination by intimidating others into staying out of a race is a perversion of the primary system. It does not serve the state or the party.[20]

Now with crossfiling gone, and with its disappearance the danger of losing a nomination to a candidate of another party also gone, the opposition to preprimary endorsements by the unofficial party organizations has grown. Politicians interested in holding office have been more and more willing to challenge endorsed candidates.

---

some 14,000 jobs have been available to the Governor for his disposal. (See James Wilson, "Politics and Reform in American Cities," in *American Government Annual,* 1962–1963, [New York: Holt, Rinehart & Winston, Inc., 1962], p. 37; and James Reichley, *The Art of Government* [New York: Fund for the Republic, 1959], p. 101n.)

[20] December 10, 1964.

Moreover, candidates have found that the contributions which the unofficial party organizations are equipped to make in their election campaigns have been reduced in importance. For one thing, both the CRA and CDC have suffered significant membership losses—their pool of available manpower resources has declined. Additionally, much of the work previously done by busy CRA and CDC volunteers can now be done by other means. Candidates can personally reach into the voters' homes via television and need not depend as much on door-to-door canvassers. Letters to every voter in a district or in the state can be printed with individualized salutations, signed, placed in an envelope, sealed, stamped, and addressed completely by machine. Further, the legislature has changed the election code to reduce the importance of CRA and CDC endorsements. In the past, voters receiving literature indicating the names of endorsed candidates were often under the impression that the CRA and CDC were the official organizations of their respective parties. In 1963 a bill authored by Jess Unruh was signed into law which provided that any endorsement of a candidate at a primary election must carry a disclaimer indicating that the endorsement is unofficial. Candidates claiming these endorsements in campaign literature and advertisements were also required to include such disclaimers.

The "truth in endorsements" bill was just one indication of the growing antagonism between party leaders holding elective public office (the "government party") and the CRA and CDC. For many government party members, the unofficial party organizations are too little concerned with winning elections for their party—the whole reason for their creation—and too much concerned with expressing themselves on public policy issues and going on ideological binges, regardless of the impact on the party's election chances. Some candidates for public office—particularly incumbents, who often feel they can win re-election on their own—argue that what they gain in votes from club or assembly campaign activities they more than lose because of the embarrassing issue positions taken by these organizations.

Government party members—particularly Democrats—complain that the CDC and CRA are ideologically too extreme or radical for their constituents. The CDC has always been a forum for what James Wilson calls "liberals of the left." Its annual conventions have adopted resolutions favoring U.S. trade with Communist China; the right of public school teachers to strike; the abolition of the House Un-American Activities Committee; the removal of State Department restrictions on travel by American citizens; abolition of capital punishment; legalization of abortions where "there is substantial risk of grave impairment of the physical and mental health of the mother or child"; a two-dollar an hour minimum wage; extension of unemployment insurance for agricultural workers; application of child labor laws to agriculture; stepped up civil rights enforcement by the Department of Justice; the Rumford Fair Housing Law; and so on. They have been consistently opposed to America's military intervention in Vietnam.

Many Democratic officeholders or officeseekers have felt compelled to dissociate themselves in one way or another from the organization because of its ideological orientation. Some have adopted a version of Jess Unruh's 1964 disclaimer that "I don't belong to that organization. It doesn't represent my views." Governor Brown, in 1966, countered a Republican attack on him for accepting the CDC endorsement by pointing out that acceptance did not necessarily mean he was embracing every CDC policy position. At times, the dissociation has been more elaborate. In 1960 state Senator Fred Farr was attacked by his Republican opponent with an advertisement in the major Monterey area newspaper pointing out that he had been a delegate to that year's CDC convention and linking him with the stand taken by the CDC on six specific issues. Farr responded with a press release stating,

> I was not present when the resolutions were adopted and had no part in them. I went there primarily to hear candidates. As a matter of fact, the resolutions were adopted by a small group after most of the delegates had left the hall.

At other times government party members have chosen to intervene rather than dissociate, to "fight rather than switch." Officeholders have often made impassioned pleas to CDC conventions for moderation in policy statements and they have frequently been successful. The most dramatic case of intervention, however, came in 1965–1966. Simon Casady had been elected CDC president early in 1965, in large part because of the support of Alan Cranston, then state Controller, and party leaders close to Governor Brown. In the months that followed Casady became increasingly outspoken in his criticism of the national administration's Vietnam policy. In September 1965, Brown called for Casady's resignation, an unprecedented move that was followed by a similar demand by the executive committee of the Democratic state central committee. It was not Casady's views on Vietnam that prompted his demand, said Brown, but the way in which Casady was using his office to wage a "statewide crusade" against President Johnson and the "contemptuous manner" in which he had engaged in "ill-considered and intemperate attacks" on a Democratic President, Democratic congressmen from California, and Democratic state officials.

Casady refused to resign. In November, twenty-nine of forty-seven members of the CDC Board of Directors voted to impeach Casady, falling short of the required two-thirds vote.[21] Brown, Cranston, and other officeholders running for re-election the following November announced they would boycott the 1966 endorsing convention if Casady was not ousted. At the February 1966 state CDC convention Casady asked the delegates for a vote of confidence, arguing that "the real issue in this controversy . . . is the issue of independence. Is CDC an independent volunteer political organization controlled from below by its membership? Or is it a captive army of camp followers and favor seekers controlled from above by the Democratic hierarchy of elected officeholders." The delegates failed to give Casady his vote of confidence and he resigned.

Following the 1966 general election, the CDC resumed its attack on the Vietnam policy of the national Democratic administration. At its 1967 convention, the delegates voted to challenge President Johnson with a "peace slate" entered in the June 1968 presidential primary if the war was not soon ended. At a special convention in September of 1967 the CDC formalized its intention to proceed with an anti-LBJ delegation slate—the first formal move in the nation to challenge the President's assumed bid for re-election within the structure of the Democratic party. Shortly thereafter Senator Eugene McCarthy announced his presidential candidacy and the "peace slate" idea of the CDC now had a candidate to give it real meaning. The organization's efforts on behalf of McCarthy's candidacy in California fell short of the mark. A slate committed to Robert Kennedy carried the state's presidential primary.

The decision to challenge Johnson and support McCarthy cost the CDC dearly. Nearly one half of the members of the Board of Directors and four of seven Vice-Presidents resigned; many clubs disaffiliated, some moving into new unofficial organizations; membership dropped; county committees withdrew their affiliation. The Democratic National Committeeman from California, Eugene Wyman, called on the CDC to

---

21 The fifteen-page bill of particulars submitted by Casady's opponents suggests that the ouster attempt was motivated by more than the President's stand on Vietnam. It charged Casady with failing to accept responsibility for strengthening the council organizationally, politically, and financially, with refusing to acknowledge the "policy-making role of the Board of Directors," with projecting "to the public an erroneous image of the council," by his "personal attacks," with attempting "to substitute his own narrow concept of the council's function for that established by the constitution and bylaws," and with "alienating the council from large segments of the Democratic party (including, among others, CDC-endorsed candidates and CDC-supported officeholders)."

disband on the grounds that "it has reached a point where now it is more harmful to the Democratic party than it can ever be good for the party." Cranston characterized the organization that was largely his creation "a sorry mess" and of "no service to the party." Others charged it with being totally committed to a single issue and no longer a forum for free debate and lively discussion.

How the events of the past four years will affect the future of the CDC is problematical. Issue-oriented organizations are always likely to have greater difficulty when their own political kin are making public policy. With the Republicans now in power in Sacramento and in the nation's capital, the CDC's combative and liberal temper may once again prove useful in revitalizing the party. At present, however, many Democratic officeholders still view it with some measure of hostility for its devil-may-care ideological escapades.

As for the CRA, in recent years it too has found a place on the ideological fringe of its party. Although the CDC has been charged with being more liberal than rank-and-file Democrats, the CRA has now been charged with being more conservative than rank-and-file Republicans. The CRA switch from its traditional moderate Republicanism to conservative Republicanism occurred at its 1964 convention. There, Barry Goldwater's presidential candidacy was endorsed over the opposition of supporters of Nelson Rockefeller. Retiring CRA president William Nelligan angrily announced that "the fanatics of the Birch variety have fastened their fangs on the Republican party's flank and are hanging on like grim death. Nobody invited these oddballs into our ranks. They muscled their way in." And Caspar Weinberger called the conservative takeover a "retreat into madness." In 1966 the CRA president acknowledged that five of sixteen CRA executive committee members were John Birch Society members.

Since 1964, CRA conventions have passed resolutions calling for "total victory" in Vietnam and an escalation of the bombing in North Vietnam; repeal of the Rumford Act; an end to the 160-acre limitation on farms that receive irrigation water from federal reclamation projects; closing of the state printing plant (which prints textbooks and other state materials) and giving the responsibility to private enterprise; passage of the so-called "Liberty Amendment" to abolish federal personal income, estate, and gift taxes; rejection of the nuclear nonproliferation treaty; ending cultural exchanges with communist countries; restoring the bracero farm labor program; repeal of the 1968 federal gun control law; and so on.

In 1967 Governor Reagan addressed the annual CRA convention in

terms similar to those frequently used by officeholders of either party
when addressing their respective unofficial party organizations:

> It is the duty and responsibility of volunteer Republican organizations not
> to further divide but to lead the way to unity. It is not your duty, responsi-
> bility, or privilege to tear down, or attempt to destroy others in the tent
> [of the Republican party]. We must always remain in a position that will
> let us effectively support candidates chosen by the entire party in the
> primary. To do less is a disservice to the party, and, more importantly, to
> the cause in which we believe.

The Governor's admonition went unheeded by his listeners. On the next
day, the CRA embarked on a course similar to that being pursued at the
same time by the CDC in its "dump-Johnson" campaign. The convention
delegates agreed that they would seek to unseat incumbent U.S. Senator
Thomas Kuchel—a Republican of moderate leanings, independent temperament, considerable seniority, and a post as Assistant Minority Leader
in the Senate—by finding a suitable candidate to run against him in the
1968 primary. Here was an unofficial party organization not merely
embarrassing an officeholder through extremist policy positions but
actually trying to destroy politically one of the state's most effective Republican vote-getters. Kuchel, of course, was eventually defeated by
CRA-endorsed Max Rafferty in the senatorial primary. The seat that
doubtlessly would have remained in Republican hands had Kuchel been
renominated, was subsequently taken by Democrat Alan Cranston, who
handily defeated Rafferty in the 1968 November election. Said Republican Assemblyman William Bagley in response to the CRA decision at its
1967 convention: the persons responsible are "political piranhas who
feast upon their own and whose appetites are satiated only by defeat
of those Republicans with whom they disagree. [They are] the same
spoilers who wrecked Dick Nixon's campaign for Governor in 1962
because he was 'too liberal'. . . . It is astonishing to me that this wrecking
crew can purport to be public spokesmen for the Republican party."
Assembly Republican leader Robert Monagan, in opposing the "dump-
Kuchel" move, argued prophetically that "the price of eating one's own
is the indigestion of defeat."

Given the ideological convulsions of the CDC and CRA and their
repeated brushes with their respective government parties, it is hardly
surprising that neither organization has been able to contain the divisions
within its midst. Competing but smaller mass membership organizations
largely comprised of strays from the CRA and CDC have been formed.
The United Republicans of California (UROC) was chartered in 1963.

It was organized by a group of conservatives who had just failed in an attempt to assume control of the CRA and had given that organization up as hopelessly too liberal. They wanted a vehicle to serve on behalf of Barry Goldwater's forthcoming presidential candidacy, and a year after its formation UROC followed the CRA endorsement of Goldwater with one of their own. Just prior to the 1966 UROC convention, its executive secretary, Rus Walton, resigned, expressing dismay over growing John Birch Society influence in the organization and saying—in a familiar theme—"I'm sorry for these people. They're the type who would prefer to go down to defeat with their flags flying than to win an election in this state." Like the CRA, UROC endorsed Reagan in 1966 and Rafferty in 1968. At one time or another it has come out for a ban on all trade with communist countries, tuition at California's institutions of higher education, U.S. withdrawal from the United Nations, an end to trade restrictions with Rhodesia, making social security voluntary, and repeal of the Rumford Act.

The newest unofficial Republican group of note was formed in 1964— the California Republican League. Meant to be a haven for party moderates, the founders of the CRL were Rockefeller supporters in the 1964 presidential primary and most were former CRA members swept aside when that organization endorsed Goldwater earlier in the year. Both the CRA and UROC, it was felt, were out of step with "mainstream" Republicanism. As the first CRL president, William Gray, said, "The past few years the groups which have served as spokesmen for the GOP have represented too narrow a view. It is time that voice and direction be given to broadly-based Republican positions." In view of Rockefeller's defeat in the 1964 primary, the defeat of CRL-endorsee George Christopher in the 1966 gubernatorial primary, and the defeat of CRL-endorsee Thomas Kuchel in the 1968 senatorial primary, it is difficult to endorse the CRL claim that it represents "mainstream" Republicanism—at least not in California. Unlike the CRA and UROC, the CRL explicitly excludes John Birch Society members from its rolls. It has taken fairly strong positions on civil rights, in defense of the Supreme Court, and in opposition to the Liberty Amendment.

As for the Democrats, the fragmentation of the CDC has been less dramatic than that of the CRA. In 1964 the Democratic Volunteers Committee was formed. Comprised largely of CDC dropouts and clubs that had never been affiliated with the CDC—mostly in southern California —the DVC was primarily a product of the initiative of Jesse Unruh. Unlike the other organizations discussed thus far, it makes no preprimary endorsements and is not interested in establishing a distinctive ideological identity. Defecting CDC members have also formed regional Democratic

Councils in northern, central, and southern California. These councils consist of local clubs in each area whose members broke with CDC because of its anti-Vietnam stand. Intending to avoid global issues and to concentrate on local and regional issues, the main objective of these units, like that of the DVC, is to elect Democratic nominees.

OTHER UNOFFICIAL PARTY ORGANIZATIONS

The CRA and CDC, and most of the groups formed as a result of the centrifugal forces within the two original organizations, share certain common characteristics. They are open membership groups, take positions on issues, and endorse candidates in party primaries. There are a number of less significant organizations which do not share these characteristics. Most of them limit their membership to certain kinds of people. The Republican Associates of California, established in southern California in 1953, and the Republican Alliance, established in northern California in 1959, are high-dues organizations primarily designed for businessmen. Neither group is concerned with stating positions on issues of public policy. And neither group makes preprimary endorsements. They serve principally to provide financial and research assistance to the Republican party and its candidates. The Committee for California was organized in 1967 as an elite group by Democrats prominent in the academic, business, and legal professions and interested in seeking out and promoting new and attractive candidates for high office.

Some groups are limited to young people. The Young Democrats and Young Republicans are the most prominent of these. Like some of the other unofficial organizations, these tend to take somewhat radical positions on issues, regularly embarrass their elders, and occasionally are plagued with vigorous ideological conflicts. Many of today's public officeholders served their political apprenticeship in the YRs or YDs. Additionally, there have been such groups as Teenage Republicans (TARS) and the California College Republicans (created in 1963 as a more moderate antidote to the YRs but rejoining the YRs in 1969).

The California Federation of Republican Women is currently the largest unofficial party organization in the state, a position it has achieved even though its bylaws prohibit preprimary endorsements. Organized at the community level, these spirited ladies contribute generously of their time, money, and energy to party efforts. In 1964, for example, it was estimated that over 42,000 of its members were involved in campaign tasks for an average of 32 hours a week, i.e., they contributed 1,350,000 woman-hours of campaign work to the party's candidates. Additionally, they raised and spent almost $400,000 during the campaign.[22] Like some of the other organizations, the CFRW has been involved in heated liberal-conservative clashes in recent years.

california party elites

"Every fight consists of two parts: (1) the few who are actively engaged at the center, and (2) the audience that is irresistibly attracted to the scene."[23] California's voters comprise the audience to the continuing battle between the state's political parties, an audience with the unusual power of determining the outcome of every round in that battle. Among the voters, however, is a small minority in the center of the arena of conflict who are "actively engaged" in partisan politics. This minority is California's political elite. Who are these people? What are they like? In what ways do Republican leaders differ from Democratic leaders? How homogeneous is each party's elite? The following discussion of these questions is based on an analysis of some 579 questionnaires completed by California party leaders in 1960 and 1964. The 1960 respondents were members of the Republican and Democratic delegations to the national party conventions of that year. Only one authentic leadership slate was presented by each party to its presidential primary voters —meaning that no group of party leaders is excluded from consideration in this analysis because its delegation slate had been defeated at the polls. As a result, and in view of the way in which the slates were selected, there is every reason to believe that Herbert McClosky's conclusion that delegation members are "as faithful a cross section of . . . party leadership as could be had without an extraordinary expenditure of money and labor"[24] is especially applicable to these two 1960 groups.

---

[22] Richard Bergholz, *Los Angeles Times* (Nov. 4, 1965). The organization's 1964 expenditures were broken down as follows:

Goldwater-Miller Campaign	$81,000
Murphy campaign	47,000
Congressional campaigns	37,000
State legislative campaigns	34,000
Maintenance of local headquarters	40,000
Various GOP dinners, testimonials, and the like	61,000
Additional campaign-related projects	86,000

[23] E. E. Schattschneider, *The Semi-Sovereign People* (New York: Holt, Rinehart & Winston, Inc., 1962), p. 2.

[24] "Issue Conflict and Consensus Among Party Leaders and Followers," *American Political Science Review*, LIV (June 1960), p. 405.

In 1964 questionnaires were sent to members of the California delegation to that year's Democratic National Convention, again a highly
representative group of the state's party elite whose only challenge in
the presidential primary came from a slate of persons almost entirely
unknown in active Democratic politics. As for the Republicans, there
were two authentic leadership slates of delegates entered in the 1964
presidential primary, with the one pledged to Barry Goldwater emerging
with a narrow victory over the one pledged to Nelson Rockefeller. Questionnaires were sent in this case to the members of both delegation slates;
the two groups of respondents are combined here for purposes of analysis
and will be identified as the 1964 Republican leadership corps.[25]

Included among the four groups of respondents considered (one for
each party in each of two years) are representatives of the various important components of California's political parties—holders of official
party office; leaders of California's unofficial party groups, such as the
CDC and the CRA; state legislators, congressmen, and other partisan
government officials; heavy financial contributors to the parties; representatives of interest groups closely associated with the parties; and
so on. Add them all up and the persons studied here are the "people
to know" in California party politics.

SOCIAL CLASS AND SOCIAL STATUS

Observers have long had an interest in the demographic characteristics
of political decision makers. For some this interest has reflected a concern for whether the leaders are "reputable," whether by virtue of their
backgrounds or training they deserve or are equipped to handle the
responsibilities of political leadership. As a group, politicians have not
been greatly admired, and many Americans believe the world of politics
is mainly inhabited by the social and mental flotsam of the nation. Few
people would like their son to become a politician or their daughter to
marry one.[26]

---

[25] The Goldwater and Rockefeller groups are compared in Edmond Costantini
and Kenneth Craik, "Competing Elites Within a Political Party: A Study of Republican Leadership," *Western Political Quarterly* (Dec. 1969). Some of the material
in these pages appears in a different form in that article, and also in Edmond
Costantini, "Intraparty Attitude Conflict: Democratic Leadership in California,"
Western Political Quarterly, (Dec. 1963), and in Edmond Costantini, *The Democratic Leadership Corps in California* (University of California, Davis: Institute
of Governmental Affairs, 1967).

[26] Walt Whitman's one-sentence description of Democratic party leaders a
century ago is among the most comprehensive and pungent statements of its kind.
Said Whitman in describing delegates to the party's 1856 national convention:
"[They are] the meanest kind of . . . officeholders, office seekers, robbers, pimps,

Paralleling this concern for the "reputability" of political leaders has been a concern for their "representativeness"—whether as a group they are a microcosm of the general public or of the rank-and-file voters of their respective parties. In part this concern is based on some variant of the notion that democracy loses its meaning and the political system becomes insensitive to mass opinion if political leaders represent only a social and economic elite. The two concerns—for reputability and representativeness—tend to have contradictory thrusts, because among the ways one establishes reputability is through superiority, rather than representativeness.

Are the leaders of California's major parties members of the state's social and economic elite? Are there differences between the parties' leadership groups that correspond to those found at the voter level? Table 6–1 presents data on the social class of the Democratic and Republican leadership groups in 1960 and 1964. For our purposes, an individual's social class is considered to be a product of his achievements in income, education, and occupation. In Table 6–2 the groups are considered in terms of social status. For our purposes, social status involves social attributes that are *ascribed* rather than *achieved,* attributes "which differentiate individuals but which (in contrast to class factors) they are powerless to produce in themselves."[27] The status factors considered are religion, nationality background, and age.

The data reveal that the leaders of both parties in California are "superior" to the general public in class achievement. Approximately 20 per cent of the entire sample has an annual income of over $50,000, whereas less than 10 per cent has an income of under $10,000. Among the 1960 Democrats, the median income was $19,000 whereas for the 1964 Democrats and for the Republican groups in both years it exceeded $25,000. Between 80 per cent and 90 per cent of each of the four groups had gone to college and significant percentages—from 35 per cent to 55 per cent—had continued on after college to professional or graduate

exclusives, malignants, conspirators, murderers, fancymen, customhouse clerks, contractors, kept-editors, spaniels well-trained to carry and fetch, jobbers, infidels, disunionists, terrorists, mail-riflers, slave-catchers, pushers of slavery, creatures of the President, creatures of would-be Presidents, spies, blowers, electioneers, body-snatchers, bawlers, bribers, compromisers, runaways, lobbyers, spongers, ruined sports, expelled gamblers, policy backers, monte-dealers, duelists, carriers of concealed weapons, blind men, deaf men, pimpled men, scarred inside with vile disease, gaudy outside with gold chains made from the people's money and harlot's money twisted together; crawling serpentine man, the lousy combings and born freedom-sellers of the earth." (Originally written in 1856.) *The Eighteenth Presidency!,* Edward Grier, ed. (Lawrence: University of Kansas Press, 1956), pp. 28–29.

[27] Suzanne Keller, *Beyond the Ruling Class: Strategic Elites in Modern Society* (New York: Random House, 1963), p. 175. See also pp. 205–210.

TABLE 6–1 SOCIAL CLASS AND CALIFORNIA PARTY ELITES

| | 1960 Percentage | | 1964 Percentage | |
	Democrat	Republican	Democrat	Republican
Annual Family Income				
Under $10,000	14	4	5	6
$10,000–20,000	40	23	28	32
$20,000–30,000	26	32	24	21
$30,000–40,000	4	4	12	13
$40,000–50,000	3	6	8	6
$50,000 and over	13	31	23	22
Formal Education				
No college	21	16	12	10
Some college	15	23	18	21
Completed college but not beyond	20	26	16	21
Professional or graduate training	44	35	54	48
*Occupation**				
Government official	38	11	18	4
Lawyer	27	20	27	23
Teacher	6	—	5	4
Other professional	6	9	9	12
Businessman	27	61	40	49
Blue-collar worker	1	—	1	1
Clerical or sales worker	—	—	2	3
Farmer	7	11	2	5
Labor union official	9	—	5	1
Other	3	—	1	2

* Multiple occupations account for the total percentage exceeding 100.

Note: The total number of respondents in each leadership group is 158 of 242 (65 per cent) 1960 Democratic delegation members; 56 of 140 (40 per cent) 1960 Republican delegation members; 180 of 319 (58 per cent) 1964 Democratic delegation members; 182 of 339 (54 per cent) 1964 Republican delegation members. Percentages in this and other tables are based on the number of persons responding to each question, and in each case this number is slightly smaller than the total number of respondents.

training. In terms of occupation, 80 per cent or more of each of the four groups are either government officials, professionals, or businessmen. Blue-collar workers (skilled, semiskilled, and unskilled employees), and clerical and sales workers—persons considered to be of relatively "low" occupational achievement—comprise only 2 per cent of the total sample. (Compare the data in Table 6–1 and 6–2 with the data presented earlier in Table 4–6, for a rough idea of the way in which party leaders differ in

TABLE 6-2 SOCIAL STATUS AND CALIFORNIA PARTY ELITES

	1960 Percentage		1964 Percentage	
	Democrat	Republican	Democrat	Republican
Religion				
Protestant	57	79	50	82
Catholic	17	15	17	12
Jewish	16	4	22	4
None	10	2	11	2
Nationality Background: *When*				
First generation (Foreign born)	5	4	9	5
Second generation	30	15	35	21
Third generation	29	40	24	30
None of these	36	42	32	44
Nationality Background: *Where**				
Northern Europe				
United Kingdom	29	36	42	55
Ireland	20	21	25	23
Germany and Austria	22	33	22	30
Other	21	42	18	24
Eastern Europe	30	6	17	3
Southern Europe	6	6	7	7
Asia, Africa, Latin America	6	—	6	4
Age				
20–30	1	—	2	3
30–40	25	13	23	20
40–50	40	30	41	27
50–60	23	35	26	31
60–70	10	20	7	13
70 and over	1	2	1	6

* Percentages exceed 100 because of multiple nationality backgrounds for many respondents.

social characteristics from party followers. If anyone believes, for example, that party leaders' income is representative of the income of the average Californian or of each party's supporters, such comparison might prove interesting.)

The superior class achievement of California's political leaders should not be surprising. Abundant evidence indicates that political leaders elsewhere are similarly successful in class terms. More leisure time and financial resources, more clearly defined stakes in political affairs, more self-confidence and highly developed political skills, greater involvement in all sorts of community organizations that overlap and feed into party organizations, a "halo" effect by which those who have met society's definition of social success are assumed also to be capable of meeting the problems of politics—these factors and others contribute to the overrepresentation of persons of high class achievement in the ranks of a party's leadership elite. Surprising or not, and however explained, the data here suggest that California's political elite is part of the state's social class elite. In this sense, they may be highly "reputable" but they are hardly "representative."

In 1960 the median family income among Republican respondents was $27,000, markedly above the $19,000 median income of the Democrats. However, in 1964 the Democratic group enjoyed the higher median income ($27,000 as compared to $24,500 for the Republicans). Perhaps this difference can be explained by the fact that the Democratic convention in 1964 was 3,000 miles away in Atlantic City, New Jersey, thus making it too expensive for some party activists to attend, whereas the Republican convention was held in San Francisco. In both years, Democrats were slightly less likely than the Republicans to have continued their formal education past high school. But they were more likely to have gone through college and into graduate and professional training. This latter difference is doubtlessly because of different career goals, with Democratic leaders having been more interested than their Republican counterparts in pursuing professional careers requiring post-college training and less interested in business careers. Indeed, in both 1960 and 1964 a greater percentage of Republicans than Democrats were businessmen, a finding consistent with commonly accepted conclusions about constituency or clientele differences between the parties. A greater percentage of Democrats were professionals. Farmers comprised somewhat more and labor union officials somewhat less of the Republican leadership group in both years, again consistent with interparty constituency or clientele differences.

One marked difference between party elites in terms of occupation involves the substantially higher percentage of government officials (almost all congressmen or state legislators) among the Democrats. Partly, this reflects the fact that there were fewer GOP officeholders to choose from when the delegations were selected. But it also reflects the crucial position of public officials within the Democratic party and how much greater they are esteemed by that party. Government officials are more important to the achievement of Democratic party goals than Republican officeholders, more important to parties of "innovation" than to parties of "consolidation." The greater organizational value of these officials to the Democrats is likely to be rewarded accordingly when delegations are selected. In contrast, Republican distrust of government may well extend to those of its leaders who are engaged in the governmental process and they may be given relatively short shrift in the delegation selection process. Moreover, government officials seem to be especially important in parties whose constituency/clientele is relatively low in social class. Because leadership in any party almost of necessity devolves upon persons of high class achievement, the best that a low-class party can do is to place special trust in those leaders who have already demonstrated, through performance, their responsiveness to lower-class needs. Few persons of high class achievement are better able to demonstrate that responsiveness than those already in the policy-making arena.

Despite the aforementioned party differences in social class among our respondents, it is not these differences that are most striking about the data in Table 6–1. Rather, it is the fact that respondents in both parties are highly successful in class terms and are hardly representative of their respective followers, Democratic and Republican voters.[28]

In considering social status we are concerned with social attributes which, in contrast to class factors, the individual is powerless to change. In the United States, as in all societies, some of these ascribed attributes have been considered to be preferable to others and to contribute more positively to one's reputability. Generally, to be a descendant of someone on the Mayflower or to be of old American stock confers higher social status than being an immigrant or the son of an immigrant; to be of English or German extraction is preferred to being of Polish or Italian or non-European extraction; and to be Protestant is considered more desirable than being non-Protestant. The data on California party leaders suggest that if one is low in *class* achievement he is likely to be out of the running when it comes to entry into the state's political elite—the chances are that he lacks leisure, money, verbal and other skills that are practically prerequisites for assuming the responsibilities of high-level political leadership. The resulting problem of elite nonrepresentativeness

---

[28] In class *origin* interparty differences become somewhat sharper and the elites become more representative. Over 60 per cent of the Democratic respondents in 1964 compared to 44 per cent of the Republicans claim that their fathers had not gone beyond high school in formal education. Thirty-nine per cent of the Democrats compared to 22 per cent of the Republicans claim that their father's occupation when they were growing up was as a clerical, sales, or blue-collar worker. Eighty-four per cent of the Democratic respondents in 1964 claim that they have improved their economic position over that of their family when they were growing up compared to 72 per cent of the Republicans.

is especially acute for the Democratic party, as it tends to have a lower class constituency/clientele than the Republicans.

But what if one is low in social *status?* Is he also to be excluded from the ranks of California's party elites? Table 6–2 suggests that those of lower social status—measured in terms of the material at hand—are not excluded. Thus the 1960 census reveals that approximately 25 per cent of the California population is "foreign stock" (i.e., foreign born or with one or both parents foreign born) and poll data reveal that one third is non-Protestant. These percentages are actually smaller than the percentage of our respondents falling into these low status categories.

Moreover, the elites of the two parties differ much more clearly in terms of status than in terms of class. And the difference corresponds to those existing between the voter-followers of each party. In general, the Democratic party leaders reflect their party's greater appeal among voters of lower status, i.e., among non-Protestants, persons of foreign birth, and those of nonnorthern European extraction. Thus in terms of religious affiliation, only about one half of the Democratic respondents compared with 80 per cent of the Republican respondents are Protestant, figures remarkably similar to differences at the voter level.[29] (See Table 4–6) Persons of foreign stock comprise almost twice the percentage of Democratic as Republican leaders in both 1960 and 1964. And in terms of nationality background, Republicans are much more likely to be of northern European—including British and German—extraction than Democrats.[30]

Another ascribed attribute that must be mentioned is age. Although the respondents from both parties are older than the general population, the Democrats are significantly younger than the Republicans. The median age for the Democratic respondents is 46 in both 1960 and 1964, and the median age for the Republicans is 52 in 1960 and 50 in 1964. Once again, the difference between parties at the elite level corresponds to the difference between party followers.

In general, the data suggest that the leaders of both California parties are "superior" in terms of social class and achieved social attributes but that they are quite similar to their followers in terms of social status and

---

[29] Moreover, a greater percentage of Democratic than Republican Protestants are affiliated with the three lower status denominations (Baptist, Lutheran, and Methodist) and a smaller percentage with the three higher status denominations (Congregational, Episcopalian, and Presbyterian).

[30] As could be expected from the small interparty difference in the percentage of Catholics among our respondents, those of Irish or Italian extraction comprise roughly equal proportions of each party's leadership groups, a finding not consistent with what is known about party followers.

ascribed social attributes. What they gain in reputability on the one hand, they gain in representativeness on the other.

PARTY INVOLVEMENT

One of the most obvious ways in which party leaders could be expected to differ from party followers is the extent of their commitment to and involvement in the affairs of their party. In many respects, being chosen to serve on a delegation to a national convention is the ultimate accolade a party has the power to bestow on its members, and the honor is generally reserved for those party "faithful" who have devoted considerable energy and time to party efforts.

Table 6–3 shows the extent of political commitment and involvement of party leaders. What emerges from these data is not just that our respondents are indeed very highly committed and involved, but that the elites of the two parties are quite different in this respect. A greater proportion of the Democratic than the Republican respondents in both years were party county central committee members, a greater proportion were state central committee members, and a greater proportion were members of the major unofficial organizations affiliated with their party. In terms of financial involvement, whereas 45 per cent of the 1960 and 59 per cent of the 1964 Democratic respondents had contributed $500 or more to their party, only 36 per cent of the Republicans in each year had contributed that generously. Moreover, the Democrats were more likely to have served on previous national convention delegations: 47 per cent of the 1960 and 56 per cent of the 1964 Democrats were "repeaters" compared to 39 per cent of the 1960 and 29 per cent of the 1964 Republicans. Even though the Democrats in both years were younger than the Republicans, they had been active in their party for about the same number of years; on the average, the members of all groups considered had been active for approximately 15 years. Given the data on previous delegation membership and years of active party involvement, the relative youth of the Democratic leaders does not seem to mean that there is greater "circulation" at the elite level in the Democratic party than the Republican party. Although the Democrats appear more successful than the Republicans in bringing "new blood" into their party's leadership elite when new blood is measured in terms of youth, they are not more successful when new blood is considered to mean newcomers to party affairs. And the Democrats seem to demand a greater organizational and financial commitment to the party by those who are to be given recognition as its leaders.

Several explanations might be proposed for these Democratic-Republi-

TABLE 6–3   ELITE DIFFERENCES IN EXTENT OF
PARTY INVOLVEMENT.

	1960 Percentage		1964 Percentage	
	Democrat	Republican	Democrat	Republican
Position in Official Party				
Member of county central committee	50	48	34	30
Member of state central committee	61	42	55	38
No official party position	27	31	34	53
CDC or CRA Member	78	45	70	35
Money Contribution to Party (1958 or 1962)				
Under $100	10	16	11	29
$100–500	45	49	30	35
$500–1,000	19	12	17	13
$1,000–5,000	17	16	27	21
$5,000 or more	9	8	15	2
Membership on Previous Delegations				
Never	53	61	44	72
Once	34	16	30	16
Twice	6	16	14	5
Three times	4	—	6	4
Four or more times	3	7	6	4
Years Active in Party				
0–5	5	7	7	17
5–10	23	13	18	15
10–15	21	37	28	16
15–20	10	4	21	20
20–25	12	24	7	11
25–30	13	2	8	7
30 or more	16	13	11	14

can differences in party commitment and involvement. First, although leadership in any party almost of necessity falls upon those of high class achievement, such achievement is less likely to be seen as sufficient for entry into the elite structure of a party with a lower-class constituency/ clientele. A lower-class party (i.e., the Democratic party) is more likely to require that its leaders demonstrate a commitment to lower-class goals by persistent and devoted activity in their behalf. Second, the Democrats may find it more difficult than the Republicans to find persons of higher class achievement to assume leadership responsibilities. As a consequence, the party may be forced to impose relatively higher organizational and financial burdens on those they do find. Third, a higher-class person holding political beliefs that tend to be lower class in orientation (i.e., to be Democrats) may wish to avoid the politically hostile environment in which his class naturally places him. Instead of involvement in normal higher-class social relationships, the upper-class Democrat may prefer to become involved in his political party where those with whom he comes in contact will be more supportive of his political beliefs. The upper-class Republican, on the other hand, need not become deeply involved in his party to avoid a politically hostile associational environment. Because his party does not fill the kind of social need for him as it does for his Democratic counterpart, the Republican leader does not become as deeply involved in its affairs. Fourth, Republicans have benefited more than the Democrats from California's antiparty tradition. And because they enjoy an advantage in nonparty political resources, the party organization has been less significant than that of the Democrats in achieving election victories. The successes of the Democrats in recent years, on the other hand, have been in large part attributable to organizational revival and effort and to the return of a partisan spirit by which their voter followers could be best mobilized. Consequently, the Democrats have put a higher premium on commitment to the party organization than the Republicans in giving elite status to its supporters.

ISSUE CONFLICT BETWEEN PARTIES

Party conflict in the United States, concludes the French author of one of the most celebrated works on comparative political parties, is "a conflict without principle."[31] The sentiment is not unique. Many Americans have a gnawing suspicion that there are no real issue differences between the Democratic and Republican parties, and consequently see our elections as virtually meaningless except as a means of replacing one set of rascals with another.

For some observers, however, the alleged tweedledum and tweedledee character of American parties is a major asset of the political system and a chief contributor to its survival. Among the essential features of our democracy, says Clinton Rossiter, is that "the parties have been the

---

[31] Maurice Duverger, *Political Parties* (New York: John Wiley & Sons, Inc., 1954), p. 418.

peacemakers of the American community, the unwitting but forceful suppressors of the 'civil war potential' we carry always in the bowels of our diverse nation."[32] Similarly John Fischer, editor of *Harper's* magazine, concluded a defense of the American party system by noting that "the purpose of European parties is, of course, to divide men of different ideologies into coherent and disciplined organizations. The historic role of the American party, on the other hand, is not to divide but to unite."[33]

For others the alleged absence of interparty conflict is cause for concern and reason for reform. Over half a century ago, James Bryce charged that our parties were two empty bottles differing only in their labels and suggested that "a time for a reconstruction is fast approaching."[34] Countless political observers have repeated Lord Bryce's charge in one way or another in the intervening years, and there have been equally countless proposals designed to achieve or to hasten the ever-approaching "time for a reconstruction."

In contrast to parties in some European countries, American parties have certainly not taken ideological positions that challenge the very fundamentals of the nation's political and economic system. But are the Republican and Democratic leaders identical? Are the tweedledum and tweedledee, "two empty bottles" characterizations accurate? The 1960 questionnaires being analyzed in Table 6–4 included nine items on specific issues of public policy; the 1964 questionnaires included fourteen issue items, four of which duplicated 1960 items. Respondents were asked to indicate whether they were "not at all," "very little," "somewhat," or "very much" in favor of each proposed policy. Table 6–4 compares the policy orientation of our party leadership groups. For ease of analysis we will consider a "very much" or "somewhat" response to signify that the individual is *in favor of* the given policy, and the table presents only the percentage of respondents in each group who fit into this category. The 1960 items were so worded that in each case a group with a higher percentage in Table 6–2 can be considered more "liberal." In 1964 the first seven issue items listed in the table were worded in the same way, whereas for the remaining seven the higher the percentage the *less* liberal the group. The notion of "liberalism" used here refers to a constellation of attitudes that include favoring a greater role for the federal government in dealing with social problems; favoring the interests of the laboring or lower-income segments of the population; having a

---

[32] *Parties and Politics in America* (Ithaca: Cornell University Press, 1960), p. 59.
[33] Unwritten Rules of American Politics," *Harpers,* **CVCVII** (Nov. 1948), p. 32.
[34] *The American Commonwealth,* rev. ed. (New York: The Macmillan Company, 1910), p. 29.

TABLE 6–4 ISSUE CONFLICT BETWEEN DEMOCRATIC AND REPUBLICAN PARTY ELITES

Percentage in favor of—	1960 Democrat	1960 Republican	1964 Democrat	1964 Republican
Increasing the federal minimum wage from $1 to $1.25	92	36		
A medical-aid-to-the-aged act tied to Social Security	96	33		
Greater economic aid to underdeveloped countries	92	60		
Federal aid to school construction	94	56		
A federal Fair Employment Practices Commission	91	44		
Diplomatic recognition of Communist China	43	4	48	19
Abolition of the House Un-American Activities Committee	69	2	57	11
Nationalization of selected basic industries	15	2	18	1
Power projects entirely developed with federal funds over those developed through federal-private partnership	84	10	54	6
A federal health insurance program covering men and women of all ages			87	36
Intensifying the federal government's "war on poverty"			91	26
A comprehensive federal government program to deal with the problems and effects of automation			95	60
United States withdrawal from the United Nations			1	22
A crackdown on state welfare recipients			35	83
Stricter enforcement of federal anticommunist legislation			29	72
Abolition of the progressive aspects of the income tax			15	42
Ending federal aid-to-education programs			5	39
The initiative repealing the Rumford ("Fair Housing") Act			7	53
Encouragement of state "right to work" (antiunion shop) laws			9	58

more conciliatory and cooperative attitude in the international arena; favoring a more relaxed government posture toward domestic communism; and favoring government policies benefiting racial minorities.

The basic conclusion to be drawn from the data in Table 6–4 is clear and unambiguous. The Democratic leaders are more liberal than their Republican counterparts. In both 1960 and 1964 Democrats responded more liberally on every single issue presented them. And the interparty differences are not trivial but significant across the board. A few notable examples will suffice. Whereas in 1960 less than 5 per cent of the Democrats were "opposed" to enactment of the program that has since become known as medicare, two thirds of the Republicans were of such a mind; whereas in 1960, 90 per cent of the Republicans were "opposed" to power projects fully developed by the federal government, only 15 per cent of the Democrats felt that way; whereas in 1964 three quarters of the Republicans were "opposed" to intensification of the "war on poverty," over 90 per cent of the Democrats were "in favor of" such an intensification.

Whether the magnitude of these issue differences between party leaders is ideal depends in part on how one feels about so-called "consensus politics" or about "conflict politics." The data *do* indicate, however, that party elites are indeed different in their issue orientation, that the difference is consistent and clear across a broad spectrum of political issues, and that it is sustained over a four-year time period during which new persons entered the elite structure of both parties and others dropped out.

ISSUE CONFLICT WITHIN PARTIES

It should be noted, however, that parties are not monoliths in which all leaders adhere to a single "line"; they are not without their own internal dynamics of issue conflict. The 1960 and 1964 survey data permit us to look at two examples of such conflict *within* California's party elites.

Earlier in this chapter reference was made to the tensions that exist between unofficial party organizations and "governmental parties." Democrats holding partisan public office frequently view the California Democratic Council with suspicion and hostility. For many, the CDC is not sufficiently concerned with winning elections and overly concerned with taking positions on issues regardless of the political consequences. CDC spokesmen often come to the opposite conclusion: Party officeholders tend to be too concerned with being re-elected and too little concerned with pursuing needed policy objectives. To this extent, the difference between the two groups is one of political "style"—one group assumes a power-orientation to politics, the other an issue-orientation. But the tension between the CDC and the Democratic officeholders may also be seen as ideological in nature, with the central tendency of the former being more liberal on policy issues than that of the latter.

To what extent does the questionnaire data considered here indicate that at the elite level of the party there is a liberal-conservative conflict between the unofficial party (CDC) and the governmental party (elected officeholders)? Twenty-six of our 1960 respondents are officers of the California Democratic Council; forty-seven hold elective partisan office in the state or national governments (almost all being either state legislators or congressmen). Table 6–5 compares the issue orientation of these two groups.

Once again, the results of the comparison are clear and unambiguous. On each and every issue, the CDC officials are more "liberal" than the government officials. However, words of caution are in order before making too much of the ideological conflict between the CDC and the party's "government party." On most issues the two groups are quite similar, with over 80 per cent of each being in favor of six of the nine issue items and with similar percentages being opposed to a seventh. Moreover, although the Democratic government officials are consistently more conservative than the CDC officers, reference to Table 6–5 reveals that there is no issue on which their responses are more conservative than that of the 1960 Republican elite. In fact, there is not one issue on which the percentage of Democratic officeholders in favor of the proposed policy is closer to the percentage of the Republican delegation members in favor of the policy than to that of the CDC officers. Finally, the questionnaire data suggest that it would be an oversimplification to view the CDC and the "government party" as two distinct components of the Democratic party. There was considerable overlap between the two groups among the delegation members. Although only 4 per cent of the elected government officials among our respondents claimed to be CDC officers, an additional 57 per cent claimed to be active members in the CDC, leaving only 39 per cent who claimed to be inactive members or nonmembers of the organization. (Indeed, the common view that the CDC had been a totally isolated and discrete structural component of the Democratic party in California is further belied by data regarding the holding of official party positions among our 1960 respondents. Of the 103 respondents serving on Democratic county central committees or on the party state central committee, 17 per cent were CDC officers and 51 per cent active members of the CDC.)

TABLE 6–5 ISSUE CONFLICT BETWEEN DEMOCRATIC PARTY
LEADERSHIP GROUPS: A COMPARISON OF CDC OFFICIALS
AND ELECTED GOVERNMENT OFFICIALS, 1960

Percentage in favor of—	CDC Officials	Elected Government Officials
Increasing the federal minimum wage from $1 to $1.25	100	88
A medical-aid-to-the-aged act tied to Social Security	100	93
Greater economic aid to underdeveloped countries	100	82
Federal aid to school construction	100	87
A federal Fair Employment Practices Commission	96	91
Diplomatic recognition of Communist China	54	31
Abolition of the House Committee on Un-American Activities	83	57
Nationalization of selected basic industries	21	12
Power projects entirely developed with federal funds over those developed through federal-private partnership	88	82

The California Republicans have been afflicted with a continuing factional dispute in recent years, a dispute that came to the fore in the 1964 Goldwater-Rockefeller presidential primary contest. By comparing the issue orientations of the members of the Goldwater-pledged and Rockefeller-pledged delegation slates presented to the 1964 Republican primary voters, we have some measure of the ideological depth of the dispute and of how issue conflict within a party can compare with issue conflict between parties.

The issue orientation of the members of the two delegations is presented in Table 6–6. The greater conservatism of the Goldwater group is clear and unambiguous. On each and every issue interfactional differences are in the expected direction. On some issues—recognition of Communist China, abolition of the House on Un-American Activities, nationalization of industries, federal versus federal-private power projects, and cracking down on welfare recipients—there is basic agreement between the two groups. But on most issues, the fissure is wide. For example, two thirds of the Goldwater group favor ending federal aid to education compared to only one quarter of the Rockefeller group, ap-

**TABLE 6–6   ISSUE CONFLICT BETWEEN REPUBLICAN PARTY
LEADERSHIP GROUPS: A COMPARISON OF THOSE ON THE
GOLDWATER DELEGATION AND THOSE ON THE
ROCKEFELLER DELEGATION, 1964**

Percentage in favor of—	Goldwater Delegation	Rockefeller Delegation
Diplomatic recognition of Communist China	5	28
Abolition of the House Committee on Un-American Activities	—	18
Nationalization of selected basic industries	—	1
Power projects entirely developed with federal funds over those developed through federal-private partnership	5	8
A federal health insurance program covering men and women of all ages	6	53
Intensifying the federal government's "war on poverty"	3	41
A comprehensive federal government program to deal with the problems and effects of automation	40	73
U.S. withdrawal from the United Nations	53	5
A crackdown on state welfare recipients	91	78
Stricter enforcement of federal anti-communist legislation	89	63
Abolition of the progressive aspects of the income tax	64	28
Ending federal aid-to-education programs	65	24
The initiative repealing the Rumford ("Fair Housing") Act	83	34
Encouragement of state "right to work" (antiunion shop) laws	84	42

proximately two thirds of the Goldwater group favor abolition of the progressive aspects of the income tax whereas only one quarter of the Rockefeller group are so inclined, less than 5 per cent of the Goldwater group are in favor of intensifying the war on poverty as opposed to 40 per cent of the Rockefeller group, over one half of the Goldwater group favor dropping out of the United Nations whereas only 5 per cent of the Rockefeller group are so inclined. On eight of the fourteen issues, the percentage of Rockefeller Republicans in favor of the proposed policy is closer to the Democratic percentage (indicated in Table 6–4) than to the percentage of Goldwater Republicans. In this sense, the Rockefeller group is about as much in conflict ideologically with their fellow Republicans supporting Goldwater as they are with the Democrats.

At the same time, despite its liberalism compared to the Goldwater elite, the Rockefeller group is still more conservative on every issue with which they were presented than the Democratic elite, as reference to Table 6–4 reveals. One of the themes of the campaign on behalf of Senator Goldwater was that if he were the Republican presidential candidate, the party would at last offer the American voters a "choice but not an echo." The present data suggest that the Rockefeller wing of the Republican party in California may be substantially more liberal than the Goldwater wing, but it is still substantially more conservative than, and not an echo of, the Democrats.

CHAPTER 7

interest group politics

elf-protection and self-promotion are powerful motives
in politics. It is reasonable to expect that people will form
organizations for the expressed purposes of protecting
and promoting their self-interests. The numerous *interest
groups*[1] actively engaged in politics constitute irrefutable
evidence of the capacity of some of our citizens to organize in their own behalf. Many hundreds of organizations in California systematically attempt to influence
public policy on behalf of their membership. There is no
area of public concern and no arena of policy making
that is not confronted by some representative of some
interest group. Legislators, executives, judges, administrators, and voters—all must deal with some variety of

---

[1] Duane Lockard argues in *The Politics of State and Local Government* (New York: Macmillan, 1963), pp. 155–156, that the
term *interest group* is less prejudicial than the term *pressure group*,
which is often used in referring to organizations designed to exert
influence or "pressure" upon public officials. We agree and will
use *interest group* to avoid any negative connotation when discussing such organizations.

interest group. Sacramento is an obvious center of interest group activity, but all units and levels of government of the state are accessible to interest groups. Interest groups are an integral part of the political life; indeed, these groups and their representatives are an indispensable part of California politics.

the role of interest groups

An interest group is an organization designed to make certain claims upon other organizations, notably governmental organizations, for the establishment, maintenance, or enhancement of specific patterns of behavior.[2] An interest group is expected to further the interests of its members by trying to constrain the behavior of other groups and individuals. Farm organizations are expected to secure favorable crop subsidies for their members; labor unions are expected to gain higher wages for their members; and manufacturers' associations are expected to procure protective tariffs for their members. Interest groups are expected to further the *common* interests of their members.[3] It is generally understood that the main purpose of an interest group is the protection and promotion of the common interests of a collection of people.

Although there is some question about the capacity of interest groups to serve the common interests of their members,[4] most such groups do

---

[2] This definition of interest group is a variation of a definition offered by David B. Truman in *The Governmental Process* (New York: Alfred A. Knopf, Inc., 1951), pp. 33–34. Our definition differs somewhat because we are interested in existing interest groups and are less concerned with potential interest groups, which form a vital part of Professor Truman's theory. Also see V. O. Key, Jr., *Politics, Parties and Pressure Groups*, 5th ed. (New York: Thomas Y. Crowell Co., 1964), pp. 17–19, for a similar definition for organizations which Professor Key preferred to call *pressure groups*. It is worthwhile to note that both authors derive part of their definitions and part of their discussions from a common source: James Madison's famous essay on factions contained in *The Federalist*, No. X.

[3] Mancur Olson, Jr. in *The Logic of Collective Action*, paperback ed. (New York: Schocken Books, Inc., 1968), has written a penetrating criticism of interest group theory. See especially his discussion of commonality and group interest, pp. 1–22.

[4] Olson, op. cit., provides a careful examination of the relationship between individual interests and group interests. A major contention of his book is that *"rational, self-interested individuals will not act to achieve their common or group interests. . . . The notion that groups of individuals will act to achieve their common or group interests, far from being a logical implication of the assumption that individuals in a group will rationally further their individual interests, is in fact inconsistent with that assumption."* (p. 2.)

He goes on to argue that unless some sort of sanction or incentive is presented claim to represent the collective, common interests of their members. Further, this claim is generally accepted by public officials more or less at face value. It is convenient for officials to accept the claim that a given union, farm organization, credit association, school districts' association, or conservation group does represent the interests of its constituent membership and that the lobbyists who speak for the interest group are expressing the collective will of the members. Even though this be myth, California government depends upon the general acceptance of this convention as a true state of affairs. Lobbyists and interest groups form a major system of linkage between officials who enact, execute, and evaluate public policy and the public.

INTEREST GROUPS AND SPECIAL INTERESTS

Interest groups pursue *special interests*. The boundary of the interests shared by the members of an organization is defined by the special or distinctive quality of these interests. The California Teachers Association, for example, is an organization that represents the special, distinctive interests of the participating educators. Its chief rival, the American Federation of Teachers, is an organization that represents the special distinctive interests of its members. Although both these organizations are concerned with the protection and promotion of the interests of California educators, each constitutes a special set of interests. The CTA, the older and traditional organization, appeals to teachers who view their vocation as a profession and who do not support the conventional techniques employed by trade unions, such as strikes, picket lines, and collective bargaining with individual employment units. The AFT, the newcomer in California, appeals to teachers who view their vocation less as a profession and more as a trade, and who do support the collective bargaining tools normally associated with labor unions. Thus, both organizations promote specially defined sets of interests that are distinctive from each other.

Many other interest groups, each with its own special interests, are involved in the politics of public education in California. Such organizations as the Small School Districts' Association, the statewide Parent-Teachers Association and its local affiliates, the many Black Students' Unions, the California Realtors Association and its local units, various

---

which forces or entices members of a large group to bear the costs involved in achievement of group interests, neither the individuals nor the group will further the goals held in common.

local school districts, several taxpayers associations, the National Education Association, and the County Superintendents Association are among the large number of interest groups that have a direct interest in education politics. Each of these organizations represents a specially defined set of interests that has some claim to recognition in the process of making educational policy at various levels of government in this state. And, of course, public education is only one of the many areas of public policy, in which specially defined interests are promoted by a variety of interest groups.

To a degree, policy making consists of sorting out the various claims made by and for these special interests, and attempting to compromise the claims and counterclaims made in the name of these special interests. Although policy making is more than simply reacting to the competitive claims of special interests and engaging in what has been called "political brokerage,"[5] there is no question that much of the information upon which public policy is made comes directly from groups promoting their own special interests.

INTEREST GROUPS AND POLITICAL LINKAGE

Legislators, administrators, judges, party officials, and voters all depend upon interest groups for vital information about the merits and effects of public policy. Interest groups, from the point of view of a person making a decision about a specific policy, furnish a number of varying interpretations of proposed and existing policy. In a system of popular government, policy makers require a variety of viewpoints to help insure that policy reflects the subtle nuances of public desire and demand. Interest groups in making claims upon government provide a means whereby a partial cross section of opinion is potentially available to public decision makers.

Interest groups perform vital functions in the decision-making process. Because the same interest group is interested in a given policy or potential policy at all stages of its development, enactment, administration, and demise, the group and its agents serve to cut across formal lines of authority. The various centers of decision making—legislative committee, governor's staff, administrative department, commissions, party organizations, courts, voting booths, and so on—to varying degrees are tied to-

---

[5] See John C. Livingston and Robert G. Thompson, *The Consent of the Governed*, 2nd ed. (New York: The Macmillan Company, 1963, 1966), pp. 88, 238–247, and 249 for a discussion of viewing politics as "brokerage," and for discussion of the ideological content of the term *brokerage politics*.

gether by the activities of interest groups. Continuity through time and space is provided by the activity of interest groups. Although the interest groups alone do not provide a total system of linkage, they do materially contribute to the coordination and exchange necessary to provide useful interaction among the various units of our highly factionated and decentralized system.

For example, Pacific Gas and Electric, which provides electrical power and natural gas to most northern California communities, is one of California's most important private concerns and one of our most powerful interest groups. It must continuously confront various units of our political system to promote and protect its interests. It has a well-trained and experienced staff of lobbyists to intervene in the legislative process. Its attorneys and research personnel always are ready to protect the company in court or to promote its interests before the California Public Utilities Commission. Members of its corporate board of directors and some of its administrative personnel use personal as well as formal contacts to exchange information with aides to the Governor, administrative units such as the Department of Water Resources, and staff members of the Department of Finance. Although it does not directly intervene in the affairs of political parties, P. G. and E. has lent support to politicians known to be amenable to its interests. Also, as most interest groups do, it communicates regularly with other organizations that act as interest groups. In short, P. G. and E., like all effective interest groups, must keep itself informed and must inform the organizations with which it does political business or it could not survive politically or economically.

Thus, interest groups provide a kind of representation and political communication. The various constituencies represented by interest groups differ significantly from those represented by legislators, administrators, judges, voters, and the Governor. In a real sense, an additional dimension of political communication is provided by the interaction of interest groups with other political actors. The linkage system and communication within it are imperfect, but the activities of interest groups do permit the transmission of ideas, desires, and demands in a systematic way not provided by our formal constitution.

INTEREST GROUPS AND WEAK PARTIES

California's system of weak political parties gives added significance to interest groups in the state's politics. It is axiomatic in American state politics that weak parties breed strong interest groups.[6] Interest groups

---

[6] See Harmon Zeigler, "Interest Groups in the States," in Herbert Jacob and Kenneth N. Vines, eds., *Politics in the American States* (Boston: Little, Brown and

are particularly active and influential in states like Oregon, Washington, and California, where parties operate under very restrictive constitutional and statutory regulations. In strong party states like Massachusetts, Illinois, and New York, electoral machinery, campaigns, management of the government, and policy making traditionally have been dominated by the party organizations and their partisans. In these states interest groups have played a secondary role to parties in processes of political communication and, in fact, often have had to work through the party structures to gain their special ends. In California and other weak party states, the tradition has been different. Interest groups have played much more important roles in elections, campaigns, and day-to-day operations of government and policy making. In California where partisan politics is prohibited in local government, interest groups have performed all of the roles played by parties in many strong party states. It is a great irony that many of the reforms promoted by the Progressives have so weakened the California party structure that special interests, a main target of the reformers, have gained in many ways the dominant position over parties in the operations of the state political system.

The classical functions of American parties—informing the public, selecting candidates, developing programs, campaigning for office, and running the government—are also carried out by interest groups in this state. Informing the public, particularly during election years, is extremely expensive. California parties spend extraordinarily large sums of money presenting the virtues and vices of various candidates to the voters. Considerably less money is spent by parties in educating the voters about the substantive issues at hand. Interest groups spread hundreds of thousands of dollars each year to make sure the public understands their specific interpretation of given policy alternatives, and during election years selected interest groups spend very large sums to gain a favorable reaction from the voters on the many initiatives and referendum items that are presented regularly on the California ballot.

California's primary system is an open invitation for interest groups to become involved in selection of candidates. Although statewide primaries are partisan contests, the parties are able to contribute little to defray the costs of contending candidates. Interest groups are a major source of money and assistance for most candidates for local and state elections. And, of course, in the nonpartisan primaries and general elec-

Company, 1965), pp. 117 and 125–128; E. E. Schattschneider, *Party Government* (New York: Holt, Rinehart & Winston, Inc., 1942, 1967), pp. 196–198; and Henry A. Turner and John A. Vieg, *The Government and Politics of California,* 3rd ed. (New York: McGraw-Hill Book Company, Inc., 1967), p. 63.

tions for local officers, parties may not legally assist the candidates at all. In the state general elections, where the parties are able to provide more funds for their candidates, there is still need for considerably more money and organizational assistance than the parties and allied organizations can provide.

The considerable difficulties in establishing effective party discipline and party government are discussed elsewhere in this book.[7] It is, however, important to note at this juncture that parties cannot force their will upon candidates elected to public office. Although there has been a resurgence of partisan leadership, particularly in the state Assembly,[8] during the past ten years, party government as known in several other states,[9] remains untested in recent California experience. One study[10] indicates that interest groups are the most important influence in the behavior of a California legislator. Whereas legislators in New York, Texas, and Ohio have shown considerable allegiance to party and party leaders, California lawmakers are notoriously fickle to both party and their party leaders.[11] Interest groups are important influences upon the operations of all our state governments,[12] but in California interest groups tend to play an extraordinary role in the management of government.

varieties of interest groups

The number of organizations acting as interest groups in California is unknown. So many groups have a specific interest to promote and protect that a satisfactory census would be very difficult to devise. Thousands

---

[7] See Chapter 6, "Party Organization and Leaders," and Chapter 8, "Party-in-Government: Politics at the State Capital."

[8] William Buchanan, *Legislative Partisanship, the Deviant Case of California* (Berkeley and Los Angeles: University of California Press, 1963), pp. 123–134, notes the beginnings of increasing partisanship in the Assembly under Speaker Jesse Unruh. This trend seems to have been strong enough that the present Speaker, Robert Monagan, more or less has followed Unruh's lead.

[9] See the essays by Dayton D. McKean, "Elections and Political Parties," and "Patterns of Politics," in James W. Fesler, ed., *The 50 States and Their Local Governments* (New York: Alfred A. Knopf, Inc., 1967), pp. 200–252 for discussion of regional patterns.

[10] See John C. Wahlke, Heinz Eulau, William Buchanan, and LeRoy C. Ferguson, *The Legislative System, Explorations in Legislative Behavior* (New York: John Wiley, & Sons, Inc., 1962), pp. 311–376.

[11] Ibid.

[12] See Zeigler, op. cit., pp. 113–142; McKean, op. cit., pp. 244–252; and Lockard, op. cit., pp. 155–160.

of organizations try to influence public policy at the various levels of government in this state.

Nearly four hundred organizations are regularly listed in the index, *Legislative Advocates and Organizations,* provided by the state legislature for each session. Many organizations—such as the John Birch Society, the American Association of University Professors, the Colorado River Association, and the Tejon Ranch—are not registered as legislative lobbies, but nonetheless they do influence public policy through contacts with decision makers. The executive branch of the state government has more than fifty-five major offices, departments, boards, agencies, and commissions; they and many subordinate units often must lobby other groups and decision makers to promote and protect their interests. Although many of the more than 5,000 units of local government in California are represented by regional and functional organizations such as the County Supervisors Association of California, each unit of local government is at least a part-time interest group.

Categorizing the many organizations that act as interest groups at the various levels of California government and politics is extremely difficult. No classification system is fully satisfactory, but for the purposes of this book a straightforward scheme proposed by another author has been adopted and slightly modified.[13] Interest groups will be divided and classified under the following general headings: (1) government officials, (2) business, (3) professional associations, (4) labor, (5) agriculture, (6) ideological organizations, (7) ethnic groups, and (8) miscellaneous.

The first five require little explanation. The eighth, "miscellaneous," is a catch-all residual category to account for organizations such as media, veterans associations, taxpayers' associations, and conservation groups that do not neatly fit into the other categories.

Wealth is such an important value in our society that most of the organizations which we normally call interest groups are primarily interested in the distribution (and redistribution) of wealth. Those organizations which would be included under our first five headings—government officials, business, professional associations, labor, and agriculture—as well as most organizations that would be included in our miscellaneous category are concerned above all with the relative distribution of resources, costs, and benefits in our public and private economies.

---

[13] Wayne L. Francis, *Legislative Issues in the Fifty States: a Comparative Analysis* (Chicago: Rand McNally & Company, 1967), pp. 118–120. Professor Francis' classification scheme includes the first five and the seventh categories, but does not have special categories for ideological and ethnic interest groups. Presumably he would include such groups in his miscellaneous category.

Most of what has been called the group struggle[14] is conflict among economic interests.

Although almost all organizations are concerned directly or indirectly with protection and promotion of their "economic" interests, some organizations are concerned more about ethnic identification and ethnic power. It is true that ethnic minorities are among the poorest people in California, but racial issues are so crucial in this state as well as the whole nation that it is important to recognize the role of ethnically defined groups in our politics.

Other organizations may be separated from the great mass of interest groups primarily concerned with wealth per se on the basis of their espousal of specific ideologies. These ideologies may include many dimensions, but the organizations that support them have as their main aim the preservation or change of the fundamental structure and processes of our polity. Groups in this category range from those which advocate revolution to those which support a specific reform of the existing constitution. Their distinguishing characteristic is their pursuit of a specific set of political principles.

Any list of California interest groups[15] will have a preponderance of organizations concerned with economic well-being. Most governmental decision making has important consequences for the relative distribution of wealth, including the distribution of the public funds generated through taxation. It is reasonable for most lobbying organizations to be concerned with the effects of public policy upon their economic position. Government officials, as lobbyists, are no exception.

GOVERNMENT OFFICIALS

Government officials constitute the largest number of lobbyists in the state. The most obvious thing about officials and governmental units as lobbyists and interest groups is that they are not "private" in the sense that business, farm, or labor groups are. When most of us think of interest groups, pressure groups, or lobbies, we usually think of people or organizations that do not have official standing in government, but do

---

[14] The idea of viewing interest group interaction as a struggle is forcefully stated by Bertram M. Gross, *The Legislative Struggle* (New York: McGraw-Hill Book Company, Inc., 1953), chapters 2, 3, 12, and 13.

[15] See Joseph P. Harris, *California Politics*, 4th ed. (San Francisco: Chandler Publishing Co., 1967), pp. 85–86; Henry A. Turner and John A. Vieg, *The Government and Politics of California*, 3rd ed. (New York: McGraw-Hill Book Company, Inc., 1967), p. 52; and Winston Crouch, et al., *California Government and Politics*, 3rd ed. (Englewood Cliffs, N.J.: Prentice-Hall, Inc., 1964), pp. 83–84.

directly participate in official decision making.[16] In this book, however, organizations with official standing in government have also been designated as interest groups. Thus, the very people who are the official decision makers are also lobbyists. Any official making a special plea before a decision-making group is lobbying.

State-level agencies such as the Department of Employment, the Public Utilities Commission, and the Justice Department are interest groups because they must lobby the Governor, the legislature, many other officials and agencies as well as private groups in order to promote and protect their interests. A number of individual cities, counties, school districts, and special districts, including the City of Los Angeles, the County of Santa Barbara, the San Francisco Board of Education, and the Metropolitan Water District of Southern California, maintain lobbyists in Sacramento. Some organizations that maintain lobbyists at the state capital represent more than one unit of government; the California Junior College Association and the Irrigation Districts Association are good examples. About one in twelve of the organizations listed by the legislature as having registered advocates are local governmental agencies or groups representing governmental agencies.

Public officials must lobby each other in the process of making public policy. Officials, as representatives of their parent organization, are concerned that specific legislative bills are passed or defeated, that particular administrative practices be initiated, maintained, modified, or ceased, that programs be established or ended, and that appropriations be secured. The survival of agencies and of individual careers require that officials engage in lobbying.

Administrative decision makers rely very heavily upon other officials for vital information. It is a truism that the most important source of new legislation is the executive branch and its many administrative agencies. What is true for the legislative process is also true for the administrative process. An indispensable source of information for executives and administrators are other members of the executive branch. Furthermore, all units of state government depend upon local government as a major source of information and ideas for policy making. There is no question that public officials perform significant lobby functions at all levels of government in California.

---

[16] See Assembly on Private Groups in Illinois Government, *Private Groups in Illinois Government,* final Report and Background Papers, Papers by James H. Andrews, January 21–22, 1965 (Urbana, Ill.: Institute of Government and Public Affairs, University of Illinois, March 1965), pp. 1–2 and passim for a discussion of the role of private groups in state government and of the distinction between private and public groups.

BUSINESS

The organizations that have a direct stake in the state's and the nation's economy are perhaps the most important set of private interest groups in California. Business organizations are the most numerous *private* lobbies in the state legislature. About half of the interest groups registered with the legislature are either single business corporations or organizations whose constituents are business firms. California appears to be well within nationwide state trends; in many states the registration of legislative lobbyists shows that business associations and business firms are numerically predominant.[17] Although numbers alone do not necessarily indicate political significance, the numerical dominance of the legislative lobby by business does give some indication of the importance which these organizations place upon legislative policy making. Unquestionably, business finds it convenient and necessary to keep close tabs upon legislators and the legislature.

One study suggests that from the point of view of legislators themselves, business groups derive more power or influence from their legislative lobbying activities than do agriculture, labor, and government groups.[18] Forms of direct lobbying appear to be as important as a group's size, membership, prestige, or potential vote in determining relative power as perceived by legislators.[19] Because business groups appear to utilize entertainment, personal assistance, and favors more than other groups, it is not surprising to find that legislators view business groups as deriving considerable power from these activities.[20] In fact, lobbyists who work for business interests appear to dominate the free lunch circuit in Sacramento, much to the discomfort of many of their competitors.

Business interests are represented by some of the most experienced lobbyists in California. Messrs. James D. Garibaldi,[21] Elmer P. Bromley,[22]

---

[17] Harmon Zeigler presents data indicating that in seventeen states, including California, business firms or business associations numerically dominate the lobby registration lists. Among the states listed, Florida and Iowa ranked lowest with 46.9 per cent of the registered interest groups categorized as "business" or "single business corporation" and Virginia ranked highest, with 81.3 per cent of registered interest groups in the same categories. See "Interest Groups in the States," in *Politics in the American States,* pp. 109–112; especially Table 4, Classification of Interest Groups in Selected States, 1964, p. 110.

[18] John C. Wahlke et al., pp. 333–338.

[19] Ibid., Table 14.10; Number of references to various reasons for power of specific groups given by legislators in four states, pp. 334–335.

[20] Ibid., p. 333.

[21] Mr. Garibaldi was listed in 1968 as an advocate for the Hollywood Turf Club,

and Albert J. Shults,[23] who collectively represents some of the most important interest groups in the state, are examples of the highly skilled and respected lobbyists speaking for California business. It should be noted that whereas these gentlemen and many others are expert practitioners of the wine and dine technique, their effectiveness as lobbyists depends upon many other factors, including their personal reputations, knowledge of politics, and ability to aid legislators with expert information. Business is successful because its lobbyists are as a group respected, hardworking, and experienced men. The same must be said for the lobbyists who represent other interests, but business lobbyists are especially able.

It would appear that business tends to concentrate its lobbying activities upon the legislature, but this does not mean that business groups neglect the executive and judicial branches and local government. Some cases are obvious and come to one's mind immediately. The railroads, Southern Pacific for example, the resource utilities, Southern California Edison as an example, and the telephone companies, Pacific Telephone and Telegraph for instance, are all regulated by the California Public Utilities Commission. The businesses that are regulated must by law and by convention engage in activities that closely resemble legislative lobbying. Open pressure lobbying is frowned upon by law and custom, but other techniques of informing officials including testimony before hearings, use of the media, letters, telephone calls, and personal contact are used by representatives of these enterprises in making their cases before the PUC and other agencies.

Although utility regulation is an outstanding example of the necessary connection between interests and nonlegislative policy makers, business interests must maintain regular contact with a vast number of state and local agencies in order to survive in the political economy of California. From time to time, some rather naïve person is shocked upon discovering that interest groups must lobby civil servants, judges, city

---

Pacific Outdoor Advertising Company, Blue Chip Stamp Company, California Beverage Distributors Association, California Association of Highway Patrolmen, All Bid Depositories Committee of California, California Court Reporters Association, and Signal Oil and Gas Company.

[22] Mr. Bromley specializes in representing utilities and in 1968 was listed as being an advocate for Pacific Gas and Electric Company, San Diego Gas and Electric Company, Southern California Edison Company, Southern California Gas Company, and Southern Counties Gas Company.

[23] Mr. Shults is a veteran representative of oil interests and in 1968 was listed as an advocate for the Atlantic Richfield Company, Gulf Oil Corporation, Humble Oil and Refining Company, Mobil Oil Corporation, Phillips Petroleum Company, Shell Oil Company, Standard Oil Company of California, Union Oil Company of California, E. I. Du Pont de Nemours and Company, and Ethyl Corporation.

managers, and other "nonpolitical" officials. Although we might be careful about casual acceptance of all such lobbying activities, there is no reason to be shocked by extralegislative lobbying. It is simply an integral part of our politics, and business groups as well as all other interest groups are expected to engage in it.

PROFESSIONAL ASSOCIATIONS

California has the standard professional organizations: government employees, teachers, college and university professors, attorneys, and medical vocations; all are organized to promote and protect their professional interests. Although these organizations are numerically insignificant when compared to governmental units and business groups,[24] they constitute an important set of lobbies in California politics. One professional group, the California Teachers Association (CTA), is considered by some observers to be the single most powerful and influential professional interest group in the state.[25] It is unquestionably true that the CTA and other associations of public employees such as the California State Employees Association (CSEA), the California Association of Highway Patrolmen, and the California Association of Secondary School Administrators are important lobbies in Sacramento as well as among local governments.

The medical profession has long been powerful in state and national politics. In addition to its concern with legislation affecting medical practices, standards, availability of medical services, and the like, the California medical profession has an institutionalized, vested interest in the operations of the public and private colleges and universities in the state and in the administrative agencies that supervise, regulate, and control the public and private medical facilities of California. University medical schools, regional mental health coordinating programs, hospital boards, county departments of public health and many other programs and institutions are the natural concern of the medical profession.

The legal profession, although usually not accorded the reputation for great power which the medical profession enjoys, is directly and indirectly an interest group of great importance. Like most professional

---

[24] According to Harmon Zeigler, op. cit., p. 110, professional groups average about 7.5 per cent of the groups registered in the seventeen states covered in his study. He indicates that professional groups constitute 4.7 per cent of the registered organizations in California. The same ratio, about one in twenty, is reflected in the 1968 edition of *Legislative Advocates and Organizations* published by the state legislature.

[25] See Wahlke et al., op. cit., pp. 317–319 and Francis, op. cit., pp. 40–41.

groups, the various bar associations (county and statewide) are actively engaged in trying to influence policy at all levels of government. Most judges but not all are attorneys. Nearly all units of government must continually partake of the professional services of attorneys. Special professional schools and professional regulations are no less important to lawyers than to doctors. Like teachers, school administrators, physicians, and others who profess special expertise, attorneys have a vested interest in expressing their expertness whenever possible.

LABOR

California in comparison with New York or Michigan is not considered a strong labor union state. Although labor groups are very active in California politics, the trade union movement has not gained the popular support and political power it appears to have in many other industrial states. Some unions, notably the Teamsters, the International Ware-housemen's and Longshoremen's Union, and the statewide AFL-CIO have considerable membership in this state. No California union rivals the United Auto Workers' in Michigan or the Teamsters in Pennsylvania. Some California unions, most recently the American Farm Workers, have had very little success trying to influence public policy makers. One could say that the AFW is so weak that it is not yet considered a legitimate union by most public officeholders.

This is not to say that unions are not important or that they are not influencial in community-level politics. In sharp contrast to Orange county and Los Angeles, the San Francisco Bay area has many strong unions that take part in local politics with over-all success. Furthermore, the statewide membership in trade unions is considerable; about 1,900,-000 in 1968. In comparison with other interest groups such as business, agriculture, and professions, however, organized labor must be considered relatively less influential.

Interestingly enough, some labor organizations are considered important lobbies by legislators. The Teamsters and the AFL-CIO were named among the most influential lobbies in a comparative study of legislative issues,[26] and the AFL-CIO was one of fifty-six interest groups indicated by name by California legislators in another study;[27] in fact, it was named among the top five interest groups in terms of salience as defined by perceptions of the legislators.[28] Thus, it appears that union

---

[26] Francis, op. cit., pp. 40–42.
[27] Wahlke et al., op. cit., pp. 316–319.
[28] Ibid., p. 318.

lobbies are active and well-known to California legislators. This does not mean that labor gets what it wants or is powerful in relation to business interests, but only that labor makes considerable effort to gain support in the legislative process. In general terms, this may mean that labor must expend more resources in order to survive than other more favored groups do in California, or it may mean that labor is really more powerful in state politics than it is in local politics or both. In any event, organized labor is a force to be reckoned with in the state.

AGRICULTURE

In the minds of many people, agriculture still is California's basic industry. Although only about 5 per cent of the state's labor force works on farms and ranches, the Council of California Growers will argue that "agriculture creates jobs" and "30 per cent of all California jobs" depends on agriculture. In a sense, the pride expressed by exponents of California agriculture[29] is fully justified. California is still one of the leading agricultural economies in the United States; there are nearly 100,000 farms and ranches in the state which produced about 5 per cent of the state's total product of nearly seven billion dollars in 1968. Agriculture no longer dominates the state's economy, but it is a vital part of our very rich and diverse productive capacity.

The public, and to a large extent, public officials have a very sentimental view of agriculture in this state. The historical importance of agriculture and the energies of agricultural interest groups have fostered a sense of agrarianism that pervades California politics. The Grange, the first of the well-organized agriculture groups and rather in decline now, the California Farm Bureau Federation, still the major force in agricultural politics, the Associated Farmers, a long-standing organization of considerable membership, and the Agricultural Council, an active statewide "public relations" association, have all worked hard at preserving and developing agriculture's good image. Excusing the pun, agriculture has real grass roots in California. It is not fortuitous that legislators are reported to rank agricultural interests among the most meritorious and respected.[30]

Agricultural interest groups, including those already mentioned as well

---

[29] See Henry Schacht, "California's Wealth and Pride in Agriculture," *California Monthly*, LXXXI, 10 (July–Aug. 1961), pp. 8–13, reprinted in C. M. Price and E. R. Kruschke, eds., *Consensus and Cleavage: Issues in California Politics* (San Francisco: Chandler Publishing Co., 1967), pp. 481–488, for a very energetic expression of the value of agriculture in California.

[30] Wahlke et al., op. cit., p. 318.

as the commodity organizations such as the California Cattlemen's Association, the California Milk Producers Federation, and the California Rice Growers Association, activity engage in lobbying at all levels of government. Together these groups constitute one of the most important lobbies among local governmental and state administrative units. It is interesting to note that although agricultural interests are viewed with great respect by legislators, they are not very numerous nor do they actually lobby the legislature as much as government, business, and labor groups. Again, this does not mean that they are not successful in protecting their interests, but merely that not much activity is required in the state legislature to protect their interests. Agriculture is so successful in California, politically as well as economically, that one could be misled by the relatively low expenditure of energy expended on lobbying the legislature.

"Agribusiness," as the growers and food-processor complex is called by friend and foe alike,[31] does have an enviable position. The California State Department of Agriculture has a strict clientele relationship with agricultural interest groups. Although the state department is not so important as it once was, its close ties with agribusiness is a tribute to the relative pervasiveness of agricultural power. The University of California, especially with its Giannini Foundation at Berkeley and flourishing Agricultural College at Davis, has long had close ties with agricultural interest groups.[32] The State Resources Agency and in particular its Department of Water Resources are amenable to the needs of agriculture. County government because of its power over land use and property taxation is a prime arena of agricultural interest; it is not uncommon for farmers to sit on the board of supervisors or planning commission in California counties. Many special districts, primarily those dealing with land or soil reclamation and conservation, or water management, are the domain of farmers and agricultural interest groups. Any fair appraisal of California politics must recognize the considerable activity and influence of agricultural interests in the state.

---

[31] See Schacht, op. cit., p. 481 and passim for favorable use of this term, and Anne and Hal Draper, *The Dirt California, Agribusiness and the University* (Berkeley: Independent Socialist Clubs of America, 1968), for unfavorable use of this term.

[32] The University of California, like many land-grant universities, historically has had very close ties with the U.S. Department of Agriculture, Federal Extension Service. For useful discussions of the agricultural extension service, with some references to the California experiences, see Charles M. Hardin, *The Politics of Agriculture* (New York: The Free Press, 1952), pp. 20–53, and Grant McConnell, *The Decline of Agrarian Democracy* (Berkeley and Los Angeles: University of California Press, 1959), pp. 1–67.

IDEOLOGICAL ORGANIZATIONS

Some organizations spend most of their energies trying to convince anyone who will listen to them that their own particular brand of political ideology is best and should be put into practice or maintained. A few such organizations have official lobbyists at the state capital and are considered to be legitimate practitioners of the lobbying art. Among the respectable groups are the Roman Catholic Church, the Council of Churches, the California branch of the Temperance League of America, and the American Civil Liberties Union. Some organizations lack complete acceptance, but are still legitimate enough to lobby with some hope of effectiveness. One might place the Young Americans for Freedom in this category.

More radical groups, from the viewpoint of the mainstream of American politics, are not likely to be very effective lobbies. Imagine the over-all effectiveness of lobbying by the John Birch Society, Students for a Democratic Society, the Communist party of California, the American Nazi party, the Minutemen, or the Independent Socialist Clubs of America.[33] Although all of these radical groups have a place in our politics and some of them appear to have direct and indirect influence on policy and policy makers, none of them seriously engages in or is accepted in the interest group politics game played by most of the organizations listed in this chapter. Although they may systematically attempt to mold public opinion, to influence officials, and to shape public policy, they are generally excluded from regular politics in California.[34]

Ideological organizations face odds that many other interest groups do not. Their goals, even among the most modest and respected of them, can, if put into practice, seriously modify the normal processes of government and politics. The more radical an ideology appears to its fellow practitioners of politics, the more difficulty it is likely to encounter in trying to get its way. Unacceptable groups often hope to and sometimes

---

[33] Surely someone is going to object and argue that some of these organizations are budding political parties or at least quasi-parties. It does appear that these organizations all want to hold office, a major test for a party. Some have actually nominated candidates for office and been on the official ballots at some level of government in California; all have tried to support candidates for office. We will argue, however, that they are not accorded the normal privileges of parties and are not able to act in the same fashion as the two major parties. They rest in a twilight zone and we view them as mostly behaving like interest groups.

[34] It is important to note that by and large, such radical groups are really different than unsuccessful interest groups that are permitted to choose to be part of regular politics. It is one thing to be excluded and another to be included but doomed to failure.

do become more legitimate through time, but it may be a very long time before the SDS becomes integrated into normal interest group politics. In fact, SDSers abhor the thought of political integration into the system as much as most politicians do. It is safe to say that ideological groups with the exception of the major political parties and their major splinter fringe organizations are of marginal consequence in the mainstream of California politics. They all are worth considering, in particular the more radical, because a set of forces are being side-stepped by our regular organized politics. It is difficult to speculate about the fate of such groups, but it is clear that many of them represent a growing, often violent dissent. One might hope that in time they will be brought into mainstream politics, but the evidence does not offer much hope at this time. Much of the so-called "New Politics" is composed of coalitions of extremist ideological and ethnic groups; mostly they are misunderstood and rejected by those of us who take part in regular politics. If the old politics and the new politics are to blend, then the demands of these groups must be accounted for in some manner.

ETHNIC GROUPS

California has many ethnic minorities. Almost any racial or national group has some representation in this state's large, diverse population. Of special importance, however, are four ethnic groups that have not been brought fully into the state's economic and political life. Negroes, who are often called Blacks nowadays, constitute the most obvious group of deprived persons, but an even larger group are the people with Spanish surnames.[35] Militants from this ethnic group refer to themselves as *Chicanos*, but they have been traditionally referred to as Mexicans, Mexican-Americans, and Latins. People whose ancestors lived somewhere in Asia form the next largest ethnic group[36] and the smallest but deprived the longest are the American Indians.[37] Aside from the fact that many of these people are not white their common denominator is their general political deprivation.

The depressing history of this deprivation in California of the Asians, Chicanos, Blacks, and Indians is too long to review in detail here. The relative gains and failures of ethnic organizations such as the NAACP, CORE, SNCC, MAPA (Mexican-American Political Association), and

---

[35] The U.S. Census of 1960 sets the Negro population of California at 883,861 and the Spanish surname population of the state at 1,426,538.

[36] In 1960, the "Asian" population of California was approximately 317,376.

[37] There were less than 40,000 American Indians in this state in 1960.

the American GI Forum are known. Although most Californians would congratulate themselves on the liberality of their personal racial attitudes and on the record of California, ethnic organizations have not been noted for their success in California politics. Even the most established ethnic politician realizes the small inroads his people have made in our state politics. It is true that there are more members in the state legislature from these groups than ever before,[38] but the historical record is not good. It is an uncontestable fact that the very poorest strata of California's total population are overwhelmingly composed of blacks, browns, yellows, and reds. There are many poor whites, but the non-white poor are more numerous in proportion to their total population.[39] The plight of the ethnic minorities is generally known and our state is responding in a fashion.

More radical groups are becoming increasingly important among ethnic minorities in California, especially among the young people. The Black Muslims, the Black Panther Party, and the Black Students' Union are the best known of the radical black organizations. The Brown Berets is the best organized and most militant organization among the Spanish-speaking population. Very recently an organization called the Third World Liberation Front has been organized to cut across boundaries of the ethnic minorities and to unite these people.

The most radical of these groups support separation of the races and the most moderate view American society as racist. The most radical demand partition of the nation and the most moderate espouse direct action and confrontation politics. These radical ethnic organizations are excluded from our regular politics. Partly this exclusion is based on their radical goals and methods; partly it is a function of their nationalism and racism; and partly it is because of the currents of racism in the white society. Whatever the reasons, these organizations represent a considerable number of young people who feel that traditional politics has little to offer them. It is a great tragedy for Californians.

MISCELLANEOUS

California has a number of organizations that act as interest groups but do not fit into any of the categories already provided. Some are very

---

[38] There are presently six Blacks in the California legislature, five in the Assembly, and one in the Senate. One *Chicano* is a member of the Assembly. There are two members of Asian descent in the Assembly and one in the Senate.

[39] In 1960, median family income among California's nonwhite population was $2,598 and among the total population it was $3,451.

active lobbies; the League of Women Voters and the Sierra Club are good examples. Some have rather specific interests, such as California's famous old-age pension lobbies. The California Institute of Social Welfare is an offshoot of the "Ham and Eggs" movement of the 1930s and under the leadership of the late George McLain and others has been an interesting and important lobby from time to time.[40] A number of other groups might be added, but the few named will serve to illustrate the many groups that are not easily classified.

VARIETY AND CONFLICT

The foregoing discussion should provide an indication of the vast numbers and kinds of organizations that may be viewed as interest groups. Although there are significant variations in the relative power of the groups both within and without the established politics of the state, there is no question that such a variety lays the foundation for continuous conflict among organized interests. According to orthodox group theory, the great variety of groups and resultant group conflicts are positive virtues for a democratic society.[41]

Organized interest groups must engage in conflict with each other, but the conflicts among groups must be contained within known bounds and rules. For without the regularized clash of interest groups, our nominally pluralistic society would not be very pluralistic.

interest group operation

California has been said to illustrate "the triumph of many interests."[42] The great variety of interests that apply organized pressure upon government officials certainly supports this contention. Although the California legislature was once dominated by a single interest group,

---

[40] The classic discussion of old-age pension groups in California is Frank A. Pinner, Paul Jacobs, and Philip Selznick, *Old Age and Political Behavior* (Berkeley and Los Angeles: University of California Press, 1959); especially pp. 1–22 and 201–264.

[41] See Robert A. Dahl, *A Preface to Democratic Theory* (Chicago: University of Chicago Press, 1956), for a statement of the orthodox theory of democratic pluralism in America; see Peter Bachrack, *The Theory of Democratic Elitism* (Boston: Little, Brown and Company, 1967), for a critique of the orthodoxy.

[42] Zeigler, op. cit., pp. 125–126. See also Buchanan, op. cit., pp. 28–48 and 60–61.

the Southern Pacific Railroad, and during the 1930s and 1940s was dominated by a coalition of groups, current events suggest that no set of interests has overwhelming influence in the legislature or anywhere else in the state government. Close examination of some local polities might reveal that a few interests dominate their politics, but this is not true about our larger towns and cities.[43] It is safe to say that California comes as close as any state to having the diverse and fractionated political structure admired by pluralists.

Interest group politics in California is competitive.[44] Not only are there a lot of interests in the state, but within the boundaries of a given interest there is likely to be more than one organization that speaks or claims to speak for the interest. Thus, in any given policy decision, a number of different organizations usually are going to confront the decision makers, each with a point of view. A word of caution: California interest group competition should not be viewed as competition among equals. One of the most obvious lessons of politics is that relative power is unequally distributed. Some interest groups are more influential than others. The main point, however, is that our state is noted for the over-all importance of the interest group struggle in policy making.

The struggle among interest groups is most obvious in the legislative process. Some people feel that lobbying is or should be restricted exclusively to the legislative branch. It is our contention that lobbying—systematic attempts to influence decision makers—occurs throughout the government. All governmental actors are potential recipients of interest group influence, and California, with a particularly pluralistic political system, provides large numbers of potential points of access for interest groups. Our intention here is to illustrate the interest group access in the California policy through discussion of several arenas of policy making.

---

[43] See Eugene C. Lee, *The Politics of Nonpartisanship* (Berkeley and Los Angeles: University of California Press, 1960), Chapter 6, "Groups, Leaders, and Influence," pp. 70–96, for a general discussion of groups and their impact on city politics in California; Ritchie P. Lowry, *Who's Running This Town* (New York: Harper and Row Publishers, Inc., 1965), for a controversial study of a small college town in northern California, which argues that a coalition of interests dominate its politics; Edward C. Banfield, *Big City Politics* (New York: Random House, Inc., 1965), Chapter 5, and Francis M. Carney, "The Decentralized Politics of Los Angeles," *The Annals of the American Academy of Political and Social Science,* 353 (May 1964), pp. 107–121, for discussions of pluralistic politics in Los Angeles.

[44] As a point of comparison, see Duane Lockard's *New England State Politics* (Princeton: University of Princeton Press, 1959). Various chapters deal with specific states. Of particular interest are his discussions of interest groups in Maine, where timber, electric power, and manufacturing dominate the legislature, pp. 107–118; in Connecticut, where many groups struggle for power, pp. 285–291; and in Rhode Island, where labor tends to dominate other groups, pp. 221–225.

Legislative policy making is a good starting point not only because of general acceptance of lobbying there but also because the history of legislative lobbying in this state has been colorful.

INTEREST GROUPS AND LEGISLATORS

The close relationship among lobbyists and legislators has led some observers to characterize the lobbies as the "third house." Lobbyists are so important in California that they are more than a third house; they actually are an integral part of the operations of both the state Assembly and Senate. The reasons for this intimate involvement of lobbyists in the legislative process are many, but in general they are all functions of a central fact: Interest groups are able to provide legislators with services not available from other organizations including political parties. Although parties and partisanship have increased in importance in recent years, it is still true that legislators are dependent upon interest groups for such crucial services as campaign resources, basic information about issues, assistance in resolving conflicts among interests, communication with clientele and constituency groups, and development of a sense of congeniality in the legislative process. The reciprocal relationship that brings legislators to intervene in behalf of interests rests upon the capacity of interest groups to make legislative life more bearable and to make political careers possible.

The extent to which legislators may become dependent upon lobbyists and interest groups for vital services is illustrated by the pre-eminence of Arthur H. Samish in the 1930s and 1940s. Mr. Samish, who never held an official position in the California legislature, was the most powerful man in that body for nearly twenty years. Not a few people, including Samish himself, felt that he was the most powerful person in the state. Whatever his total power in the state, Samish's role as broker for some major interests permitted him to become the single most important man in the legislative process.[45]

Although Samish was a shady operator, much of his power and much of his corruption were functions of the political environment of the times.[46] The state legislature of the 1930s was not an attractive place

---

[45] The definitive treatment of Samish is Elmer R. Rusco, "Machine Politics, California Model: Arthur H. Samish and the Alcoholic Beverage Industry," unpublished Ph.D dissertation, Dept. of History, University of California. Berkeley, 1960. See also Buchanan, op. cit., pp. 24–25 for a list of specific lobbies for which Samish labored.

[46] This theme is developed by Buchanan, op. cit., pp. 13–27.

to work. Salaries of the legislators were woefully inadequate;[47] both parties were in disarray; lobbyists had free run of the state capital and the legislative chambers; staff assistance was almost nonexistent; room to work was impossible to secure; and rules of conduct were poorly enforced.[48] To be a member of the legislature was a dubious privilege. If one was not wealthy, it was an intolerable economic burden. The impoverishment of the individual legislator was the secret of Samish's success; one could not survive without additional resources and Mr. Samish was willing to provide them—at a price.

Samish was able to develop an organization that served as a central clearing house for many interest groups. His "brokerage firm" was able to distribute to individual legislators funds provided by groups. The free dinners, extra expenses, campaign contributions, and organized assistance made the difference for many legislators between a continuing career in politics and losing in the next campaign. Once Samish was able to graphically illustrate the relative efficiency of his operation, other lobbyists, additional interest groups, and increased numbers of legislators began to openly partake of his services. Thus, he became an able broker among interests and legislators.

Although Samish's operations were entirely known within the environs of Sacramento and his role as broker was detailed in a report in 1939,[49] it is significant that his decline as boss of the legislature did not come until 1949 with the publication of two exposé articles in *Collier's*,[50] and his demise as an influence in the legislature until 1953 when he was imprisoned for federal income tax violations. The legislature evidently found the Samish system of brokerage as profitable as did the interest groups.

---

[47] A legislator's salary was $1,200 per year in 1930. This plus per diem was insufficient to cover even the basic living expenses. See ibid., pp. 19–20.

[48] Ibid., pp. 18–21, for details.

[49] A report, known as the Philbrick Report, exposing corruption in both houses of the legislature was completed in 1938. The incoming governor, Culbert Olson, had copies made and distributed. The Senate's copy was published in its *Journal* on April 4, 1939, but all copies were ordered destroyed and the *Journal* was reprinted without the Philbrick Report. Although publicity resulting from this report forced the retirement of several legislators, Samish remained in power for ten more years. See Buchanan, op. cit., pp. 24–25.

[50] A famous article in which Samish boasted that he ran California and that he was more powerful than Governor Warren was published in 1949; see Lester Velie, "The Secret Boss of California," *Collier's* (August 13 and 20, 1949), reprinted in David Farrelly and Ivan Hinderaker, *The Politics of California* (New York: The Ronald Press Company, 1951), pp. 197–205.

This national exposure brought pressure upon the legislature to reform its relationships with lobbyists, but Samish continued to act as a lobbyist until 1953.

The famous "Secret Boss of California" articles in *Collier's* brought about a public outcry for more control over the activities of lobbyists. A special legislative session passed the California Lobbying Act in 1949. This statute, patterned after the Federal Regulation of Lobbying Act of 1946, requires the registration of "legislative advocates" (paid lobbyists) and others who receive money or any other thing of value to be used in aiding the enactment or defeat of any legislation.[51] Each lobbyist or advocate must register with the legislative analyst and file monthly reports listing bills he has been paid to support or oppose, monies received for services and expenditures made as advocate. Other individuals and organizations not using paid advocates but attempting to lobby are required to file statements listing all contributions of $100 or more, expenditures of $25 or more, and total expenditures. Responsibility for administering this statute rests with the legislature, which has delegated it to the committees on legislative representation in each house. These committees certify the registrations, issue periodic reports listing registrations, and review the statements filed by lobbyists and organizations.

A study published in 1956 indicated that the California Lobbying Act had done a great deal to prevent the recurrence of the open corruption of the Samish era, but that lobbyists continue to wield considerable influence in the California legislature.[52] It appears that California's law which ". . . has been more fully and precisely interpreted than other state [lobby regulation] laws . . ."[53] is not administered in a manner to inspire confidence. Although recently there have been improvements, the Assembly and Senate Committees on Legislative Representation are not overly zealous administrators of the regulation statute. Willie L. Brown, Jr., chairman of the Assembly Committee on Legislative Representation in 1967, served notice that he was going to try to strictly enforce the Lobbying Act,[54] but his action is exceptional and there is little over-all evidence of legislative interest in the improvement of the regulation of lobbying. Thus, although California's lobby regulation statute is impressive when compared with other states, its value as a means of actually controlling any but the most corrupt of practices is questionable.[55]

---

[51] Excluded from the provisions of this statute are public officials acting in official capacities, persons merely testifying before committees, representatives of churches, and the press and media. Political committees that are under regulation of the Election Code are exempted from having to file contribution and expenditure reports.

[52] Mary Ellen Leary, "The Legislature," *California State Government: Its Tasks and Organizations* (Stanford: California Assembly, 1956).

[53] Edgar Lane, *Lobbying and the Law* (Berkeley and Los Angeles: University of California Press, 1964), p. 165; see also pp. 162–168.

[54] *Sacramento Bee*, January 1, 1967.

[55] Lane, op. cit., pp. 154–168.

Among the most valuable services provided the legislator by the lobbyists and interest groups is assistance in campaigning. It is sufficient to say here that few legislators can afford to finance their own election campaigns. Interest groups provide most of the money, much of the organizational support, and many of the workers necessary to run even a losing campaign. Even though parties are the official organizations responsible for elections and campaigning in California, the lobbies dominate the campaigning process.

California legislators are past the days when wining and dining provided by lobbyists was a main source of subsistence.[56] The lunch or dinner provided by the lobbyists is still very productive. In general, it provides a setting for relaxed and congenial discussion of what is happening during the session, hearing, or party caucus. The friendly and gentlemanly relationships developed over food and drink go a long way in making the legislator feel needed, loved, and respected. Much of the good feeling and understanding that lobbyists require to be effective are developed in the wine and dine circuit. Eating lunch with the correct lobbyists or legislator is an inside status symbol that neither can do without. The clubby congeniality that characterizes the in-groups of the California legislature is maintained by the very large amounts each lobbyist spends each session.[57]

It is generally understood that lobbyists are vital sources of information for legislators.[58] Not only are lobbyists and other representatives of interest groups of consequence in the legislative hearings, but they appear to be a significant source of information outside the hearing room.[59] The relative lack of staff assistance and research facilities among

---

[56] The voters approved a constitutional amendment in 1966, which raised the salary of the legislator from $6,000 to $16,000 annually. This adequate salary and the establishment of annual sessions has gone a long way toward making the holding of a seat in the legislature a full-time job.

[57] During the 1967 session, an estimated $1,122,165 was officially spent by lobbyists (*Sacramento Bee*, Sunday, October 29, 1967). A check of individual expenditure reports shows that a considerable amount of this total, perhaps as much as 60 per cent, is spent on restaurant, bar, liquor store, and hotel bills.

[58] See: Lester W. Milbrath, *The Washington Lobbyists* (Chicago: Rand McNally & Company, 1963), pp. 209–235 for material about the information function of lobbyists in Washington, D.C.; and Harmon Zeigler and Michael Baer, *Lobbying: Interaction and Influence in American State Legislatures* (Belmont, Calif.: Wadsworth Publishing Company, Inc., 1969), pp. 162–171 for an assessment of the information function of lobbyists in the state legislatures of Massachusetts, North Carolina, Oregon, and Utah.

[59] See Zeigler and Baer, op. cit., pp. 167–170. Data gathered by Professor Wayne L. Francis for *Legislative Issues in the Fifty States: a Comparative Analysis* indicate that California legislators view lobbyists as a major source of information about issues. All fifteen respondents from California indicated that interest group representatives or administrators were significant sources of information in assisting the legislator in making up his mind to support or oppose a particular bill

the state legislatures as compared with Congress are offered as reasons why state legislators are more prone to depend upon lobbyists as sources of primary information. California, however, probably has the best staffed and supported legislature among the fifty states. Thus, California legislators have good personal and committee staffs for research, but still depend upon lobbyists for data both through the hearing process and by personal contact.

Lobbyists also assist in securing support in both houses for bills introduced by legislators. An interesting case in point is a bill introduced by Assemblyman Jim Bear (Democrat, 79th District, San Diego) during the 1967 session, a bill to expand the California State Scholarship program, which permits deserving students to attend institutions of higher learning in this state. Mr. Bear, who was a professor of law and Assistant Dean of the College of Law at the University of San Diego, knew the value of these scholarships to students and to colleges and universities.[60]

Assemblyman Bear faced little difficulty securing passage of his bill in the lower house. It was modified slightly and passed from the Assembly Education Committee's Subcommittee on Higher Education with a favorable "do pass" recommendation. The bill's next hurdle was the Assembly Ways and Means Committee, which must pass on all money bills. During hearings before this committee, the state Department of Finance, an arm of the Governor's Office, opposed the bill because of its anticipated costs (for 1971–1972, $8,030,400) and because of the then-current conflict over the "tuition question" for the state colleges and state university. The Democratic majority of the committee did not agree with the Department of Finance and passed the bill from committee with a "do pass" recommendation. The bill was passed from the Assembly by a vote of 57 ayes and 3 nays.

The state Senate posed a more difficult task for Mr. Bear and his scholarship bill. The bill was quickly passed through the Education Committee with a "do pass" recommendation. The bill was next reviewed by the powerful Senate Finance Committee. In the days before the public hearings, lobbyists representing the Association of Independent California Colleges and Universities, the California State Colleges, and the University of California made personal contacts with members of the Senate Finance Committee expressing their support of Mr. Bear's bill.

---

when he is uncertain. California respondents also mentioned as frequently as administrators and interest group representatives, both of the following: legislator-specialists and community leaders from the district.

[60] Miss Kim Eileen Gilbert did most of the research for this discussion of scholarship legislation.

The lobbyist for the Association of California Independent Colleges and Universities, Mr. Morgan Odell, was especially important to the passage of this bill in the Senate; he made sure members understood the importance of the bill to his group. This bill proved to be the most vital bill of the session for his organization. Much of the organization's energies were expended in mailing letters and circulars to prominent alumni, suggesting they write to legislators and to the Governor in support of the bill. Despite strong opposition throughout from the Department of Finance, the bill passed the Senate, 29 to 3, and was signed into law by Governor Reagan.

This narrative illustrates several essential points about interest groups in the legislative process. First, it would be difficult to push a bill through both houses of the legislature without support from lobbyists. Mr. Bear was able to "lobby" his bill through the Assembly, but the Department of Finance might have succeeded in derailing it in the Senate or killing it at the gubernatorial level without the political support provided by the various interest groups and their lobbyists. The united front presented in favor of this bill by the major lobbies of higher education in California no doubt encouraged speedy passage in the Senate and signature by Governor Reagan. Second, the interests helped legislators choose sides by lining up public and private support and opposition for the bill. The coalition of the higher education lobbies made it clear that "education" supported Mr. Bear's proposal. The issue of more scholarship support became cast into a conflict between "economy" (Department of Finance) and "educational opportunity" (higher education) and legislators could make a rational choice between contending sides. Third, public agencies, the university and the state colleges, threw their support behind a bill more beneficial to the private institutions of higher learning than to them. The scholarship program is a boon to private schools that lack large-scale public support. The lobbyists representing the public institutions were willing to support the private lobbyist because of long-run common needs and goals; a united front that exists over time can be an effective force in the legislature. Fourth, the lobbyists and their organizations provided excellent "press" and communication with constituency groups for Mr. Bear and the other Assemblymen and Senators who joined him in cosponsoring the bill as well as the Governor who signed the bill into law.

Thus, in this case, private and public organizations and their lobbyists performed all of the normal legislative functions we have come to expect from interest groups. They provided support, information, communication, and publicity. It is easy to see that interest groups are crucial elements in the political linkage system. Perhaps Mr. Bear's bill would have fared well without active support (and opposition) from specific lobbyists; this is questionable,[61] but even if true, the groups and their lobbyists enhanced the record of the individual politicians involved and provided a vital means of exchanging information within the legislative process.

INTEREST GROUPS AND ADMINISTRATORS

Open lobbying that characterizes the legislature is almost unknown in executive departments. Most lobbying of administrators outside official hearings is done behind closed doors. The covert nature of administrative-interest group contact leads some people to believe or pretend it does not exist. The popular belief that lobbying takes place in the legislature and not in the executive branch is not true, but it is buttressed by California law.

Most administrators in this state are covered by civil service regulations; very few are actually political appointees. The merit system, in which officials are recruited, placed, promoted, and compensated on the basis of merit, has been fully operational in California since 1934. Civil servants are further protected from "political influences" by California's version of the Hatch Act, which severely constrains an appointed public official under the merit system in his partisan political activities.

The merit system umbrella, however, does not prevent interest group activity from intervening in the executive departments. As powerful decision makers the Governor and the other elected members of the executive branch are naturally centers of interest group activity. Appointed members of some boards and commissions are also crucial decision makers and receive their share of interest group attention. The same is true of the noncivil-service positions in the higher levels of the various departments. And, in spite of the merit system, lower-level public servants also are potential contacts for interest groups and their lobbyists.

In fact, interest groups are less likely to try to influence the Governor or other top official than the other administrators of the executive departments. The reason is simple. Interest groups are usually interested in

---

[61] It is interesting to note that state Senator Mervin Dymally introduced a bill in the same session to create 500 new state scholarship subsistence grants at the college level for economic disadvantaged students who display academic ability. This bill had a considerably more difficult time passing through the legislature and was vetoed by Governor Reagan. It lacked support from the independent college and universities lobby; no letters, editorials, circulars, and old grad pressure was forthcoming in support of this bill. It was not strongly lobbied and lacked the bipartisan legislative and public support of Mr. Bear's bill.

a very specialized, specific thing. They want to zero in on the particular agency or administrator who is responsible for the specific policy in which they are interested. If the agency is removed from partisan politics, so much the better. The more isolated from partisanship and public control an agency is, the better the lobbyist likes it. Nothing is better than to engage in influence politics in a situation where the people involved are "nonpolitical" and "above politics."

The interaction between interest group and agency is a delicate, carefully balanced relationship. The interest group tries to secure a regular channel of influence and the agency tries to build support for its programs by securing regular clients. A good example of this is the relationship between the Department of Fish and Game and the many public and private interest groups it serves.

A series of controversies over proposed changes in the operations of the state Department of Fish and Game illustrate the extent to which the fortunes of interest groups and agencies become merged.[62] The Department of Fish and Game along with its policy-advisory boards—the Fish and Game Commission, the Wildlife Conservation Board, and the Marine Research Committee—is responsible for the management and protection of California's abundant wildlife resources. The agency performs its functions under considerable pressure from private sportsmen and conservation groups. The clientele relationship is especially strong because of the special financial structure of the agency. Except for some capital funds coming from the Wildlife Conservation Board, the department has been funded almost entirely from fees paid by individual sportsmen. Sportsmen, paying the major share of the costs of the department's operations, have come to view it as their agency. They assume it is primarily intended to serve their demands and they expect to have a powerful voice in policy making and administration in the department.

There are an estimated 1,500,000 to 2,000,000 sportsmen in California. About 10 per cent of this number take part in the affairs of sportsmen's associations. The state has many local clubs and sportsmen represent one of the most fragmented lobbies in state politics. Under encouragement from the Department of Fish and Game, the California Wildlife Federation was organized in 1954 as an affiliate of a national body. This was an attempt to federate the 640 local clubs into nine regional councils. The department felt that it could better deal with regional council than individual clubs. The federation was not very successful in uniting the sports-

---

[62] Most of the material upon which this discussion is based is taken from John R. Owens, *A Wildlife Agency and Its Possessive Public*, Inter-University Case Program, Inc., No. 87 (Indianapolis: The Bobbs-Merrill Co., Inc., 1965).

men and most local groups continue to go their own way. Thus, the department continues to face an array of organizations, each making its demands and each urging the decision makers to act in many and often conflicting ways.

In 1956, the Department of Fish and Game decided that the only way to secure the additional funds needed for its many programs was a general raise in basic hunting and fishing fees. The department recommended to the legislature during the 1957 session that license fees be raised. The sportsmen's groups took a dim view of this suggestion and attempted to secure opposing legislation. A major question was the formula for the fee increases. The department favored across the board increases, which was opposed by many individual groups and clubs. During the hearings to consider the department's proposals and alternative legislation, representatives from the department, legislature, the California Wildlife Federation, Associated Sportsmen of California, the Sacramento-Sierra Sports Council, and the state Chamber of Commerce testified. All agreed that the department was in difficulty, but they could not agree on what should be done; in particular, which fees should be raised. Under pressure from unhappy sportsmen's groups, the issue was compromised. Fee raises, using a different formula, were legislated and a study was ordered to see if the department could be more efficiently administered.

The firm of Booz, Allen and Hamilton (BAH) was given the contract to study the operations of the Department of Fish and Game. The department did not welcome this study and was most unhappy with some of its major recommendations concerning reorganization of the top levels of the department. The department found itself in the awkward position of resisting recommendations made on behalf of its main clientele groups, the sportsmen. Agency administrators, through delay and playing off factions of sportsmen's groups against each other, were able to blunt the most critical of the recommendations made by BAH.

Our examination of the Fish and Game Department demonstrates the rather delicate balance of relationships between administrators and interest groups. The department felt strained when confronted with a diversity of groups and opinions. Its natural inclination is to attempt to consolidate its clientele groups into a single manageable entity. As our case illustrates, however, an agency seldom enjoys this luxury. There is not likely to be a one to one relationship between agency and organization. An agency is more likely to face a multitude of claims from not a few groups, each with its own special interpretation of what should be done. A second point is that the agency attempts to influence clientele groups as much as groups try to influence the agency. Although the Department of Fish and Game is not overly successful in their attempts, their mode of operation suggests they would like a little more influence among sportsmen's associations. Agencies need support, not criticism, before legislative committees and hearings. A final point. The balance of power in the reciprocal relationship between agency and clientele groups is likely to rest with the agency. Although the Department of Fish and Game got into trouble over the fee raises, the fees were raised and the department was able to resist most of the reforms suggested by BAH. Interest groups win battles, but public agencies prevail.

INTEREST GROUPS AND THE PUBLIC

The public is expected to intervene in California government; it is official doctrine that citizens should participate in their own government. Public opinion is supposed to influence governmental decision making. Citizens are expected to nominate and select their rulers. Voters are required to actively take part in law making through direct democracy. Interest groups, always anxious to seek their opportunities and take advantage of them, must be concerned with the public at large and with voters in particular.

The activity of interest groups in elections and campaigning for public office is discussed in detail elsewhere in this book. Here we are more concerned with the capacity of interest groups to secure specific legislative victory through direct appeal to the voters. There is no question that much indirect influence upon government may be exercised by interest groups through the cultivation of a good image and the education of the people. Resultant public opinion often has considerable influence upon politicians, especially those who follow the public opinion polls. In California, however, it is possible for interest groups to supplement or bypass their governmental lobbying activities and to appeal to the people through the mechanics of direct democracy. Although many states have provisions for recall, referendum, and initiative,[63] California is surely the dreamland of direct democracy.

The instruments of direct democracy—*recall, initiative,* and *referendom*—were adopted in California in 1911 by the Progressives. Direct democracy was intended to put government into the hands of the people in order to thwart powerful interest groups and the political parties.

---

[63] Twenty-one states provide for initiative or referendum; twelve states permit recall elections at the state level; many states provide for recall at local levels. See Winston W. Crouch, *The Initiative and Referendum in California* (Los Angeles: Haynes Foundation, 1950), for the definitive interpretation of the California experience.

Direct democracy may weaken parties but in California there is evidence to suggest that it actually increases the relative influence of interest groups. Although recall has not been used extensively in California, the initiative and referendum have. Most direct legislation not put on the ballot by the legislature has been put there by interest groups.

Recall elections are intended to remove from public office persons who have proven to be poorly qualified, corrupt, or incompetent. A recall petition must be prepared which states the charges against the official(s) whose removal is sought. For statewide officials, the petition must be signed by electors equal in number to 12 per cent of the total vote cast for that office in the preceding general election and the petition must be signed in each of five counties by voters equal in number to at least 1 per cent of those voting for candidates for that office. Recall petitions for local officials or state officials elected from a subdivision of the state must be signed by electors equal in number to 20 per cent of those voting for candidates for that office in the preceding election.

Petitions are sent to the appropriate certifying official; in the case of state offices, it is the Secretary of State. He verifies and certifies the signatures and petition, and then sends the petition to the Governor who must institute the second stage of the recall process: the election. He must call an election not less than sixty nor more than eighty days after certification.

The citizen is actually asked to vote twice. He must choose to recall the incumbent and to name his successor. Individuals who want to run for the contested office may become candidates by filing a petition signed by electors equal in number to 1 per cent of the vote cast for that office in the preceding election. The challenged incumbent must face the recall charges and run against other candidates at the same time.

To prevent undue use of this device and to give elected officials a chance, a recall petition cannot be circulated against a public official (who is not a member of the legislature) until he has held office for six months. Legislators may face recall petitions five days after the start of a legislative session or six months after election to office, whichever is earlier.

Although these provisions seem permissive and perhaps a little reckless, recall has not been actively used except in local politics.[64] Our last two Governors, Pat Brown and Ronald Reagan, had recall petitions circulated

---

[64] As pointed out in Turner and Vieg, *The Government and Politics of California,* p. 88, the recall has been used primarily in California in cities, most notably in Los Angeles where four mayors have faced recall elections and two were removed from office.

by persons taking exception to their management of the government, but the petitions failed to contain sufficient certified signatures for calling an election. The most famous recent case of recall involved the Tax Assessor of Sacramento County, Dr. Irene Hickman. Although the recall petition was successful, the election was not and Dr. Hickman retained her office. It is hard to take recall procedure seriously, especially at the state level. In any event, interest groups have shown little interest in recall at the state level and it remains an unused artifact of reformers' passion.

Referendum and *initiative* procedures have proved much more useful to interest groups. In a strict sense *referendum* applies to those issues which are brought before the electorate by action of the voters rather than the legislature.[65] These petition referendums may be used to require a measure that has been enacted into law by the legislature and signed by the Governor to be submitted for approval by the voters. Although certain measures are exempted from petition referendum—including acts calling for elections, revenue and appropriation bills, and emergency measures passed by two-thirds vote of both houses—most legislation is subject to referendum within the sixty-day period after adjournment of the regular legislative session or the ninety-day period after adjournment of a special legislative session. During this period before the legislation goes into effect, a petition signed by qualified electors equal in number to five per cent of the vote in the previous election for governor and certified by the Secretary of State will prevent a piece of legislation from becoming law and will require its submission to voters for approval. A majority of the voters must approve it or the bill is defeated.

The third form of direct democracy, the *initiative*, permits voters to propose statutes and constitutional amendments. After a proposal is drafted, it is submitted to the Attorney General who prepares a statement describing the proposed legislation in 100 words or less. This statement is attached to the petitions circulated by supporters of the proposal. To be certified and placed on the ballot, the petition must have the signatures of qualified voters equal to 5 per cent (for statutes) or 8 per cent (for constitutional amendments) of the vote in the last gubernatorial election. A majority vote is necessary for passage of initiative measures. It should be noted that initiative measures are attractive to interest groups because they can be amendments to the constitution and

---

[65] The referendum has two distinct forms in California. The *required* or *compulsory* referendum pertains to constitutional amendments and bond issues passed by the legislature; these must be submitted to the voters for approval. The *protest, optional,* or *petition* referendum permits citizens to vote on statutes passed by the legislature upon petition by a specified number of electors.

once passed cannot be declared unconstitutional by state courts. Thus, it may be tempting to try to use the initiative for securing a locked-in provision; the fact that eighty-four of the 142 initiative measures proposed since 1911 have been constitutional amendments testifies to this temptation.[66]

What has been the utility of the initiative and referendum for interest groups? In general, it is argued that direct democracy, principally the referendum and initiative, have done more to increase than to reduce interest group power. Table 7–1 summarizes the success of initiative and referendum proposals in California.

TABLE 7–1   CALIFORNIA STATEWIDE INITIATIVE AND REFERENDUM PROPOSALS, 1911–1968*

	On Ballot	Passed
Initiative constitutional amendments	84	23
Initiative statutes	58	16
Referendums†	35	14
Totals	177	53

* After Henry A. Turner and John A. Vieg, *The Government and Politics of California*, p. 92.
† Not included here are 458 constitutional amendments, statutes, and bond issues submitted to the voters by the legislature.

The table shows that about three initiative or recall measures have been presented to the voters per year and about four fifths have been initiative measures. In relation to the number of bills introduced into legislature each session—over 3,000 in the 1968 session alone—the total number of 177 ballot measures does not seem very impressive. If one considers, however, that some of the most controversial and vital issues in California have been ballot propositions, then the use of initiative and recall becomes relatively more impressive.

Among the eighty-four constitutional amendments proposed by initiative have been the 1956 Proposition 4 permitting the development of California's offshore oil resources and the 1968 Proposition 9, which was designed to curtail the use of property taxes for certain purposes. The defeat of these measures seriously affected the state's public and private

66 Turner and Vieg, op. cit., p. 91.

economies. The oil and gas measure was supported by the major oil interests and was opposed by conservation groups and the smaller oil companies. The property tax proposal was supported by the California Real Estate Association, the California Apartment House Owners Association, some farm groups, and several local taxpayers groups. A wide range of interests including labor, education, the state Chamber of Commerce, many local governmental units, the California Taxpayers Association and the Governor opposed this measure and supported an alternative measure, Proposition 1A on the same ballot.

Probably the most famous of recent ballot proposals, at least outside of California, was Proposition 14 of 1964.[67] This initiative would have invalidated the Rumford Act and other fair housing statutes. The main legislation in question was introduced during the 1963 legislative session by Assemblyman W. Byron Rumford and it quickly became the most controversial piece of legislation that year. The bill had the support of various civil rights groups, the CDC, some of the Democratic leaders of the legislature, including Speaker Jesse Unruh, and Governor Pat Brown. After considerable controversy and delay, the bill passed out of the Senate and was signed by Governor Brown. The Rumford Act did not go into effect until after the ninety-day period set aside for circulation of referendum petitions. The interest groups that had opposed the bill in the legislature, notably the California Real Estate Association, chose not to try to secure a protest referendum but instead opted for a constitutional initiative for the next general election. The Rumford Act became law on September 20, 1963.

The Rumford Act was a bitter defeat for conservative interest groups in the state. The act states

The practice of discrimination because of race, color, religion, national origin, or ancestry in housing accommodations is declared to be against public policy.

This part [of the Health and Safety Code] shall be deemed an exercise of the police power of the State for the protection of the welfare, health, and peace of the people of the state.

---

[67] Most of this discussion of Proposition 14 is taken from Thomas W. Casstevens, *Politics, Housing and Race Relations: California's Rumford Act and Proposition 14* (Berkeley: Institute of Governmental Studies, University of California, June 1967).

An analysis of voting behavior on this initiative is contained in Raymond E. Wolfinger and Fred I. Greenstein, "The Repeal of Fair Housing in California: an Analysis of Referendum Voting," *American Political Science Review,* LXII (Sept. 1968), pp. 753–769.

This legislation seriously threatens conventional interpretation of property rights as viewed by many real estate firms and apartment owners. In response to this threat, the California Real Estate Association and the California Apartment Owners' Association formed the Committee for Home Protection. The organization was to develop support for and to sponsor an initiative constitutional amendment to repeal the Rumford Act and other fair housing laws. Proposition 14, as the initiative was listed on the 1964 election ballot, came as a result of a petition signed by about 600,000 qualified voters, somewhat over the 468,259 required.

In general, the initiative sought to severely restrict the police power of the state in the regulation of housing practices. In part, it read

> Neither the state nor any subdivision or agency thereof shall deny, limit, or abridge, directly or indirectly, the right of any person, who is willing or desires to sell, lease, or rent any part or all of his real property, to decline to sell, lease, or rent such property to such person or persons as he, in his absolute discretion, chooses.

The language is very broad and challenges much of California's fair housing statutes. Opponents tried to prevent the proposal from being put on the 1964 general election ballot, but the writ of mandamus sought by a NAACP attorney was denied and the initiative became the fourteenth proposition on the 1964 ballot.

A bitter and highly controversial campaign followed. Opponents urged political leaders and groups to take a stand on Proposition 14, and many did. The Committee for Home Protection developed a statewide network of local committees to develop support for their initiative. The opponents, with the assistance of civil rights groups such as the NAACP, CORE, and the ACLU, also attempted to form local support groups, but they were noticeably less successful. Although some radical right groups embarrassed the Committee for Home Protection, with considerable financial and organizational support from local real estate firms and associations, it ran a smooth campaign aimed at defending traditional property rights from infringements by this Rumford Act.

Considerable funds were expended during the campaign. California law requires expenditure reports to be filed with the Secretary of State;[68] these official records gave some idea of the relative amounts spent by the two sides. Total expenditures on Proposition 14, as reported, were

---

[68] State law requires that any person or organization spending $1,000 or more on a statewide ballot measure must file a report with the Secretary of State. It is unlikely that anything near the actual amounts spent are reported; for example, some people have estimated that more than two million dollars was spent on Proposition 14 as compared with the less than one million dollars officially reported.

$879,000; the proponents reported $379,000 and the opponents reported $500,000 was spent. Although more money has been spent on other initiative campaigns,[69] this is a sizeable sum. Nearly nine tenths of a million dollars represents a considerable investment for any set of interest groups.

The Committee for Home Protection proved to be an effective mobilizer of public opinion. Proposition 14 was passed by the voters on election day by nearly a two-to-one margin (4,526,460 "yes" to 2,395,747 "no"). This victory, however, was not the end of the struggle among interest groups over the Rumford Act and Proposition 14. Civil rights groups immediately set about to challenge the initiative in the courts. The initiative was declared invalid, in conflict with the fourteenth Amendment to the U.S. Constitution, on May 10, 1966, by a five-to-two vote of the California Supreme Court.

The Proposition 14 campaign illustrates the high investments which interest groups will make in appealing to the public. It also demonstrates the most common causes of complaints against the initiative and referendum system. Such campaigns are very expensive and have become highly sophisticated. Only well-organized, rather affluent coalitions of interests can afford to pursue the kinds of professional public relations campaigns associated with most ballot measures. The campaigns are often bitter, emotional contests in which the voter is not likely to make a choice between carefully argued positions. Instead, the voter is likely to be asked to respond to false images and half truths. Finally, it is relatively easy for an interest group to put a measure on the ballot. Although most interest groups are not disposed to use ballot measures unless defeated in the legislature, important issues have been put on the ballot through initiative and referendum. Direct democracy makes it easier, not harder, for interest groups to ply their trade.

interest group power in california

Interest groups are among the most influential forces in California politics. Their influence is felt in the political parties, the electoral campaigns, the making of public policy, and the administration of govern-

---

[69] Turner and Vieg, op. cit., p. 95, report that more than 4.8 million dollars were spent in the 1956 campaign on the oil and gas initiative. This is probably an all-time high for a single proposition, but in 1964, more than $500,000 was spent on each of the four initiative measures according to these authors.

ment. To a large extent, the exercise of public authority in this state reflects the needs and desires of the many powerful interests. In a sense, California does represent the victory of interest group politics.

Their pervasive influence presents some crucial questions about the functions of interest groups in California. Some groups are ineffective; it is essential to determine what makes an interest group effective. Functional representation is provided by interest groups; this representation has its own special bias. The public good requires control and regulation of interest groups; this control and regulation is relatively ineffective. The balance of our discussion will be devoted to a consideration of these points. As has been stated forcefully elsewhere, it is best to know "Whose game do we play?"[70]

WHAT MAKES AN EFFECTIVE INTEREST GROUP?

The answer to this question depends a great deal upon whom you ask. Lobbyists are inclined to argue that personal skill and hard work are the key variables. Legislators often reply that accurate information makes a lobbyist reliable and therefore influential. Some commentators will say money and some will say organization. It is probable that they are all correct. Skill, effort, money, and organization are characteristic of most of the interest groups which we would consider effective. Other things such as the legitimacy of the group, the size of population represented, and the experience of the individual lobbyist are also of consequence. For the sake of orderly discussion, let us divide our consideration of variables determining interest group effectiveness into the following categories: acceptance of the group's place in politics, resources available to the group, and skills and experience of the individual lobbyist.

Acceptance by policy makers and other interest groups is the most vital differentiation among interest groups. Some groups, the League of Women Voters for example, are effective primarily because they have gained a high degree of acceptance among public officials. A radical group, the John Birch Society for example, may have extreme difficulty lobbying because of its over-all illegitimacy in the eyes of officials. Thus, an effective interest group must work very hard at achieving acceptance by the public and by decision makers. A considerable amount of the public relations efforts of interest groups is expended on developing legitimacy and acceptance.

[70] E. E. Schattschneider, *The Semi-Sovereign People* (New York: Holt, Rinehart & Winston, Inc., 1960), pp. 47–61.

Resources make the difference for many interest groups. The cost of organized pressure politics is very high. Our discussions of campaigning, initiative and referendum elections, and legislative lobbying have indicated the high dollar costs involved in interest group competition. Money is one of the most essential resources, but organization, membership, and time are also crucial. The California Teamsters Legislative Council, considered as one of the more influential labor groups in the state, is a good example of all resources coming together forcefully. The lobbyists for the Teamsters are not among the high spenders and although the council undoubtedly spends considerable amounts of money in their lobbying effort, their relative effectiveness vis-à-vis other labor groups and nonlabor groups is not solely dependent upon the amount of money expended on the lobbying effort. The Teamsters are noted as being among the best organized set of unions in the state. Their membership in the combined locals is considerable. The time spent by their lobbyists and supporting staff is significant. In general, the Teamsters are considered one of the best organized, hardest working, and efficient lobbies in California.

Thus, effective lobbies must have surplus funds, organizational energy, and time to expend. Relatively poor lobbies are not effective. Groups that do not make large investments in lobbying activities or which are not efficient in the management of these activities are not likely to be very effective. The high costs of lobbying obviously weights interest group politics toward those interests—business firms, large landowners, large unions, professional organizations with sizeable membership, and so on—which can "tax" their organization and membership from the resources necessary for effective competition with other interests.

It is no secret that among the most effective and highly paid lobbyists in Sacramento are ex-members of the legislature. They are effective not only because of whom they know, but also because of what they know, because of their *experience* and *skill*. In short, they know how the California legislature operates. California, as many other states, has a number of free-lance lobbyists whose livelihood depends in large measure upon how experienced and skilled they are. Many administrative agencies through trial and error have found which of their staff can effectively lobby and this reputation follows the person throughout his career. Lobbying is a highly specialized and demanding profession. Only a select number of people are actually very good at it; they are likely to be people who worked their way up through the ranks as assistants to other lobbyists or as staff members of legislative committees or as members of the legislature.

Legislators consistently rank the personal approach of the lobbyist as one of the crucial factors in his success. It is difficult to tell what is the best personality and the best style for a lobbyist because they as a group include many different kinds of people. Lobbyists do, however, have to be persons of great patience and understanding. They must be able to make the person being lobbied feel that he is not being lobbied. They are professional salesmen who must not allow their personality to interfere with the personality of their sales targets. There is no doubt that lobbying is a subtle business and that lobbyists must be artful and prudent men.

THE BIAS OF INTEREST GROUP POLITICS[71]

The struggle among interest groups has two interesting effects. First, it places a premium upon strong organizations that have considerable resources and which are relatively efficient in their lobbying effort. Accordingly, it has been argued that this produces a class bias in interest group politics. Second, the continuing struggle among interest groups, particularly at the level of actual lobbying, tends to encourage coalition formation. This suggests that competition and countervailance among groups may not be so pervasive as one might think. Both of these conclusions imply that there is a definite bias in the representational functions of interest group politics.

It is generally accepted that political participation in organizations varies with socioeconomic status. People with lower status are less equipped and less inclined to engage in organizational politics than are people of higher status. Thus, it is argued that the high premium placed upon organizational activity by interest group politics biases it toward the middle and upper classes and against the lower classes.[72] It is not true that *everyone* or even nearly everyone actually takes part in interest group activities. Interest group politics, as a result, does not reflect the interests of all the people of California. Interest group politics is highly selective; it is primarily the instrument of a segment of the total population.

Unfortunately, large numbers of individuals and many potential interest groups are opted out of interest group politics in California.[73] The

---

[71] See Schattschneider, op. cit., and Mancur Olson, Jr., *The Logic of Collective Action, Public Goods and the Theory of Groups* (New York: Schocken, 1968), for good discussions of the basic limitations of group theory and of group politics.

[72] Schattschneider, op. cit., pp. 30–36.

[73] Professor Schattschneider, op. cit., p. 35, suggests that probably as many as 90 per cent of the national population is outside the pale of organized interest group activity. His estimate may seem a bit extreme, but the point is well taken.

costs of effective pressure are too high for many people and for many organizations. This is not to condemn interest group politics, but merely to point out one of its most serious limitations; many people cannot depend upon interest groups to represent their interests.

The problems associated with coalition formation have long been recognized by group theorists, but it is worth discussing them here because of the over-all significance of group competition in California. If all interests were well organized (and costs and resources were rather equitably distributed) and if the organizations and lobbyists operated in an open and highly competitive market, then interests would tend to cancel each other out and in the long run no set of interests would dominate group politics. None of these ideal conditions exists in California. Instead, organizations in their search for scale economics, particularly at the level of the lobbyists, tend to overcome their differences and form coalitions. These coalitions can be rather stable through time and the competition among organizations begins to take on the characteristics of a closed oligarchy. This, of course, biases interest group politics against late comers and new groups. Entrance costs into the rather limited competition are very high. Although new groups can and do enter and new coalitions are formed, the neat counterbalance system is not likely to exist at all. The net result of the class bias and the competitive bias of California interest groups is the blockage of some kinds of political demands and the overrepresentation of some interests at the expense of others.

CONTROL AND REGULATION OF INTEREST GROUPS

Past experience with powerful interests in California during the days of the Southern Pacific Railroad and the Artie Samish era has demonstrated that, when left alone and unrestrained by outside authority, interest groups tend to become rather overbearing and ruthless. Open political corruption is the legacy of unrestrained interest group competition. The record of the attempts to control the potential excesses of interest groups, however, has not provided us with any definite answers as to how best to control and regulate interest group activities. Some reforms, notably the initiative and referendum, have been highly unsuccessful. Some attempts, the legislative advocate registration procedures for example, have been more successful in curtailing the major excesses of interest groups. Political reformers are still concerned about possible interest group corruption and the attempt to increase the control and regulation of interest groups goes on.

Among the recurring suggestions one is likely to hear are increased publicity concerning interest group expenditures; increased disclosures of the recipients of funds, gifts, and favors from lobbyists; stricter control of campaign costs and funds; registration of lobbyists who appear before administrative agencies; limitations upon the total expenditures that may be made in an initiative or referendum election; better enforcement of existing statutes such as the Lobbying Act; higher pay for public officials; and legal prohibition of all lobbying. All of these reforms, excluding the last, have considerable merit. Interest group politics and lobbying are political facts. Lobbyists perform crucial functions for decision makers. Interest group representation is necessary in our society. We cannot do away with them without irreparable consequences for all of us. We can, however, make better attempts to prevent interest group politics from getting out of hand. All of the reforms just mentioned can be put into practice only if both citizens and public officials make concerted efforts to change existing laws. Such efforts, like all organized behavior, will be very costly. It is questionable that such effort will be made unless some major scandal develops and is exposed. The experience with Mr. Samish offers this lesson.

CHAPTER 8

party-in-government: politics at the state capital

t he primary goal of a political party is to win public office and control government. Indeed, the governing function, or the willingness of the party to accept responsibility for the operations of government as a whole, is what most sharply distinguishes it from other political organizations. In a democracy, the party's right to govern rests on the assumption that it is the best agent to represent the popular will. The people can not govern directly but must speak through elections. They choose from a set of candidates nominated by the political parties those who best reflect their views on public issues. The party that elects a majority of its candidates then proceeds to organize the government and carry out its program. Simply stated, this is the theory of party government.

However, even a casual observer of politics realizes that the party-in-government does not conform to this theory.[1] The process of governmental policy making is a

---

[1] Regardless of the merits of party government, most scholars agree that the doctrine represents a model of how government

complicated and disorderly business. Political parties do not wield exclusive authority over public policies in any of the fifty states or the nation. Governmental policy making has a more pluralistic basis and is influenced by a variety of public and private individuals and groups. The party may be the most important of these groups but certainly it does not dominate every aspect of the policy-making process. Furthermore, even if the political party was in a position to control policy making, it is doubtful whether it could internally agree on any coherent party program. Admittedly, party platforms exist in abundance, but too often these consist only of campaign rhetoric, and candidates fail to take them seriously once in office. In a sense, the party that wins the election differs from the one that runs the government. The governmental party, consisting of all the elected legislative and executive officials, usually cannot discipline its members to carry out the promises of the electoral party.

Why is it so difficult for the governmental party to fulfill the policy-making role prescribed for it by the theory of party government? A partial explanation rests with the nature of the two-party system and the kind of major parties it creates. In most places in the United States effective political competition takes place only between the major parties. Republican and Democratic candidates are the only alternatives presented to voters. In a country as complex and diversified as the United States, this division of the electorate into two parts is a fantastic act of political simplification. A consequence of this political dualism is the establishment of socially heterogeneous, loosely organized, and nondoctrinaire major parties. The Republican and Democratic parties are loose-knit political coalitions representing a wide variety of policy views. The task of the political leader is to manage the diversity within his party and to control those differences which threaten constantly to tear it apart. The price of such harmony is a nonideological party, or one that plays down political issues and concentrates on the goal of winning office.

The formal structure of government probably has an even greater effect than these political factors on the operations of party government. The separation of powers doctrine inhibits the development of a party policy reconciling differences within the governmental party. The power to govern is not centralized in the hands of a cabinet as it is in the parliamentary system but is purposely divided among three separate and

should operate rather than a statement of how it operates in fact. The doctrine of party government has provoked controversy for some time among political scientists. Austin Ranney puts the issue in a historical context and analyzes both sides of the controversy in *The Doctrine of Responsible Party Government* (Urbana: University of Illinois, 1962).

constitutionally independent branches of government. Conflict rather than cooperation is the intent of separation of powers. The legislature, executive and, in a special way, the judiciary share power for policy making; each jealously guards its prerogatives from encroachments by the others. Thus, although the same party might control the legislature and executive, there is no guarantee that they will cooperate on policy. Separation of powers was designed to prevent governmental tyranny rather than provide governmental efficiency.

Primarily this chapter deals with political parties as they function in government. It focuses on the California legislature, the central policy-making institution of government, and on the role parties play in this political milieu. Some attention is also given to the legislative role of the Governor and to his responsibilities in the area of initiating legislation and mobilizing support for his proposals.

political trends in the california legislature

Legislatures can function legally without benefit of political parties, but all states except Minnesota and Nebraska organize their legislatures along partisan lines. Types of partisan politics in legislatures, however, vary greatly from state to state, and even within a particular state at different times. We find in many southern states, for example, legislatures dominated by a single party. Conflict in these cases is not between the major parties, but rather between factional divisions within the dominant party. Today California is classified among those states with the two-party competitive legislative politics. According to Jewell and Patterson, California ranks among the ten states with the strongest legislative competition; legislative control alternates between the major parties and party control of the legislature tends to approximate control of the governorship.[2] In the twenty-five year period from 1945 to 1969, the Republicans in California have controlled the Assembly for fifteen years, the Senate for thirteen years, and the governorship for seventeen years.

Of course, this classification of California as a two-party competitive legislative state is based only on the years since World War II. Before then, the role of parties was quite different in the legislature, and the

---

[2] Malcolm E. Jewell and Samuel C. Patterson, *The Legislative Process in the United States* (New York: Random House, Inc., 1966), p. 144.

Republicans and Democrats were not so competitive. In fact, the degree of partisanship in legislative matters appears to compare directly with the degree of partisanship among the electorate as a whole. As long as the nonpartisan spirit dominated California's electoral politics, party government had little opportunity to develop in Sacramento.

FOUR PERIODS: PROGRESSIVISM TO PARTISANSHIP

From a partisan perspective it is possible to divide California's legislative history in this century into four distinct periods: (1) Progressive era, 1910–1932; (2) frustrated partisanship, 1933–1941; (3) nonpartisan revival, 1942–1953; and (4) partisan era, 1953 to the present.[3] The Progressive era, beginning in 1910 and continuing to the early 1930s, set into motion the nonpartisan tradition that influenced every aspect of California's politics, including its legislative politics. Progressive reforms, particularly the practice of crossfiling, created independent-minded legislators who felt little or no obligation to their party. The legislature operated in terms of factional rather than partisan division, with the battle lines drawn between Progressives and conservatives. Party unity was totally lacking, and the caucus and other instruments of party government were ineffective. Parties were present in the legislature, but control of the legislature was not in their hands.

The forces of California Progressivism began to run down in the late 1920s and early 1930s, offering an opportunity for the revival of two-party competition in the legislature. The conservative and Progressive factions that replaced political parties could no longer be sustained by the Republicans, and so these functions began to split along two-party lines. The conservatives took over control of the Republican party while most of the Progressives moved into the Democratic party. The election of Franklin D. Roosevelt and the advent of the New Deal accelerated the exodus of the Progressives from the GOP.

With these developments, the fortunes of the Democratic party improved considerably. In 1934 Democratic registrants outnumbered the Republicans for the first time in the state's history. In the same year the Democrats elected thirty-eight of the eighty members of the Assembly, and two years later won control of the lower chamber. Finally, in 1938 they elected a Governor, Culbert Olson, the first Democratic holder of this office in this century. The Republicans retained control of the Senate probably because of the malapportionment of that body.

---

[3] William Buchanan, *Legislative Partisanship* (Berkeley: University of California Press, 1963), passim.

The stage was now set for more partisanship in the legislature. The Democratic members of the Assembly exhibited strong party unity and, on a straight party vote, elected Paul Peek as Speaker. The Democrats then waited for leadership from Governor Olson who, failing to provide it at this crucial juncture, contributed to the collapse of party unity. Olson's ineptness was partly the result of ill health and partly bad judgment, but basically he lacked the necessary political skills to manage his own party and develop bipartisan support. In the following session of the Assembly, a group of economy-minded Democrats joined with the Republicans and defeated the incumbent Speaker. With this action the Democratic efforts to organize the legislature along partisan lines failed.

The 1942 election of Earl Warren to the governorship led to the revival of nonpartisan politics in the legislature. Although Warren had been active in Republican party affairs, he recognized his party's minority position and realized his need for bipartisan support to win. He also understood, better than his opponent Governor Olson, the deep anti-party feelings harbored by many California voters. The theme of Warren's campaign was "leadership, not politics," and he was endorsed as the "nonpartisan candidate" by most of the larger newspapers in the state as well as by prominent Democrats. Once in office he maintained this nonpartisan posture. He seldom identified himself with other Republicans in the state or nation. Though he made sure his supporters controlled the Republican party, he personally played no role in party affairs. Warren fashioned a bipartisan coalition that cut across the Progressive elements of both parties, appointing to public office both Republicans and Democrats loyal to him. He was a strong and energetic Governor who worked constantly for legislative acceptance of his program. During his long administration, the legislative battles were seldom between Republicans and Democrats, but rather between factions for or against Warren.

Goodwin Knight, Warren's successor, sought to operate his administration in the nonpartisan Johnson-Warren tradition. Broader political developments, however, moved California's electorate in partisan directions. Essentially, nonpartisanship was a sensible strategy for the Republicans because, as Mary Ellen Leary noted, "nonpartisanship was the device by which they made themselves palatable to the Democratic majority."[4] For the Democrats, however, nonpartisanship restrained the party from capitalizing on its superiority in registration. Thus, it is understandable why the Democrats (in the 1950s) launched a drive toward stronger and more effective political parties.

Two important developments took place in 1952 and 1953 that serve

[4] Ibid., p. 94.

as important landmarks in the movement toward partisanship. In 1952, the voters modified California's crossfiling system for nominations by requiring that all statewide and legislative candidates be identified by party on the primary ballot. In 1953, the California Democratic Council (CDC) was formed as a statewide organization of local Democratic clubs. The CDC's purpose was to strengthen the grass roots organization of the party and to provide preprimary endorsements for legislative and other candidates. These developments were instrumental in returning the Democrats to power in 1958. They elected Edmund G. Brown as Governor, captured control of the Assembly, and for the first time in this century won a majority in the Senate. One of the first acts of the Democratic legislature was to abolish the system of crossfiling for partisan nominations.

The spirit of nonpartisanship had acquired enough momentum to influence the legislature for a few more years. In 1961, however, the Assembly elected Democrat Jesse Unruh as Speaker. Under Unruh's leadership, legislative affairs became increasingly more partisan.

Despite these developments, California's legislature is still not a highly partisan body. Deeply ingrained traditions do not easily disappear and legislative behavior is still influenced by nonpartisan traditions. Moreover, most of the increase in partisanship is reflected in the Assembly. The Senate still adheres more firmly to its Progressive heritage. The 1965 Senate reapportionment, however, is bound to speed the upper house along the path to party government.

legislative apportionment

In October 1965, the California legislature approved a reapportionment scheme that drastically redistricted the state and provided for a legislature with representation in both houses based on population. Thus, California implemented the "one-man, one-vote" principle set down by state and federal court decisions, and abandoned its thirty-five-year-old "Federal plan" of apportionment. But, most significantly, the 1965 reapportionment redistributed political power within the state and, particularly, within the legislature.

LEGISLATIVE APPORTIONMENT, 1849–1930

The legislature, by definition, is a representative body—but representative of what or whom? In general, Americans espouse a system of representation based on political equality, but historically the nation has deviated from this system by allowing factors other than population to serve as a basis of representation. In adopting the "Federal plan" California voters chose a system of dual representation, providing for an upper house comprised of forty Senators, each elected from districts based primarily on area, and a lower house of eighty Assemblymen elected from districts based on population. This arrangement, in practice, clearly favored the political interests of citizens in the rural northern section of the state.

The Constitutions of 1849 and 1879, consistent with the equalitarian tradition of the frontier and common practice in other states, provided for a bicameral legislature with electoral districts in both houses apportioned on a population basis. This system was relatively effective until the turn of the century when the urban population of the state surpassed the rural, and southern California began to grow at a more rapid rate than the north. Because the Constitution required the legislature to reapportion with every decennial census, the implication of this demographic pattern was that control of the legislature would soon pass from the residents of the San Francisco area and the northern rural countries to the urban center in the south. And, as a result of this growing regional conflict, legislators found it increasingly difficult to agree on reapportionment plans. After a prolonged dispute in 1910, they settled for a makeshift compromise but in 1920 they failed to agree on any plan at all.

FEDERAL PLAN

A sustained deadlock in 1923 and 1925 forced the legislatures to pursue initiative procedures as a solution to the reapportionment problem. A constitutional amendment appearing on the 1926 ballot, supported mainly by southern interests, called for the retention of population as the most democratic basis for apportioning seats in both houses. This amendment also established a Reapportionment Commission empowered to act in the event that the legislature failed to agree on a plan. In opposition to the proposal, farm groups throughout the state, backed by the San Francisco Chamber of Commerce, qualified a ballot proposition calling for a legislature based on the Federal plan. California voters rejected the southern-backed proposition with 60 per cent of the vote, while 55 per cent of the voters accepted the constitutional amendment providing for a legislature based on the federal principle.

Thus, the amendment established a Senate composed of forty geographic districts giving no county more than one senatorial district, and allowing no more than three counties to comprise a single senatorial district. Representation in the eighty-seat Assembly would still be apportioned on the basis of population, regardless of geography. In addition, the amendment provided for a Reapportionment Commission consisting of four statewide elected officials empowered to reapportion if the legislature failed to do so. This plan finally went into effect in 1930, despite an unsuccessful referendum attempt to throw out the Federal plan in 1928.

Although the Federal plan purposely subordinated population as a factor in Senate apportionment, population developments in the state created greater disparities in the sizes of districts than first anticipated. Limitations on the number of counties that could be combined, and on the number of Senators per county, established an inflexible apportionment formula that made difficult even modest adjustments to population changes.

California's population "exploded" during the Depression and war years, with southern California, particularly Los Angeles County, experiencing the heaviest population gains. Los Angeles County's population increased from 2.2 million in 1930 to almost 7 million in the mid-1960s. Under the Federal plan, these 7 million residents were represented by one state Senator, while only 17,000 inhabitants of three rural counties in the North also had one Senator. In other words, in theory at least, a resident of one of these three rural counties had 425 times the "voting power" in the state Senate than a resident of Los Angeles. Moreover, the eight counties of southern California, with nearly 60 per cent of the state's population, had only 20 per cent of the Senate seats. A majority of the Senate seats were controlled by counties with less than 11 per cent of the population.

California's initiative procedures offer an opportunity for dissatisfied interests to take their case directly to the general electorate. In the late 1940s, groups opposing the Federal plan began placing before the voters a series of constitutional amendments designed to modify the plan. In 1948, the California Federation of Labor sponsored a constitutional initiative aimed at re-establishing population as the basis of representation in the Senate; the only limitation was that no one county could have more than ten Senators. The impetus for this move was the feeling of organized labor that its interests were not being adequately represented by the rurally dominated Senate. Labor often supported legislation that, after passing the Assembly, was buried in a Senate committee controlled by hostile interests. Voters apparently did not share labor's dissatisfaction with the Senate because they defeated the proposed initiative by more than a two-to-one margin. The measure failed to receive a majority in any county, including Los Angeles, which stood to gain nine seats.

In 1960, another group, headed by Frank Bonelli, chairman of the Los Angeles County Board of Supervisors, placed a reapportionment initiative on the ballot. This measure called for a redistricting of the Senate to provide for more representation of the larger urban counties. Despite the fact that Los Angeles County would gain the most seats, urban centers other than Los Angeles, namely the San Francisco and East Bay areas in the north, also to make substantial gains in Senate representation. Obviously, the proponents of this measure hoped to break the normal sectional deadlock over reapportionment by forging an alliance between urban centers in the north and south. This strategy failed, however, and the voters defeated the proposition by a large majority. This defeat can be explained, at least partially, in terms of extenuating circumstances. On the same ballot was the $1.7 billion statewide water project, which authorized construction of facilities to transport water for the first time from northern to southern California. Apparently, many voters felt that the south's water problems were more important than reapportionment, and that they might jeopardize passage of the water bonds by supporting the Bonelli plan. Governor Brown, an advocate of Senate reapportionment, opposed the 1960 proposal on these grounds.

Nevertheless, Governor Brown had promised that if the voters defeated the measure, he would appoint a blue ribbon commission to study the issue and make recommendations for a more equitably apportioned Senate. After the election, he appointed a commission that finally reported a modest plan to the legislature recommending that Los Angeles County receive three more Senate seats. The Senate blocked any action on this proposal. Consequently, Supervisor Bonelli and his supporters placed another reapportionment proposition on the 1962 ballot. This measure called for an increase in the size of the Senate to fifty members, the new seats being allocated to the largest metropolitan counties. Although coming closer to success than previous propositions, this measure won 47 per cent of the vote and was defeated along with its predecessors.[5]

For diverse reasons, a majority of voters continued to support California's dual system of legislative representation. Among the strongest defenders of the Federal plan were rural interests throughout the state. Although the agricultural industry is critical to California's economy, rural interests have never been strong enough to defeat, without significant help, popular efforts to overturn the federal scheme. Fortunately

---

[5] For a comprehensive history of these reapportionment developments, see Don A. Allen, Sr., *Legislative Sourcebook* (Sacramento: Assembly of California, n.d.), pp. 5–39.

for the agricultural interests, they were able to enlist the support of northern urban areas in defending the Federal plan from an onslaught of attacks. This particular alliance was possible because of the deep-seated regional antagonisms characterized by northern fears of the rapid and burgeoning population in the south.

Ideological reasons also explain why some interests preferred to keep the Senate unchanged. The Senate, at least since 1930, was a defender of the status quo. Critics charged that it was a graveyard for liberal legislation passed by the Assembly. Many of the strongest supporters of the Senate were conservative corporate interests. For example, public records filed with the Secretary of State reveal that three fourths of the funds spent to defeat the 1962 reapportionment proposal came from sixteen large corporations, including a large public utility, several oil companies, large banks, and the railroads and one New York public relations firm.[6]

Clearly, the contestants in the reapportionment battle had reached an impasse following the defeat of the 1962 proposition. The legislature, particularly the Senate, had rejected even minimum modification of the Federal plan. Moreover, when opponents took the issue to the people, they suffered three defeats in a fifteen-year period. Still, it seemed certain that a system that allocated one Senator to represent 7 million people could not be defended indefinitely. The resolution of the reapportionment dilemma, however, came from an unexpected source—the Supreme Court of the United States.

1965 REAPPORTIONMENT

In 1962 the Supreme Court of the United States dramatically declared in the landmark case *Baker v. Carr* that legislative apportionment was a legitimate judicial issue and that citizens could invoke the Equal Protection Clause of the United States Constitution to test the fairness of state legislative apportionment schemes.[7] This case reversed an earlier court decision in which the court had refused to intervene in a reapportionment dispute on the grounds that the issues were not justiciable.[8] Two years after the Baker decision, the Supreme Court, in the lead case *Reynolds v. Sims,* declared that "as a basic constitutional standard, the Equal Protection Clause requires that the seats in both houses of a

---

[6] Joseph P. Harris, *California Politics,* 4th ed. (San Francisco: Chandler Publishing Company, 1967), p. 106.

[7] *Baker v. Carr,* 369 U.S. 186 (1962).

[8] *Colegrove v. Green,* 328 U.S. 549, 556 (1946).

bicameral state legislature must be apportioned on a population basis."[9] The Supreme Court's application of the "one-man, one-vote" principle to both state legislative chambers raised doubts about the constitutional validity of California's Federal plan of legislative representation. Ironically, Chief Justice Earl Warren, who had defended California's federal plan while Governor, delivered the opinion of the court.

Extension of the Reynold's doctrine to California came quickly. A number of cases were pending in federal courts specifically challenging the apportionment of California's Senate, but *Silver v. Jordan* was the first on which a court reached a decision.[10] On December 3, 1964, the Los Angeles Federal District Court in a two to one *per curiam* order held that the "present plan of Senate apportionment by districts in California in unconstitutional." The court ruled that a population disparity of 425 to 1 between the smallest and largest districts is "an invidious discrimination of citizens' rights and violative of the Equal Protection Clause of the Fourteenth Amendment to the United States Constitution." The court further stated that the federal analogy was irrelevant to California because the counties were not sovereign units, but merely administrative subdivisions of the state. Finally, the court ordered the California legislature to reapportion the Senate by July 1, 1965, and noted that if the legislature failed to do so by that date, the court would assume the responsibility to act.

The California Senate faced a disagreeable and difficult task when it convened in January 1965: the court, in effect, ordered incumbent Senators to abolish their own districts.[11] Before undertaking this task, the Senate explored other conceivable alternatives. One that held the most promise was a constitutional amendment promoted by U.S. Senator Everett Dirksen, which called for a reversal of the Reynold's decision. Despite strong support by the California legislature, this amendment was not approved by the United States Senate. Other alternatives considered by the legislature included (1) electing all forty Senators on an at-large basis; (2) increasing the size of the Senate so that fewer incumbents would lose their seats; (3) establishing a unicameral legislature; (4) and dividing California at the Tehachapi Mountains into two states. This last proposal, in fact, actually passed the Senate, but was quietly junked in the Assembly.

---

[9] 377 U.S. 533, 568 (1964).

[10] *Silver v. Jordan*, 241 F. Supp. 576 (1965).

[11] For a detailed legislative history of the adoption of the 1965 Legislative Reapportionment Law, see John Gallagher, Karl Lamb, John R. Owens, John P. White, *The Politics of Representation in California: State and Local Governments* (Washington, D.C.: American Enterprise Institute, in press) Chapters 8, 9, 10.

After an agonizing five months the Senate passed a reapportionment bill dividing the state into thirty-five senatorial districts, with one Senator each from eighteen districts, two Senators each from five districts, and twelve Senators from Los Angeles County. Although this bill shifted thirteen seats to the south, allowing for a total of nineteen southern and twenty-one northern seats, critics argued that it still did not meet the "one-man, one-vote" mandate of the court. This became a moot issue, however, when the legislature adjourned without Assembly approval of the measure. It appeared that the stalemate between the two chambers would force the federal court to reapportion the legislature. But before the federal court could act, the California Supreme Court entered the fray and declared that the Assembly as well as the Senate violated the "one-man, one-vote" injunction, and then ordered both houses to re-apportion immediately. To guide the legislature, the California court set down the standard that the population of a legislative district could not deviate more than 15 per cent from the ideal size. The Governor called the legislature into special session, and after additional months of grueling work it passed the Reapportionment Act of 1965.

The 1965 law established a population standard for representation in both houses, and districts relatively equal in population. All of California's legislative districts now range within 15 per cent above or below the population standard. The smallest Assembly district is the 16th with a 1960 population of 168,397, and the largest, the 26th, with a population of 222,971. Thus, the largest district has only 1.3 times as many people as the smallest. The Senate districts vary in size from the smallest, the 2nd, with a 1960 population of 334,477, to the largest, the 12th, with a population of 444,387; resulting in a population variance of 1.3 to 1. At least 48 per cent of the state's population is required to elect a majority of the members of both houses. (See Figures 8–1, 8–2.)

Certain short-run effects of reapportionment, deserve comment. It is obvious, for example, that the balance of political power in both chambers has shifted to southern California; eight southern counties have forty-six of the eighty Assembly seats, and twenty-two of the forty seats. Los Angeles County alone has thirty-one Assemblymen and fourteen Senators. (Los Angeles shares another seat with Orange County.) Moreover, despite the difficulty of pigeonholing every legislative district into an urban-rural classification, now there are fewer rural districts. If we define rural districts as those without a population center of 50,000 or more, only 10 per cent of the Senate and 14 per cent of the Assembly districts can be classified as such. Moreover, reapportionment did bring about the highest turnover of legislative membership in California's history. Approximately 50 per cent of the legislative seats changed hands; twenty-three newcomers joined the Senate and thirty-three freshmen joined the Assembly.

In partisan terms the Republican party benefited most from reapportionment. In 1966 the Republicans gained seven Assembly and five Senate seats and in 1968 they picked up an additional three seats in the lower house. Even with these gains there is still some evidence that the Democrats did pull off a slight gerrymander.[12] The Democrats in 1966 with 48.6 per cent of the statewide Senate vote and 46.3 per cent of the Assembly vote won 52.5 per cent of the seats in each house. Moreover, the Republicans had to win 54 per cent of statewide Assembly votes in 1968 in order to gain 51 per cent of the seats and control that house. The crucial legislative elections, however, will come in 1970 and then the party that wins control of the legislature will have the power to reapportion both houses for the decade.

It is too early to comment on the long-run consequences of reapportionment. The 1967 and 1968 legislative sessions provide no easy revelations about the future direction of legislative policy making in California. Certainly, the legislature did not make any major moves toward accommodating increasing urban demands. In time, no doubt, the cities of California will benefit some from a legislature more oriented to peculiar urban problems and needs. Nonetheless, we should not believe reapportionment to be the only or the most important factor influencing legislative policy choices. How the legislature acts on policy depends on many more things than how its seats are apportioned.

legislative elections

The freshman legislator appreciates the importance of the political party long before he arrives in Sacramento. Legislators, of course, gain their positions through partisan elections. They must rely upon the electoral party, or the rank-and-file citizens who vote Democratic or Republican, to put them into office. The political party in this broad sense determines the fortunes of all legislative candidates. However, the political party defined in the restricted sense as the legal party organization, plays a much more varied role in legislative elections. In some districts, for example, candidates depend only marginally on the formal party organization, seeking only to run under the party label on the ballot; but in other districts, the party organization strongly influences the selection of candidates and their chances of election to office.

---

[12] Ibid., Chapters 11, 12.

(COUNTIES—ASSEMBLY DISTRICTS)

1. Del Norte, Lassen Modoc, Plumas, Shasta, Sierra, Siskiyou, Tehama, Trinity, Humboldt
2. Humboldt, Mendocino, Sonoma
3. Sacramento
4. Butte, Colusa, Glenn, Lake, Sutter, Yolo
5. Napa, Solano
6. Alpine, Amador, Calaveras, El Dorado, Inyo, Mariposa, Mono, Nevada, Placer, Tuolumne, Yuba
7. Marin, Sonoma
8. Sacramento
9. Sacramento, Yolo
10-11. Contra Costa
12. San Joaquin
13-17. Alameda
18-20. San Francisco
21. Kings, Tulare
22. Santa Clara
23. San Francisco
24-25. Santa Clara
26-27. San Mateo
28. Kern
29. Kern, San Luis Obispo, Tulare
30. San Joaquin, Stanislaus
31. Merced, San Benito, Santa Cruz
32. Fresno
33. Fresno, Madera
34. Monterey
35. Orange, San Bernardino
36. Santa Barbara, San Luis Obispo
37. Ventura
38-68. Los Angeles
69-71. Orange
72-73. San Bernardino
74. Riverside
75. Riverside, Imperial
76-80. San Diego

FIGURE 8–1   ASSEMBLY DISTRICTS

292

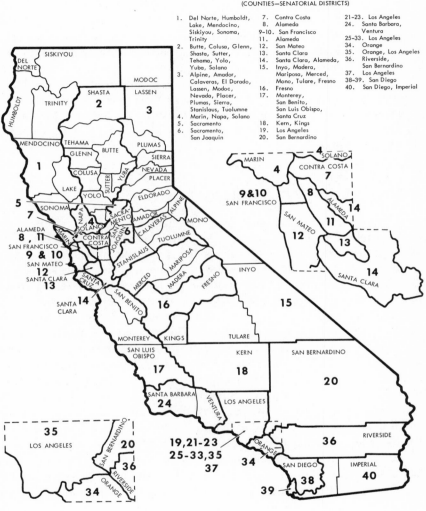

(COUNTIES—SENATORIAL DISTRICTS)

1. Del Norte, Humboldt, Lake, Mendocino, Siskiyou, Sonoma, Trinity
2. Butte, Colusa, Glenn, Shasta, Sutter, Tehama, Yolo, Yuba, Solano
3. Alpine, Amador, Calaveras, El Dorado, Lassen, Modoc, Nevada, Placer, Plumas, Sierra, Stanislaus, Tuolumne
4. Marin, Napa, Solano
5. Sacramento
6. Sacramento, San Joaquin
7. Contra Costa
8. Alameda
9-10. San Francisco
11. Alameda
12. San Mateo
13. Santa Clara
14. Santa Clara, Alameda
15. Inyo, Madera, Mariposa, Merced, Mono, Tulare, Fresno
16. Fresno
17. Monterey, San Benito, San Luis Obispo, Santa Cruz
18. Kern, Kings
19. Los Angeles
20. San Bernardino
21-23. Los Angeles
24. Santa Barbara, Ventura
25-33. Los Angeles
34. Orange
35. Orange, Los Angeles
36. Riverside, San Bernardino
37. Los Angeles
38-39. San Diego
40. San Diego, Imperial

FIGURE 8–2   SENATORIAL DISTRICTS

293

The degree to which a legislator responds to partisan cues depends to some extent on his sense of obligation to the political party. An individual involved in politics on his own initiative, nominated without party support, and capable of mobilizing his own campaign organization would feel minimally obliged to the party organization. Once in the capital he could be expected to act more independently than a legislator who had been heavily dependent on his party during the election. The partisan character of the legislator's district also affects the way he responds to the dictates of the legislative party. A legislator from a highly competitive district might have closer ties to the party organization than a legislator from a one-party district. An unstable political base forces on him a greater concern about partisan politics and his party's position in the legislature.

CROSSFILING AND LEGISLATIVE NOMINATIONS

The nonpartisan spirit that long dominated California politics seriously shackled political parties in legislative elections. In recent years, however, the significance of parties has increased as California sheds more and more of its Progressive inheritance. This development is particularly evident since the abolition in 1959 of the system of crossfiling for nominations. Crossfiling had its greatest impact on state legislative elections because more candidates crossfiled for the legislature than for statewide or federal offices. The ultimate of this method of nomination was to make many legislative elections meaningless; simply, there was no election contest because a candidate won the nomination of both parties. The following figures demonstrate the noncompetitive character of many legislative contests. From 1914 to 1954 (the latter date representing the year party labels reappeared on the primary ballot), 50.5 per cent of all Assembly races and 62.3 per cent of all Senate races were decided in the primary.[13] Obviously, a candidate receiving the nomination of both parties was a relatively free political agent in the legislature; and, indeed, the period (1940–1950) when legislative candidates used crossfiling most widely coincided with a period of extensive nonpartisanship in the legislature. In this decade, 70 per cent of the Assembly and 84 per cent of the Senate contests were decided in the primary.[14]

---

[13] Dean Cresap, *Party Politics in the Golden State* (Los Angeles: The Haynes Foundation, 1954), p. 4.
[14] Ibid.

The specific effects of crossfiling on the minority party also inhibited partisan politics in the state legislature. Apparently, incumbents benefited most from crossfiling. Denied the party label as a means of identification, primary voters tended to vote for incumbents because their names were more familiar. Furthermore, incumbents frequently had the advantage of being unopposed for renomination, whereas the out-party usually had greater difficulty uniting behind a single candidate. As the dominant force during the years of crossfiling, the Republican party reaped the advantages of the system.

PARTISAN COMPETITION IN DISTRICTS

Since the late 1950s, a reasonable degree of political competition has marked most elections for statewide and federal offices in California. This competition, however, has not existed in most state legislative districts. Although a functional definition of *competition* is difficult to derive, a legislative district in which the victor wins less than 55 per cent of the two-party vote will be considered competitive. Table 8–1 summarizes the various degrees of competitiveness in California legislative elections for the period 1960–1968.

The abolition of crossfiling first of all resulted in a sharp decline in the number of uncontested elections and, therefore, contributed to the increase in party competition throughout the state. Table 8–1 shows that

TABLE 8–1 DEGREE OF TWO-PARTY COMPETITION FOR CALIFORNIA SENATE AND ASSEMBLY SEATS, 1960–1968

Level of Competition	Senate		Assembly	
	Number	Percentage	Number	Percentage
Safe seats	100	83.4	336	84.0
Dem. unopposed	5	4.2	9	2.3
Dem. 60 per cent above	41	34.2	133	33.3
Dem. 55.1–59.9 per cent	15	12.5	52	13.0
Rep. 55.1–59.9 per cent	14	11.7	42	10.5
Rep. 60 per cent above	22	18.3	97	24.2
Rep. unopposed	3	2.5	3	0.7
Competitive seats	20	16.6	64	16.0
Dem. less than 55 per cent	10	8.3	35	8.8
Rep. less than 55 per cent	10	8.3	29	7.2

from 1960 to 1968 only 7.0 per cent of the Senate races and 3.0 per cent of the Assembly races were uncontested. The table also shows a fairly large number of legislative districts fall in the safe classification. The data reveal that, including the uncontested races, 83.4 per cent of the Senate and 84.0 per cent of the Assembly elections during this period were won by at least 55 per cent of the two-party vote. Even accepting 60 per cent as the breaking point between safe and competitive races, still over 60 per cent of the seats are safe. According to these figures, only 16 per cent of the seats in each house are competitive and these are evenly divided between Republicans and Democrats. Clearly, political competition is not characteristic of most legislative contests. Moreover, an incumbent is particularly difficut to unseat. From statehood until 1965, only 86 of the 892 elected Senators were subsequently defeated in an election, of the 3,055 Assemblymen, only 131 were subsequently defeated.[15]

Generally, the absence of effective two-party competition in most legislative districts results from gerrymandering, or can be explained in terms of the social composition of the major parties. Despite the recent creation of districts that are substantially equal in population, gerrymandering will continue to create one-party districts. Although the 1965 legislature reapportioned both houses according to the "one-man, one-vote" principle, the number of competitive districts did not increase appreciably. Moreover, although the major parties are socially heterogeneous, they do draw support disproportionally from social groups. Thus, the parties are stronger in those areas where social groups identified with them tend to concentrate. For example, because Negro and lower-income groups are predominantly Democratic, and because they also live in the central or slum areas of large cities, the Democratic party dominates these legislative districts.

The most significant implication of this persistent strain of non-competitiveness in California legislative districts is its effect on the partisan climate of the legislature. A legislator with a relatively safe district tends to be more independent of his party than one who requires the support of his party to ensure his re-election to office.

ROLE OF PARTY IN RECRUITMENT, NOMINATIONS, AND CAMPAIGNS

One of the most important functions of the political party is the recruitment of candidates for public office. Clearly, political careers are not sufficiently prestigious or rewarding that people eagerly wait in

---

[15] Allen, op. cit., p. 195.

line to run for these offices. Evidence indicates that California parties play a minor role in recruiting legislative candidates. John C. Wahlke and his associates in their research on the California legislature reported in 1957 that only 42 per cent of the Democratic and 22 per cent of the Republican respondents said (in interviews) that their political party sponsored their legislative careers.[16] It appears also that recruitment patterns are a function of urbanization and interparty competition. Inasmuch as urban areas develop the strongest party organizations, urban party leaders are more likely to actively recruit candidates than their colleagues in rural areas. In competitive districts the nomination process appears to be more open, allowing for self-recruited candidates as well as candidates recruited by nonparty groups.[17] In politically lopsided districts, however, the minority party has to play a more active role in conscripting candidates because its nominees have little chance of winning.

Partisan considerations might also be important to a legislator with extensive experience in his party's internal affairs, particularly if he has been a party officer, central committee member, or active campaigner for other candidates. This kind of involvement helps to socialize an individual to think in partisan terms. In California, however, party service is no prerequisite to a public career. Wahlke reported that 52 per cent of the legislators had never held previous party office or, more significantly, had never been active in party work of any kind.[18]

Despite a wide variation in legislative campaigns, most legislative candidates are fairly independent agents. There are no party slates in primaries and most legislative candidates run independently of other officeseekers on the ballot. Most candidates recruit their own workers, raise their own funds, and plot their own strategy and tactics. Thus, campaigns are highly personalized, emphasizing face-to-face contact with voters through organized meetings and rallies, door-to-door canvassing, factory gate and shopping center visits. Newspapers and outdoor billboards are popular campaign media and most candidates send out at least one direct mailing. Television, however, is used sparingly, because most stations cover a viewing area much larger than the legislative district, thus making TV an uneconomical means of communicating with voters.

Although the principal responsibility for the campaign rests with

[16] John C. Wahlke et al., *The Legislative System* (New York: John Wiley & Sons, Inc., 1962), p. 98.

[17] Lester G. Seligman, "Political Recruitment and Party Structure: A Case Study," *American Political Science Review*, Vol. LV (March 1961), pp. 77–86.

[18] Wahlke et al., op. cit., p. 97.

individual candidates, parties provide some aid and assistance. The formal party organization, however, has never been particularly effective at the local level. As mentioned in Chapter 6 the law even fails to provide for any party units below the county committee. Development of extralegal party units (CDC, CRA) in recent years significantly strengthened the grass roots organizations of both parties. These groups, in addition to regular (legal) party units, have provided a reservoir of experienced party workers that is a valuable resource for legislative candidates.

In recent years, the state organizations of both parties have also become increasingly concerned with legislative races. An indication of this growing interest is the so-called Cal Plan, developed by the GOP State Central Committee under the leadership of its former chairman, Gaylord Parkinson. The Plan called for concentrating all available party resources in key marginal legislative districts with the hope of gaining eventual control of both houses of the legislature. The special election campaign of state Senator Milton Marks from San Francisco in 1967 exemplifies the efficacy of this approach; he won the seat in a heavily Democratic area, defeating a popular Assemblyman. His election can be attributed in part to the support of party workers from all over California who came to San Francisco to campaign at the precinct level.

Information about financial assistance to legislative candidates by party groups is incomplete and unreliable. It is obvious, nonetheless, that legislative campaigns are costly. (See Chapter 5.) Although party units raise money, probably only a small amount of the total is channeled into legislative races. The Republican party, with a more efficient system of centralized fund raising, probably outdoes the Democratic party in providing direct financial assistance to legislative candidates.

In recent years Democratic candidates have turned to the Speaker of the Assembly for financial assistance more often than to the State Central Committee. As an outgrowth of his legislative leadership, Speaker Jesse Unruh served as a broker for campaign contributions. As Speaker he could raise $100,000 or more from a testimonial dinner with lobbyists reputedly buying a good part of the tickets to these dinners.[19]

In conclusion, the political party in California plays only a marginal role in legislative elections. Most legislative districts are dominated by one party. Once elected to office, a legislation stands a good chance of reelection. Most candidates are self-starters—they are not directly recruited by the party. They are responsible primarily for their own campaign and receive minimal support from the legal party organization. Thus, the absence of any extensive socialization by the political party

---

[19] Hill, op. cit., p. 161.

results in a legislative body composed of members responsible mainly to themselves and their own perceived interests.

legislative leadership and political organization

Each house of the California legislature conducts its business through a formal organization according to procedures set down in an official body of rules. The organizational structure consists of permanent and temporary presiding officers, majority and minority leaders, a number of minor housekeeping officials, and the procedural and substantive committees. Superimposed on this legal structure is the partisan organization that represents the Republican and Democratic parties; it consists of the party caucus, caucus chairmen, and party whips (Assembly only). Because the theory of party government prescribes that the majority party control the formal organization, the California system is a curious blending of the official and the partisan structures. The presiding officer of the Assembly, for example, combines in the same office the role of legislative and party leader. On the one hand, he is elected by the full chamber to preside fairly and impartially over its affairs, on the other hand, he leads the majority party and is responsible for its program. Consequently, legislative leaders must operate through both the official and party apparatus and it is nearly impossible to draw sharp distinctions between the two.

The leadership role of the majority is more complex than the theory of party government suggests. Essentially, the leadership's job is to build a majority coalition in support of controversial issues. Its strategy depends on a number of circumstances, some internal and others external to the legislature. The political temper of the time clearly influences the amount of legislative partisanship. A nonpartisan political climate in the state as a whole leads to weak and ineffective parties unable to articulate political differences. Under these circumstances, the real conflict in the legislature may not be between the parties, but within them or among powerful interest groups competing for public favors. The size of the margin the majority enjoys over the minority affects legislative behavior. If the margin is close, then naturally the leadership plays down partisanship because it must depend on votes from across the aisle. Attitudes held by individual legislators regarding their legislative roles, especially their partisan roles, influence their response to leadership. A plea for party loyalty will mean less to a senior legislator accustomed to crossfiling than to one nominated according to the present partisan rules. The degree of partisanship is also influenced by the character of the party legislative organization, how well organized it is, how often it meets, and whether important matters are brought before it. The leadership's ability to command also depends on the sanctions it can employ to discipline recalcitrant members.

ASSEMBLY ORGANIZATION

The elected leaders of the Assembly consist of the Speaker, Speaker pro tem., majority and minority floor leaders. By far the most important of these officials is the Speaker; indeed only the Governor outranks him as an important figure in California government. Legislative power tends to be centralized in the hands of the Speaker, and he can dominate the affairs of the Assembly. A listing of his formal powers demonstrates the range of his influence: (1) he appoints the chairman of the Rules Committee and the chairman and vice-chairman and members of all Assembly standing and special committees, (2) he refers all bills to committees, (3) he acts as chairman of the committee of the whole, (4) he serves as an ex-officio member, without a vote, on all committees, (5) he exercises all the powers of a presiding officer, e.g., recognizes members, interprets rules, and decides points of order, (6) he exercises all the privileges and prerogatives of regular members, e.g., he votes and participates in debate.

The Speaker is elected by the full membership and serves for the duration of the legislative session. In general, California Speakers have held office for a short period of time. Four incumbents have served for six years, seven for four years each, and all others for two years or less.[20] The ex-Speaker, Jesse M. Unruh, took office in 1961 and had been re-elected for every subsequent legislative session until 1968, thus serving longer than any other Speaker. Robert Monagan was elected Speaker in 1969 after the Republicans won control of the Assembly.

The election of a Speaker often provokes a bitter struggle. In fact the choice of a Speaker reveals much about the actual distribution of power in the Assembly. His election does not follow strict party lines, as does the choice of the Speaker of the U.S. House of Representatives. Although the California Speaker invariably comes from the majority party, he is not nominated by his party caucus, nor is his election guaranteed by party regularity in voting on this organizational matter. The contest is

---

[20] Henry A. Turner and John A. Vieg, *The Government and Politics of California*, 3rd ed. (New York: McGraw-Hill Book Company, Inc., 1967), p. 109.

seldom between a candidate from each party, rather, it generally involves candidates representing factions of the majority party. An examination of the competitive Speaker races since the 1930s reveals only two instances when the Speaker was elected in a strictly partisan manner, i.e., each party put up its own candidates and the vote was entirely along party lines. These two occasions were the elections of Paul Peek in 1939 and of Jesse Unruh in 1968.

The election of the Speaker, however, does follow a fairly traditional pattern. Once a vacancy occurs, aspiring candidates in the majority party attempt to forge a winning coalition through a complex series of negotiations with members of their own party. Because the absence of party discipline makes it usually impossible for a candidate to win with votes only from his own party, he must move across the aisle for support. If the minority party put forth its own candidate, or even maintained unanimity in bargaining with opposing candidates, it could hold the balance of power in the Speakership race. Individual minority members, however, are tempted to bargain independently. An important inducement in the negotiations for a winning coalition is the promise of committee chairmanships and assignments. The Speaker makes all appointments to committees and is not bound to his own party in appointing chairmen. Frequently, the result of all this preliminary maneuvering is that one candidate clearly emerges with the necessary votes, thus eliminating his opponents and assuring his formal choice without opposition. In fact, incumbent Speakers have faced opponents in only ten elections since 1930.

This type of open race for the Speakership obviously limits the party's ability to control legislative programing. The Speaker is not a very effective leader of the majority party, indeed, at times he represents what amounts to a bipartisan coalition. On several occasions, the Speaker received more votes from members of the minority than from his own party. Moreover, important committee chairmanships, as well as the control of committees, fall to members of the minority party. The Speaker has traded away these positions in exchange for minority support. He does attempt, however, to retain the balance of power on these committees by controlling the swing vote. On the whole, Assembly Speakers have been forced to operate in a nonpartisan fashion and as a result, successful candidates for the job usually come from the political center of the majority party rather than from any extreme faction. Although the Speaker does not always lead a partisan majority, he must nevertheless lead and represent moderate views if he is to carry out the intermediary and conciliatory tasks within and between the parties.

The foregoing is a fair description of the Speakership until the early

1960s when the political climate of the state and the legislature began to grow more partisan. This change coincides with the election of Jesse Unruh to the Speakership. He has been called the first truly partisan Speaker since the beginning of the Progressive Era. Unruh came to the Assembly in 1954, the year partisan labels first appeared on the primary ballot, by defeating a crossfiling Democrat for a Los Angeles seat. He served as Governor Brown's southern campaign manager in 1958, and in reward for his services, Brown endorsed his appointment as chairman of the powerful Assembly Ways and Means Committee. When in 1961 Governor Brown announced he would appoint the incumbent Speaker, Ralph Brown, to a newly created appellate judgeship in Fresno, Unruh indicated he would be a candidate for the Speakership. Gordon Winton, Jr., of Merced, the Democratic party floor whip also announced he would seek the post. Winston's strength reached a high point of 38 votes, but he failed to squeeze out the additional three votes needed to win and Unruh was elected. The race followed the traditional pattern with both candidates bargaining with Republicans for support. It was rumored that Unruh received vital backing from a number of Republicans whose seats he had saved in the 1960 reapportionment.[21]

Despite the fact that Unruh's election followed the pattern of non-partisan contests, he soon displayed his preference for strong party leadership. He realized that California politics was changing and that if a Democratic administration was to move in new policy direction, it would have to make more effective use of its normally partisan majority. He began to develop the partisan role of the Speaker, he strengthened the legislative party organization, and he began to strengthen party discipline. The Republican minority increasingly resented his power and forged a united opposition. The minority party holds an important weapon in that the budget and emergency measures must receive a two-thirds vote. By closing their ranks, Republicans were able to delay passage of the 1962 budget and force Unruh to make certain concessions. When they repeated this tactic in 1963, Unruh promised to break the unity of the Republican caucus, and made the unprecedented move of locking the chamber doors and refusing exit to anyone opposing him on the budget. Angered by the growing unity of the minority party in 1963, Unruh revealed his commitment to the partisan organization of the Assembly by amending the rules to provide for the election of the Speaker by party caucus, and stipulating that all committee chairmen and vice-chairmen come from the majority party. This change put the organization of the Assembly for the first time on a strictly partisan basis. It promised

---

[21] Buchanan, op. cit., pp. 132–133.

wide-ranging consequences, but the rule was never put into effect because the Speaker relented and restored the old rule in 1964.

Admittedly, as speaker, Unruh was a controversial political figure. Regardless of one's attitude toward him, even his enemies admitted that he was a strong leader. Although he never publicly commented on his conception of the Speakership, he obviously had a well-developed notion of the office and its leadership responsibilities. Certainly, he thought of his function as more than procedural, involving only the management of the business of the Assembly in a neutral manner. He perceived his role in the broadest political terms; he was interested in mobilizing political power toward specific goals. His enemies characterized him as an ambitious political boss, seeking and using power for personal and selfish ends; but his supporters countered this assertion by arguing that his exercise of power was legitimate and necessary in the political arena to achieve desired public policies. Most importantly, Unruh understood that effective legislative leadership is tied to success as an independent political figure. Clearly, his partisanship extended beyond the walls of the legislature; he was deeply involved in legislative campaigns, both in the recruitment of new candidates and the provision of financial assistance to them. As contrasted with previous Speakers, Unruh reportedly served as a clearing house for contributions from lobbyists, by receiving and distributing large sums of money, and making critical decisions about which candidates should receive campaign contributions. Moreover, Unruh successfully sought a role in national politics; he served in 1960 as John F. Kennedy's campaign manager in southern California. In fact, as long as Kennedy was in the White House, Unruh was much more influential in Washington than Governor Brown. Continuing his connection with the Kennedy family, he headed Robert Kennedy's delegation to the Democratic convention in 1968.

It remains to be seen whether the present Republican Speaker, Robert Monagan, will act in as partisan a manner as his predecessor. The leadership style of the Speaker depends to some extent on the incumbent's temperament and personality, and Monagan is a much less controversial figure than Unruh. It is apparent, however, that many of the changes in the Assembly made by Unruh have now become so widely accepted that they have become institutionalized. Significantly, Monagan declared upon assuming the speakership in early 1969 his intention to keep intact the system of legislative staff aides and committee consultants instituted by Unruh. The speaker needs the assistance of staff people if he is to fulfill his political leadership role.

The Speaker is assisted in his leadership responsibility by the Speaker pro tem., the Majority Floor Leader, and the Assembly Rules Committee.

The Speaker pro tem. presides in the absence of the Speaker, and serves a generally ceremonial function. The Majority Floor Leader is appointed by the Speaker, and serves as his personal liaison with the majority party on the floor of the chamber. During the 1930s, it was customary for the chairman of the Rules Committee to serve also as Majority Floor Leader; but in the 1950s the Assembly rules were revised to extend formal recognition to this position. The rules also provided at the same time for a Minority Floor Leader. As the title suggests, he attempts to coordinate his party's efforts in the legislature. It is significant, however, that the rules establishing this office do not specifically designate that the Minority Leader will, in fact, represent the minority party. The rule says, "The minority, if any, or *any* organized segment of the membership may, through caucus or other means, designate a member to act as floor leader for it." (Emphasis added.) Clearly, the Assembly does not assume that political organization within the body will always form along strict party lines.

The administration of the Assembly is managed by the Speaker through the Rules Committee, and the latter is a significant adjunct to the Speaker's powerful internal apparatus. The committee consists of seven members, three appointed by the majority party caucus, three appointed by the minority party caucus, and the chairman appointed by the Speaker. The Speaker, Majority Leader, and a number of other legislative leaders, serve as ex-officio members. The committee provides certain housekeeping functions, including the allocation of office space in the capital, the appropriation of money for interim committees, and, most significantly, the hiring of committee staffs.

The only truly partisan body existing in the legislature is the party caucus. During the Progressive Era, the caucus was not in regular or effective use; but during the late 1930s it was revived and has since become an important legislative institution. Speaker Unruh, particularly, used the Democratic caucus in an effective fashion. The caucus, chaired by an Assemblyman elected by the party, has a professional staff to provide necessary services and a generous budget. The party caucus meets weekly to discuss the legislative program in terms of strategy and tactics, and the scheduling of significant bills. The caucus rarely attempts to develop party positions on legislation, nor does it discipline its members or enforce the party line. However, with the election of Republican Governor Ronald Reagan, the Assembly Democratic caucus began cautiously to develop some alternatives to the policies of the Governor. The Democratic caucus also provides such partisan political services as the drafting of press releases for distribution in the district, assisting in campaign organization, and generally helping in the re-election of incumbents.

Republicans did not keep pace with the Democrats under Unruh in the development and use of the party caucus. Although the Republicans met regularly to discuss legislative issues, they did not provide the kinds or extent of services undertaken by the Democrats. However, since taking control of the Assembly in 1969, Speaker Robert Monagan has increased the staff of the Republican caucus and has promised to increase its services to party members.

SENATE ORGANIZATION

Although the Senate and the Assembly are in many ways organizationally similar, the process of leadership and legislative decision making differs significantly. In general, patterns of leadership in the Senate are more informal than in the Assembly. Leadership is a shared function, not concentrated in the hands of a single powerful presiding officer as in the Assembly. Senate members, like U.S. Senators, see themselves as participants in an exclusive club, and emphasize the importance of seniority and primary loyalty to the club. Thus, adherence to party and partisanship in much less crucial than in the Assembly. The reasons for these differences are complex; still, a partial explanation can be found in structural and political factors. Senate membership, of course, is one half the size of the Assembly, and the tenure of office is twice as long. A body of forty members permits sustained face-to-face contact, thus allowing a less structured leadership and more informal means of achieving consensus. Also contributing to this style of decision making is the fact that only one half of the membership is up for election every two years; the Senate, therefore, has a more stable membership than the Assembly. Also, turnover in the Senate averaged only 15 per cent over the last two decades, as opposed to a 30 per cent rate in the Assembly. These facts result in longer tenure for Senators and, understandably, an increased importance of seniority as a factor in Senate leadership. The 1965 reapportionment, however, has significantly altered the makeup of the Senate. Under the Federal plan, leadership reflected the northern rural bias of the Senate; but since reapportionment the basis of representation has changed and recent evidence indicate the Senate may be undergoing profound changes in its leadership patterns and distribution of political interests.

In contrast to the Assembly, the actual leader of the Senate is not its presiding officer, the Lieutenant Governor; rather, it is the President pro tem., an elected legislator. If he is of the same party as the Governor the Lieutenant Governor does exercise a degree of power, inasmuch as he serves as the executive's voice in the Senate, but his influence has declined significantly since 1939. Before that time he was a powerful official who appointed the standing committees and served as chairman of the important Rules Committee. The power of committee appointments fell to the Rules Committee in 1939, and eventually the President pro tem. was designated chairman of this committee. Despite this increase in power for the President pro tem., his status does not compare with that of the Speaker of the Assembly. Effective power in the Senate lies with the committee chairmen; thus, the system does not allow for any concentration of power in the hands of a single leader. The power of the chairmen is based on their responsibilities for making critical decisions about legislation that passes through their committees. It is clear, therefore, that power is shared among a collection of powerful Senators; this collegial group consists generally of the President pro tem., the members of the Rules Committee, and the chairmen of the important committees on finance, government efficiency, revenue and taxation.

Recent developments indicate, however, that the style of Senate leadership is undergoing a change and the Senate is now becoming a more partisan body. The formation of political party caucuses in 1967 and 1968 is one manifestation of the growing importance of parties in the Senate. Previously, the caucus was, in effect, nothing more than a general meeting of the entire Senate convened to deal with the bipartisan business of the body. The 1965 reapportionment produced changes in the composition of the Senate that increased its partisan orientation. Changes included an increase in the number of Senators from urban areas, especially from southern California, and the addition of a number of former Assemblymen who capitalized on redistricting by moving from the lower house to the Senate in the previous election. These former Assemblymen were accustomed to the greater partisan orientation of the Assembly, under the leadership of Speaker Unruh, that provided extensive professional staff and political services. They were less dependent on a leadership arrangement involving a relatively small bipartisan clique of old guard legislators. In May 1967, a number of freshman Democratic Senators, joined by two veterans who were excluded from the traditional leadership group, formed a Democratic caucus. Initially, the Senate's leadership was reluctant to participate in the caucus and expressed doubts about its usefulness. The Democratic President pro tem., Hugh M. Burns, argued that party caucuses were fraught with danger—commitments formed in caucus often conflict with constituency preferences, and the close division between parties in the Senate required a coalition between both parties to achieve legislation—but concluding that the caucus could not be stopped, the old guard leadership began to attend meetings and participate in caucus activities. Finally, they accepted the caucus, formalized it, and elected a chairman acceptable to them. At the opening of the 1968 session, Republicans followed the Democrats' example and established a party caucus of their own.

The role of the caucus in the Senate is still not clearly defined. Established Senate leaders, although extending a degree of legitimacy to the caucus system, are nonetheless reluctant to allow the caucus to become a major vehicle of party leadership. Caucus meetings have been infrequent, serving more as a source of information than of leadership. For example, the Republican leadership in the 1968 session called a caucus to consider the budget developed by the Democratically controlled Finance Committee, but caucus action was limited to a general discussion of the legislation. No attempt was made to work out a party position on the budget; rather, individual members expressed their dissatisfaction with parts of the bill, and the floor leader was directed to bargain with the Finance Committee on a number of these points. Although the leadership is uncomfortable when the caucus attempts to deal directly with partisan legislative matters, it has allowed the caucus staff to provide to individual legislators certain political services that do not touch on legislative matters. For example, the Democratic caucus staff includes several campaign technicians who provide advice and direction to Senators. Recently, the staff took on the complex arrangements for a fund-raising dinner to support Democratic candidates seeking re-election. The staff has also participated in special elections held for the purpose of filling legislative vacancies. As in the Assembly, the Senate leaders are beginning to understand that the loyalties of individual legislators can be swayed significantly when they receive such services from the legislative party.

The replacement of President pro tem. Hugh Burns during the 1969 session provides another illustration of the trend toward greater Senate partisanship. Burns typified the old regime that dominated the Senate for decades. Although a Democrat, he first won election as President pro tem. in 1957 with the help of dissenting Republicans, and he conducted the business of the Senate in such a nonpartisan fashion that he was re-elected without opposition in every session until 1968. Even after the Republicans gained, by victories in special elections, a 20–20 split in 1967 and a one-vote majority in 1969, Burns continued to retain his post. The secret of his success lay in his ability to maintain the loyalty of a number of Republican Senators who were part of the bipartisan Senate establishment. Eventually, however, in May 1969, a coalition of Republicans and "young Turks" among the Democrats ousted Burns and elected Howard Way (Republican, Tulare) as President pro tem. Despite the fact that a handful of Republicans supported Burns to the last, a larger number of Republican Senators felt they owed it to their party to take over the leadership of the Senate. Republican party workers had labored diligently in regular and special elections to win a Senate majority and it seemed only right that the majority should assume the reins of leadership.

Moreover, Burns's nonpartisanship contributed to his problems within his own party. His nonpartisanship was one of the reasons that persuaded the "young Turks" to cross party lines and support Howard Way. The "young Turks," most of them former Assemblymen accustomed to the partisan style of the lower chamber, grew uneasy with the clubby, nonpartisan manner in which Burns operated the Senate. They were irritated by the fact that Governor Reagan had, on a number of occasions, stated that he had full confidence in Burns as Senate leader. To make matters even worse, Burns committed the partisan sin of supporting Richard Nixon for President in 1968 and refusing to endorse Alan Cranston, his own party's U.S. Senatorial nominee.

COMMITTEE ASSIGNMENTS

An examination of the committee system, and the methods of appointing legislators to committee positions, helps in understanding the organization and the exercise of power and influence in the legislature. As in most states, committees in the California legislature make the key decisions affecting legislation. Most issues are very complex consequently, the legislature must depend on the smaller units of committees to perform the tedious but necessary technical evaluation and investigation of bills. Only infrequently does the full body disregard the recommendations of its substantive committees. Thus, control of committee assignments provides the leadership with a powerful sanction over the rank and file. If an individual legislator wishes to maximize his influence, he must seek appointment to committees that provide him access to the points of decision on bills in which he is most interested. Likewise, the powerful economic interest groups in the state also seek to influence this key area of legislative policy making.

Although the number of committees has varied over the years, in recent sessions of the legislature there have been twenty-six standing committees in the Assembly and twenty-two in the Senate. Most Assemblymen serve on three committees, and Senators serve on as many as five. Obviously, not all committees are equally important. In both houses, the Rules Committees control the critical procedural business of the body, and therefore exert great influence over the entire proceedings of the legislature. Also, committees on taxation and appropriations control tax and budget bills and must approve all bills that require the expenditure of state funds. This category of bills is large, and an estimated one third of all bills passes through the Ways and Means Committee in the Assembly. Other high-ranking substantive committees include education, transportation, and insurance and finance.

California legislative rules allow more discretion in the assignment of committee positions than the rules of more highly partisan legislatures. Unlike the national Congress, the majority party neither control all chairmanships, nor even a majority of seats on all committees. Responsibility for making committee assignments in the Assembly, as we have already noted, rests with the Speaker, and in the Senate, with the Rules Committee. The rules of the Assembly specify only that the Speaker must take into consideration individual preferences of the legislators. In the Senate on the other hand, the rules call for a consideration of member preference, seniority, experience, and geographical balance. Despite the failure of the rules to mention party as a criteria, partisan affiliation is a crucial factor to both houses in determining committee assignments. The place of party in committee chairmanship assignments is suggested by the figures in Table 8–2.

The table demonstrates clearly that, although party control does not result in complete domination of all chairmanships, the vast majority of these positions fall to the majority party. Even during the period of crossfiling and nonpartisanship (1945–1952), nearly three fourths of the Senate and Assembly chairmanships went to the majority party. During the recent period of increased partisanship (1959–1966), the number

TABLE 8–2 STANDING COMMITTEE CHAIRMANSHIPS; SENATE, ASSEMBLY, BY PARTY, REGION (SELECTED PERIODS)

Senate (Percentages)

	Rep.	Dem.	North	South
1945–1952 (Rep. control)	72.8	27.2	82.8	17.2
1959–1966 (Dem. control)	21.2	78.8	88.8	11.2
1967–1969 (Rep.–Dem. control)	49.2	50.8	52.3	47.7

Assembly (Percentages)

	Rep.	Dem.	North	South
1945–1952 (Rep. control)	75.5	24.5	45.4	54.6
1959–1966 (Dem. control)	15.8	84.2	57.7	42.3
1967–1969 (Rep.–Dem. control)	50.7	49.3	53.4	46.6

of majority party chairmanships naturally increased slightly, but roughly one fifth of the chairmanships still remained with the minority party. Thus, the California legislature evidently is not fully committed to a partisan organization and style. This situation will persist as long as party discipline is lacking in voting for the Speaker; under this condition, the Speaker is encouraged to trade chairmanships for minority party support. The figures for 1967–1969, when seats were almost evenly divided between parties, show that division of chairmanships was roughly related to party division of seats in both houses. Moreover, the closer the balance between the two parties, the greater the need for a bipartisan style of leadership in order to form the necessary majority coalitions to pass legislation.

Evidence from table 8–2 also indicates that the Assembly adheres more closely to party loyalties in the choice of chairmen than the Senate. An explanation for this difference is that factors other than party, e.g., sectionalism and seniority, play a larger role in the Senate. Before reapportionment, Senators from the northern region enjoyed a near monopoly of important committee chairmanships; but the 1965 redistricting shifted seats to the south, and, consequently, more committee chairmanships. The table reveals, on the other hand, that the distribution of chairmanships in the Assembly has traditionally reflected a more equitable division of seats between north and south, because of its reliance on population, rather than geography, as a basis of representation.

The Senate has managed to blunt the effects of reapportionment through the continued use of seniority as a determining factor in committee assignments. An analysis of committee chairmanships in 1967 showed on the four top committees, the average tenure of their members was 14.8 years; on the ten minor committees, average tenure was only 4.8 years. In fact, the eleven Senators with the longest tenure—all elected before 1960—controlled a majority of the seats on the four top committees.[22]

governor and legislative leadership

Power in government has shifted in the twentieth century from the legislature to the chief executive. The most dramatic demonstration

[22] "Strategy and Culture in Legislative Committee Assignments: California in 1967," Richard Brandsma and Alvin D. Sokolow, paper prepared for presentation at Western Political Science Association, Seattle, Wash., March 21–23, 1968, pp. 20–25.

of this phenomenon is the increase of presidential power. The chief executive influences and mobilizes national opinion on the full range of policy questions. Indeed, the President, not Congress, leads the quest for answers to the nation's domestic and foreign problems by generating ideas, formulating policies and programs, proposing legislation, and assuming the major responsibility for congressional passage of these programs. This form of presidential leadership is the model for state government, particularly in the large urban states where problems reflect those of the nation as a whole. The doctrine of separation of powers restricts, to some degree, the expansion of this executive role. Because of the tensions created by this constitutional mode, the success of any Governor in exercising his political power is largely dependent on his personal abilities and, of course, political skills.

LEGISLATIVE LEADER

Characteristically, California's Governors have since the days of Hiram Johnson, sought and exercised strong executive leadership. These governors, including C. C. Young, Earl Warren, and Edmund Brown, have articulated the state's needs, developed their own solutions to the state's problems, presented programs to the legislature, and employed every constitutional and political means to influence decisions made in the legislature. Today, the major source of a total program of state legislation, geared to the broad requirements of the state, is the chief executive. Although individual legislators carry personal programs to meet constituency demands, the legislature does not generate a comprehensive program.

The success of any Governor in effectively pursuing this strong executive role is dependent on his abiilty to exercise peculiarly political skills. He must be able to mold and mobilize public opinion, rise to a position of party leader, and create a sense of partisan solidarity. His position as the state's chief executive allows wide opportunity to lead. The Governor receives more than 400 speaking invitations each month and travels widely in the state carrying his message to the people. In weekly televised press conferences, the Governor is allowed a platform from which to exhort the legislature, express opinions on his program and the opposition, and to influence public opinion. Recently, Governor Reagan has appeared on special television broadcasts in order to develop support for issues of particular importance to him, much in the same manner as Franklin D. Roosevelt's "fireside chats." Reagan's apparent recognition of the highly political character of these broadcasts is suggested by the fact that the Republican state central committee pays the bill. Clearly, the Governor's public leadership and influence is tied to his role as a party leader. Increasingly, the public recognizes the Governor as party leader, particularly, as in the case of Reagan, when he extends his political role into national affairs. Clear evidence of Governor Reagan's leadership was presented by former Republican Party Chairman James Halley. He reported that the Governor raised more than $3 million for the GOP since 1966 and that he campaigned in forty-seven Assembly districts and twenty Senate districts. "No one has done more to rebuild and strengthen the party," said Halley.[23] Nevertheless, control of party machinery has been only grudgingly, and partially, surrendered by the powerful legislative party leadership. In fact, as already noted, California law still permits control by legislative personnel of the state central committees and conventions.

The Governor relies on several legal-constitutional powers that aid him in dealing with the legislature. He reports annually on the condition of the state—a sort of "state of the state" address. This message to the legislature, the major policy statement of the Governor in any year, outlines his legislative aspirations and usually makes a number of specific program suggestions. In an election year, this speech usually points up the accomplishments of an incumbent's administration, or synthesizes the campaign rhetoric of a newly elected Governor. Importantly, California provides for an executive budget, which means the Governor is fully responsible for the preparation of annual estimates of expenditures and revenue. The relative allocation of funds in any budget reveals a good deal about the policies of the government. With centralized control of the budget, the Governor can employ his discretion in emphasizing any program contained in the budget. Although ultimate review of the budget rests with the legislature, the chairman of the powerful Ways and Means Committee in the Assembly is usually approved by the Governor when his party controls the Assembly, and in effect serves as his representative on the floor of the lower house. Moreover, through the power of budgeting, the Governor can effectively manage the growth, develop, and administration of his executive departments and agencies. Each of these agencies perceives itself to some degree as an independent entity, and feels some urge to bargain directly and individually with the legislature for funds; the centralized budget, however, encourages these agencies to operate through the Governor.

The constitution allows the Governor twelve days after any bill is passed either to approve or veto it, or take no action (in which case the bill becomes a law). The Governor may also exercise an item veto over budget matters that allows him to eliminate or reduce any item in the

---

[23] *Sacramento BEE,* January 27, 1969.

budget. In 1966, the power of the Governor to pocket veto a bill was restricted when the constitution provided for a special veto session during which any measure vetoed by the Governor could be overridden by a two-thirds vote of the legislature.[24] Finally, the Governor can call special legislative sessions; but the 1966 constitutional amendment diminished this power of the Governor by providing for annual sessions of the legislature, thus eliminating the short budget sessions in even-numbered years and reducing the need for special meetings of the legislature. During the special session, the legislature must consider only those issues specified by the Governor when calling the session.

LEGISLATIVE LIAISON

As the Governor's leadership role expands, the office necessarily becomes more institutionalized. A personal staff of assistants and advisers aids the Governor in carrying out his responsibilities to the legislature, the party, and the voters. The organization of a Governor's staff usually reflects his personal requirements and preferences. In most cases, the appointment of a special assistant for legislative relations takes on added importance. Governor Reagan, deviating from the tradition of a single legislative secretary, appointed a personal representative for each house of the legislature.

Although these assistants deal with a broad range of legislative relations, they are not necessarily directly involved in the formulation of specific legislative programs. The key to any Governor's program is the "state of the state" message. Based on this speech, the governor sends to the legislature specific, detailed bills which, in effect, become his legislative program. The sources of this program vary. The governor himself, of course, advances a series of campaign promises and recommendations that will eventually become a policy base for legislative programming. A special legislative task force, appointed by Governor Reagan in October 1966, when his election seemed imminent, supplemented and complemented the new Governor's ideas by presenting more proposals. The Governor, also, is inundated by legislative proposals from the numerous administrative agencies and departments. The coordination of gubernatorial policies with the aspirations of the agencies, however, creates some conflict in developing a cohesive administration program. These agencies amount to special interest groups within the governmental scheme and are continually attempting to press their own cases to the

---

[24] No Governor's vetoes have yet been overridden in the special veto session and there is talk about abolishing it.

legislature. The Governor's task, therefore, is to impose some coherence and conformity, consistent with his own policies, ideology, and aspirations, on this fragmented arrangement of program development. Although institutionalization of a system for executive clearance of departmental proposals is not fully developed, as in the federal government, some regularization of procedures is emerging. Finally, the Governor is a target, often a willing one, of the barrage of information, requests, and advice of the special interests that are represented by lobbyists in the state capital. Of course, Governors of different political orientations are generally accessible to those groups most consistent with their own persuasions.

The staff attached to the office of the legislative secretary has become an important permanent adjunct to the Governor's office. The functions of the staff include the technical analysis of every bill of any interest to the Governor. From this careful analysis, the staff classifies bills according to whether the Governor should oppose, support, or not concern himself directly. In addition to this evaluation process, the staff also carefully watches the fate of each bill in the legislature—especially the Governor's bills. They, of course, are in constant contact with the legislature, guaranteeing that bills are handled by the appropriate legislators and that votes are collected for support. Also, the staff analyzes the final bills and recommends that the Governor either sign or veto individual bills. The executive power of veto does, of course, provide the Governor with a useful weapon against a recalcitrant legislature. Only seldom will the legislature override an executive veto, in fact since 1923, the legislature has overridden a veto only twenty-nine times. In 1967, at the end of the regular session, Governor Reagan vetoed eighty-three of the 1,808 bills passed. Democrats, in the special veto session in September, unsuccessfully tried to overturn eleven of the eighty-three vetoes. Significantly, each party voted strictly along party lines, and the Democrats were unable to muster the two-thirds majority.

Operating without effective coercive force or leverage, the Governor and the legislative secretary must employ good relations, persuasion, and faith in moving individual legislators to support administration bills. During his first term, facing a legislature dominated by Democrats, Governor Reagan received approval of 50 per cent of his proposed measures. Reagan was in a difficult position, and his first year's record was not particularly promising, especially considering the "honeymoon" period usually granted to first-term governors. Moreover, the solidarity of the Democratic party in the Assembly, under the leadership of Unruh (who even battled Democrat Pat Brown) proved a formidable obstacle in the path of Reagan's legislative program. However, a historical perspective indicates a solid trend toward expansion of executive power. Also, now that the Republicans control the Assembly and Senate, Governor Reagan can expect greater success with his program.

party and voting

Probably the most critical test of the party's strength in the legislature is its ability to ensure the votes of its members on important roll calls. The theory of party government calls for strict party regularity, with the party exercising sanctions over its members to insure a "united front." Although this is the case, for example, in the British Parliament, neither the national Congress nor the fifty state legislatures function with this amount of party discipline and control. In fact, the degree of party competitiveness from one state to another affects significantly the degree to which party loyalty is enforced. In a one-party state, for example, cleavages on policy tend to follow factional lines within the dominant party, and differences between the Republican and Democratic parties are unimportant. But in more competitive states, the political party becomes a stronger influence on the voting behavior of the legislature.

Earlier studies on voting in the California legislature showed that, despite a certain degree of party competition for electoral office, the legislature revealed little evidence of party regularity. To some extent, this phenomenon can be explained in terms of the state's tradition of nonpartisanship. All legislative behavior, however, cannot be viewed in terms of parties alone. Legislators are influenced by a variety of pressures including sectional conflicts, urban-rural differences, factional divisions within parties, and so on. These factors, not party divisions, explain some roll call votes. In fact, some observers assert that the most critical divisions in California politics are the divisions between the state's northern and southern sections because, before the 1965 reapportionment, the system of representation in the Senate conformed to these sectional divisions. A study that attempted to test this assertion of sectional conflict in legislative voting during the 1957, 1959, and 1961 sessions found that north-south conflicts in the Assembly were insignificant. The only two major policy areas suggesting a sectional basis for voting were water and transportation. The split on the water issue resulted from the scarcity of water resources in the south, and an abundance in the north. The transportation dispute was over the formula for allocating highway funds throughout the state. In the Senate, however, the study found that sectional conflicts were more important and rivaled in significance the conflict between the two parties. Yet neither factor provides a consistent predictor of legislative voting.

The same study attempted to link urban-rural distinctions to voting behavior but failed to turn up any significant conflict aside from the water issue. There is no sharp conflict between the cities and the countryside because California is predominantly an urban state and population centers often coexist in counties that also have a high level of agricultural production.[25] The reapportionment of the Senate, combined with some resolution of the state's water problems, diminishes even further the potential for sectional or urban-rural conflicts in the legislature. Moreover, the last vestiges of nonpartisanship are giving way gradually to an increased partisan style and orientation in the Assembly and, to a lesser degree, in the Senate. Thus, the party has now become a relatively stable factor influencing voting behavior in the legislature.

ROLL CALL ANALYSIS

A number of measures can be applied in determining the role of party in legislative voting. Not all issues, or roll calls, are relevant to the analysis of party voting. In fact, the majority of bills considered in a regular legislative session deal with technical, noncontroversial issues that receive unanimous or near unanimous support. The first step, therefore, is the establishment of some standard that provides a basis for selecting "controversial" votes. The traditional definition of such a bill is when at least 10 per cent of the voting members of the body oppose it. A minimum definition of a party vote is when a majority of one party opposes a majority of the other party on a roll call; a stricter definition would encompass only those roll calls on which at least 90 per cent of one party opposed 90 per cent of the other. For the purposes of this analysis, a 50 per cent opposition is a "partisan" vote, whereas the 90 per cent standard defines "party line" votes. A more sophisticated measure of "cohesion" (party unity on a vote) is Stuart A. Rice's index of cohesion.[26] This index measures the degree to which a party votes together on a single roll call or collection of roll calls. For example, a party that splits its membership 50–50 on a vote would have an index of zero. Because

---

[25] Charles M. Price, "Voting Alignments in the California Legislature: A Roll Call Analysis of the 1957, 1959, 1961 Sessions" (unpublished Ph.D. dissertation, Department of Political Science, University of Southern California, 1965); see Chapters VI, VII, and VIII.

[26] Stuart A. Rice, "The Behavior of Legislative Groups," *Political Science Quarterly*, Vol. 40, 1925, pp. 60–72.

statistical methods assume that chance alone would produce a 50–50 division, any deviation above this random distribution will produce a higher index of cohesion. For example, a party line vote, previously defined as 90 per cent of the members of a party voting together, would produce a cohesion index of 80.[27]

Before proceeding to an analysis of more recent data, it is valuable first to examine a number of earlier studies on legislative voting behavior. One of the first studies, by Cresap in 1949, found that 31 per cent of the contested Assembly roll call votes were "partisan," and 21 per cent in the Senate.[28] Buchanan's study of the Assembly in 1957 reported 34 per cent "partisan" roll calls, and 1 per cent "party line" roll call votes.[29] A comparison of this 1957 data to 12 other competitive party states revealed California ranked lowest in party voting.[30] Substantiating this low assessment of the importance of party in voting, a part of the 1957 Wahlke study reported that only one legislator in twenty ranked party first as a source of opinion conflict. Most Assemblymen placed north-south differences ahead of party, whereas Senators ranked north-south, city-county, and liberal-conservative cleavages as more significant than party.[31]

The most recent and comprehensive study of voting in the California legislature is Robert K. Binford's analysis of roll call votes in the Assembly for the period 1953–1963.[32] Although this study contains no data for the Senate it should provide some indication of voting patterns in the legislature as a whole. One value of Binford's investigation is that it extends from the time immediately following Warren's strong non-partisan administration through the early 1960s when partisanship was beginning to assert itself. Binford's findings are summarized in Table 8–3.

The table presents data derived from an analysis of only contested roll call votes. These votes averaged nearly 400 per session. Columns three through six summarize in raw numbers and percentages the "partisan" and "party line" votes for the ten-year period 1953–1963. Although the year 1959, when the Democrats took control of both houses

---

[27] The algebraic formula for the vote index of cohesion (i) is $\dfrac{M-m}{M+m} = i$, where M is the majority and m is the minority.

[28] Cresap, op. cit., pp. 52–63.

[29] Buchanan, op. cit., pp. 127–131.

[30] Malcolm E. Jewell, *The State Legislature* (New York: Random House, Inc., 1962), pp. 51–52.

[31] Buchanan, op. cit., p. 116.

[32] Robert K. Binford, "Party Cohesion in the California State Assembly, 1953–1963" (unpublished M.A. thesis, Department of Political Science, Stanford University, 1964).

TABLE 8–3 INCIDENCE AND COHESION OF ROLL CALL VOTES, CONTESTED AND PARTISAN, IN THE CALIFORNIA STATE ASSEMBLY—1953 TO 1963*

1	2	3	4	5	6	7	8	9	10
	Numbers and Percentages of Roll Call Votes					Party Cohesion			
	Contested	Partisan		Party Line		Democrats		Republicans	
Year	10 Per Cent of Voting Membership Opposed	50 Per Cent of Repub. Voting Opposing 50 Per Cent of Dem. Voting	Per Cent of Contested	90 Per Cent of Repub. Voting Opposing 90 Per Cent of Dem. Voting	Per Cent of Contested	Partisan	Party Line	Partisan	Party Line
General Session									
1953	345	87	25.2	2	.6	46.7	96.0	40.6	93.0
1955	303	66	21.7	1	.3	45.6	100.0	39.2	100.0
1957	345	127	36.8	4	1.2	44.1	88.0	45.1	92.0
1959	509	242	47.5	14	2.8	60.7	na	50.9	na
1961	476	210	44.1	18	3.8	70.3	94.6	46.0	94.3
1963	311	161	51.7	31	10.0	75.9	95.5	63.1	95.6

* Adapted from Robert Keith Binford, "Party Cohesion in the California State Assembly, 1953 to 1963" (unpublished M.A. thesis, Department of Political Science, Stanford University, 1964), p. 35.

for the first time in this century, produces the highest percentage of "partisan" votes, the clear trend is a continuously increasing number of "partisan" votes. In fact, the number of "partisan" votes in 1953 was 25 per cent, compared to the 1963 figure of 51 per cent, a twofold increase. Using the stricter test of a "party line" vote, the table demonstrates again that the figure increased from a mere .6 per cent in 1953 to 10 per cent in 1963, a fifteenfold increase. Clearly, these data substantiate the earlier descriptive analysis showing the growing role of party leadership and organization in the legislature. Although both analyses fail to show concretely that the party is the single disciplinary force affecting roll calls, a fair inference is that some causal relationship exists between the increased partisan voting and the increased role of the party in the legislature. Still, whatever the relative importance of a variety of influences on voting, the number of strict "party line" votes, indicating true party discipline, is low. The figures show that the number of such votes in 1963 is only 10 per cent of the contested roll calls.

The table 8–3 also presents indices of cohesion (defined earlier) for the same ten-year period and for each party. The significant conclusions derived from these data is that, excepting the 1963 session, Republicans have maintained a constant, but moderate, level of party unity; on the other hand, the Democrats maintained a fairly constant level but increased substantially their cohesion indices from 1959 to 1963. The low Republican cohesion rating from 1953 to 1957 is largely the result of the nonpartisan culture in the legislature. The Democratic increase beginning in 1959 coincides with their emergence as a majority party and the end of crossfiling and other Progressive traditions. Generally, this indicates that the majority party can be expected to achieve more cohesion than the minority. Any legislative successes of the minority party are, in part at least, dependent upon the support of members of the majority party. In short, extreme partisanship on the part of the minority is dysfunctional for achieving legislative goals. At some point, however, the sustained solidarity of the majority party serves as a catalyst for increased internal solidarity of the minority party. This hypothesis serves as an explanation for the significant increase in cohesion of the Republicans in 1963. Moreover, although Table 8–3 does not deal with the current situation, the leadership of the Republican Governor serves to increase the unity of his party in the legislature. And, on certain critical measures such as the budget and emergency legislation, a small minority, if it is extremely cohesive, can exercise a veto as these measures require a two-thirds approval.

Although the figures dealing with the number of "partisan" and "party line" votes help to understand the role of party in voting, strict party voting is meaningless unless party divisions are related to important policy issues. In fact, perhaps the largest function of the party is the organization of opinion and votes around significant questions. What policy areas, therefore, produce the sharpest divisions between the two legislative parties? Binford's classification of "partisan" and "party line" bills into subject matter categories allows an analysis of the relative impact of policy on party voting. The areas generating the greatest party division in the period 1961–1963 were, in the following order: welfare, human rights, education, elections, government, taxes and revenue, labor, and rules. Clearly, these represent meaningful programmatic issues and are also the most sharply debated on the national level. Moreover, Binford found, in comparing this ranking to an earlier period (1953–1955), a change in the nature of issues resulting in the greatest party division. The earlier period revealed more conflict around administrative issues like taxes, revenue, and governmental organization, compared to the current emphasis on social issues such as welfare, education, and human rights. Conflict producing issues are becoming broader, more fundamental in philosophical terms, and are affecting larger numbers of people in the society. These issues, in turn, are increasingly the basis for party differences.[33]

These conclusions apply most specifically to the Assembly. Hard and fast findings about the Senate are impossible without empirical data but some tentative generalizations can be offered. Political parties continue to exert less influence on voting in the Senate than in the Assembly. Moreover, until the 1965 reapportionment, issues dividing the Senate tended more heavily to reflect sectional conflicts than in the Assembly, now, however, a completely reapportioned body will probably work to undercut this difference. The trend toward partisanship, though stronger in the Assembly, can be expected to increase and continue in the Senate.

In consclusion, the legislative party, more than any other single variable, helps to explain voting behavior and patterns in the state legislature. Moreover, the party is destined to become increasingly significant. Admittedly, certain areas, such as water and transportation, do result in votes that cut across partisan lines but, compared to the full range of legislative decisions, this kind of voting is relatively rare. Finally, some controversial issues defy explanation in terms of traditional conflicts of party, section, urban versus rural, and so on. A legislator's voting behavior sometimes depends on factors peculiar to himself or to his constituency, and it is difficult to generalize about these idiosyncratic forces.

---

[33] Binford, op. cit., pp. 48–53.

CHAPTER 9

epilogue

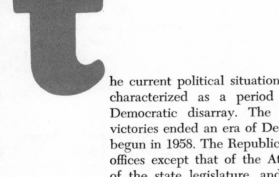he current political situation in California might well be
characterized as a period of Republican revival and
Democratic disarray. The 1966 and 1968 Republican
victories ended an era of Democratic dominance that had
begun in 1958. The Republicans now control all statewide
offices except that of the Attorney General, both houses
of the state legislature, and one U.S. Senate seat. The
Democrats still have a slight majority in the Congressional delegation. The Republican party appears to be in
fine organizational health whereas the Democrats are
divided and feuding.

REPUBLICAN REVIVAL

Governor Ronald Reagan continues his tremendous
popularity. The California Poll, conducted by the Field
Corporation, consistently has shown that no fewer than
two thirds and as many as three fourths of the people in
California feel that he is doing a good job. He has been
successful in dealing with the public, his party, and the

legislature. Governor Reagan has ably used television in capitalizing
on his successes, and unlike Dr. Max Rafferty, he is a glamorous personality who comes across well on this cool medium. Mr. Reagan in some ways
is the perfect product of California political technique.

The GOP has control of both legislative chambers for the first time
in twenty years. Although the Republicans hold only a slight margin
in both houses, they hope to strengthen their position in 1970. An indication of the party's growing power in legislative districts is its continued success in special elections; Republicans have won all four special
legislative elections since 1966.

The Republican party is a revitalized organization. It has plenty of
money and under the Governor's leadership, has become an effective
campaign instrument. The volunteer organizations are cooperating better
with the party than in the past. Republicans are providing their party
with local workers and support on a scale not known for some time.

The 1970s look bright. Governor Reagan is assured renomination
if he wants it and his re-election is only a little less certain. The GOP
looks forward to increased legislative power after the 1970 election
and feels that it will gain enough seats to control the reapportionment.
This would insure them of increased influence in both houses of the
state legislative and the U.S. House of Representatives for a number of
years.

DEMOCRATIC DISARRAY

Democrats lack unified leadership. The Attorney General, Thomas
Lynch, is not an effective party leader. U.S. Senator Alan Cranston won
an impressive victory in 1968, but is likely to focus on Washington, D.C.,
and national politics. The situation is not bad, but the Democratic
members of the state Senate are split between the "young Turks" and
the old guard. Jesse Unruh remains an important figure but his power
has slipped in the Assembly since Republican Robert T. Monagan was
named Speaker by the GOP majority.

All signs point to a severe leadership struggle in the 1970 primary
among Jesse Unruh, Joseph Alioto and possibly others. There is some
question about the capacity of the Democratic party to go through the
primary campaign and emerge without debilitating splits. If there is a
difficult primary struggle, the party will be so weakened and divided
that it will not be able to offer the Republicans much opposition in the
general election. In fact, the disarray of the Democrats is a main contributing factor to the high expectations of the GOP in 1970.

Although some CDCers hope that common enemies, Governor Reagan and President Nixon, will unite this once powerful arm of the Democratic party, it is unlikely that the CDC will prove effective. It too is in disarray and can not offer the strong support it has provided the party in the past. The main hope of the Democrats is their three-to-two edge among registered voters.

IMPLICATIONS OF THE REPUBLICAN REVIVAL

Republicans seem willing and able to continue the trend toward increasing partisanship begun by the Democrats in the 1950s. Crossfiling is no longer around to encourage maverick behavior. Governor Reagan is not following the bipartisan strategy of Earl Warren. Instead, he has proven to be an effective partisan leader. In the Assembly, Speaker Monagan shows no signs of relaxing the partisan lines developed under the Democrats. GOP leaders may be able to maintain party leadership in the Senate.

California politics has taken a turn to the right under Republican rule, with more and more concern about law and order, fiscal responsibility, welfare abuses, and race. Although the state's budget continues to grow under Republican leadership, education, welfare, health, and antipoverty programs face hard times. It may be that conservatism in this state is part of a national trend, but to liberals it appears that California is setting a trend.

As the mainstream of our politics moves to the right, the fringes carry on the California radical tradition. On the right, the John Birch Society proposes to set up their own grade schools and universities. On the left, students are increasingly making use of confrontation methods to press their demands. Other young people have organized LUV (Let Us Vote) and are seriously trying to secure the franchise for the 18–20 year olds. Minority groups are becoming more militant in pressing their demands. There is no reason to suspect that these trends will not continue into the 1970s.

These developments have serious implications for traditional politics. The eighteen-year-old vote would upset many established patterns. The radicals and minorities are becoming better organized at a time when it is difficult to secure positive response to their demands. Our regular politics will continue to be challenged by outside groups. There is a real question about the capacity of our traditional organizations to withstand the continued pressure of these alienated people. Hopefully parties, interest groups, and other organizations can be opened and expanded to include many of these disenchanted people.

THE STATE AND THE NATION

Republican revival in California and elsewhere in the West has important implications for national politics. California's vital role in presidential politics makes Republican predominance here a crucial factor in the fortunes of both national parties. There is every indication that the increasing good fortune of the GOP in California means continued success for it in national party competition.

A FINAL WORD

California politics continues to befuddle people. They do not know whether to take our politics seriously or to consider them a curiosity—interesting and entertaining to be sure, but certainly not to be emulated in any way. As one commentator recently put it, "Is California a laugh or a lesson?" Clearly, California politics is too important in too many ways to be dismissed. Because of its size alone people must pay attention to what California does politically. Yet it is more than size that makes California politics important to the rest of the nation. California is no longer the "great exception"; its political style is becoming increasingly more relevant to other states. T. George Harris, a *Look* editor, puts it succinctly, "California . . . provides a preview of conditions coming on more slowly in older regions. For better or worse, the politics of the future now starts here."[1]

---

[1] *Look,* Sept. 25, 1962, p. 73.

index

327